Abraham Lincoln

Also by George Anastaplo

The Constitutionalist: Notes on the First Amendment

Human Being and Citizen: Essays on Virtue, Freedom, and the Common Good

The Artist as Thinker: From Shakespeare to Joyce

The Constitution of 1787: A Commentary

The American Moralist: On Law, Ethics, and Government

The Amendments to the Constitution: A Commentary

The Thinker as Artist: From Homer to Plato and Aristotle

Campus Hate-Speech Codes, Natural Right, and Twentieth Century Atrocities

Liberty, Equality, and Modern Constitutionalism: A Source Book

Abraham Lincoln

A CONSTITUTIONAL BIOGRAPHY

George Anastaplo

ROWMAN & LITTLEFIELD PUBLISHERS, INC.
Lanham • Boulder • New York • Oxford

ROWMAN & LITTLEFIELD PUBLISHERS, INC.

Published in the United States of America
by Rowman & Littlefield Publishers, Inc.
4720 Boston Way, Lanham, Maryland 20706
http://www.rowmanlittlefield.com

12 Hid's Copse Road
Cumnor Hill, Oxford OX2 9JJ, England

British Library Cataloguing in Publication Information Available

Library of Congress Cataloging-in-Publication Data

Anastaplo, George, 1925–
    Abraham Lincoln: a constitutional biography / George Anastaplo.
        p.   cm.
    Includes bibliographical references and index.
    ISBN 0–8476–9431–3 (alk. paper)
    1. Lincoln, Abraham, 1809–1865—Political and social views.
    2. Lincoln, Abraham, 1809–1865—Views on the Constitution
    3. United States—Politics and government—1783–1865.   4. United
    States—Constitutional history.   5. Lincoln, Abraham, 1809–1865—
    Political career before 1861.   I. Title.
    E457.2.A54   1999
    973.7'092—dc21   99-14721
                                                                    CIP

Printed in the United States of America

♾ ™ The paper used in this publication meets the minimum requirements of
American National Standard for Information Sciences—Permanence of Paper for
Printed Library Materials, ANSI/NISO Z39.48–1992.

To
MY CHILDREN'S CHILDREN
and to their Children
with the Reminder that their patriotic Forebears
were among the brave Men
North and South
who both counseled against and fought in
the American Civil War

"Captain [Levi] Preston, why did you go [sixty-seven years ago] to the Concord Fight, the 19th of April, 1775?"

"Why did I go?"

"Yes, my histories tell me that you men of the Revolution took up arms against 'intolerable oppressions.'"

"What were they? Oppressions? I didn't feel them."

"What, were you not oppressed by the Stamp Act?"

"I never saw one of those stamps, and always understood that Governor Bernard put them all in Castle William. I am certain I never paid a penny for one of them."

"Well, what about the tea-tax?"

"Tea-tax! I never drank a drop of the stuff; the boys threw it all overboard."

"Then I suppose you had been reading Harrington or Sidney and Locke about the eternal principles of liberty."

"Never heard of 'em. We read only the Bible, the Catechism, Watts' Psalms and Hymns, and the Almanack."

"Well, then what was the matter? And what did you mean in going to the fight?"

"Young man, what we meant in going for those red-coats was this: we always had governed ourselves, and we always meant to. They didn't mean we should."

—Mellen Chamberlain

What tremendous news this is about [the assassination of] Lincoln! As they have infringed the Constitution so much already, it is a pity Grant, for his own sake, cannot go a little further and get rid of such an incubus as Johnson. If Lincoln had been killed two years ago it would have been an immense loss to the North, but now he has done his work. All the recent matters have raised America in one's estimation, I think, and even this assassination brings into their history something of that dash of the tragic, romantic, and imaginative, which it has had so little of. *Sic semper tyrannis* [shouted by John Wilkes Booth] is so unlike anything Yankee or English middle class, both for bad and good.

—Matthew Arnold

During the early part of the second World War there came to light the story of a farmer from the back country of Oklahoma—one of the yet unspoiled—who, upon hearing of the attack on Pearl Harbor, departed with his wife to the West Coast to work in the shipyards. His wife found employment as a waitress and supported the two. Unable to read, the new worker did not understand the meaning of the little slip of paper handed him once a week. It was not until he had accumulated over a thousand dollars in checks that he found out that he was being paid to save his country. He had assumed that when the country is in danger, everyone helps out, and helping out means giving.

—Richard M. Weaver

The sources of the three epigraphs on the preceding page—epigraphs that come out of this Country's three greatest wars—are:

Mellen Chamberlain, John Adams, the Statesman of the American Revolution, with Other Essays *(Boston: Houghton Mifflin, 1899), 248–49 (an interview of 1844).*

Cecil Y. Lang, ed. The Letters of Matthew Arnold *(Charlottesville: University Press of Virginia, 1997), 2:409 (Paris, April 27, 1865).*

Richard M. Weaver, Ideas Have Consequences *(Chicago: University of Chicago Press, 1948), 121.*

Contents

Prologue   *1*

1   The Declaration of Independence:
      An Introduction   *11*

2   The Declaration of Independence:
      On Rights and Duties   *31*

3   The Northwest Ordinance   *39*

4   Slavery and the Federal Convention of 1787   *51*

5   The Common Law and the Organization
      of Government   *69*

6   Alexis de Tocqueville on Democracy
      in America   *81*

7   John C. Calhoun and Slavery   *113*

8   Southern Illinois's Abraham Lincoln   *123*

9   The Poetry of Abraham Lincoln   *135*

10   The "House Divided" Speech   *149*

11   The Lincoln–Douglas Debates   *157*

12   The First Inaugural Address   *177*

13   The Fourth of July Message to Congress   *185*

14   The Emancipation Proclamation   *197*

15   The Gettysburg Address   *229*

16   The Second Inaugural Address   *243*

17   Abraham Lincoln's Legacies   *251*

Epilogue   *257*

Notes   *263*

Index   *361*

About the Author   *373*

Prologue

The implications of a principle are likely to become clearer as
the principle becomes ingrained; the barons who forced King
John to promulgate Magna Carta probably had no sense at all
that commoners would someday invoke the great charter's principles [against barons].

—Albert W. Alschuler

I

Abraham Lincoln recognized that he was "very little inclined on any occasion to say anything unless [he] hope[d] to produce some good by it."[1]
Much that we have from the mature Lincoln, therefore, was carefully prepared for specific occasions, usually of a political character. Is not this the
trait of a remarkably practical man?

I attempt to follow in Lincoln's tracks to this extent: all of the discussions collected here (adapted somewhat to this dialogic context) were
prepared by me for specific occasions between 1961 and 1998. In them I
address issues in American history, political philosophy, and constitutional
law to which I have returned again and again. These issues are illuminated by, and in turn illuminate, observations about current affairs. An effort
is made to permit each of the chapters of this Collection to stand alone.
This means that some overlapping among the chapters is unavoidable, not
least because each chapter was designed to be comprehensible on its own
when it was originally prepared. This also means that one can proceed, as
reader, in whatever order one prefers through this Collection, although my

---

This Prologue includes material from a talk given at the Faculty Workshop,
Loyola University of Chicago School of Law, April 28, 1992. (Original title "*Somerset v. Stewart*: On Taking the Low Road to High Places.") It has been previously
published in 17 *Oklahoma City University Law Review* 715–24 (1992).

The epigraph is taken from Albert W. Alschuler, "Rediscovering Blackstone,"
145 *University of Pennsylvania Law Review* 1, 51 (1996).

more or less chronological order is recommended. *Considerable overlapping is to be found in the extensive notes, which tie the chapters together, as does the index.* (In addition, I repeat quotations from Lincoln as needed in each chapter. The circumstances of the development of this book do not permit me to be as confident of the accuracy of all of the quotations used here, especially those taken from the press, as I am entitled to be about quotations taken from Lincoln and checked against a reliable edition of his works.)

Lincoln, as a practical man, was largely shaped by his career as a lawyer who was very much interested in politics. Critical to the politics of his day was, of course, the status of slavery in the United States. Particularly important for him was the 1857 *Dred Scott* case, which dramatized the issues relating to what the permanent status in this Country would be of persons of African descent and whether slavery would be permitted to take root in the Territories (and hence in a dozen future States) of the Union.[2]

The opening portion of this Collection (Chapters 1–7) suggests the constitutional, political, and social background out of which Lincoln emerged. The career of Lincoln, up to his Presidency, is sketched in the central portion of this Collection (Chapters 8–11). The concluding portion (Chapters 12–17) examines Lincoln as President, working for the most part from his major addresses, messages, and proclamations. I have, during three decades of preparing materials for various occasions, worked with a view to this Collection in which aspects of Lincoln's constitutional biography would be surveyed and assessed. The detailed commentaries provided by me on the Emancipation Proclamation and the Gettysburg Address indicate how carefully all of Lincoln's mature works should be read. These commentaries are anticipated by the discussions in this book of the Declaration of Independence and of a chapter in Alexis de Tocqueville's account of the America in which Lincoln grew up.

It should be useful, at the outset of this book, to remind the reader of the greatest slavery-related litigation in Anglo-American law before *Dred Scott*: the English case of *Somerset v. Stewart*.[3] *Somerset* suggests what the fate of slavery could have been in the United States, a Country grounded in the principles of Magna Carta and the Declaration of Independence. (I remind the reader, in the Epilogue, of what could once be said about those unfortunate [but fortunately rare] human beings who may be by nature slavish.)

II

The *Somerset* case was decided on June 22, 1772, by the highest common-law court in England, a court presided over by the great commercial-law judge, Lord Mansfield. Mansfield and his colleagues, who were evidently reluctant to decide this case, had had jurisdiction over this matter for about a year and had ordered five separate hearings. One report we have reads:

> On return to [a writ of] *habeas corpus,* requiring Captain [*John*] *Knowles* to shew cause for the seizure and detainure of the complainant [*James*] *Somerset,* a negro—The case appeared to be this—
>
> That the negro had been a slave to Mr. [*Charles*] *Stewart,* in *Virginia,* had been purchased from the *African* coast, in the course of the slave-trade, as tolerated in the [North American] plantations; that he had been brought over to *England* by his master, who intending to return, by force sent him on board of Captain *Knowles's* vessel, lying in the river; and was there, by the order of his master, in the custody of Captain *Knowles,* detained against his consent; until returned in obedience to the writ [in December 1771]. And under this order, and the facts stated, Captain *Knowles* relied in his justification.[4]

Much about this case, and especially about the statements made by Mansfield, is prosaic in tone, in marked contrast to the eloquence of counsel during the extended arguments in this matter. It was evident both that the case had aroused considerable interest and that the cause of personal liberty was more popular than the cause of property claims on this occasion, as reflected in what is conceded again and again by counsel for the slave owner. Mansfield himself recognized the high caliber of the arguments before the court and said he was gratified that so many young lawyers had been present to hear them.

Somerset anticipates the 1857 *Dred Scott* controversy in this Country. That is, it may be seen here that special problems can be expected when one tries to move around with one's slaves, especially into and out of jurisdictions where slavery is not explicitly provided for by law.[5]

What did the *Somerset* case do? Mansfield himself tended to emphasize its limited scope: his court placed a restraint upon the forcible removal of a particular slave from England. The ruling did not simply forbid all such removals; rather, it provided that anyone claimed as a slave who was threatened by such removal and who applied in time to an appropriate court in England was entitled to an order that he be released. No provision was made for any other claims (for example, for wages) that such a person might have. Nor were forcible removals of slaves formally discouraged—and, for all I know, such removals continued after *Somerset,* at least in those instances where a petition for a writ of habeas corpus was not resorted to on behalf of a slave who was known to be threatened by forcible removal.

Put this way, *Somerset* can be seen not only as prosaic in its terms but also as quite narrow in its scope. We shall see that the same can be said of President Lincoln's Emancipation Proclamation almost a century later. For example, some complained, in 1862 and 1863, that Lincoln's proclamation emancipated only slaves in those parts of the United States where the Union Army was not in control, inasmuch as it referred only to those slaves (in States or parts of States still in rebellion) that could not be immediately reached by their would-be emancipators.

Even so, *Somerset* did recognize that slavery was, to say the least, a dubious institution, something that Englishmen had learned by that time from John Locke's *Second Treatise on Government* (1690), if they did not already know it. So dubious is slavery, *Somerset* taught, that only positive law (whether legislation or well-established custom) can support it. We notice in passing that the principles of natural law (or of natural right) are not considered enough by the Mansfield court to invalidate positive law when that law has been clearly provided for by the relevant authority. Does this not suggest something about the limited status of judicial review in Anglo-American law in the 1770s?

III

But however narrow *Somerset* may have been technically in 1772, it has been almost legendary in the impact it has had for more than two centuries now. For one thing, it immediately lowered a legal cloud over all slavery in the British Empire. The extent of its influence testifies to what is intrinsic to the case, the principles that are somehow drawn upon by the court.

We are reminded thereby of the vitality of the principles that a healthy system of laws depends upon and reaffirms. This can be seen in what the barons got from King John at Runnymede in 1215. These nobles' subjects could in turn eventually invoke against them the principles that the barons themselves had invoked against their king in Magna Carta. This can be seen as well in what the Continental Congress, including of course owners of slaves, let loose among themselves when they invoked against King George III the self-evident truth that all men are created equal. And we have been seeing, for some decades now, how the principles implicit in the Fourteenth Amendment have taken on a life of their own in turn. This development was anticipated by what was said and done in the Emancipation Proclamation, something that had been recognized by Frederick Douglass from the outset, despite the limited scope of Lincoln's prosaic-sounding proclamation.[6]

IV

Somerset, it can be said, was not "really" about slavery but rather about conflict-of-laws issues and about the problem of the relation of municipal law to the general principles of the common law. These matters can be put, as Mansfield puts them, in rather prosaic terms. Mansfield's purported desire to go no further than he had to is reflected in the efforts he made to avoid having to decide this case at all. In effect, he issued several warnings to the would-be owners of slaves in England. Everyone was put on notice as to what the court was likely to do if it was pressed to decide the case. Mansfield made a point of noting that several such controversies had been settled out of court in recent years, evidently by simply emancipating or otherwise satisfying in each instance the slave in question. (Had the owners of emancipated slaves been compensated by other slave owners in England who wanted to avoid a definitive ruling?)

It is obvious that Mansfield gave the owners of other slaves being held in England time both to have this particular controversy settled and to get out of the country with their slaves at once if they planned to leave, especially since they had evidently come to rely on the security of their property in England. One wonders, considering Stewart's failure to respond to the threat implicit in Mansfield's remarks, whether this was a contrived case, with abolitionists really behind Stewart, the ostensible owner of Somerset. Although I have seen no evidence of this, the situation does look odd. However that may have been, Mansfield recognized that there were thirteen thousand to fourteen thousand slaves being held at that time in the country, with a total value of some £700,000.[7] This, in short, was serious business. It was clear that Mansfield wanted everyone to understand that the law could not be cavalier about the property and expectations of so many people, especially in the light of "official" remarks (however ill-conceived) that had been made some decades before about the status of property in slaves in England. Assurances had once been given to owners of slaves, it seems, and now some warning was needed before a critical change in the effective rules could be announced, even if that announcement merely recognized a change of opinion that had already taken place.

If liberty is to mean anything, Mansfield seems to say, property and not-unreasonable expectations must be respected. This must have seemed only fair. The very liberty sought by slaves depends upon moderation, including respect for recognized property rights. This approach is to be expected from a great commercial-law judge such as Mansfield: the significance of what he holds is enhanced by his obvious insistence upon the rule of law.

We are reminded, by the concerns which Mansfield had to balance, that there often is, for deep-rooted legal issues, no simple solution. There are likely to be contending equities to be recognized. This may be seen in the affirmative-action controversies we encounter today. It may be seen as well in such bold advances as the prohibition of slavery in the Northwest Territory and the issuance of the Emancipation Proclamation. The Northwest Ordinance was obliged to provide, along with its categorical prohibition of slavery in a vast territory, for the return of fugitive slaves; the Emancipation Proclamation was obliged to recognize, if its status as a sound military measure was to be maintained, the continued toleration of slavery in the parts of the United States already subject to the control of the Union Army. This approach may further be seen in Lincoln's policy toward slavery throughout the Civil War, with his repeated recommendations of the gradual, compensated emancipation of slaves.

V

I return to the immediate effects of *Somerset* in England. Evidently slaves were still held there after June 1772, at least for a while. It also seems that contracts of sale dealing with slaves all over the Empire and elsewhere could continue to be recognized in English commercial litigation. Perhaps the masters of slaves who wanted to have their servants with them in England could come to treat them somewhat as indentured servants.

Such owners, however, may have risked difficulties if and when they wanted to leave England with their slaves. In many instances, of course, the slaves may not have known that they had the right to resist forcible removal. In other instances, the slaves may have wanted to leave, perhaps to return to their families or a better climate back in the West Indies or in the American Colonies. Later travelers to England from the Americas often took the precaution of having their slaves sign "contracts" for labor before coming over, contracts that were expected to permit an owner to remove a slave forcibly if need be.[8]

But despite all of these qualifications, evasions, and adaptations, the *Somerset* case had considerable significance throughout the British Empire and later (but to a lesser extent) in an independent United States. It seemed to recognize fundamental principles both of the common law and of natural right (or natural law) that called slavery into question. *Somerset* could even be considered, as in Massachusetts shortly thereafter, to have abolished slavery throughout the British Empire.[9]

VI

However limited its technical holding, *Somerset* seems to have prepared the way for the 1833 act of Parliament that abolished slavery in the British Empire. It is revealing that this act was considered necessary by abolitionists in England. Similarly, Lincoln pressed for the Thirteenth Amendment, knowing that however important, and hence valid, his Emancipation Proclamation had been as a military measure, something of a more legislative character was needed for the long-term security of persons of African descent in this Country.

It is instructive to notice in *Somerset* the ways in which legislative supremacy is taken for granted. Mansfield understands that there are serious difficulties in providing for a general emancipation of slaves, or for a recognition of such emancipation, by means of a judicial opinion alone. (This observation may also apply to such controversies as the status of abortion rights in the United States in our own time.) Mansfield reminds the parties to this case about the prerogatives of Parliament with respect to a comprehensive regulation of the institutions of slavery in England.[10]

Although *Somerset* could not invalidate positive law, it could be used by those who wanted to repeal or reform positive law, whether that law was found in legislation or in long-established customs. Mansfield, even as he acknowledged the authority of positive law, used language that he must have recognized would be celebrated and made good use of "in states unborn and accents yet unknown."[11] Consider, for example, his concluding remarks in *Somerset*:

> The return states, that the slave [*Somerset*] departed and refused to serve; whereupon he was kept, to be sold abroad. So high an act of dominion must be recognized by the law of the country where it is used. The power of a master over his slave has been extremely different, in different countries. The state of slavery is of such a nature, that it is incapable of being introduced on any reasons, moral or political; but only [by] positive law, which preserves its force long after the reasons, occasion, and time itself from whence it was created, is erased from memory: It's so odious, that nothing can be suffered to support it, but positive law. Whatever inconveniences, therefore, may follow from a decision, I cannot say this case is allowed or approved by the law of *England*; and therefore the black must be discharged.[12]

That Mansfield was able to leave such a legacy as is found in these words without sacrificing his reputation as a judge sensitive to the sacred rights of

property testifies to judicial statesmanship of the highest order, statesmanship that is buttressed by well-honed rhetorical skills.

VII

We have observed that the Declaration of Independence is another of those
documents that reach, in their implications and consequences, far beyond
their immediate circumstances and purposes. That document, with its dramatic "created equal" language, helped Americans secure their independence and advance the cause of self-government.

But we are again reminded of the often puzzling complexity of such
matters when we further notice that one consequence of this founding
document was to get Americans out of an imperial system that was to be
governed a half-century later by a general act of emancipation of all slaves.
Thus, Americans, as one result of their eloquent invocation of liberty in
1776, deprived themselves of the salutary effects of the Abolition Act
enacted by Parliament in 1833. (That was about the time that John Calhoun and his desperate associates were sinking deeper and deeper into a
perverse justification of slavery as a positive good, not merely as a necessary evil.) Had separation from Great Britain not happened, it can be
argued, the American Civil War might have been avoided, assuming that
Great Britain could have enforced its 1833 abolition statute in all of its
American Colonies. We should be thankful, at least, that the American War
of Independence was not provoked by a British attempt to emancipate
American slaves.

No doubt, we can see applications down to our day and beyond of
various of the lessons taught by *Somerset,* including something that applies
to any circumstances that find a country divided into factions that have little if any interest in each other's well-being. For example, consider how
the following condemnation of slavery, which is taken from the oral arguments in *Somerset,* bears upon both our troubled race-relations circumstances and any deepening class divisions among us today:

> [Slavery] is dangerous to the state, by its corruption of those citizens on
> whom its prosperity depends; and by admitting within it a multitude of
> persons, who being excluded from the common benefits of the consti-
> tution, are interested in scheming its destruction.[13]

We can turn now in our thoughts in this book-length dialogue, on the
statesmanship of Abraham Lincoln, to the lessons taught us by his career, a

career within that venerable constitutional system which presented him such achievements as Magna Carta, *Somerset v. Stewart,* and the Declaration of Independence, as well as such atrocities as chattel slavery and *Dred Scott.* It is easy to neglect the fortunate aspects of Lincoln's wonderfully successful career, not least perhaps in how and when he left the political stage. Guidance is provided here for the unduly ambitious by an observation in a 1956 letter by Leo Strauss:

> I wish power and understanding were more united than they are. But I am afraid that the efforts which sensible men would have to make in order to acquire power would detract from the most reasonable employment of their reason. So we have to go on trusting on occasional friendly gestures of *fortuna* . . .

That is, this Collection, which investigates these and related matters, could well be subtitled *A Dialogue on Prudence.* Here, indeed, the Declaration of Independence is a good place to start as well as to end.

1

The Declaration of Independence: An Introduction

All the political sentiments I entertain have been drawn, so far as I have been able to draw them, from the sentiments which originated, and were given to the world from this hall [Independence Hall] in which we stand. I have never had a feeling politically that did not spring from the sentiments embodied in the Declaration of Independence. . . . I have often inquired of myself, what great principle or idea it was that kept this Confederacy so long together. It was not the mere matter of the separation of the colonies from the mother land; but something in that Declaration giving liberty, not alone to the people of this country, but hope to the world for all future time. It was that which gave promise that in due time the weights should be lifted from the shoulders of all men, and that *all* should have an equal chance. This is the sentiment embodied in that Declaration of Independence.

—Abraham Lincoln

I

Any examination of Abraham Lincoln's constitutionalism can usefully take its bearings, as Lincoln himself did, by the Declaration of Independence. We, in our capacity as citizens of the United States, recognize at the outset of this inquiry that the Declaration of Independence is primarily a public document.[14]

This talk was given at the Hillel Foundation Jewish Student Center, University of Chicago, February 12, 1961. (Original title "The Declaration of Independence: Explanation and Reminder.") It has been previously published in 9 *Saint Louis University Law Journal* 390–408 (1965).

The epigraph is taken from *The Collected Works of Abraham Lincoln,* ed. Roy P. Basler (New Brunswick, N.J.: Rutgers University Press, 1953), 3: 240 (Philadelphia; February 22, 1861).

The Declaration was issued for public purposes, at home and abroad. One can see in it passages designed to influence British and French readers, as well as passages designed to secure public support in the Colonies for the year-old rebellion.

It is a public document also in that it draws on what was commonly accepted by those—of the revolutionary persuasion, at least—who had long discussed the issues dealt with in the Declaration. Thus, John Adams could observe many years later, "There is not an idea in it but what had been hackneyed in Congress for two years before."[15] And Thomas Jefferson could respond that it was the purpose of the Declaration

> not to find out new principles, or new arguments, never before thought of, not merely to say things which had never been said before; but to place before mankind the common sense of the subject, in terms so plain and firm as to command their assent, and to justify ourselves in the independent stand we were compelled to take. Neither aiming at originality of principle or sentiment, nor yet copied from any particular and previous writing, it was intended to be an expression of the American mind, and to give to that expression the proper tone and spirit called for by the occasion. All its authority rests, then, on the harmonizing sentiments of the day, whether expressed in conversation, in letters, printed essays, or in the elementary books of public right, as Aristotle, Cicero, Locke, Sidney, &c.[16]

Finally, the Declaration is a public document in that Jefferson's draft was carefully reviewed, and altered in many respects, by the Continental Congress, a body of men more moderate than he, which eventually adopted and promulgated the Declaration. The Congress added the appeals to "the Supreme Judge of the World" and for "the Protection of divine Providence," struck out the fierce condemnation of the slave trade penned by Jefferson (and defended by Adams), and indeed made so many other changes that Jefferson considered his work mutilated. No doubt, Jefferson anticipated many of the points on which the Congress would insist; even the draft originally submitted to the Congress (which was cut down thereafter by one-fourth) cannot be taken as simply reflecting Jefferson's thought to the extent that other of his public utterances might be.

Each of these considerations affects how the document should be read and provides support for Ralph Waldo Emerson's description of it as one of those "acts of great scope, working on a long future and on permanent interests, [which honor] alike those who initiate and those who receive them."[17]

II

The contents of the Declaration of Independence, the document Daniel Webster regarded as "the title-deed of [American] liberties,"[18] suggest a division into seven parts. It is characteristic of the Declaration, however, that even the delineation of its parts, to say nothing of their meaning, is far from unambiguous and invites continuous reappraisal. Here, for example, is a simpler, three-part division of the Declaration: "This is what we believe about government. This is what has been done to us. This is what we have to do now."

We confront, first in a seven-part division, the elaborate *title* which indicates that this is a declaration, adopted on July 4, 1776, by "the REP-RESENTATIVES of the UNITED STATES OF AMERICA, in GEN-ERAL CONGRESS assembled." The second part consists of a long sentence in which there is stated the purpose of the document, including the worldwide tribunal to which it is directed. *Venue,* so to speak, is established. There is next the *commencement* of the argument, which contains a statement of the general principles, the self-evident truths and deductions drawn from those truths, upon which the colonists' course is based. The fourth and central part of the Declaration is by far the longest, containing well over half of its more than thirteen hundred words: it is a *statement* of the cause of action, of the grievances resulting from a series of improper acts on the part of the King of Great Britain, closing with the complaint that the Colonists' "repeated Petitions" had been "answered only by repeated Injury" and with the observation, "A Prince, whose Character is thus marked by every act which may define a Tyrant, is unfit to be the Ruler of a free People." There is next the *conclusion* to be drawn from the foregoing conjunction of principles and injuries: the Colonists must exercise a people's inalienable right to abolish a form of government thus shown to be destructive of the proper ends of government. The sixth part of the document includes the formal *declaration* of independence, a restatement of the resolution that had been submitted to the Congress a month earlier,[19] as well as the mutual *pledge* in support of this declaration. Finally, there is the list of the signers of the Declaration, collected according to States.

It should be noted that even the term "declaration" is not without significance, for it reminds readers both of the legal form by the same name and of the historic political declarations that preceded the Declaration of Independence. The legal form is, in pleading, "a specification, in a methodical and logical form, of the circumstances which constitute the plaintiff's cause of action."[20] Or, to take another definition, it is "a formal statement intended to create, preserve, assert or testify to a right."[21] The terms we are able to ascribe to the parts of the Declaration conform not only in language but also in sequence to the common-law form of declaration: title, venue, commencement, statement, conclusion, and even the formal declaration (with its pledge). Thus, the case for the Americans was set forth in a tribunal comprised of both God and mankind.

Of the historic declarations preceding the Declaration of Independence, there are three of which special note should be taken here, one English, two American. The most famous, the English Declaration or Bill of Rights, the 1689 document incorporating the terms of the Glorious Revolution of the year before, consists of three parts:

> a recital [by Parliament] of the illegal and arbitrary acts committed by the late king [James II], and of their consequent vote of abdication; a declaration, nearly following the words of the former part, that such enumerated acts are illegal; and a resolution that the throne shall be filled by the prince and princess of Orange, according to [specified limitations].[22]

The Continental Congress no doubt drew in its Declaration of Independence upon the precedent of the Convention Parliament and its condemnation of a usurping monarch, even to the extent of placing the Colonists on firm constitutional ground by reporting that King George III had "abdicated Government here." But there is, of course, a vital difference: the 1689 Parliament reformed the monarchy; the 1776 Congress repudiated both parliament and monarch.

That the misdeeds of Parliament, more than those of the monarch, were responsible for the rupture in 1776 is clearly indicated in two earlier American declarations, both of them also issued by the Continental Congress: "The Declaration and Resolves of the First Continental Congress," October 14, 1774, and "The Declaration of the Causes and Necessity of Taking Up Arms," July 6, 1775. The principal complaint in both declarations is, in the words of the Declaratory Act of 1766, that the British Parliament claimed "a power, of right, to bind the people of America by statute in all cases whatsoever." In 1774, the Colonists were prepared to oppose only by "peaceable measures" the various "grievous acts and measures" to which they had been subjected. In 1775, after once again stating their grievances, having considered themselves "bound by obligations of respect to the rest of the world, to make known the justice of [their] causes," they announced that they must take up arms "for the preservation of [their] liberties." At the same time, they assured their supporters in Great Britain, "We mean not to dissolve that union which has so long and so happily subsisted between us."[23]

A year later, however, they must "acquiesce in the Necessity" of declaring independence. Since allegiance to the British Crown was to be cast off—for it was this, not any authority Parliament might claim, that they seem to have considered to provide their only constitutional link with the British Empire—the emphasis is placed in 1776 upon the misdeeds of the King of Great Britain, the acts of Parliament being laid at his door by virtue of the royal assent that he had given to this legislation. The rhetorical advantages of this course are evident, however specious it may seem to the constitutional historian. Thus, the United States of America came into being.

The Athenians, Thucydides reports, were obliged at the beginning of the Peloponnesian War to solemnize a public funeral of the first slain in that war. On that occasion, we are told, "the man chosen to make the oration was Pericles, the son of Xantippus, who, when the time served, going out of the place of burial into a high pulpit to be heard the farther off by the multitude, spake unto them in this manner."[24] The authors of the Declaration of Independence also chose a high pulpit for the occasion on which they delivered the decisive pronouncement of *their* commonwealth: for they so elevated the thought and style of their sentiments that their words, like those of Pericles, stir aspiration even as they defy imitation.

III

We turn now to the text of the Declaration of Independence. It is convenient to direct our efforts to discussing—or, rather, to raising questions about—five teachings of the Declaration, teachings that bear on the equality of men, on forms of government, on the right of revolution, on divine sanctions in political affairs, and on the ends of government.

The Declaration asserts as the initial politically relevant self-evident truth, if we overlook for the moment the very recognition that there are self-evident truths, that "all Men are created equal."

What can this mean? Certainly, the men responsible for the Declaration knew what we know: human beings not only differ in such physical characteristics as strength and beauty, to say nothing of color, but also, and much more important, they differ even at birth in intellectual and perhaps even in moral equipment. One could continue to enumerate differences among human beings, some of which would be politically relevant.[25] Yet, would not the very enumeration rest upon an implicit recognition of the fact on which the self-evident truth about "all Men" draws? That is, the distinctions to be enumerated are made among *human beings,* among creatures who resemble one another more than any one of them resembles any of the other creatures of the earth.

This emphasis upon, as distinguished from the age-old recognition of, the essential equality of men rests on considerations of justice: why should this human being be treated differently from that one unless and until good reasons for differential treatment are advanced? This consideration of justice, which may have come to seem practicable, at least in economic matters, as a result of the material abundance promised by modern science and its technology, is reflected in the second of the "self-evident" truths enunciated by the Declaration: all men "are endowed by their Creator with certain unalienable Rights [and] among these are Life, Liberty, and the Pursuit of Happiness."[26] The rights to life, liberty, and the pursuit of happiness are called "unalienable," a term that suggests nature and the natural: an alien, who is to be made a citizen, goes through what the Declaration calls "Naturalization."

Some rights cannot be alienated, they cannot properly be given up or taken away without good cause (and any such attempted alienation must be either mistaken or under protest and may properly be repudiated). But, as we all know, life and liberty can certainly be forfeited. There is found in the Fifth Amendment to the Constitution of the United States, for example, a recognition of this distinction: one cannot be deprived of life, liberty, or property without due process of law. Thus, an arbitrary taking—one which is a deprivation that cannot justify itself and thereby denies the essential similarity among human beings—fails to take due account of the inalienability of critical rights.

It has been said (and even by Abraham Lincoln, the most distinguished commentator thus far on the Declaration of Independence) that, strictly speaking, the enunciation of the principle that all men are created equal was "of no practical use" for the immediate purpose at hand: separation from Great Britain.[27] Yet, was not this principle convenient, perhaps even necessary, for the argument that culminated in the affirmation of the right of any people "to alter or to abolish" any regime that fails to serve the ends appropriate to government? Thus, to go one step further, the equality of men seems vital to the argument that *this* community of human beings, this people, is entitled as much as any other people to independence.

This *people* is distinguished, or distinguishable, from "the rest of Mankind." True, "Consanguinity" inclines the Americans toward their "British Brethren," but this tie does not require acquiescence to tyranny over "a free People." What makes a "people"? What, for example, is the basis for the designation of Quebec as "a neighboring Province" rather than as one of "these Colonies"? Certainly, the "merciless Indian Savages" are not considered part of *this* people, nor perhaps are the slaves whose "domestic Insurrections" the Colonists fear. There is reference, on the other hand, to "fellow Citizens" who have been compelled (after having been "taken Captive on the high Seas") "to bear Arms against their Country" and to become "the Executioners of their Friends and Brethren, or to fall themselves by their Hands."

There is something called a "Country," which is somehow related to "a free People," "the good People of these Colonies," and "one People." Is it made up of "Friends and Brethren"? But not the "British Brethren"; and friendship, we are told, is governed by war and peace. *Is* there any test, any formula, any clear way of determining what is included or excluded? Many "nations" in Africa, Asia, and Europe today face this problem. The American Civil War testifies to the almost fatal difficulty in definition, perhaps even to the arbitrary character, of the term "one People." Perhaps, indeed, the problem of determining what constitutes a people for political purposes suggests why the intellectual virtue referred to in the Declaration is *prudence* rather than *wisdom*.[28] Prudence can dictate political action on the basis of assumptions that may be ultimately unexamined, resulting in judgments that are probable or simply commonly accepted. Wisdom, on the other hand, strives for a nonpolitical certainty: it cannot settle for "the Rectitude of . . . Intentions" or leave unquestioned the "self-evident" truths with respect to the equality of men, the meaning and significance of "Life, Liberty, and the Pursuit of Happiness," or the basis of the distinction of this people from that.[29]

It is evident that the Declaration, despite its form, is not a logical demonstration. Demonstrations certainly do not rely on appeals to Heaven: to "the Supreme Judge of the World" and to "divine Providence." The "separate and equal Station" "among the Powers of the Earth" is provided for by the "the Laws of Nature and of Nature's God." Somehow, the world is asked to believe, it is appropriate that this should be "one People" who are entitled to "dissolve the Political Bands which have connected them with another." The world has gone on to believe—partly as a result of the American example and even more as a result of the American insistence upon the equality of men (especially as reflected in the Wilsonian doctrine of self-determination)—that all self-defining bodies of men are equal, one to another, if they but choose to insist upon the point.

We are occasionally reminded that slave owners signed the Declaration of Independence as readily as those who did not own slaves. But this does not cast light so much on the meaning of the "created equal" language as it does on the inability of human beings always to give full effect to their principles in the circumstances by which they may be confronted. Whatever the private views on slavery of the authors of the Declaration, the public language they employed provided, and continues to provide, the classic statement of the equality maxim to which the Emancipation Proclamation, the Gettysburg Address, and the Thirteenth, Fourteenth, and Fifteenth Amendments are decisive contributions.[30]

It is good to remind ourselves today of Lincoln's inspired view "of the *meaning* and *objects* of that part of the Declaration of Independence which declares that ''all men are created equal.'''[31] "The authors of that notable instrument," he said in 1857,

> did not mean to assert the obvious untruth, that all were then actually enjoying that equality, nor yet, that they were about to confer it immediately upon them. In fact, they had no power to confer such a boon. They meant simply to declare the *right,* so that the *enforcement* of it might follow as fast as circumstances should permit. They meant to set up a standard maxim for free society, which should be familiar to all, and revered by all; constantly looked to, constantly labored for, and even though never perfectly attained, constantly approximated, and thereby constantly spreading and deepening its influence, and augmenting the happiness and value of life to all people of all colors everywhere. . . . Its authors meant it to be, thank God, it is now proving itself, a stumbling block to all those who in after times might seek to turn a free people back into the hateful paths of despotism. They knew the proneness of prosperity to breed tyrants, and they meant when such should re-appear in this fair land and commence their vocation they should find left for them at least one hard nut to crack.[32]

We can see here how Lincoln put the Declaration to political use in 1857, emphasizing that aspect of its teaching appropriate to the circumstances of *his* age, and we can also see why he often referred to it as an "instrument." Indeed, the "hard nut" had been subjected to powerful hammer blows. The assertion of the equality of all men had recently been condemned on the floor of the United States Senate as "a self-evident lie." Other influential men, including Chief Justice Roger B. Taney and Senator Stephen A. Douglas, conceded the validity of the "created equal" assertion but denied that the African was meant to be included within its terms. Even Lincoln later recognized that the "self-evident" of earlier generations had been undermined by "a great civil war" and by the controversy that had led to that war: he was obliged to speak at Gettysburg of "the *proposition* that all men are created equal."

It is curiously indicative of our own equivocal attitude toward the founding sentiments of this republic that the deservedly celebrated 1954 United States Supreme Court decisions striking down public school segregation in this Country failed to mention—assuming that such segregation represents a denial of the principle that all men are created equal—the Declaration of Independence, relying instead upon the much more questionable and far less elevated findings of social science research.[33] Perhaps, indeed, we have moved so far from the dogma of "self-evident" truths that we sometimes seem to agree with the Chief Justice who had assured us a few years before,

> Nothing is more certain in modern society than the principle that there are no absolutes, that a name, a phrase, a standard has meaning only when associated with the considerations which gave birth to the nomenclature. . . . To those who would paralyze our Government in the face of impending threat by encasing it in a semantic straitjacket we must reply that all concepts are relative.[34]

The "principle that there are no absolutes" is not one to which men can pledge themselves in forming or re-forming "a free People." It is as a reminder of absolutes, and indeed of the nature of human beings, that the Declaration of Independence remains our founding instrument.

IV

What is the relevance today, for law-abiding Americans, of the calm insistence in the Declaration of Independence that whenever any form of government becomes destructive of the proper ends of government, "it is the Right of the People to alter or to abolish it, and to institute new Government"?[35] Do Americans need to be reminded of this two-century-old reservation, which is but another of the self-evident truths? Do they need to insist on this reservation even in an age when they are generally satisfied with their form of government?[36]

Not that the revolutionary principle has been altogether lost sight of. It is, for instance, reflected in the distinction in positive law between rebels and pirates. It may well be, however, that Americans have greater need to be explicitly reminded today of this principle, and all that it implies, than at any other time in their history. The men of 1776 could speak of "self-evident" truths. We no longer do so—at least, not the educated and sophisticated among us—whereas they would have said that it is precisely the educated who are best equipped to discern what is self-evident.[37] Rather, we

are more disposed to speak of that to which "we" are accustomed or conditioned, as distinguished from that to which "they" are conditioned or
accustomed, without delving into the basis of the distinction between "we"
and "they." Indeed, such an insistence upon the "we" means that there must
be no possibility of questioning what "we" believe or do: it means, ultimately, that the very assertion of the right to question—the assertion of the
principle of the right of revolution—is itself grounds for suspicion if not
evidence of disloyalty.[38]

To insist upon the right "to alter or to abolish" when those in power
become destructive of the ends of government is more than a recognition
of how human beings respond in desperate circumstances to the actions of
their rulers; rather, it is an insistence upon those ends, upon ends which
transcend all forms of government, including that form which happens to
be incorporated in our Constitution. That Constitution can certainly be
said, at this time, to promote those ends for the American people. But what
if a government, proceeding pursuant to the forms of the Constitution,
becomes destructive of the ends of government? What, that is, if the Constitution itself should come to be, or should be made to be, destructive of
the proper ends of government?

It is assumed by the Declaration that there are, under any form of government, ends beyond the government by which the activities of governments might be judged. These are ends that can inform and guide actions
and decisions in circumstances far less serious than those in which an appeal
must be made to arms. The ends are left to human beings to discover and
define; we are reminded here of the traditional recourse to natural law.[39]
These ends have something to do with "the Laws of Nature and of Nature's
God," something to do with "certain unalienable Rights," *among which* are
the rights to "Life, Liberty, and the Pursuit of Happiness." Men can—
indeed they must—rely upon governments to effect these ends; but even if
they try to do so, they cannot legitimately surrender to others the most
valuable of man's inalienable rights, most valuable because of its reliance
upon that which distinguishes human beings from the other creatures: they
cannot surrender the right, and the duty, to examine and assess the deeds
of their governors and of themselves.

The Declaration reminds us thereby of the old-fashioned proposition
that there are standards outside and above the agreements and teachings of
men, government, and era, standards superior even to what "the People"
might at any moment believe or choose. In short, the right of revolution
implies an insistence upon the supremacy of reason in human affairs.[40]
Those today who rebel against the principle of "the right of revolution" act
more in self-defense than they realize: not because of any present prospect

of forcible overthrow of the Government of the United States, of course, but because of the hollowness in much of current thought that is exposed by an awareness of what the right of revolution must mean. This revolutionary principle remains in our time "one hard nut to crack" for those who "might seek to turn a free people back into the hateful paths of despotism," the despotism either of tyrannical governors or of self-indulgent multitudes.[41]

It should not be left at this. There runs through the Declaration a qualification that has been ignored by people of other times or in other lands who seize upon it as a simply revolutionary precedent and justification, and that is the qualification that reason must be exercised and the reasonable raised up. The "Opinions of Mankind" are to be respected: the causes impelling a people to separation should be declared. To state causes requires the use of reason as well as the application of principles common to, or generally accepted by, mankind. Not only are "Facts . . . submitted to a candid World," but also there is advanced a kind of argument starting from self-evident premises and proceeding to probable conclusions. Particularly significant here, not least of all as testimony to the gravity of the "long Train of Abuses and Usurpations" that led to the disruption, is the list of more than two dozen "Oppressions" of the Colonists visited upon them or assented to by the British monarch.

Thus, there is a right to alter or to abolish a form of government that is destructive of the ends of government, but it is a right that does have as one condition the proper exercise of reason: "Prudence, indeed, will dictate that Governments long established should not be changed for light and transient Causes." The Declaration recognizes explicitly a *duty* "to throw off" offending governments, but it also recognizes the duty to move carefully and with good cause before so serious a step is taken. It relies upon the good sense, as well as the natural inertia, of human beings who "are more disposed to suffer, while Evils are sufferable, than to right themselves by abolishing the Forms to which they are accustomed."

What moved *this* people to act at *this* time? We must say something about the long list of "Abuses and Usurpations" for which the King is declared responsible. It is sufficient for our purposes here, which are only incidentally those of the scholar, to make a threefold division: there is the opening set of charges relating primarily to the refusal of the King to govern or to permit others to govern properly; there is the central portion in which there are found the "Usurpations" reflected in acts of Parliament to which the King has assented; and there is the concluding part in which murders, burnings, and other acts of violence and cruelty are predominant, following upon the announcement, "He has abdicated Government here,

by declaring us out of his Protection and waging War against us." It is
rhetorically sound that the opening and closing parts of the Declaration
incorporate "Abuses" most apt to persuade readers generally, even in
monarchical France. The charges range from the anarchy of no government to the anarchy of lawless and predatory government. Buried in the
center of the list, and hence less apparent to the casual reader, are the
"Usurpations" that are keyed more to American conditions and to the
expectations of those familiar with the British constitution. These charges
are least likely to appeal to outsiders, or even to many Americans, although
it is among them that we find most of the specific complaints that had
been agitated for a dozen years.[42] The elaboration of this list of two dozen
"Oppressions," following upon the statement of general principles, is
intended to provide support for the conclusion that Colonial government
by Great Britain had clearly become destructive of the ends to which it
should have been dedicated.

Yet, the problem remains, how is it to be determined whether such
conclusions are proven, whether a particular revolution is justified? There
is, of course, for this revolution as for any other, the practical consideration
recognized by Ulysses S. Grant in 1885:

> Now, the right of revolution is an inherent one. When people are
> oppressed by their government, it is a natural right they enjoy to relieve
> themselves of the oppression, if they are strong enough, either by with-
> drawal from it, or by overthrowing it and substituting a government
> more acceptable. But any people or part of a people who resort to this
> remedy, stake their lives, their property, and every claim for protection
> given by citizenship—on the issue.[43]

But neither the prospect of success (or failure) nor the gravity of the
oppression can be decisive, however important such considerations may be.
For there is a recognition, even in the Declaration of Independence, that
not even the most serious denial of inalienable rights can in every instance
justify revolution or attempted revolution. The slaves in North America
were clearly denied the right to liberty: the fierce passage Jefferson had
penned for the Declaration and that was stricken by the Congress seems to
recognize this denial.[44] Yet, there is listed among the complaints against the
British the charge that "domestic Insurrections" had been excited among
the Colonies. Thus, it was advanced and no doubt regarded as a serious
grievance that slaves had been induced by the British to exercise the right
to abolish the rule of Colonists who were denying the Africans far more
vital rights than most if not all of those referred to in that part of the Declaration reciting the list of royal oppressions.

How is this to be understood? To what extent, to use Lincoln's justification of the acquiescence to slavery in the 1770s and thereafter by the authors of the Declaration, does "the necessity of the case" govern? Such questions presuppose an understanding of the ends that transcend all forms of government, an understanding that distinguishes between principle and doctrine, between political philosophy and ideology. The proper implementation of the answers to such questions depends in large part upon the precepts and examples of public-spirited men of virtue whose "Rectitude of . . . Intentions" can be trusted.

V

The proper relation between the Constitution of the United States and the Declaration of Independence is often obscured, partly because the importance of the Declaration as the fundamental constitutional document is largely overlooked, partly because of the remarkable success of the form of government laid out in the Constitution.

For, we have to remind ourselves, the American Constitution, with its provision for what it calls "a Republican Form of Government," is but one among the alternatives left open by the Declaration. We are told that governments are "instituted among Men" to secure "certain unalienable Rights"; and we are told further that "whenever any Form of Government becomes destructive of these Ends, it is the Right of the People to alter or to abolish it, and to institute new Government, laying its Foundation on such Principles and organizing its Powers in such Form, as to them shall seem most likely to effect their Safety and Happiness." The ends of government are based on "self-evident" truths; but the means to effect the ends of government cannot be so certain. It is recognized by the Declaration that forms of government might have to be experimented with, that the "most likely" has to be settled for; and it seems that what appears best at one time might not be appropriate on another occasion. One prince is declared "unfit to be the Ruler of a free People," but not all princes? We see in the "most likely" qualification a striking instance of tentativeness in an instrument otherwise marked by its bold and confident assertions.

And yet, the Declaration is often understood as authority for the superiority of what is now called "democratic government." What has led to this sometimes mischievous doctrine? There is, of course, historical accident playing its part: *the* form of government appropriate to the sentiments of the Declaration has been identified with the form of government that has been developed by the people of the Declaration. Even in the instrument itself there is reference to "the Right of Representation in the Legislature," a right described as "inestimable" to "those People"—"inestimable," it should be noted, not "unalienable"—and "formidable to Tyrants only." Democrats seem to derive support as well from the assertion that a people may on occasion replace one government with another that seems most likely *to them* to fulfill the purpose of government. But this, we have seen, recognizes that no single form of government is best in all circumstances. Consider, for instance, the government best (if only temporarily) either for "the merciless Indian Savages" or for the slaves whose "domestic Insurrections" are dreaded.

Perhaps even more important in establishing, not implausibly, the connection between democracy and the Declaration of Independence in the minds of people everywhere is the emphasis in the Declaration upon the proposition that governments derive "their just Powers from the Consent of the Governed." Where does "Consent of the Governed" lead? Does *consent* make the exercise of powers *just*? That might, at first glance, seem to be suggested, but a careful reading does not require this interpretation. Perhaps consent relates not to the justice of the exercise of the powers of government but rather to the legitimacy of a particular government. Perhaps it should also be said that once consent is given, it cannot be withdrawn until the government becomes destructive of the ends of government. Legitimacy, once secured, is preserved by justice. Moreover, a people is entitled to retain (and may be obliged to defend) the just government to which it has consented.[45]

How is consent expressed? The reference to "the consent of our Legislatures," which would seem to require positive legislative action, suggests a requirement of action by the people as well if their consent is to be secured. But what kind of action? May not a popular vote or plebiscite establish a spurious consent? Are there not means other than a referendum to determine or establish consent? Perhaps the common feeling of the people, reflected in contentment, peaceableness, and prosperity, is a sufficient, even a better, indication of consent. But, we must ask further, what if a people is deceived into acquiescence? What if misery and conflict are mistaken for happiness and harmony? What if rank injustice and cruelty are mistaken for a just and civilized regime? Are mistaken or deceived peoples able to give consent to rulers and regimes that have become destructive of the ends of government? By proceeding along these lines, we bring closer together the criteria of legitimacy and justice. Are they kept as far apart ultimately as are prudence and wisdom, as far apart as the realm of action and the realm of thought? Must we have recourse here as well to a reliance upon "the Rectitude of our Intentions?"[46]

VI

We see in the Declaration's references to divinity an oblique anticipation of the separation of powers established in the Constitution. There are four references of this kind (and it is rhetorically appropriate that they should be placed, in pairs, at the beginning and at the end of the document):

1. "the Laws of Nature and of Nature's God"

2. "endowed by their Creator"

3. "appealing to the Supreme Judge of the World"

4. "with a firm Reliance on the Protection of divine Providence"

The first reference to God, and perhaps the second as well, regarded God, as *legislator:* it is He Who orders things, ordaining what is to be. He first comes to sight as the lawgiver or lawmaker. (Just as in the Constitution, so in the Declaration, the legislative aspect of government is primary, both in the order of enumeration and in importance.) Next, God is seen as *judge.* Finally, He is revealed as *executive,* as One Who extends protection, enforcing the laws that have been laid down (with a suggestion as well of the dispensing power of the executive).

Thus, the authors of the Declaration of Independence created even the Government of the World in the image of their political institutions.[47] We should further note that the first two references to divinity were inspired by Jefferson: God is seen and known as reflected in Nature, as something that can be grasped by man's reason without the aid of revelation. The third and fourth references, on the other hand, which were added on the floor of the Congress to the Jeffersonian draft, come closer to the God of the Bible, the God of revealed religion. In fact, one must observe that the Congress in its pious contributions may have been more "realistic" politically than the free-thinking Jefferson. The testimony of George Washington in his Farewell Address of 1796 is relevant here:

> Of all the dispositions and habits which lead to political prosperity, religion and morality are indispensable supports. In vain would that man claim the tribute of patriotism, who should labor to subvert these great pillars of human happiness, these firmest props of the duties of men and citizens. The mere politician, equally with the pious man, ought to respect and to cherish them. A volume could not trace all their connections with private and public felicity. Let it simply be asked: Where is the security for property, for reputation, for life, if the sense of religious obligation desert the oaths which are the instruments of investigation in

courts of justice? And let us with caution indulge the supposition that morality can be maintained without religion. Whatever may be conceded to the influence of refined education on minds of peculiar structure, reason and experience both forbid us to expect that national morality can prevail in exclusion of religious principle.

It was from such material that Lincoln developed the "political religion" he thought vital to "the perpetuation of our political institutions."[48] The hand of Divine Providence could be discerned by him in many incidents relating to the Declaration of Independence. Even in casual remarks in response to a serenade, the President could observe:

How long ago is it?—eighty odd years—since on the Fourth of July, for the first time in the history of the world a nation by its representatives, assembled and declared as a self-evident truth "that all men are created equal." [Cheers.] That was the birthday of the United States of America. Since then the Fourth of July has had several peculiar recognitions. The two men most distinguished in the framing and support of the Declaration were Thomas Jefferson and John Adams—the one having penned it and the other sustained it the most forcibly in debate—the only two of the fifty-five who signed it being elected President of the United States. Precisely fifty years after they put their hands to the paper it pleased Almighty God to take both from the stage of action. This was indeed an extraordinary and remarkable event in our history. Another President, five years after, was called from this stage of existence on the same day and month of the year; and now, on this last Fourth of July just passed, when we have a gigantic Rebellion, at the bottom of which is an effort to overthrow the principle that all men are created equal, we have the surrender of a most powerful position and army on that very day. [Cheers] . . . Gentlemen, this is a glorious theme, and the occasion for a speech, but I am not prepared to make one worthy of the occasion.[49]

These remarks and their theme are refined and elevated in the Gettysburg Address. There is to be seen in that address, as in Lincoln's Second Inaugural Address, a sublime blending of the political and the religious.[50] The anticipation of such blending by the Declaration of Independence may be detected not only in its separation of powers in the Government of the World but even in its designation of "Honor" as "sacred."

Thus, we can discern not only in the history of the framing of the Declaration and in the sentiments of our greatest statesmen, but even in the language of the Declaration itself, the tension, possibilities, and problems with respect to the proper relation between religion and politics that come down to our day.

VII

We have left, for the conclusion of this introduction to the Declaration of Independence, our return to that which is the starting point of the enterprise, the temporal ends of government. The purpose of government, we are told, is to secure "certain unalienable Rights, . . . among [which] are Life, Liberty and the Pursuit of Happiness." Further along, we are induced to infer that government must be instituted with a view to the likelihood of effecting here on earth the "Safety and Happiness" of the people. The right to life and perhaps to liberty may be seen in the effort to guarantee the safety of the governed; the right to liberty and the pursuit of happiness may be reflected in the effort to promote the happiness of the governed.

Emphasis is placed throughout the instrument upon the invasions of liberty, and consequently of life, property, and the common good, at the hands of "the present King of Great-Britain." There is revealed, it is alleged, a "Design to reduce [Americans] under absolute Despotism"; the direct object of "the repeated Injuries and Usurpations" is "the Establishment of an absolute Tyranny over these States"; the King's character is marked "by every act which may define a Tyrant"; he "is unfit to be the Ruler of a free People." Thus, liberty is central not only to the famous trilogy—whether expressed in the form found in the Declaration or in the traditional (and less revolutionary) version of "life, liberty and property" affirmed in the American Bill of Rights—but also (it seems) to the view of the authors of the Declaration of how happiness might be achieved and life preserved. They may even be taken as agreeing with what Pericles said of the Athenian dead, that they placed happiness in liberty, and liberty in valor.

The Periclean formula cannot be understood without consideration of its context, for Pericles goes on to urge his fellow citizens, in imitation of the honored dead, to "be forward to encounter the dangers of War."[51] The emphasis is placed upon valor, because war is currently the arena in which the fate of the city is to be decided. In times of peace, however, we should expect justice (or perhaps friendship) more than valor to be the secret of liberty (or perhaps mutual respect). That, too, is what the authors of the Declaration seem to suggest: their "British Brethren" are rebuked for having been "deaf to the Voice of Justice and of Consanguinity." The tie of blood should have particularly inclined Britons to listen to repeated complaints; the demands for justice, reflected in the list of royal measures that offend against laws both written and unwritten, should make all men listen, especially when the demands are supported by deeds of valor.

We are reminded of a proposition advanced by Washington, the proposition "that there exist in the oeconomy and course of nature, an indissoluble union between virtue and happiness." Both valor and justice are needed if the ends of government are to be secured: prudence dictates where the emphasis is to be placed, whether it is a time for war or a time for peace. Indeed, prudence must guide human beings not only in the development and administration of their constitution, but even in the determination of the appropriate occasions for praising the merits or exposing the defects of their revered constitutional documents.

Now we, as does the Declaration, must draw to the end of this phase of our discussion, an end which is a new beginning, a beginning which recognizes that we have, in the words of Benjamin Franklin, "no more durable preeminence than the grains in an hour glass." (We hear echoes of Benjamin Franklin's words in the mortality-minded poetry of Abraham Lincoln that we examine in Chapter 9 of this Collection.) The Declaration opens with the haunting phrase, "When in the Course of human Events," an expression that marks the practical character of the enterprise even as it reminds us of the fragility of human affairs and human existence. Yet reason and the civilization to which reason and reverence have led human beings make their demands and offer their hopes. It was in this spirit that the two giants of the Congress of 1776 continued their association into old age. It was in this spirit that Thomas Jefferson wrote to John Adams in 1813,

> I have thus stated my opinion on a point on which we differ, not with a view to controversy, for we are both too old to change opinions which are the result of a long life of inquiry and reflection; but on the suggestion of a former letter of yours, that we ought not to die before we have explained ourselves to each other.[52]

Indeed, these men, as partners and rivals, helped to lay the foundations for a government by explanation: for it is the willingness to explain oneself that displays a decent respect for the opinions and, therefore, for the reason and moral sensibilities of mankind. But, unfortunately, explanation is the mode of peace and sacrifice, the mode of war. And it is, for the Declaration of Independence, a time of war. We are assured at the conclusion of the instrument by a pledge to each other of "our Lives, our Fortunes, and our sacred Honor." The right to life is put in the balance, for each man signed in the Declaration his own death warrant, as a traitor, in the event of failure. The right to the pursuit of happiness, the fortunes that lie before them, is also put in jeopardy.

Liberty, as well, is thrown into the scale, but not as are the other two great rights. For liberty is offered up immediately, rather than in the event of failure: the liberty of choice, the liberty of action, is sacrificed to the common cause. There is a dedication, a dedication sealed by a pledge of honor—by the pledge, that is, not to exercise their liberty to abandon the cause that they dare proclaim to the world.

2

The Declaration of Independence: On Rights and Duties

> There is no truth more thoroughly established, than that there exists in the oeconomy and course of nature, an indissoluble union between virtue and happiness, between duty and advantage, between the genuine maxims of an honest and magnanimous policy, and the solid rewards of public prosperity and felicity. . . . [W]e ought to be no less persuaded that the propitious smiles of Heaven, can never be expected on a nation that disregards the eternal rules of order and right, which Heaven itself has ordained. . . . [T]he preservation of the sacred fire of liberty, and the destiny of the Republican model of Government, are justly considered as *deeply,* perhaps as *finally* slaked, on the experiment entrusted to the hands of the American people.
>
> —George Washington

I

We, in our capacity as students, bring to the Declaration of Independence the teachings of political philosophy, and especially Classical political philosophy.[53] These teachings may affect one's view of the Declaration. They may even make one wonder just what should be thought of that venerable instrument. It is such wonder that can move the student temporarily absolved of the certitudes and allegiances of citizenship to ponder and inquire, if only to prepare himself to assess properly the blandishments of revisionist fashions.

This talk was given in the College, the University of Chicago, October 10, 1963. (Original title "Another Look at the Declaration of Independence.") It has been previously published in 9 *Saint Louis University Law Journal* 408–15 (1965).

The epigraph is taken from George Washington's First Inaugural Address, April 30, 1789.

But, first, the student might wonder whether it is necessary to try to understand the instrument, to confront the problems that it poses. Perhaps if he were always to remain a student, he would be entitled to direct his attention exclusively to other matters. But it is likely, considering the nature of our regime, that he will one day assume the duties of a citizen in a republic.[54] It is partly with that likelihood in view that he is obliged to address himself to an instrument that is critical to the life of his Country.

A people takes its meaning from such founding statements as the Declaration of Independence, from such public expressions of its political soul. Thus, in order to comply with the ancient, even divine, commandment to know one's self, one must examine and know well and continually reexamine fundamental statements. Not all great peoples can be entrusted with such a commandment,[55] but only those that have been formed by constituting statements that do bear examination, that, despite the defects that any public utterance must have, nevertheless continue to instruct and elevate student and citizen alike.

II

Governments are instituted among men, we are told, in order to secure the inalienable rights with which all men are endowed by their Creator. Among the rights that governments are instituted to secure are "Life, Liberty, and the Pursuit of Happiness." Thus, the objectives of governments are said to be those of making human beings safer, freer, and happier than they would otherwise be; they are summed up by the Declaration as "their Safety and Happiness." And safety, we suspect, is desired for the happiness that it permits. Thus, the emphasis is somewhat different from what it would be for one who maintains that the objective or end of government is to secure the virtue of the people, to make human beings better than they would otherwise be. Roughly speaking, then, happiness seems to be made more of in the Declaration than is virtue.

Of course, happiness, properly understood, must be seen in terms of virtue. One has only to recall Aristotle's discussion in the first book of the *Nicomachean Ethics,* where he argues that virtue is a critical (but not the only) component of happiness. There may be, for instance, a truly virtuous man beset by a painful illness or by powerful enemies: he would be happy, or at least less unhappy, if circumstances changed for the better.[56]

But, as Aristotle is also aware, men's opinions about happiness vary widely, and this creates political as well as ethical problems. Some identify happiness with bodily pleasure, others with political honor, and a few even with critical activities of the mind. Is there not an inevitable tendency, then, to regard happiness as something resting not only on opinion, but particularly on one's own opinion? That is, men are more apt to differ in the everyday world about what happiness is than about what virtue is. The man who would consider himself entitled, if not even obliged, to express firm opinions about whether a particular act on the part of his neighbor is honest or brave might still be heard to say, in evaluating another's way of life, "Well, that's what makes him happy!" Thus, when happiness is held up as a goal for a community, it can suggest and permit not only a variety of approaches to its achievement but also, in effect, a variety of goals, each dependent upon individual temperament and personal circumstances.

But, it must be immediately asked, can a variety in goals define or hold together a community? Does this variety deprive most human beings of the firm guidance they need in the conduct of their affairs, making them more likely to be dependent, for that guidance, upon transitory leaders and fashions that cater to their baser instincts? The result would be either to encourage softness and selfishness in decent men or to discourage them from taking anything seriously.

Is that people likely to be happiest, then, that does not think primarily of its happiness, but rather of what is the good, of what is the right or even the noble thing to pursue?

III

When a man, or at least a modern man, thinks of virtue, he tends to think of obligation; when he thinks of happiness, it is to his preferences or even to his desires that his thoughts are likely to turn. And this, in turn, suggests the distinction between duties and rights. Duties imply one's view of the community and of the relation of the citizen to that community. Rights, on the other hand, are concerned primarily with what one, as an individual, has coming to him. The constitution implied by the Declaration of Independence seems to be one constructed more with rights than with duties in mind. Even the uses of the two words reflect the difference in emphasis: "right" or "rights" is used almost a dozen times in the Declaration, "duty" only once. This use of duty—"to throw off" any government tending toward despotism—seems to be a corollary to the "Right of the People to alter or to abolish" any form of government destructive of the ends of government.

No sense of obligation can long dominate such an emphasis upon rights. One may forgo one's rights; one may choose not to insist upon them; or one may balance one right off against another. One may, legitimately, even forget about them. But with a stress on duties, the emphasis shifts; an obligation exists; one is not left free to ignore duties; one may not legitimately forget about them. Good citizenship is implied more in the observance of duties than in the insistence on rights, except in those instances where the citizen considers himself obliged to insist on his rights for the political health of the community. Generally speaking, duties make us move somewhat in accordance with the good of the city; rights leave us to move as we happen to wish.

An invocation of rights that have been denied has obvious rhetorical advantages, especially in an instrument designed to win ordinary people to support with passion a call to arms. But free citizens more concerned with their rights than with their duties are likely to develop, in times of prosperity and peace, an attitude that will see civic virtue threatened by the pursuit of private pleasures, by a crude utilitarianism.[57]

IV

A further difficulty with an emphasis upon rights, and somewhat related to what has been said here about civic virtue, may be seen when the invocation of rights threatens the safety, if not also the very existence, of the community.

Some rights are said to be "unalienable." This suggests the natural, that which is so much a part of man, in society or out, that it would do violence to his humanity to strip him of it.

But the Declaration also speaks of "Acts and Things" that independent states may of right do, such as levying war, concluding peace, contracting alliances, and establishing commerce. All independent states can lay claim to these as incidents of "the separate and equal Station" to which "the Powers of the Earth" are entitled according to "the Laws of Nature and of Nature's God." This suggests, in turn, that states, at least in their relations with one another, have a status or significance independent of whether the inalienable rights of citizens are being secured within those states. The power of one state to contract a treaty of commerce with another, for instance, would not ordinarily be affected by the degree of liberty of the citizens of one of the contracting parties.

Thus, both the citizen and the state are said, in effect, to ground their rights in nature.[58] There is no apparent difficulty when the citizen and his state are allies—when, for instance, the state acts to secure the liberties of its citizens from foreign encroachment. But what should happen when the citizen and the state differ as to priorities? What if the government regards the preservation of life as the most important end of government, while the citizen stresses liberty? Such a difference of opinion is reflected in the controversy among us since the Second World War about freedom of speech. The determination of the proper role of freedom of speech must be made, then, on the basis of a priority dictated by the American tradition, if not on consideration of whatever end of government might lie beyond both life and liberty.

This conflict among rights grounded in nature becomes even more acute when one considers another of the inalienable rights, the right of the people to alter or to abolish a particular form of government when it becomes destructive of the ends of government. But among the rights of a state, which it has power to implement, is that of levying war against enemies domestic as well as foreign. One could argue, on this basis, that the right of the state to suppress rebellion is implied by Nature and Nature's God as one of those "Acts and Things" that every state "may of right do." To what standard does one have recourse in adjudicating between these two claims based on natural rights, if not to some notion of justice and the common good which rises above the more mechanical concept of rights and which may imply the perfection of the human being.[59]

Thus, an irreconcilable conflict can be said to be implicit among the doctrines of the Declaration of Independence. This conflict was smoothed over for Americans at the time of the Revolution by the coincidence of the two sets of rights: the right to wage war was exercised by the governments of the Colonies against the British nation on behalf of a people whose rights, as citizens, were said to have been invaded by that nation. This conflict between the two sets of rights was much more evident, however, in the American Civil War, when the government's right of self-defense was challenged by citizens invoking their inalienable rights.[60] Abraham Lincoln attempted to resolve this conflict by an insistence upon the Constitution. But he was eventually driven to higher ground where he had recourse, in the Gettysburg Address, to "a new birth of freedom." The British, in the American War of Independence, do not seem to have been able to find ground above what they took to be constitutionalism. They could not rise above the dogmas of a quieter past.

This conflict, between the rights of a state and the rights of citizens, continues to our day and may be reflected in the current affirmative-action controversy. To what extent would a recourse to prudential considerations of virtues and hence duties (rather than rights) tend to resolve such a conflict, the virtue particularly appropriate here being justice?[61]

V

What can be said now of the expediency of the separation of the American Colonies from Great Britain?

This is not an issue today, except as we consider the merits of a larger union, such as a Western Hemisphere community in association with the European Union or even a world government. But this question does serve to direct us to the further question of whether our political institutions were wrenched out of their natural setting, thereby inhibiting or distorting the maturation there would have been. Whether such inhibition or distortion should be considered desirable depends, in part, upon how one views the nature of a state: to what extent should a political community be based on reason, to what extent on tradition? It is easy to forget, especially when one is young, that tradition tends to incorporate or reflect passion and to make allowances for the peculiar circumstances of a place or a people.

The separation of the Colonies from Great Britain meant, among other things, the repudiation of English social institutions. Thus, there was a tendency to retain selected English political forms without retaining as well the network of social institutions (such as the educational system, the ecclesiastical establishment, and the class structure) which supported the political and which had helped form the Founding Fathers, probably the most talented class of politicians Americans have ever had. The result was an almost inevitable democratization of the regime: this seems to follow generally (whatever Plato's *Republic* may seem to say) from the replacement of tradition by rationality, accentuating even more an emphasis upon rights in lieu of virtue or duty.

Thus, the question of the expediency of separation encourages us to consider the adequacy of our social institutions for our political life.

VI

When we turn from the question of the expediency of separation to that of the justification for the revolt, we can weigh considerations suggested by the Declaration itself.

Central to the list of grievances are the legal issues that had been made so much of in the period leading up to the Revolution. Thus, the Colonists relied to a surprising extent, for their statement of grievances, on their understanding of the British constitution.[62]

To what extent is the statement of the cause of action by the authors of the Declaration repudiated by the very language and tone of the document? That is, does the document reflect a level of civilization and political maturity that should make the reader wonder whether the Colonists had indeed been mistreated or enslaved? Whatever differences had developed between Britain and its Colonies, was it not likely that an honorable resolution within the limits of the British constitution could have been achieved without recourse to arms by rivals of the caliber suggested by the language of the Declaration?

But, it can be countered, if the authors of this instrument were as elevated as their eloquence suggests, should they not be regarded as the best judges of both the expediency and the justice of the separation for which they fought? That is, they knew the circumstances and issues better than we are likely to know them, however superior we may be in arguing from consequences that no one could have foreseen. It is possible, as well, that the British constitution itself, with its remarkable heritage of liberty, was given a turn for the better, or was at least deterred from a turn for the worse, as a result of the difficulties encountered in America by British rulers imprudently insistent on *their* rights. Thus, we can see the continuing relevance of even this question, whether the revolt was justified, to an understanding of our political institutions.

It should also be evident that the answers to the questions we have raised, and even the questions themselves, depend in large part upon the emphasis one chooses to give to a variety of factors. The reader has no doubt noticed the tentativeness of much of what has been suggested here. This reminds us of the provisional character of much that anyone can reasonably say about political matters. We can acknowledge the importance of political philosophy even as we recognize the attractiveness of other fields of study with their promises of greater precision and certainty. Once again we suspect a contest between virtue and happiness, as these are commonly understood.

VII

We are obliged, especially in our capacity as citizens, to follow our suggestions of the problems that confront the student of the Declaration of Independence with an immediate reminder of the virtues of that instrument.

The effectiveness, and perhaps even the prudence, of the "authors of that notable instrument" is reflected in the vitality that the American Republic has retained to this day—in the prestige, freedom, and prosperity that it enjoys among "the Powers of the Earth." This vitality, as well as some current problems, may be traced back to that powerful source.

The tone and language of the Declaration of Independence reflect a style and a kind of life that indicate the standards that are needed today, especially in an age when good taste and republican simplicity are routinely threatened. The tone and language of the Declaration presuppose an audience, a people, of an elevated character. The cast of thought rises above the mundane: the best in the citizen is aroused and nourished, even where the language is couched in terms of his self-interest. A dedication to duty permeates the instrument, whatever the long-run effects of the argument may happen to be. This dedication is sealed by the solemn pledge with which the authors of the Declaration of Independence close their challenge to constituted authority.

The citizen who keeps the Declaration before him is made to look at political life through the eyes of men who employed the accents of nobility in describing what they saw. This model of nobility, which recalls Classical forerunners, can instruct us regarding what we should encourage as well as what we should condemn in the life we shape and share with our fellow-citizens.[63] Even the rights we have touched upon, when properly interpreted, can be seen to involve standards of human excellence and to imply a dedication to civic virtue. Thus, these rights can be seen to suggest that very perfection of the human being that we seek.

It is well to be again reminded of the most important right, duty, and power relied upon in the Declaration of Independence, that of rightful rebellion.[64] The proper exercise of this power, the only one designated therein as both a right and a duty, presupposes an adequate examination of circumstances, politicians, and issues. It means, in effect, the most searching and continuous examination of public life by the responsible citizen. This obligation and opportunity can be seen in our institution of freedom of speech.[65]

Freedom of speech, thus understood as both a right and a duty, does not constitute a threat to our community or to its constitution but, rather, makes it possible to correct any tendencies there may be among us toward apathy, tyranny, or mere selfishness. The serious and yet respectful examination of the nature, virtues, and limitations of our political institutions calls for the lifetime dedication of the dutiful citizen.

3

The Northwest Ordinance

Pray what was it that made you [Southern Ohioans] free? What kept you free? Did you not find your country free when you came to decide that Ohio should be a Free State? It is important to enquire by what reason you found it so? Let us take an illustration between the States of Ohio and Kentucky. Kentucky is separated by this river Ohio, not a mile wide. A portion of Kentucky, by reason of the course of the Ohio, is further north than this portion of Ohio in which we now stand. Kentucky is entirely covered with slavery—Ohio is entirely free from it. What made that difference? Was it climate? No! A portion of Kentucky was further north than this portion of Ohio. Was it soil? No! There is nothing in the soil of the one more favorable to slave labor than the other. It was not climate or soil that caused one side of the line to be entirely covered with slavery and the other side free of it. What was it? Study over it. Tell us, if you can, in all the range of conjecture, if there be anything you can conceive of that made that difference, other than that there was no law of any sort keeping it out of Kentucky? while the Ordinance of '87 kept it out of Ohio. If there is any other reason than this, I confess that it is wholly beyond my power to conceive of it. This, then, I offer to combat the idea that that ordinance has never made any State free.

—Abraham Lincoln

This talk was given at the Basic Program of Liberal Education for Adults Weekend, University of Chicago, Starved Rock State Park, Illinois, May 14, 1976. (Original title "The Northwest Ordinance of 1787: Illinois' First Constitution.") It has been previously published in 75 *Illinois Bar Journal* 408–15 (1965).

The epigraph is taken from *The Collected Works of Abraham Lincoln,* ed. Roy P. Basler (New Brunswick, N.J.: Rutgers University Press, 1953), 3: 455 (Cincinnati, Ohio, September 17, 1859).

I

July 13, 1787, was a fateful day in the history of the United States. An action taken by "the United States in Congress assembled" on that Friday the thirteenth was decisive in shaping this Country for at least two hundred years, perhaps for so long as it shall continue in its present form. For on that day the Congress, sitting in New York pursuant to the Articles of Confederation, enacted the legislation we know as the Northwest Ordinance (or the Ordinance of 1787). This was "an Ordinance for the government of the territory of the United States North West of the river Ohio," the territory that became (during the next sixty years) the States of Ohio, Indiana, Illinois, Michigan, and Wisconsin.[66]

The enactment of this Ordinance can be said to be one of the three great actions of the Continental Congress under the Articles of Confederation.[67] The other two were the prosecution, to a successful conclusion, of the Revolutionary War and the provision for the development and ratification of the present Constitution of the United States.[68]

Daniel Webster spoke of the Northwest Ordinance in these terms: "We are accustomed . . . to praise the lawgivers of antiquity; we help to perpetuate the fame of Solon and Lycurgus; but I doubt whether one single law of any lawgiver, ancient or modern, has produced effects of more distinct, marked, and lasting character than the Ordinance of 1787."[69] Others have referred to this law as "the great Ordinance," the "Magna Charta of American Freedom," even as something that had been "the pillar of cloud by day and of fire by night in the settlement and government of the Northwestern States."[70]

Such sentiments have been inspired, in part, by the significance of the provision in the Ordinance prohibiting slavery in the Northwest Territory: "There shall be neither slavery nor involuntary servitude in the said territory, otherwise than in the punishment of crimes, whereof the party shall have been duly convicted." It was for this reason that much was made of the Ordinance in the great Webster-Hayne debates in the Senate in 1830.[71] It figured as well in the Lincoln-Douglas debates in Illinois in 1858. Lincoln himself celebrated, on more than one occasion, Jefferson's role (that is, the role of a great Southerner) in the prohibition of slavery in the Northwest Territory.[72]

Thus, the Ordinance of 1787 was fateful in that it indicated clearly and authoritatively the original constitutional stance in this Country toward slavery, insofar as there was a *national* stance. It indicated as well that there would be additional States added to the Union from time to time and that those States would be on the same footing as the original thirteen States. This confirmed not only that the United States would not be a colonial power, but also that the new States, so far as the Northwest Ordinance anticipated them, would be States spared from their outset the curse of slavery. That slavery was indeed regarded as a curse by the Founders—that is, by the principal thinkers of the founding period—should be evident to anyone who studies both their public statements and their private papers. It was a curse that not only required compromises and adjustments but also demanded ultimate repudiation. One cannot hope to begin to understand those men unless one recognizes that they detested both the institution of slavery and (to a lesser extent, perhaps) the harsh necessities to which they were obliged to conform because of it.[73]

The fatefulness of the Ordinance of 1787 can be summed up in this fashion: The Ordinance gave, with respect to slavery, a decisive shaping to the future of the Country. This meant, among other things, that a civil war would probably have to be fought. That is, the Ordinance could not go far enough in confining and thus eventually eliminating slavery—but it did make it likely that any war that came would be won by the free States of the Union, if they were so minded.

II

These are indeed remarkable effects to be attributed to one act of Congress, and to an act of the by then relatively ineffectual Continental Congress at that. But before I attempt to justify these broad attributions, we must look at the document itself. It is one of the curious features of American constitutional development that there is an intimate relation between the most portentous events in the Country's history and some quite prosaic features in its constitutional documents. This is partly because these documents are, by and large, "working papers"—that is, they are not high-flown statements of principle (although principle is involved) but primarily guides for immediate, particular actions.[74]

I have suggested that at the root of the prohibition of slavery in the Ordinance of 1787 were the reservations that most sensible men of the time, in the South as well as in the North, had about that institution. Of course, more prosaic accounts of the adoption of the slavery prohibition, and indeed of the entire Ordinance, are also available and are not without merit. Thus, a scholar could, early in this century, speak of the enactment of the Ordinance in these words:

Gratification and surprise has frequently been expressed that the Ordinance should have unanimously passed the Continental Congress at a time when there were represented in that body only three northern states and five southern states. Briefly summarized these are among the considerations that led to this happy result:

1. The desire of Congress to discharge its obligations to the Revolutionary [War] soldiers who were pressing their claims and willing to take western lands in payment.

2. The insistence of the Ohio Company, composed of Revolutionary [War] officers, upon the inclusion in the Ordinance of certain fundamental principles.

3. The assurance that the settlement of the territory northwest of the Ohio would protect the settlement south of that river from the incursions of the Indian.

4. The presence in Congress of new members from the South—especially from Virginia, with new ideas in regard to the industrial and social results of free labor under the Ordinance as finally framed.

5. The limitation of the new Ordinance to the territory of the United States northwest of the River Ohio.

6. The opening up of the Mississippi River to free navigation.

The delegates from the South ceased to oppose the Ordinance when it was limited to the territory northwest of the Ohio River and a provision was added to the anti-slavery clause authorizing the return of fugitive slaves. William Grayson, one of the delegates from Virginia, in a letter to James Monroe tells why the sixth article of compact [the prohibition upon slavery] was supported by delegates from the South: "The clause respecting slavery was agreed to by the southern members for the purpose of preventing tobacco and indigo being made on the northwest side of the Ohio, as well as for other political reasons."

The southern delegates evidently thought it would be advantageous for them to have a monopoly of cheap labor south of the River Ohio.[75]

It is inevitable that less as well as more elevated accounts should be available to explain the origins of the more notable things of this world. One sees in such divergences a reflection of fundamentally opposed opinions about the very nature of things—about the place in human things of matter as well as of ideas.[76]

Attention to the prosaic can help us see better the technical side of American constitutionalism. The prosaic is particularly evident in the Northwest Ordinance, that constitution-like statute. One can see there the prosaic side of the founding period—in the importance, for instance, of private property and hence for the individualism of which Americans always make so much. It can be seen as well in the detail in which procedures are spelled out. A respect for procedure makes for predictable (and hence efficient) government. Efficiency and liberty are not unrelated: one is put on notice as to what is likely to happen, and one is free to conduct oneself accordingly. A fixed and known process means that a people's sense of natural justice has an opportunity to make itself felt. Furthermore, assurances with respect to procedure may be essential if there is to be security for private property. (Is not *Robert's Rules of Order* a peculiarly American development?)

III

Before we turn to the heart of the Northwest Ordinance, let us consider the body of it as a whole. That body can be divided into five parts (in addition to the title with which it opens and the enactment clause with which it closes). Each of our five parts is introduced by some form of "Be it ordained."[77] Part 1 provides for the district (or districts) of the Territory to which a "temporary government" shall apply; Part 2 provides for the transfer of property (whether by descent, by sale, or by other means); Part 3 provides for the selection of officers of government and for the operation of a temporary government; Part 4 provides for "the fundamental principles of civil and religious liberty" and for the future establishment of States in the Territory; and Part 5 provides for the repeal of earlier attempts to minister to the Territory.[78]

The principle of order among these five parts seems to be this: Part 1 identifies the Territory to which the Ordinance applies; Part 2 addresses the problem of property, that property around which life in the territories turned. (Part 1 also can be seen as addressed to the problem of property, in the form of the designation of the territory of the government to be established.) Once the extent of the territory and the status of private property are recognized, the establishment of government can be undertaken in Part 3. Much of that government's activity will have to do with regulations of property (within specified limits). Part 4, with its concern for new States and their establishment, lays down the terms or guarantees under which they are to come into the Union. Finally, in Part 5, earlier provisions for the government of this Territory can be set aside.

Within Parts 2, 3, and 4 there are complicated arrangements that are generally evident to the reader upon inspection. I will refer to Parts 2 and 3 further on. It is useful to notice, with respect to Part 4, the following arrangement of its six articles: Articles 1 and 2 deal with rights of individuals; Article 3 with education and the proper treatment of Indians; Articles 4 and 5 with relations among States; and Article 6, with slavery.[79]

There is something rather practical about all of these arrangements—whether the five parts of the Ordinance or the six articles of Part 4 (which is like a bill of rights). There is the minimum statement of principle; there is much more the provision of practical guarantees and procedures. The practical bent of things may be seen from the outset. It is recognized in the opening lines of the Northwest Ordinance, and elsewhere, that the opinion of Congress may change from time to time as to what is "expedient": "future circumstances" may require periodic reassessment of what should be done. A framework is provided within which such reassessments may be done properly (that is, in a known and predictable manner).

One can see in these arrangements the work of sensible men. This is not to suggest that they were men without aspirations, but their aspirations were firmly grounded. Or, as we would say, they were "realistic."

IV

The heart of the Northwest Ordinance may be found, I have indicated, in its provisions with respect to property. The Ordinance of 1787 exhibits, in this respect, a plebeian—one might say, a democratic—version of the concerns of Magna Carta five and a half centuries earlier. An obvious concern of the barons in 1215 had been that the King respect their property and associated prerogatives.

Property is critical in various ways in the Ordinance. This seems appropriate enough, since the principal reason that most early settlers went out to the Northwest Territory was to acquire land of their own that they could work. Property was vital to life in the new territories: each settler was to be his own man; each was to be independent. The emphasis was upon the opportunity afforded to all (or, at least, to unprecedented millions) to act much as they happened to desire.[80]

The Northwest Territory was later to become the heartland of America. There each man could be (or, at least, could seem to be) on his own, bound the least of all Americans by European customs. The new States formed under this dispensation (in a sense, these are the first truly American States) profoundly affected the character of the entire Union including the old, or original, States. People thus cut off from ancestral ties and traditions—people thus left remarkably free to govern themselves as they chose—became a people most open to change, to chance, and to constant adaptation to "future circumstances."[81]

Of course, these people were not left completely free from the outset to govern themselves as they chose. Restrictions were placed, at least until

Statehood was achieved, upon what they could do to and with private property. Such restrictions were evidently necessary to reassure potential purchasers of land from the Government of the United States. Property had to be protected, it seems, against the depredations of local self-government. Guarantees were therefore written into the Ordinance. But once property was widely distributed among many families, the regime became one in which private property shaped the character of future generations, so much so that its protection could safely be left to the vigilant care of local duly constituted self-government.[82]

Consider the ways in which respect for property is provided for in the Ordinance: Residence is not essential for effective ownership of property. (Notice that the property primarily discussed here is landed property; that seems to be the critical property from which all other wealth, it is assumed, derives.) Provision is made for wills, sales, and other means of alienation of property. The importance of property may be seen in the qualifications for both officers and electors. The only qualifications for any office are citizenship, length of residence, and amount of property. Residence means that one has had time to learn about the area; property means that one will have a permanent interest in the welfare of the locality.

Property rights are further protected by the guarantee provided against the impairment, by territorial legislation, of contracts that have been entered into.[83] But the respect for property—that is, for the right of a man both to be assured of what he has and to be able to do with it pretty much as he wishes—is not without limits. The framers of the Ordinance, in acting upon an opinion as to how property should be distributed at the death of its owner, placed limits upon what one might do with one's property. Not only is it spelled out in some detail what happens to property when one dies without a will, but there are clear provisions, even if a will should be left, for the share to be taken by the widow.[84]

Perhaps the most important limitation upon the property rights that some might claim is the perpetual prohibition of slavery in the Northwest Territory. It may be implied in the Ordinance, by the attendant concession made with respect to fugitive slaves, that the only States that shall be entitled to permit slavery are the original thirteen.[85] But even by 1787 slavery had begun to take root in the territories south of the Northwest Territory.

V

Still, slavery was struck a mortal blow by the slavery prohibition in the Northwest Ordinance. It is, I have suggested, a provision that helped determine the outcome of the Civil War.

The Union—the Union as it came to be, the Union of Abraham Lincoln and of the eventually victorious North—was anticipated by the Ordinance of 1787. One can see again and again in the Ordinance provisions and understandings that are developed further in the Constitution of 1787, provisions and understandings that were significant departures from those found in the Articles of Confederation drafted a decade before.

For one thing, Congress displays itself in the Northwest Ordinance as a body with considerably more power than seems to be provided to it by the Articles of Confederation.[86] Thus, Congress laid down conditions for fashioning, from the Northwest Territory, States like those that originally made up the Union. Such States would naturally have more of a national view of things, since they would owe their very establishment to the Union. States formed in this way must have found it hard to conceive of themselves as existing independent of the Union. On the other hand, the very existence of national territories, and thereafter of the five States fashioned out of the Northwest Territory and elsewhere of other States like them, testified to the integrity of the Union as much more than a temporary league of more or less independent sovereignties.[87]

The Ordinance also advances the understanding that there should be a national constitution and that the American people, wherever they are found, should be self-governing. Such a constitution, it seems to be said, should have a bill of rights. But, perhaps more important for the shaping of the Constitution, a separation of powers seems to be indicated as desirable. Congress under the Articles of Confederation and in its governance of the territories exercised both executive and legislative powers. For the Northwest Territory itself, however, the Ordinance provides a governor rather than a territorial legislature to exercise executive power. There is some way yet to go, however, before the separate executive takes the form found in the Constitution of 1787.[88]

The Northwest Ordinance anticipates the Constitution of 1787 in still another critical respect: directions are given on how to go about putting the government into motion, and it is expected that these directions should suffice. This expectation, in both the Ordinance and the Constitution, recognizes that Americans are remarkably adept at self-government. How they got to be that way is a long story, one that can be barely touched upon here. It is the story of a people somehow dedicated to the liberty of human beings who are recognized to be by nature equal.

It is assumed that these people—that such people—can, should, and will be self-governing. No doubt, their British heritage—a heritage that all Americans draw upon in the language, literature, and institutions they inherit—is in large part responsible for their ability to govern themselves. No doubt, also, a propertied experience in self-reliance has contributed to the self-confidence, as well as to the talents, necessary for self-government.

VI

The presuppositions of the Northwest Ordinance are critical, and yet they can sometimes be difficult to notice. It is presupposed, for example, that there is a substantial uniformity among the original thirteen States. Thus, it is provided in the Ordinance of 1787 that if something has been made law by one of the States, it may be adopted as local law (pending the establishment of a territorial legislature) by the governor and judges of the Northwest Territory.[89]

The Ordinance also presupposes that the common law of England, however modified on this side of the Atlantic, is to continue to be the basis for legal institutions in the Northwest Territory. Thus property (which is put in terms of English acres, not in terms of French hectares, etc.) does not have to be defined in Part 2 of the Ordinance. What property is and how it is determined are very much taken for granted.

But whatever hopes are held out for the character, background, and political talents of Americans, precautions are taken against the darker workings of human nature. We have already noticed the slavery prohibition. But consider as well the reminder that some Indian property titles are valid and that they should be respected. It does seem appropriate that the concern for education and the concern for proper treatment of Indians should be brought together in the Ordinance.[90]

Self-government, which is also taken for granted in the Ordinance, is not relied upon without qualification. Not only must the institutions and practices in the Territory be republican, but they also must be "in conformity to the principles contained in these articles." The more democratic form of self-government is qualified by the provision that judges are selected for life, whereas the other officers of government serve for fixed terms. Those officers, unlike the judges, need to be subjected to periodic reassessment, while the opinions of judges are to be subjected routinely to review by other judges.

And, of course, the restrictions in Part 4 of the Ordinance—many of which come from existing State constitutions and would later find their way into the national Bill of Rights—reflect an awareness that even popularly elected legislatures cannot be trusted with unlimited power. The protection of one's "mode of worship" and "religious sentiments" is mentioned first in this list of rights. But it is evident, however obscured this may be in our day, that one's privileged religious beliefs do not license all conduct that one might consider oneself obliged by one's beliefs to engage in. One's actions, however keyed to religion, can be judged and punished just as such actions would be in the cases of those who do not purport to do what they do on the basis of some religious belief.

VII

Education, it would seem from the language of the Ordinance of 1787, is the community's primary means for supporting religion and morality. Education is not limited, however, to what happens in the schoolroom. The Ordinance has itself had, I have suggested, a profound educational influence in the United States at large, not in the Northwest Territory alone. It has had much to do with shaping the character and institutions of the Country.

We have noticed that the Ordinance is permeated by a dedication to equality. Obligations are to be shared equally, so much so that the settlers in the Northwest Territory are to pay their equal share of the national debt. The rights and powers of citizens in the Northwest Territory under the Constitution, especially when new States are formed, are to be equal to those enjoyed and exercised on the Atlantic seaboard. The men of 1787 could see no reason, it seems, why future citizens and future States should stand on a different footing from their predecessors, even from their most venerable forefathers. Old republics create new republics—and all republics are, in a sense, equal.

These sentiments are rooted, we have also noticed, in the authoritative American opinion that all men are created equal. That principle of equality made plausible the addition to the Northwest Ordinance of the prohibition of slavery. No doubt, as we have seen, less elevated causes contributed to the promulgation of a slavery prohibition, but the nature of the regime was such as to permit this particular prohibition to take hold.

This meant, among other things, that there could begin the movement west of the Appalachians of the millions of people who recognized, if only on the basis of self-interest, that the institution of slavery demeaned the honest toil upon which their very existence, their property, and their own sense of dignity depended. It is surely no accident that there came from the States formed out of the Northwest Territory not only so many of the soldiers but even the President and the Commanding General of the military might which would suppress the desperate efforts of the Southern States to save themselves from what had come to seem their fate as subordinates in a Union being decisively shaped by the Ordinance of July 13, 1787.

The characterization of the Northwest Ordinance by Lincoln, in the 1859 Cincinnati speech quoted from in the epigraph to this chapter, indicates how morality may be legislated, how the character of a people may be molded or at least reinforced by the institutions it inherits and adopts. Lincoln, from early on, respected and attempted to strengthen the moral obligations of politicians and the law.[91]

This recognition of the vital importance of law is critical to a proper assessment and celebration of the great revolutionary efforts by the men of 1776 and of 1787 both in opposition to any law imposed upon them without their consent and in support of an enduring law freely established by themselves. Particularly enduring, with profound implications for this Republic, has been that justly celebrated law of laws, the Northwest Ordinance of 1787.

4

Slavery and the Federal Convention
of 1787

General Pinkney [of South Carolina] said it was the true interest of the [Southern] States to have no regulation of commerce;
but considering the loss brought on the commerce of the
[Northern] States by the revolution, their liberal conduct
towards the views of South Carolina [with respect to permitting
the importation of slaves], and the interest the weak Southern
States had in being united with the strong [Northern] States, he
thought it proper that no fetters should be imposed on the
power of making commercial regulations; and that his constituents, though prejudiced against the [Northern] States,
would be reconciled to this liberality—He had himself, he said,
prejudices against the [Northern] States before he came here,
but would acknowledge that he had found them as liberal and
candid as any men whatever.

—In the Federal Convention of 1787

I

Slavery is always with us. There are always some in every country who are
enslaved by their circumstances, their passions, their limitations. And some
of these, and many others as well, may also be enslaved by law, as were millions of people of African descent in this country until 1865. Vestiges of that
legalized slavery remain to be dealt with by American communities for
generations yet to come.

It should not require much argument to establish that the ethical and

This talk was given at the Loyola University of Chicago School of Law, April
18, 1985. It has been previously published in 20 *Texas Tech Law Review* 696–716
(1989).

The epigraph is taken from Max Farrand, ed., *The Records of the Federal Convention of 1787* (New Haven: Yale University Press, 1937), 2: 449–50 (August 29,
1787).

political issues facing the Federal Convention of 1787 continue to be relevant for us today. One question for us now, as for both the Framers and the Civil War generation, turns upon opinions about the best possible relations among the races of mankind. This question may be seen in discussions about the compatibility of races, about natural differences (if any) among the peoples of the earth, and about the consequences of centuries of developments (including the consequences of African enslavement and of American Indian extermination). In a sense, however, the race-relations question is now settled in this Country; that is, it does seem to be generally recognized, at least for the time being, that merit selection should be ultimately decisive, no matter what the activity is for which the community as such is responsible. This principle of equality, which is grounded in the Declaration of Independence, has been acknowledged to have been decisively reaffirmed for Americans by the United States Supreme Court in *Brown v. Board of Education.*[92] The important arguments we hear now are "merely" as to the means for implementing a generally acknowledged principle. This is not to suggest, of course, that serious problems—and consequently bitter disputes—do not remain to be dealt with, including the perennial problem of the extent to which governance by judiciary is to be justified, especially when the consent of the governed is vital to the regime.

But it is not only with respect to racial matters that the ethical implications of the 1787 handling of the institution of slavery remain relevant for us. Several current issues remind us that it is not slavery alone that can provoke what seems to be an "irreconcilable conflict." The pre–Civil War abolitionists are often echoed by contemporary critics of widespread abortion, just as the pre–Civil War defenders of slavery made arguments on behalf of both their liberty[93] and the law of the land—arguments that can remind one of what "pro-choice" people say today. If the parallels here are instructive as to what is likely to happen among us, then it is the pro-choice people, like the pro-slavery people before them, who will have to back off, especially since it is far more difficult for the antiabortion people, like the antislavery people before them, to compromise principles believed to be more deeply rooted in human dignity and divine law than are the positions of their opponents.[94]

The thoughtful lawyer is familiar with the dilemmas faced here, including ethical dilemmas that require even more of the lawyer than is prescribed by the canons of ethics. He knows, for example, that the right thing to do in a variety of situations depends not only upon his moral standards but also upon his civic-mindedness and his prudential judgment. Prudential judgment, in turn, presupposes information and understanding, which are things that the sensible lawyer of experience can be relied upon to appreciate.[95] In any event, a sound morality, like the serious politics serving morality, means that one has to allow for the interests and prejudices of others. The concessions one has to consider making—concessions with respect to one's own personal concerns for the sake of even higher ethical ends—are particularly demanding and instructive when one acts in a public body such as a constitutional convention or a legislature.

II

The concessions made to slavery in the Federal Convention of 1787 provoked the more radical nineteenth-century abolitionists to condemn the Constitution as "a covenant with death and an agreement with hell."[96] I note in passing that the language resorted to by these abolitionists draws much more upon Biblical images than that of the Founding Fathers ever did. (A highly refined version of such use of language may be seen both in Lincoln's Gettysburg Address and in his Second Inaugural Address.) This is related to the considerable change in the tenor of public discourse from the somewhat more measured tones of the founding period.

Even so, the records we have of the Federal Convention reveal that slavery was generally considered by delegates to be a dubious institution, however much a few of the Southern States considered themselves obliged not only to protect but even to advance it. The nearest anyone came to praising slavery on the floor of the convention may have been the observation by a South Carolinian: "If slavery be wrong, it is justified by the example of all the world. . . . In all ages one half of mankind have been slaves."[97] But this is an exception. In fact, it would be protested from time to time that this or that proposed measure threatened to "enslave" a particular State or group. Thus, a delegate from Maryland condemned a proposal on behalf of three large States (Massachusetts, Pennsylvania, and Virginia) as constituting "a system of slavery for 10 states."[98] Slavery, whether actual or metaphorical, was clearly regarded as a bad thing. James Madison (of Virginia) remarked, "Where slavery exists, the Republican Theory becomes still more fallacious."[99] And Luther Martin (of Maryland) said of one provision which recognized slavery that "it was inconsistent with the principles of the revolution and dishonorable to the American character to have such a feature in the Constitution."[100] But it was left to Gouverneur Morris (of Pennsylvania), a hardheaded champion of commerce and a friend of Alexander Hamilton (of New York), to make the most devastating attack upon slavery in the Federal Convention:

It was a nefarious institution—It was the curse of heaven on the States where it prevailed. . . . Travel thro' [the] whole Continent & you behold the prospect continually varying with the appearance & disappearance of slavery. . . . Proceed Southwardly, & every step you take thro' [the] great regions of slaves, presents a desert increasing with [the] increasing proportion of these wretched beings. . . . The admission of slaves into the Representation when fairly explained comes to this: that the inhabitant of Georgia and S.C. who goes to the Coast of Africa, and in defiance of the most sacred laws of humanity tears away his fellow creatures from their dearest connections & damns them to the most cruel bondages, shall have more votes in a Govt. instituted for protection of the rights of mankind, than the Citizen of Pa. or N. Jersey who views with a laudable horror, so nefarious a practice.[101]

Morris concluded his attack upon slavery with the insistence that he "would sooner submit himself to a tax for paying for all the Negroes in the U. States, than saddle posterity with such a Constitution."[102] No doubt, Morris's attack here was provoked by the prospect of having the relative political power of his constituents in the General Government reduced by the proposed counting of slaves in the Southern population. No doubt, also, selfish motives can be found for the disparaging remarks about slavery just quoted from Madison and Martin.[103] Even so, what is significant is that remarks of this character could be made by delegates to the Convention with the expectation that others would not take offense at them. And while the Convention was sitting in Philadelphia, the Congress, assembled in New York pursuant to the Articles of Confederation, enacted the Northwest Ordinance. That Ordinance, it will be remembered, virtually concludes by forbidding slavery in the Territory.[104]

This, then, was the stance toward slavery of the men of 1787. The "positive good" argument on behalf of the institution of slavery did not become standard Southern doctrine, if it ever really did, until well into the nineteenth century. In the eighteenth century, and certainly at the Federal Convention, the toleration of slavery was regarded as no better than "the lesser evil."

III

I have been indicating what was *said* about slavery in the Federal Convention. I turn now to an examination of what was *done* about it in the Constitution itself, drawing primarily upon Madison's *Notes* for evidence about what the delegates were thinking of as they went about their task. There are, in the Constitution of 1787, three provisions dealing directly with slavery: the provision for counting slaves in the population for representation and taxation purposes; that for permitting the international slave trade to continue until 1808; and that for dealing with fugitive slaves. (In addition, slavery is glanced at in the provision for protecting a State against domestic violence.)

The slavery-related provision in the Constitution that proved the most controversial in the nineteenth century happened to be the one about which Madison recorded the least discussion: the Fugitive Slave Clause in Article IV, Section 2. It was quite late in the Convention before a proposal was made about fugitive slaves. (This was on August 28. The Convention had assembled in May and was to adjourn in mid-September.) Pierce Butler and Charles Pinkney (both of South Carolina) moved "to require fugitive slaves and servants to be delivered up like criminals." But James Wilson (of Pennsylvania) observed that this "would oblige the Executive of the State to do it, at the public expense." And Roger Sherman (of Connecticut) added that he "saw no more propriety in the public seizing and surrendering a slave or servant, than a horse." Butler then withdrew his proposal in order to try again.[105]

It did not seem to be doubted that some provision would have to be made for the recovery of fugitive slaves, especially if the borders between the States were to be as open for trade and travel as the Convention seemed to contemplate. Not to provide for fugitive slaves in those circumstances would have amounted to a considerable de facto subversion of slavery in the South. This seems to have been understood as well by the Confederation Congress then sitting in New York City, for it had added to its dramatic prohibition of slavery in the Northwest Territory the awkwardly phrased proviso "that any person escaping into the [territory], from whom labor or service is lawfully claimed in any one of the original states, such fugitive may be lawfully reclaimed and conveyed to the person claiming his or her labor or service as aforesaid."

On August 29, Butler of South Carolina tried again, offering this suggestion to the Constitutional Convention:

> If any person bound to service or labor in any of the U— States shall escape into another State, he or she shall not be discharged from such service or labor, in consequence of any regulations subsisting in the State to which they escape, but shall be delivered up to the person justly claiming their service or labor.[106]

This was agreed to in the Convention without any recorded opposition.

When the Committee on Style and Arrangement submitted to the Convention (on September 12) what turned out to be virtually the final draft of the Constitution, the Fugitive Slave Clause was substantially like that agreed upon on August 29, except that the language "the person justly claiming their service or labor" was changed to "the party to whom such service or labour may be due." That is, "justly claiming" was replaced by "may be due," a somewhat more neutral term. On the other hand, "person bound to service or labor" was changed to "person legally held to service or labour."[107] This was further changed on September 15, the next-to-last meeting of the Convention, when "legally" was removed and "under the laws thereof" was added, so as to read, "No Person held to Service or Labour in one State, under the Laws thereof." This was done, we are told by Madison, "in compliance with the wish of some who thought the term [*legal*] equivocal, and favoring the idea that slavery was legal in a moral view."[108] Thus, as we shall see, no more than a bare acknowledgment is made in the Constitution of the slavery laws of any State, with words such as "justly" and "lawfully" removed. Is not the dubiousness of slavery reflected in these changes? Of course, the fact that such a clause was needed (a sort of "Berlin Wall" provision) further testified to the vulnerable character of slavery, especially in an association that is one country in large part because of the principles stated in the Declaration of Independence, principles that call slavery into question both as a repudiation of the created-equalness of all men and as a form of tyranny.

IV

The second constitutional provision dealing directly with slavery is the arrangement made in Article I, Section 9 with respect to the importation of slaves from Africa. This provision leads off the Bill of Rights–like list of Section 9—restraints upon the General Government (and especially Congress), even taking precedence (so to speak) over the provisions relating to "the Privilege of the Writ of Habeas Corpus" and to bills of attainder and ex post facto laws. This slave-trade provision reads:

> The Migration or Importation of such Persons as any of the States now existing shall think proper to admit, shall not be prohibited by the Congress prior to the Year one thousand eight hundred and eight, but a Tax or duty may be imposed on such importation, not exceeding ten dollars for each Person.

This provision reminds us of the differences in interests among the

Southern States themselves, for it was South Carolina, North Carolina, and Georgia alone who vigorously resisted, acknowledging in Congress immediate authority to stop something that Convention delegates could (without recorded contradiction) refer to as "iniquitous" and as an "infernal traffic [which had] originated in the avarice of British Merchants."[109] No doubt, there must have been slaveholders in States such as Virginia and Maryland who hoped to profit from sales of surplus slaves to the Carolinas and Georgia (which had evidently been depleted of slaves during the Revolutionary War), just as there were Northern shipowners who stood to gain from a continued international slave trade. Even so, the detestation of that slave trade, both inside and outside the Convention, seems to have been genuine and general. Such detestation, which is only natural and hence not surprising, is reflected in an exchange between Gouverneur Morris and the elderly Virginian George Mason. An exasperated Morris was "for making the clause read at once, 'importation of slaves into N. Carolina, S— Carolina & Georgia [shall not be prohibited &c.]'" Mason was "not against using the term 'slaves' but against naming N— C—, S— C. & Georgia, lest it should give offence to the people of those States."[110] So unpopular was the 1808-slave-trade protection in the Constitution that its handful of proponents took precautions in Article V (the amendments article) lest that protection be removed from the Constitution immediately after the document was ratified.[111] The equality of the States in the Senate was similarly protected; it, too, was thought by many to be an improper concession, but one that (like the slave-trade concession) was considered necessary if all thirteen States were to be governed in the Union under the new constitution.

Perhaps the slave-trade concession did not have to be made. The Carolinas and Georgia did threaten to leave otherwise.[112] Could and would they have done so? How would the other Southern States, especially during the Ratification Campaign, have responded to such an attempt? What risks should the delegates have run here? Among the risks they did run, and which were pointed out, was that of increasing even more the vulnerability of the Southern States by permitting an increase in their slave populations, thereby requiring for those States additional national protection against insurrections.[113]

How important was the Union for the slaves? Little is said in Madison's record of the Federal Convention about the interests of the Africans themselves, although it is recognized that it was barbarous to purchase innocent people in Africa and to transport them as slaves to North America. A very large proportion of the eventual total slave population in the United States was evidently brought in during the twenty-year "window of opportunity" permitted by the Constitution.[114] One can well wonder what the long-term interests of the newly enslaved Africans truly were, especially when one takes into account the fate and eventual importance within the United States of their descendants, as compared with that life in Africa which may have helped make slavery possible. One can also wonder how much the concessions made in the Federal Convention to South Carolina and Georgia, and the unwillingness of the delegates to call their bluff, can be attributed to the urgency to finish what had already been quite a long meeting in Philadelphia.

The 1808-slave-trade provision in the Constitution does have the merit of leaving slavery under a cloud, thereby tacitly instructing subsequent generations of alert citizens. The importation privilege *was* limited to "the States now existing"; it had to be further protected by a limitation upon the import tax that could be levied, lest Congress use its revenue power to circumvent the prohibition placed upon it with respect to immediate suppression of the slave trade; and, as we have seen, precaution had to be taken elsewhere in the Constitution against any attempt by three-fourths of the States to eliminate this provision from the ratified instrument altogether by an amendment.[115] Thus, although the slave trade may have been the only activity dealing with an article of commerce explicitly protected in the Constitution, it seems also to have been the only one that it was expected that Congress would be eager to suppress, which it did as soon as it was free to do so (that is, as of January 1, 1808).[116] And so, a generation later, John Marshall (of Virginia) could speak of the international slave trade as "a horrid traffic detested by all good men"; and he could note with some satisfaction that "America had been the first [among the nations of the world] to 'check' the monstrous traffic."[117]

Americans could be reminded, even by the troublesome concessions made to slavery in the Constitution, that there was something fundamentally wrong with the institution. After all, it went against the grain of the dedication to equality upon which the Country very much depended, that dedication which is even reflected in the closing provision of Article I, Section 9 (the very section which had opened with temporary protection of the international slave trade): "No Title of Nobility shall be granted by the United States: And no Person holding any Office of Profit or Trust under them, shall, without the Consent of the Congress, accept of any present, Emolument, Office, or Title, of any kind whatever, from any King, Prince, or foreign State." Americans were obliged to wonder, therefore, how there could be hereditary slavery if there cannot be hereditary nobility (or mastery), just as the Declaration of Independence made them wonder how the indispensable "Consent of the Governed" requirement applied to the slaves among them.

V

The remaining 1787 constitutional provision dealing directly with slavery is that in Article I, Section 2:

> Representatives and direct Taxes shall be apportioned among the several States which may be included within this Union, according to their respective Numbers, which shall be determined by adding to the whole Number of free Persons, including those bound to Service for a Term of Years, and excluding Indians not taxed, three fifths of all other Persons.

This was by far the most controversial provision dealing with slavery, so far as the Federal Convention itself was concerned: it was the most difficult to prepare, with the delegates returning to it again and again. Particularly troublesome for many Northerners, we have noticed, was the prospect of permitting Southerners to use their human property in making the count of persons that would determine relative power both in the House of Representatives and, in effect, in Presidential elections. The fear was repeatedly expressed that such a political bonus would even encourage more importation of slaves.[118] It was also anticipated that free men in the North would resent being put on a footing with slaves.[119]

This "three-fifths of all other Persons" formula goes back to the Congress under the Articles of Confederation, where the concern had been primarily with counting people with a view to determining the taxation requisitions to be made by Congress to the States.[120] Since all the States were regarded as equal in the Congress under the Articles of Confederation, population differentials did not affect voting strength. This was true for voting in the Federal Convention as well. But in the course of efforts to determine how much each State should pay into the common treasury under the Articles of Confederation, there had been recourse to population estimates—with the Southerners not wanting to have their slaves counted at all, and with the Northerners wanting to count them on a par with their masters. Northerners believed that only thus would the South's full economic capacity, and hence ability to pay, be properly gauged.[121] The compromise hit upon by the Federal Convention was to connect a State's vulnerability to direct taxation with its voting strength in the House of

Representatives.[122] It could not be definitely known at the time, although there was some anticipation of this, that direct taxation would not be a major source of revenue for Congress. It was not until after the Civil War, and then only in the form of the income tax, for which a constitutional amendment was eventually fashioned, that direct taxation became for Congress a major source of revenue.[123]

Even so, the "three-fifths of all other Persons" provision did have an instructive effect. For one thing, it was noticed in the Federal Convention that the delegates, like the men who had written the Articles of Confederation, were ashamed to use the words "slave" and "slavery" in the document itself.[124] Abraham Lincoln, on the eve of the Civil War, was to make much of the delegates' reticence, suggesting that their avoidance of certain words in the Constitution reflected their recognition that slavery was nothing to be proud of, however much they had been obliged to accommodate themselves to it. This three-fifths formula is regarded, especially in our time, as demeaning for the slaves. And in the Convention itself, there were heard protests against putting anything in the Constitution that would concede that "there could be property in men."[125] (Such sentiments had also been expressed in the course of discussions about whether the slave trade should be subject to an import tax.)[126] But does not the three-fifths formula look in the other direction? Can it not also be seen—should it not be seen—as recognizing the humanity of slaves, especially when compared to other property?[127] The South, it has been noted, would have been willing, for *representation* purposes, to count its slaves as fully human—and this was several times argued for by some Southern delegates.[128]

To argue that the slaves should be counted as full human beings supported, in effect, the teaching of the Declaration of Independence that all men are created equal. The Civil War changed the three-fifths rule to a five-fifths rule, something that was thereafter confirmed by the second section of the Fourteenth Amendment. In a sense, then, the three-fifths rule reminded the Country of the potential of those human beings who had been unfortunate enough to be enslaved.

VI

Now that we have reviewed the constitutional provisions dealing with slavery, we can add to what we have already said about the ethical problems that negotiators can confront in such circumstances. Suppose these concessions to the institution of slavery had not been made in 1787. What would have happened? Or rather, what were the Federal Convention delegates entitled to fear would be the likely consequences of "no compromise with slavery"?

If there had been absolutely no accommodation for slavery, then it is likely that there would not have been a constitution that recognized considerably more powers for the General Government than had been recognized under the Articles of Confederation. This would have meant, among other things, that a great opportunity would have been lost for establishing on a firm footing, for the first time in recorded human history, a republican government for a large country, a government that (despite its grudging allowance of slavery) could be understood to stand for the inalienable rights recorded in the Declaration of Independence. This sentiment is reflected in an observation by Hugh Williamson (of an ambivalent North Carolina), who said in the course of the slave-trade debate that "both in opinion & practice he was against slavery; but thought it more in favor of humanity, from a view of all the circumstances, to let in S—C & Georgia on those terms, than to exclude them from the Union."[129]

If the 1787 Constitution had not been agreed upon, the Articles of Confederation government would probably have remained in force in its weakened condition for perhaps another decade. That national government would also have had to leave slavery alone—and it would not have been able to do anything about the international slave trade either, before or after 1808, whatever State governments might have done. The Federal Convention delegates could further justify what they were doing by reassuring each other that slavery was on its way out, that one State after another would gradually do away with it. One particularly troublesome problem remained, however, for which no one had a satisfactory solution, and that was what was to be done with slaves in the event of a general emancipation. George Washington, who (at considerable cost to his estate) emancipated all of his slaves in his will, was disturbed by the prospects that lay before the slaves for whom he felt a deep obligation. (He refused to sell any of his slaves, once he had thought through what slavery meant.) In any event, the approach of Roger Sherman (of Connecticut), recorded on August 22, probably represented that of the typical delegate to the Federal Convention:

> He disapproved of the slave trade: yet as the States were now possessed of the right to import slaves, as the public good did not require it to be taken from them, & as it was expedient to have as few objections as possible to the proposed scheme of Government, he thought it best to leave the matter as we find it. He observed that the abolition of slavery seemed to be going on in the U.S. & that the good sense of the several States would probably by degrees compleat it. He urged on the Convention the necessity of despatching its business.[130]

Of course, one argument against any compromise on that occasion could have been that one cannot anticipate developments that may upset what had been counted upon to justify the compromise. But it should be evident upon examination that the unanticipated can also make the refusal to compromise seem foolish. Does not one simply have to do the best one can on the basis of the information available at the time? Things did happen that made the pro-slavery position more formidable in the early nineteenth century than it had been in the late eighteenth century. First, there was the Santo Domingo slave uprising in 1791, which terrified the South, making it most fearful of its own slave population. Then there was the remarkable growth of the cotton industry, which appealed to all too many people's avarice. (The cotton gin was invented in 1793.) And then there was the unexpected growth of the North, whereas it had been anticipated in the Convention and elsewhere that the growth in population (both by foreign immigration and by domestic migration) would be in the South and Southwest.[131] This meant, among other things, that the South came to feel threatened by Northern power (which could be seen, for example, in the tariffs imposed in the 1820s), and so the South tended to feel ever more on the defensive, especially about its least defensible institution, slavery. (The 1787 Convention delegates would have been surprised to learn that the constitutional refuge of the South would eventually be neither the Presidency nor the House of Representatives but the Senate, where population did not matter. But, as it turned out, free laborers [and hence votes for both President and the House of Representatives] were drawn to States where there was no slavery to demean the laboring man.)

We conclude our speculations about what might have happened without the slavery compromises in the 1787 Convention by touching upon the problem of what a dissolution of the Union could have meant. The South would have been left as an independent, slavery-dominated country. There were reasons to believe that it would have been, or would have become, an expansionist power, moving with its slave codes into the Gulf of Mexico, Cuba, Mexico, and even farther South. What, then, was in the interest of the slaves—to be abandoned completely to the control of a country governed altogether by the slaveholding interests or to be left in a country in which compromises had to be made with slavery in order to preserve a Union that was (or at least could become) fundamentally hostile to slavery? These, then, are some of the concerns aroused by the nineteenth-century abolitionists' determination to have nothing more to do with the Southern States.

VII

Perhaps we can usefully continue our ethical assessment here by considering, if only briefly, what would not have happened if the 1787 compromises had not been made. Perhaps the best evidence as to what would have been lost is what did happen under the Constitution.

Among the things that happened under the Constitution was that the Government of the United States could and did control somewhat the expansion of slavery on the North American continent, even as the strength of the North grew relative to the South. The South knew from the beginning that the North was, or was likely to become, antislavery: after all, the South knew that the North was free to give expression to the doubts about slavery that the South itself felt but had to suppress because of its circumstances. The fact that the Union was recognized by the South to be ultimately antislavery may be seen in the decisions of Southern States to secede in 1860 and 1861; that is, the South had come to the conclusion that it was "now or never," that it was steadily falling behind relative to the North, and that an aggressive antislavery movement was growing in the North. The South also knew that there could be found in the Constitution of the United States various powers that would eventually be used against slavery, once the antislavery movement was in full control of Congress and the Presidency. Consider, for example, the implications of the provision that had tied the hands of Congress until 1808 with respect to the international slave trade. Did not this very provision concede that, without its limitations, Congress would have been able to act at once, pursuant to its commerce power, against the international slave trade? And if so, did it not further suggest that Congress had the power to deal with the slave trade within the United States as well? It was Southern fear of what was likely to happen when the Government of the United States was fully controlled by the North that had led to the fierce decades-long struggles about admission of States to the Union, for that affected the one safeguard remaining for the South (that is, in the Senate). (These struggles were abated, but only temporarily, by the Missouri Compromise of 1820.) The election to the Presidency of Abraham Lincoln in 1860, on a platform that ruled out the admission of any more Slave States to the Union, appeared ominous for the South—and so it made its "now or never" move.

Such a Southern move to go it alone probably could not have been stopped in 1787. The antislavery sentiment in the United States, as well as worldwide, was not then powerful enough to support the massive Free States sacrifices that may have been required to force the South to remain in the Union. Nor was the sense of Union—the sense of being one people worth maintaining as such—yet deep enough to promote sustained efforts to keep the Country together. It took several generations of intimate association under the Constitution to achieve that. Besides, it also took fourscore years for the North to become significantly stronger than the South, compared to what it had been in 1787. Thus, the longer the Union stayed together, the weaker the South became in it—and the better able the North would be to suppress secession and, in effect, slavery, *if it should want to do so.*

Whatever the effects of the compromises of 1787, then, there remained enough vitality in the Declaration of Independence to permit and equip Northern Republicans to argue for the effective containment of slavery and to organize enough of the Country to bring this about. The Spirit of the Declaration of Independence could be discerned again and again in the Federal Convention as delegate after delegate acknowledged the ultimate dedication of the American people, North and South, to the principle of equality.[132]

VIII

Although Northern delegates in the Federal Convention accommodated themselves to slavery, the Southern delegates made even more substantial concessions. In fact, we have noted, the Southern concessions can be considered to have been eventually fatal for the slavery interests, for which Southerners should now be grateful. One must even wonder about the extent to which the more thoughtful Southern statesmen, who did hate slavery, were aware of this from the beginning and were willing to leave matters to develop as they did.

Southern concessions in the Convention included the provisions for the entry of the Western States into the Union on an equal footing with the original States; for the strengthening of the National Government, especially with respect to the regulation of commerce and the levying of taxes; and for the allowance of unlimited immigration into the United States. It was partly because of these concessions, we have noted, that the North was able in the 1860s to put into the field, and to equip properly, the massive armies that crushed the desperate Southern rebellion.

It was repeatedly recognized in the Convention itself that there were quite different interests in different parts of the Country.[133] Madison, among others, kept saying that the serious division in the Convention was not between the large States and the small States but between the Slave States and the Free States.[134] And it was further noticed by delegates that various provisions being considered for the Constitution, such as what could be done about taxing imports and exports or about regulating commerce or about allocating political power, very much bore upon the slavery question.[135] Thus, it can be said that the South sensed from the beginning what it was getting into—and, as Patrick Henry insisted back in Virginia, what it was not going to be able to get out of once it got in.

There was, then, the sense that a bargain had been made in 1787, and this proved critical to what happened as President Lincoln and his associates marshalled the North to resist Secession. A bargain meant that the Northern States were bound by such things as the Fugitive Slave Clause. But it also meant that the Northern States could, in the Civil War period, invoke the rule of law and hence the moral standing of the Union cause.[136] Such constitutionalism was difficult for the South to counteract, especially since slavery itself usually very much depends upon the legal as well as the social conventions that happen to have been established. That is, slavery depends upon considerable respect for recognized property.[137] Property in turn depends upon the rule of law. But law, if it is to maintain its vitality, must ultimately be grounded in justice and reasonableness—and the Constitution itself, and the fact that it was recognized to be to a remarkable extent the product of peaceful deliberation of a high order, seemed to everyone an extraordinary manifestation of what law could be. But however much toleration of slavery could be acquiesced in as "the lesser evil," slavery itself could not be defended as reasonable and just; it simply could not be generally accepted as a permanent institution rooted in the inalienable rights and duties of human beings.

To the extent that Americans North and South took constitutional government seriously, to that extent the institution of slavery remained under a cloud. This meant, among other things, that the South had agreed to a bargain that virtually assumed that its "peculiar institution" eventually had to go, that the principles of the American regime were against it. It is the misfortune of the South that it was not able to continue into the nineteenth century the gradual elimination of slavery that the Federal Convention had observed to be going on throughout the Country since 1776. And yet the delegates had been several times reminded in the Convention that only a just system of government could reasonably be expected to endure.[138] Their sensitivity with respect to these matters was evident even in their deliberations about slavery. Thus, as we have seen, when the Fugitive Slave Clause was being worked out, such expressions as "justly claiming" and "legally held" were removed, with the delegates settling for the bare reference to persons "held to Service or Labour in one State, under the laws thereof."[139] Madison explains in his *Notes,* as we have also seen, that this was done "in compliance with the wish of some who thought the term *legal* equivocal, and favoring the idea that slavery was legal in a moral view."[140] Even here, that is, the delegates were reminded that the truly legal, as distinguished from the dubious legislation that must be put up with from time to time, has to be grounded in, even as it should promote, the moral. In this and in other ways, it is salutary to recognize that the Constitution of 1787 was, despite its compromises and limitations, fundamentally anti-slavery in its presuppositions and aspirations.

IX

One great advantage for us of the slavery issue has been that it, through many of the formative years of the Republic (and perhaps down to this day), has obliged and permitted us to be always aware of the relation between law and morality as well as of the limits of any doctrinaire moralism. Proper reflection upon the dilemmas that decent people confront, partly because of their circumstances can help us curb that self-righteousness which can be crippling and even suicidal. We should be alert to the sorts of things one should take account of when trying to make the best of a bad situation—and this applies to matters as diverse, and yet as similar, as the controversies today about abortion and about nuclear and biological weapons.

Vital to the efforts of American statesmen has been the determination, both in the 1780s and in the 1860s, that the Union be preserved; the full realization of the principles set forth in the Declaration of Independence was believed to depend upon that. Thus, one must wonder whether it is possible for a politically active man to be moral simply by being "pure." Would a refusal by all antislavery people (whether in 1787 or in the pre–Civil War period) to compromise with respect to slavery's continuation have been truly in the interest of the Country, or of the North, or of republican principles, or of the South, or of the slaves themselves? The younger one is, the easier it may be—and perhaps the more praiseworthy it can be—to stand on principle "at all costs."

It should be evident that we have been very much occupied here with prudence, that virtue which is peculiarly concerned to reconcile the demands of the common good with the aspirations of the moral virtues. Lawyers, because of their experience in reconciling the private and the public, are particularly well equipped to appreciate the dictates of prudence. (Abraham Lincoln, it should never be forgotten, was a very good lawyer. Would he at, say, twenty-five have been able to respond as effectively as he did at the age of thirty-seven to the somewhat demeaning, yet dangerous, infidelity charges discussed in Chapters 15 and 16 of this Collection?) Lawyers tend to recognize, at least when properly instructed by their profession, that one needs to be clear (if not even absolutist) in one's objectives even as one is somewhat flexible in one's means. But this requires, among other things, that one's objectives be sound, something that one's circumstances can make difficult if not (after a while) virtually impossible to ensure.

Thus, the South, before the Civil War, could not be truly prudent, shackled as it was by an institution that was widely recognized as unjust. And this tension contributed, it seems to me, to a deep irrationality in Southern life, with the depths of this seen not in the recourse to Secession itself but, a generation earlier, in the desperate sophistries of that brilliant South Carolinian John C. Calhoun, perhaps the last Southern leader who could have returned his people to that goal of the gradual elimination of slavery that his more thoughtful predecessors during the founding period had taken for granted.[141] This is not to suggest that serious mistakes were not made in the North as well, especially when the desire to make money led both to a reckless and provocative use of the Congressional tariff power and, especially after the Civil War, to a pervasive cultural and political coarseness.[142] But it was the South that was most crippled by an inability to defer to the dictates of prudence. Indeed, it can even be said that the South had to rely upon others to do its thinking and its judging for it, in order that the good which was latent in the South might be given an opportunity to manifest itself and thus enrich the Country. Similar observations apply to our contemporary situation, especially when we deal with countries around the world that are crippled by one form or another of slavery.[143]

5

The Common Law and
the Organization of Government

The true interpretation and effect [of contracts and other instruments of a commercial character] are to be sought, not in the decisions of the local tribunals, but in the general principles and doctrines of commercial jurisprudence. Undoubtedly, the decisions of the local tribunals upon such subjects are entitled to, and will receive, the most deliberate attention and respect of this court; but they cannot furnish positive rules, or conclusive authority, by which our own judgments are to be bound up and governed. The law respecting negotiable instruments may be truly declared in the language of Cicero, adopted by Lord Mansfield in *Luke v. Lyde,* 2 Burr. 883, 887, to be in a great measure, not the law of a single country only, but of the commercial world.

—Justice Joseph Story

I

We celebrate this month [September 1988] the two-hundredth anniversary of the opening in the Northwest Territory of the first court with a common-law jurisdiction, a court set up (here in Marietta, Ohio) pursuant to the Ordinance of 1787. This court was among the institutions provided for by the Northwest Ordinance, institutions that have shaped us all in the Midwest and thereby the Country at large, and not least Abraham Lincoln, a great lawyer in the common-law tradition.[144]

This talk was given as the Manesseh Cutler Lecture, Bicentenary of the First Court Session in the Northwest Territory (organized by Robert S. Hill), at the Washington County Courthouse, Marietta, Ohio, September 15, 1988. (Original title: "The Northwest Ordinance, Natural Right, and the Common Law.")

The epigraph is taken from *Swift v. Tyson,* 16 Pet. (U.S.) 1, 19 (1842). See note 155 below.

To celebrate in these circumstances is to rededicate ourselves—and
that, in turn, depends upon knowledge of what it is we are commemorat-
ing. An investigation is called for, then, in which our first question is, What
was implied by the provision in Section 4 of the Northwest Ordinance for
courts with "a common law jurisdiction"? Such courts were considered
vital to the rights of settlers in the Territory, as may be seen in the guarantee to them of access to "judicial proceedings according to the course of
the common law." (Article II).

I will say more on this occasion about the common law, returning
thereby to the Northwest Ordinance. It suffices to note immediately that
at the heart of common-law proceedings was the understanding that there
have always been, as there still are, standards of good and bad, of right and
wrong, that may be sought and discovered by thoughtful human beings.
Such standards, though they are enduring, take account of a variety of
changing circumstances. In fact, the very flexibility in responses that is permitted, if not required, by the common law contributes to the permanent
appeal of the standards drawn upon. Whether there truly are such standards
has been perhaps the fundamental question of jurisprudence during the
past century, and not only in this Country. This is a question from which
many others radiate, such as how those standards are discovered, how they
are to be applied, and by whom.

That there are enduring standards—which exist and have some effect
independent of legislation, judicial determinations, or other formal enactments of the day—was insisted upon at the Nuremberg Trial following the
defeat of Nazi Germany in the Second World War.[145] Various crimes against
humanity were prosecuted, and defendants were convicted and executed
for such crimes, despite the lack of prior statutory authority either for the
Nuremberg tribunal or for the specific offenses charged. Another defense
rejected at Nuremberg was the plea that the defendants were merely executing the orders of their political and legal superiors. Judges of the King's
Bench had disposed of such a defense in this manner centuries earlier, in
the course of the trials following upon the restoration of Charles II after
the execution of Charles I:

> Memorandum, That upon the Tryall of one Axtell, a Soldier, who
> commanded the Guards at the King's Tryall and at his Murder; he jus-
> tified that all he did was as a soldier, by the command of his superiour
> Officer, whom he must obey or die. It was resolved that was no
> excuse, for his Superiour was a Traitor, and all that joyned him in that
> Act were Traitors, and did by that approve the Treason; and where the
> command is Traiterous, there the Obedience to that Command is also
> Traiterous.[146]

In short, the English judges said three centuries ago, one should know and hence do better. It is with this opinion that the common law somehow or other works, the firm opinion that people can be required to know what they should do. When people fail to conduct themselves as they should, properly trained judges are available to help set them straight.

II

The guarantee in the 1787 Ordinance of common-law courts gave a much needed assurance to potential inhabitants of the Northwest Territory that things would continue much as they had in the States from which the settlers would come.

It is significant that the common law was regarded as indeed common. Provisions were made for proceedings that would be similar to what the settlers had had to deal with, no matter what States they had come from. The substantial convergence among the States was far more striking than any occasional local divergences because of special circumstances. It was evident that the common-law practitioners were in touch with a great tradition, one rooted ultimately in a grasp of the reasoning that human beings could apply in developing their natural apprehension of what was right and wrong.

It was also evident that these rules as to both criminal and civil matters were regarded as immediately effective in the territory. The courts of common-law jurisdiction would be able to go to work as soon as judges were appointed. It would not matter what States those judges had originally come from. Provisions were made in the Northwest Ordinance for how property was to be distributed (for example, whenever the owner died intestate) and for how government was to be organized. The details here testify to how much was assumed by the many other rules, barely referred to in the Ordinance, that governed everyday life.

The provisions for organizing the government are guided by one critical principle that we have already touched upon: the governments of the people in the Northwest Territory would be like the governments in already existing States. This, in turn, took it for granted that the people in the Territory would be like the people in the original States.

Critical to the territorial enterprise, then, was the recognition of the principle of equality—*the equality of free men* organized in communities that would be comparable to those communities already organized by free men on the Eastern seaboard. This was not to be the equality of men under despotism. These arrangements meant, furthermore, that in due time the people in the Territory would be *entitled* to organize themselves as States that would take their places in the National Union on an equal footing with the original thirteen States.

All this bears upon the status of slavery in the Northwest Territory. It was the pervasive influence of equality in the American regime, at least from the Declaration of Independence on if not before, that always made the institution of slavery so vulnerable in the United States, so much so that its eventual repudiation nationwide was anticipated by the Northwest Ordinance.

We can also learn from the Northwest Ordinance other things that were taken for granted in the Constitution of 1787, drafted in Philadelphia during the same summer that the Ordinance was enacted in New York City. We can see as well in the Ordinance the course laid down for the development of future territories of the United States.

III

Fundamental to the old system, and carried on in the new, is the significance of property. So critical is property that John Locke, perhaps the leading secular intellectual influence in early America, could tend to see all the rights of men in terms of "property." Let us notice again how property figures in the Northwest Ordinance.

The opening section of the Ordinance deals with the property of the Territory—how it is to be divided for governmental purposes. This is the first "Be it ordained" phrase in the Ordinance.

In Section 2 (with the second "Be it ordained" phrase), the property of persons is accounted for, especially with a view to its transfer from one person to another. This is property that goes back to grants made by the United States, whose paramount title probably serves as the basis for most land grants in the Northwest Territory. The rules laid down in Section 2 are to be followed by territorial courts until an appropriate legislature changes them. The ultimate authority of Congress, at least so long as the territorial status continues, is evident throughout the Ordinance of 1787.

It was important, I have suggested, that assurances be given with respect to property: it was the prospect of property, to be acquired and worked, that was expected to bring settlers out to the Territory. So firm were the assurances about property, and so plentiful was the land to be appropriated, that people naturally came to believe (however mistakenly) that their entitlements to property did not at all depend upon government.

Equality is seen in the ready availability of land to all. It is seen also in the abolition of the rule of primogeniture: all the children of a family are to inherit equally if it is left to the law to decide. Such changes reflect general propositions about equality and republican government, whose significance may now be lost sight of. It can also be lost sight of how much not only property but even the family itself is dependent upon laws, which rely for their effective implementation on the taxes we pay. This can be particularly lost sight of by those who regard the property allocations of their day as virtually natural, if not divine, in origin.[147]

IV

Once property is arranged for (in Section 2), the Northwest Ordinance can look to provisions for government in its various branches and functions (Sections 3–12). We have here the third "Be it ordained" phrase in the Ordinance.

Americans have long been recognized to be a practical people with respect to political organization. The framers of the Ordinance of 1787 knew what had to be said in order to get various parts of government working, including provisions for how those parts were to deal with one another. A similar practicality may be seen in the way the Constitution of 1787 was put together in Philadelphia. Notice again how the United States Constitution is anticipated in the Northwest Ordinance: there are a separation of powers, a bicameral legislature, and diverse yet interwoven functions for various officers of government. All this was done by the Confederation Congress, which was itself unitary, combining legislative, executive, and even some judicial functions in one body. But it was generally recognized that the way the national government had had to be organized for a decade under the Articles of Confederation could not be permanent. The Confederation government was a wartime expedient, to be corrected and placed on a sounder basis in due time.

It cannot be observed too often these days that the Articles of Confederation, the Northwest Ordinance, and the Constitution of 1787 very much rely upon common-law terms and relations. For example, many, perhaps all, of the rights that are affirmed in those documents are common law in origin. We should also notice that when the First Congress reaffirmed in 1789 the Northwest Ordinance, it adjusted the ordinance's provisions to have them conform to separation of powers and other aspects of the then recently ratified Constitution.[148]

V

Among the governmental bodies set up by the Northwest Ordinance, and inviting further examination on this occasion, are the common-law courts we have been talking about. Everyone seems to have known what they were. Those courts would participate in law-making, along with the governor, until legislatures could be established. (Section 5) Even so, they were to draw for the laws they promulgated upon what had been done elsewhere in the Country, perhaps primarily by the legislative bodies in the original States. We can again see what was assumed about the common heritage of the American people.

An encyclopedia of our day describes the common law and its operations in North America in this fashion:

> The common law is a system of principles and rules grounded in universal custom or natural law and developed, articulated, and applied by courts in a process designed for the resolution of individual controversies. In this general sense, the common law is the historic basis of all Anglo-American legal systems. It is also an important element in the origin and plan of the United States Constitution.
>
> Though sometimes characterized as "unwritten" in reference to their ultimate source, the principles and rules of the Anglo-American common law are in fact found in thousands of volumes of written judicial opinions reporting the grounds of decision in countless individual cases adjudicated over the course of centuries.[149]

Underlying all of the common law, in addition to the great constitutional rights and civil liberties rooted in historical developments, is a doctrine of natural right, or a sense of natural justice.[150] The common law applies the general sense of justice in the community to varying circumstances; this general sense of justice includes due regard for local precedents and reasonable expectations. It seems to be presupposed by the Constitution and the Bill of Rights that this general sense of justice would continue to be respected. Thus, the standards to be applied and the way they are to be used are truly common understandings.

But this should at once be added: to say that the common law applies the community's sense of natural justice to a variety of controversies does not mean that that sense develops naturally. It does not mean, that is, that a people can always be depended upon, without any guidance, instinctively to do what is right.

Consider, for example, what is said in Article III of the Northwest Ordinance about the rights of Indians:

> Religion, morality, and knowledge, being necessary to good govern-
> ment and the happiness of mankind, schools and the means of educa-
> tion shall forever be encouraged. The utmost good faith shall always be
> observed towards the Indians; their lands and property shall never be
> taken from them without their consent; and in their property, rights and
> liberty, they never shall be invaded or disturbed, unless in just and law-
> ful wars authorized by Congress; but laws founded in justice and
> humanity shall from time to time be made, for preventing wrongs being
> done to them; and for preserving peace and friendship with them.

The Indians' rights, it seems to be indicated, exist independently of the
enactments of any American government. And, perhaps even more important for our instruction today, is it not implied by the placement *here* of this
concern for the rights of Indians that white settlers were not apt, without
proper guidance, to recognize those Indian rights? There can be seen here
what was all too evident in the slavery controversy as well: self-interest can
distort the development, the promptings, and the applications of a people's
sense of natural justice, something that may be seen in the affirmative-
action debates of our day.

Not even the common-law judges are the final authority in these
matters. There is an old saying that the opinions of the judges are not the
law but rather that they are evidence of what the law is. Thus, neither the
common law nor the Constitution is what the judges say it is. This
approach is in quite a different spirit from that found when so-called legal
realists hold sway.[151]

However important the opinions of the common-law judges are, then,
they are not sovereign. Rather, those opinions and the holdings they
explain have repeatedly to be tested by reason, especially as circumstances
change. A properly developed thoughtfulness has to be applied to what
nature provides and indicates.

VI

We again notice that the Northwest Ordinance assumed that even land
titles, however much they may be affected by the most local of rules, tended to be uniform from one State to another in the United States.[152] This is
consistent with the understanding, evident in the Ordinance itself, that
principles do not depend upon a sovereign authority; rather, they are there
to be discovered and developed by reasoning human beings sensitive to the
demands of natural justice.

Consider, for example, the use in Section 14 of the phrase, "It is hereby ordained and declared." The "ordained" here evidently refers primarily to the provisions that follow "for the establishment of states, and permanent government therein, and for their admission to a share in the federal councils on an equal footing with the original states" (Section 13) The "declared," on the other hand, evidently refers primarily to "the fundamental principles of civil and religious liberty, which form the basis whereon these republics, their laws and constitutions are erected" (Section 13). Most of the arrangements in the Ordinance are temporary, but the concluding "articles of compact" are regarded as "forever ... unalterable, unless by common consent." (Section 14) (Does not this assume that separation, or secession, by one or more States is *not* anticipated?) The rights set forth there are not merely the product of legislative determination; they are not merely something to be "ordained." Rather, their being "declared" suggests that they exist prior to governmental determinations. (This approach may be seen also in the Ninth Amendment, where it is said, "The enumeration in the Constitution, of certain rights, shall not be construed to deny or disparage others retained by the people."[153] It may be seen as well in the references to "Privileges and Immunities" in Article IV of the Constitution and thereafter in Amendment XIV, references that imply the existence of critical rights prior to, or independent of, the Constitution. This may be similarly implied by due process protections in Amendments V and XIV for the life, liberty and property of *persons,* not just for the life, liberty and property of *citizens.* Such protection is naturally, and justly, due to everyone, it seems, not just to citizens who have a special relation with a particular government.)

It is not only rights that stand independent of government or a sovereign authority but even more the principles, especially the principle of justice, that these rights serve. Among the rights of Americans is the right to organize themselves (State by State as well as Nationwide) with proper governments, a right that is dramatically reaffirmed in the Declaration of Independence. In this way, too, justice and the common good are served.

It is salutary to emphasize again how much Americans in the Northwest Territory took for granted the things they held in common no matter what States they had come from. Such commonality is still evident in serious political discourse and in addresses by lawyers to juries.

VII

An emphasis upon the enduring principles of right and wrong shared by Americans is not fashionable today among legal scholars, especially those known as "legal realists." The fashionable opinion of our time is illustrated by what Justice Holmes said in a 1928 dissenting opinion:

> Books written about any branch of the common law treat it as a unit, cite cases from this court, from the circuit courts of appeal, from the State courts, from England and the Colonies of England indiscriminately, and criticize them as right or wrong according to the writer's notions of a single theory. It is very hard to resist the impression that there is one august corpus, to understand which clearly is the only task of any court concerned. If there were such a transcendental body of law outside of any particular State but obligatory within it unless and until changed by statute, the courts of the United States might be right in using their independent judgment as to what it was. But there is no such body of law. The fallacy and illusion that I think exist consist in supposing that there is this outside thing to be found. Law is a word used with different meanings, but law in the sense in which courts speak of it today does not exist without some definite authority behind it. The common law so far as it is enforced in a State, whether called common law or not, is not the common law generally but the law of that State existing by the authority of that State without regard to what it may have been in England or anywhere else.[154]

This argument, which looks much more to *will* and *power* than to *reason* and *moral principle* in accounting for law, has become the approach of all too many modern intellectuals. It tends to be relativistic; there is little if any respect for anything "transcendental." It is supposed to be "realistic" to argue thus. The common law, Justice Holmes once proclaimed, is not "a brooding omnipresence in the sky." This was intended to be a denial of both the old-fashioned doctrine of natural right and the long-standing teaching about natural law.[155]

But, we have noticed, to say that there is natural-right guidance available to human beings does not mean that what should be done in any particular situation is readily apparent. Debate has to be resorted to, debate informed by proper inquiry and supported by disciplined passions. And, of course, in many disputes there are equities on both sides. This could be seen in the slavery controversy in the mid-nineteenth century, and it can be seen in the abortion controversy in the late twentieth century. It may be seen as well in debates about the relation between one's willingness to risk one's life in war and one's qualifications for high political office. Thus, it should be evident, reliance upon natural right is no substitute for serious thinking. Rather, natural right means that thinking can be taken seriously in determining how we should act.

VIII

We return to the property concerns with which the Northwest Ordinance opens, concerns dealt with in a pair of provisions at the beginning and another pair of provisions at the end of the Ordinance. We have already noticed that the universality of their principles meant for Americans in the Territory that property and other arrangements and rules could anticipate and promote the establishment of reliable local governments.

In the opening provision of the Ordinance, districts "for the purposes of temporary government" of the Territory are arranged (Section 1). In the next-to-last provision of the Ordinance, arrangements are made with respect to the permanent government of the Territory: precise directions are given for preparing three to five future States for the Union (Article V). This, then, is one set of provisions, about the "political" property of the Territory. Now we turn to a set of provisions, following immediately upon these, about the "private" property available in the Territory.

In the second provision in the Ordinance, arrangements are made for the property of persons, how it is to be transferred, and so on (Section 2). In the final substantive provision of the Ordinance a limitation is placed on slavery (Article VI). Why should this have been last? It perhaps suffices to suggest that this represents a last-minute concession by the Southern States in the Congress, a concession tied to an assurance about the return to them of fugitive slaves. But notice that even this assurance applies only to slaves fleeing from one of the original States, which perhaps reflects the dubious character and hence limited claims of the institution of slavery.

It is, furthermore, fitting that the slavery provision should conclude the Ordinance as it does. This concluding provision places limitations upon property. If property is as important as the Ordinance assumes from its outset, slavery can indeed be a considerable temptation for some in that it permits citizens to acquire and use property in a most comfortable way. We can appreciate the attractiveness of slavery when we consider our own appetites for labor-saving devices.

IX

The antislavery provision with which the Northwest Ordinance concludes once again reminds us of the foundations of the new American way, a way grounded in the equality of men very much used to living in a free country. The slavery provision can be taken to warn against permitting practical and material concerns to rule our lives, something especially to be guarded against in a community where much is made both of property and of the liberty of each free man to acquire whatever he can.

The common law, as an embodiment of natural right with its dedication to natural justice, was always in principle resistant to slavery, as was the fundamental equality presupposed by the American system. We have noticed that the antislavery provision of the Northwest Ordinance decided, in effect, the fate of the United States: it decided how the Civil War would come out—or rather, it reinforced, for those dedicated to the abolition of slavery within the Union, both the principles and the resources with which to accomplish their great mission. All this bears as well upon how one interprets the accommodations to slavery in the Constitution of 1787, a document that is far more antislavery in spirit than is generally recognized today.[156] In coming to this conclusion about the spirit of the Constitution, one does no more than recognize in the greatest of the Founders at least as much of a dedication to justice and the common good as we claim for ourselves. It remains to be seen whether we can be as astute as they were in putting to good use the elevated moral principles to which human beings everywhere may be somehow directed by nature.

6

Alexis de Tocqueville
on Democracy in America

Dare, my guest, to scorn riches; fashion yourself to be worthy of
deity.

—Virgil

I

Alexis de Tocqueville's *Democracy in America* is a huge book with a great reputation. Whether it is ultimately, or primarily, about the United States can
be debated. But that the American regime of the 1830s is used, and in a
most instructive way, to examine perennial questions has long been evident.
The meanings and effects of both equality and liberty, and the proper relation of one to the other, are examined at length. Tocqueville recognizes
from the outset the decisiveness of equality for his study, and in the modern world, an equality that is made even more dramatic when seen through
the eyes of a European aristocrat. Thus, it is reported in the author's introduction: "So the more I studied American society, the more clearly I saw
equality of conditions as the creative element from which each particular
fact derived, and all my observations constantly returned to this nodal
point."[157] Among the consequences, at least in America, of triumphant
equality had been the development of a vigorous individualism—and this,
too, the author endeavored, in a statesmanlike way, to put in its place.

This talk was given at the Basic Program of Liberal Education for Adults
Weekend, University of Chicago, Alpine Valley Resort, East Troy, Wisconsin,
November 8, 1980, and in an expanded version at the Claremont Institute for the
Study of Statesmanship, Claremont, California, January 24, 1986. (Original title:
"On the Central Doctrine of Tocqueville's Democracy in America.") It has been
previously published in Ken Masugi, ed., *Interpreting Tocqueville's "Democracy in
America"* (Savage, Md.: Rowman & Littlefield, 1991), 423–61.
The epigraph is taken from Virgil, *Aeneid,* VIII, 364.

On this occasion, in an effort to suggest how one might begin to think about this massive book and what it reveals about the Country in which Abraham Lincoln (with his insistence that "all Men are created equal") found himself in his twenties, I propose to look at one Tocqueville chapter in some detail. This seems to me consistent with the understanding of things proposed by the author himself. Thus, he argues for the importance, in the continental American nation, of local township government (and of the family as well).[158] These are the vital materials of which the great American edifice is constructed. A part, he seems to suggest, can reveal much about the whole. But which part should we settle upon? Why not that which is at the heart of the work, the central chapter of the ninety-three chapters of the entire book?[159] For this purpose, the sizes of the chapters do not matter, just as the sizes of localities and families (so long as they remain localities and families) do not matter for some purposes.

The central chapter of *Democracy in America* is found in the second volume of the book. This means the author had the entire work before him when he placed this chapter where he did. This short chapter, Chapter 8 of Part 2 of Volume 2, is entitled "How the Americans Combat Individualism by the Doctrine of Interest Well Understood." (What is here translated as "interest" is often translated by others as "self-interest.") I found, on settling upon this chapter as central to the book, that it had been designated as vital by other students of the book as well, albeit on other grounds.[160]

A careful, however awkward, translation is needed for the detailed commentary I offer here. As I go along, I will try to speak to questions, including old questions about the relations of moderns to ancients, that are raised not only by each paragraph in succession but also by the entire chapter and to some extent by the book as a whole. Those who know this book better than I do should be able to tell us what major differences there may be between the first and second halves of the book (when divided according to chapters). I have found it convenient to divide the central chapter into the following sections:

- Section 1: Paragraphs 1 and 2

- Section 2: Paragraphs 3, 4, 5, 6, and 7

- Section 3: Paragraphs 8, 9, and 10

- Section 4: Paragraphs 11 and 12

- Section 5: Paragraphs 13, 14, and 15

- Section 6: Paragraphs 16, 17, 18, 19, and 20

- Section 7: Paragraphs 21 and 22

This entire Tocqueville chapter is set forth in italics, paragraph by paragraph, in the course of my commentary upon it here.

II

The opening section of this chapter (made up of Paragraphs 1 and 2) is devoted to "history," a recapitulation of the doctrine that had once prevailed, and to an introduction to another doctrine, which is now about to prevail.

First, then, the recapitulation, as found in the opening paragraph of this central chapter of *Democracy in America* (brackets indicate my additions):

> *[1] When the world was conducted by a small number of powerful and rich individuals, these liked to form for themselves a sublime idea of the duties of man; it pleased them to profess that it is glorious to forget oneself and that it is fitting to do good without [regard to] interest, as God himself [does]. That was the official doctrine of the times in matters of morality.*

A pervasive opinion is reported here, one that is presented as having once been generally accepted, at least in the West ("the world"). Was that a time in which a few stood out—and in which truly political judgments were not relied upon? Is this suggested by the use of "conducted" in place of a word such as "governed"? That is, were human affairs in those times *managed* rather than being subjected to political ordering? The managers were a few "powerful and rich individuals." The usual translations here accommodate themselves to the English idiom, making the passage read, "rich and powerful individuals." But this reversal of "powerful" and "rich" conceals questions left by the French original. Were these few managers rich because they were powerful? Did they seek power in order to secure wealth?[161]

These few are designated "individuals." They stood out from all the others; perhaps they even considered everything around them *theirs*. Were they the only ones who "counted"? Certainly, they, as the visible ones, were the only ones who had access to glory; for them, sublimity meant something and was perhaps attainable. It is difficult for more than a few to share in glory, since its effect is heightened (if not even made possible) by its rarity. The "duties of man" are spoken of, but, it seems, these were duties that only a few could be expected to perform. Only a few could, under this dispensation, be truly human. To be truly human meant, for them, to be godlike. An imitation of God, by conduct that was concerned for goodness

alone without regard to personal advantage, was their aspiration.[162] A great
distance is opened between these few and all the others. One is pleased to
forget oneself; but one does derive considerable satisfaction from the recognition that one is thereby a benefactor and otherwise virtuous. Still, whatever the implications of the text here, that one does enjoy doing the right
thing should not be held against one. Indeed, is it not the mark of a virtuous man that he takes pleasure in doing the right thing, knowing that it is
the right thing?[163] Or are we to assume that all superiority is spurious or
otherwise undeserved?

    Whether it is indeed virtuous to forget oneself, however glorious that
can be in some circumstances, remains a question. May not one have at
times a duty to preserve oneself? Besides, habitual disregard for oneself can
encourage one to be unaware of, if not even callous toward, the modest
needs of others. One must be careful about the tendency of the noble to
"do right" without sufficient regard for consequences, especially in circumstances where deprivations and pains are shared by all while the glory
and related pleasures are monopolized by a few. What is truly moral remains
a question here.

    All this is referred to as "the official doctrine of the times." When
these times were is not made clear. They precede the present era, of course,
but how far back do they go? They seem to run back through the Christian era—there are indications of that in what is said about sacrifice and
great abnegations—but not so far back as the Classical period. A line of
development—perhaps even a virtually inevitable line of development—
may be assumed. Little, if anything, is said in this chapter about what
prompted this development.[164] One has the impression, here as elsewhere,
that all this is viewed from the French, or at least from the Continental,
perspective: for them, there are all around them—in buildings, in names
and language, and in history—many reminders of the claims upon them
of nobility.

    To say that the doctrine was "official" may be to suggest that it was not
necessarily adhered to generally. Still, an official doctrine, even when taint-
ed by the hypocrisy to which any long-established profession of faith is
liable, can set the tone of a time. For lack of something better—a general
unease, if not resentment, is *not* something better—the official doctrine of
a time shapes, by and large, the general opinions of that time. In this case,
the official doctrine could even be understood to provide meaning to
much of what might otherwise seem a bleak and exploited life. To refer to
it as a *doctrine* may recognize that it is a *teaching* or an *instruction,* a set of
opinions that, whatever their truth, it is considered salutary to transmit and
support. In this way, both the few and the many were once taught and reas-

sured about how all that went on around them, as well as within them, could be understood.

We can now turn, in the next paragraph, to the doctrine that, according to the author, was coming to prevail in his time:

> [2] *I doubt that men were more virtuous in aristocratic ages than in others, but it is certain that the beauties of virtue were talked about incessantly; they studied only in secret the side of it which is useful. But, to the extent that the imagination takes a less lofty flight and that each concentrates on himself, moralists are frightened at this idea of sacrifice and they no longer dare offer it to the human spirit; they are then reduced to inquiring whether the individual advantage of citizens would not work to the happiness of all, and, when they have discovered one of those points where particular interest does meet with the general interest, and conforms to it, they hasten to place it in the light; little by little like observations are multiplied. What was an isolated remark becomes a general doctrine, and one comes finally to perceive that man in serving his like serves himself, and that his particular interest is to do well.*

The official doctrine of a former age had been set forth in the first paragraph of this chapter. When the author turns to more recent times, he walks in the path marked out, two centuries earlier, by an even greater French questioner of official doctrine, René Descartes. Thus, our author, like his predecessor, begins here with an expression of personal doubt. Other traces of the Cartesian approach may be seen elsewhere in this book and even, further on, in this chapter. The author seems to call into question, if only to give full force to the contemporary alternative, the received opinion of the preceding age.[165]

What is meant by the suggestion that men were not "more virtuous in aristocratic ages than in others"?[166] Does this judgment depend upon an assessment not of a few men then and now but rather of the bulk of men in both kinds of times? Certainly, there is an indication later in this chapter (in Paragraph 15) that a time could come when the best men would not be as remarkable as the best men once were. Does the author draw the comparison he does here, at the outset of this discussion, to make as plausible a case as possible for the contemporary doctrine and its consequences?

It is a case that is to rely much upon utility. To prepare the way, the author seems to disparage those who talked "incessantly" about "the beauties of virtue." No doubt, such talk can be little more than the expression of vanity and ostentation; it is consistent with a way of life that made much of glory and the sublime. Yet, to take pleasure in doing what is right—which I have already spoken of as the mark of the truly virtuous human being—is to be drawn to the attractions of virtue as something worthy for its own sake, not just for its consequences. Is not this included in any insistence upon "the beauties of virtue"? Does not such an insistence somehow ratify human existence as something desirable in itself, as a thing of beauty, especially when well conducted, however transitory it may be?[167]

Why were aristocrats inclined to study "only in secret" the usefulness of virtue?[168] Is there something shameful about any recognition of utility here? Is there something ugly in making much of an effort to show that virtue pays—or, at least, is there something ugly about those who are taught to expect this to be shown to them?[169] Not only is it thereby tacitly recognized that virtue is inherently painful—why else endeavor to make so much of its supposed utility?—but also it is virtually conceded that one need not act virtuously in those instances when the personal utility of a virtuous act cannot be shown. To proceed pursuant to the expectation that honesty in such circumstances is the best policy may encourage one to resort to dishonesty when honesty obviously does not "pay." At the least, an unseemly calculating spirit can be promoted.

Be all this as it may, the author seems to say, these times are less high-minded. Moralists and statesmen must adapt themselves, therefore, to a lowering of sights if they are to be effective in what they teach and do. We are not told here how it was that the flight of the imagination became "less lofty" when each "concentrate[d] on himself." The new general doctrine, which leads one "to perceive that man in serving his like serves himself," is designed to minister to men in their more self-centered condition; it does not seem to have brought men to this condition; something else, it seems, is responsible for that.

In any event, the "idea of sacrifice" is no longer resorted to. Why are "moralists" so "frightened" by it? Only because it is no longer persuasive? Or because it is too dangerous in its persuasiveness, in that it has been invoked all too often with disastrous consequences? Does this latter consideration suggest that human beings have an innate tendency toward self-sacrifice and its awful beauties, so much so that a reliance upon the useful is apt to be temporary or at least vulnerable?[170]

Much is now made of the correspondence between "the individual advantage of citizens" and "the happiness of all." We notice that it is here that the citizen emerges in this chapter. Citizens had been made much of in antiquity, we recall; but there may not have been much room for citizens in the post-Classical aristocratic ages evidently referred to in the first paragraph. Only a few were full citizens then—and those few were as much individuals (long before the term became fashionable) as they were citizens: their own glory meant more to them, perhaps, than "the happiness of all."

Must not modern citizens be distinguished from their predecessors? Is not the tendency of modern citizens (particularly in democratic times) to make much of "all," of their "like," of "the general interest," rather than of local allegiances? Do we not hear echoes here of the Rights of Man and of the brotherhood of man (or at least of European man)? Does this come, at least in part, from the legitimation of the "particular interest" of each citizen, teaching him that he is entitled to identify himself with all others like himself as human beings, especially if much should be made of his economic interest with its dependence upon repeated transactions with peoples of other lands? Thus, modern man moves en masse first into the citizen-body and then into the bourgeoisie.

Does the author suggest here that the isolated instances of correspondences between particular interests and the general interest do not really add up to the "general doctrine" they are gathered together to make? Still, it is this general doctrine that has replaced the earlier official doctrine. Why is it not designated the new official doctrine? Perhaps because there is not yet an authoritative body, in the new age, to provide such ratification? May the authoritativeness of any body be in principle improper in a truly egalitarian age?

So much, then, for the history of two doctrines, the official doctrine of aristocratic ages, which is fading away, and the general doctrine of modern times, which is emerging to take its place to some extent. The reference in Paragraph 2 to "light" may anticipate the call for enlightenment with which this chapter concludes and upon which the modern project is believed to depend.

III

The second section of this chapter (made up of Paragraphs 3–7) testifies to the application of the newly emerging general doctrine among a particular people and to the consequences of that application.

The author informs the reader,

> [3] I have already shown, in several places in this work, how the inhabitants of the United States almost always know how to combine their own well-being with that of their fellow-citizens. That which I want to point out now is the general theory which helps them get there.

The Americans first come to view in this chapter as "the inhabitants of the United States." This designation seems more geographical, and even scientific, than political or racial. But is not the geography such that the

emphasis on "all" and "his like" in Paragraph 2 can easily be shifted to "fellow-citizens" here? That is, Americans live where virtually all the whites
they come in contact with happen to be fellow citizens. They need not
trouble themselves, at least not to the extent that Europeans must, to medi-
ate between the demands of humanity and those of citizenship.

Even so. the emphasis is upon the welfare of human beings in their
several capacities, whether as individuals or as all of one's fellow citizens.
The welfare of the Country, or the community, is not made anything of.
Does not this mean, among other things, that the emphasis is apt to be
upon the present generation, not upon any identification with the past or
any concern with the future?

The author's work as a whole is intended to show, among other things,
how well the American system works. The question remains, of course, how
and why it works as well as it does. The author intends to notice "the general theory which helps" Americans "almost always . . . to combine their own
well-being with that of their fellow-citizens." Is that "general theory" itself
but a tool, not something which provides ultimate guidance? This is said to
help Americans do what they do. It, by itself, may not be enough. Perhaps it
is not even the principal factor in determining how Americans act. In any
event, this "almost always" reminds us that the application of any general
theory must be tested by a higher standard if we are to be able to judge
whether that which is aimed at by the use of such a theory is indeed
achieved. That higher standard, it would once have been said, is looked to by
statesmanship. Whether statesmanship can be built into a democratic system,
or whether a self-governing people can be statesmanlike, remains a problem.

The next paragraph tells us something about the application by Americans (in a statesmanlike way?) of the general theory they employ:

> [4] In the United States, it is hardly ever said that virtue is beautiful. It is main-
> tained that it [virtue] is useful, and it is proved every day. American moralists do
> not pretend that one must sacrifice oneself for one's like because it is great to do
> so; but they boldly say that such sacrifices are as necessary to him who imposes
> them upon himself as to those whom they profit.

Why do not Americans say that virtue is beautiful? Because it is not
so? Or if it is so, do they not say so either because they do not recognize it
to be so or because they do not believe it prudent to say it is so? Are Americans fully modern in preferring to rely upon, or at least to voice, "realistic" reasons for what men do?[171]

If it should not be believed that virtue is beautiful, what then is the
status of the beautiful? If beauty should be kept separate from morality,

which is by and large a community concern, then beauty tends to be a private matter, perhaps even something left (more than virtue is) to each man's taste. Again we notice that beauty may be tacitly left to the noble-minded, with their illusions (or pretensions?) and their exotic individuality.[172]

American moralists, unlike European moralists, are "bold," not "frightened," in confronting the idea of sacrifice. Why is this? The answer may depend upon why European moralists were frightened. In any event, American moralists make much of sacrifices as mutually beneficial. Do they advocate this because they believe it or because it is useful to say so?

May not the greatness of sacrifice be sacrificed to this new way of seeing things? Perhaps greatness at large is also sacrificed. Is an emphasis upon utility and mutual benefit much more likely in a commercial republic? Do bodies matter more than spirit in such republics, or at least more so than in aristocracies? Does this shift in emphasis have something to do with the political elements in the talk and lives of Americans? A somewhat self-conscious republic may be more inclined to speak in terms of interest than is a monarchy or an aristocracy (which is more likely to be moved by considerations of pride). Does it not make more sense for a republic to be concerned with utility than with honor? After all, a community is obviously in large part bodily.[173] Utility, then, may have more to do with the broadest base of sovereignty; pride, and hence beauty, may have more to do with the few.[174]

Whatever the soundness of the American position, it reflects an accommodation to the times. Thus, it is noted in the next paragraph:

> *[5] They have seen that, in their country and in their time, man is brought back to himself by an irresistible force and, losing hope of arresting it, they have dreamed of no more than to conduct him.*

The American moralists, it seems, are aware of the limitations both of the arguments for the position they espouse and of any efforts to arrest the development that makes such a position useful. What the ultimate cause is of this "irresistible force" remains unstated here. Again we see that a standard is resorted to in the light of which the public position is taken by the moralists. How much they understand, beyond an awareness of what is immediately needed, is not clear.

The use here of "conduct" can again remind one of Descartes.[175] Conducting takes the form of the proposition reported in the next paragraph:

> *[6] They therefore do not deny that each man may pursue his interest, but they do their utmost to prove that the interest of each is to be honest.*

Selfishness, it would seem, is not to be condemned; rather, it is to be redirected. One is to be shown what is truly in one's interest, what an informed selfishness leads one to. And so we return to the notion of the utility of virtue, with special emphasis placed here on the virtue of honesty. This word *(honnete)*, which has as well the connotations of honorable, upright and just, may be particularly appropriate for a commercial republic, one in which men have to rely on one another's fidelity in the transactions they undertake.[176]

It should be noticed that man (not citizen?) is thus being addressed in this appeal to interest. It should also be noticed that it seems to be suggested that the argument made in the appeal is difficult to prove: it has always been far easier to see that one's honesty helps another than to see that it advances one's own interest as well.[177]

The second section of this chapter, which testifies to the application of the newly emerging general doctrine about interest among the Americans, concludes with a recognition of what American moralists have and have not accomplished by their arguments:

> [7] *I do not want to enter here into the details of their reasons, as that would divert me from my subject; it suffices for me to say that they have convinced their fellow-citizens.*

One might wonder, of course, whether Americans are better or worse for having been thus convinced of what may be a dubious argument. That is, does not such convincing speak well of their moral concerns, less well of their intellectual powers? But then, the author himself is less concerned with the validity of the argument here than he is with its consequences and usefulness. In this respect, he may be (at least for the moment) very much an "American," concerned more with utility than with beauty.

IV

The third section of this chapter (made up of Paragraphs 8, 9, and 10) looks to antecedents of the doctrine of interest well understood and considers the varied responses to that doctrine in America and Europe.

Thus, the first paragraph in the third section reports:

> [8] *A long time ago Montaigne said: "If I did not follow the straight road for its straightness, I should follow it from having found, by experience, that in the final reckoning it is commonly the happiest and the most useful."*[178]

This could serve as the culmination of the second section of this chapter (rather than, as I have put it, as the beginning of the third section), suggesting further that utility is to be preferred, at least in practical affairs, to beauty (which is to be seen, presumably, in "straightness"—in virtue for its own sake). But the author also hints at the roots, at least in recent centuries, of the doctrine of interest well understood. He does not go directly, or by the straight road, to Montaigne in his reliance upon him here. Montaigne does speak, in a passage to which we will return when we get to Paragraph 18, about the relation of utility to honesty—and perhaps we are intended to be reminded of that discussion by Montaigne. But the Montaigne passage drawn upon here (if the editors of *Democracy in America* are to be trusted in their suggestion as to what *is* drawn upon) is not concerned with the problem of utility; indeed, it is far from saying what Tocqueville here restates it as having said. Consider the supposed source, the opening sentence of Montaigne's essay "Of Sleep": "Reason orders us always to go on the same path, but not always at the same pace; and whereas the sage should not allow human passions to make him deviate from the right course, he may well, without prejudice to his duty, let them hasten or retard his steps, and not plant himself like a Colossus, immobile and impassable."[179] It is useful to Tocqueville to paraphrase loosely what Montaigne says here, and especially to add a reliance upon the notion of utility in determining what path one is to follow with a view to happiness.

Perhaps a kind of analogy is intended. That is, Tocqueville suggests that there are better and worse reasons for doing what one does; the important thing (as may be seen, for example, in Abraham Lincoln's career as President) is to persist in doing what one should, to keep in mind one's primary objective. Thus, where Montaigne varies the pace of one's movement along the path, Tocqueville varies the reasons for following the path. In both instances, the path is followed and, presumably, the goal is reached.

Would not even more be indicated by the explicit reliance upon this particular passage from Montaigne if it should be evident that another passage (directly on point) could have been used?[180] Perhaps we are meant, in any event, to reflect upon the chapter that is used here, the chapter on sleep. There Montaigne shows how certain men were able to sleep soundly despite their circumstances (that is, despite an impending battle or an impending suicide).[181] What are we to make of such men, that they were able to forget themselves completely? Or was it rather that they always had an ability to sense what they could and could not do for themselves, regardless of their circumstances (which others around them took so much more seriously)? Were they being highly individualistic? To sleep is to retreat from the everyday world, the world of affairs and of "reality." (Again, one can be reminded of Descartes's inquiries into these matters.) Is all this to be seen, somehow, as a commentary on the nature and prospects of "interest well understood"? To sleep is to be most private, to be most on one's own. Thus, for example, everyone can be an invincible sovereign while asleep.[182] Does this suggest the limits of any concern for the public? Certainly, the Montaigne chapter alluded to in Paragraph 8 raises questions about the body, about life itself, and hence about the importance of self-interest (however understood)—that is, about the things with which most human beings are very much concerned.[183]

Whatever Montaigne and Tocqueville are, it would seem, they are not simply straightforward (and the talk about a straight road points this up?). Is not their subtlety an aristocratic, rather than a democratic, trait? Does not subtlety, especially in the form of irony, reflect an awareness of inequalities? One must wonder what moves each of them, what each is driving at.

In any event, Montaigne has been used (in a preliminary fashion), and we can proceed to the next paragraph:

> *[9] The doctrine of interest well understood is then not new; but, among the Americans of our day, it has been universally admitted; it has become popular there: one finds it at the root of all actions; it runs through all discourse. One does not encounter it less in the mouth of the poor than in that of the rich.*

To speak of this doctrine as "then not new" may suggest that Montaigne (or perhaps Montesquieu?) is a distant source of what the Americans generally believe. It is here spoken of, for the first time (since the title of this chapter), as the "doctrine of interest well understood." Is it among the Americans, perhaps first—or at least more than anywhere else—that it is regarded as a *doctrine,* as a received teaching for all, or almost all, to accept?

It is a popular doctrine, we are told, so popular that both rich and poor mouth it. (Does this say something about the expectations of the poor in the United States? That is, that they do not expect to remain poor indefinitely? that they believe the American way of life serves their interest at least as much as it serves the interest of the rich? and that, since fortunes in the United States are so changeable,[184] the rich are more vulnerable in America than in Europe?)

We must wonder, however, whether a popular doctrine can be correct, whatever its usefulness may be. And, if it is not correct, may not a day of reckoning come? Perhaps not, it can be responded, if the use of the doctrine is conducted by those (those few?) who know what they are doing. Certainly, the thoughtful statesman knows that few things are useful in all circumstances.

American experience with this doctrine is to be compared with that of peoples elsewhere. This may be seen in the next paragraph:

[10] *In Europe, the doctrine of interest is much more coarse than in America, but at the same time it is less widespread and especially less exhibited, and every day great abnegations are feigned, which are no more.*

Curiously, the American version of this doctrine is more refined than the European, whereas one expects the Europeans generally to go in for more refinements than the Americans. But, then, the Americans have taken this doctrine more seriously and have had to live with it—and that can promote refinement.

This doctrine is still suspect in Europe: One does not parade it as in the United States. This seems to be, at least in part, because greatness is still aspired to in Europe, in the form at least of great self-sacrifice, a monumental forgetting of oneself for the sake of others (or is this primarily for the sake of the glory referred to in Paragraph 1?).

True greatness is not apt to be widespread; certainly it cannot find popular expression, however widely it may be acclaimed in time. But, we are told, these expressions of greatness are feigned; they are not to be taken seriously; they are illusions of grandeur, resorted to by those who do not recognize that times have changed and that the sublime has been made obsolete.

America, we are given to understand, is the way of the future; Europe looks too much to the past. We are obliged, if we are to be sensible, to reconcile ourselves to arguments from utility, to a doctrine which counsels human beings that it is truly in their interest to act morally toward their fellows. This, we are further given to understand, is to be sensible—and life will generally be better if the hopeless aspirations of the past for genuine virtue (that is, for virtue for its own sake—or was it for the glory of virtue?) should be surrendered as ineffectual.

V

But, then, we have in the fourth section of this chapter (made up of Paragraphs 11 and 12) a curious interlude, if not a digression. For we see indicated here, in the central paragraphs of the chapter, perhaps decisive reservations about a doctrine whose general acceptance is advocated.

The first of this pair of revealing paragraphs reads:

[11] The Americans, on the contrary, are pleased to explain, by the aid of inter-est well understood, almost all the acts of their life; they exhibit complacently how an illuminated love of themselves constantly brings them to assist one another and disposes them willingly to sacrifice to the good of the State a part of their time and their wealth. I think that in this they often do not do them-selves justice; for one sometimes sees in the United States, as elsewhere, citizens abandoning themselves to the disinterested and unconsidered impulses which are natural to man; but the Americans hardly ever avow that they concede anything to movements of this kind; they like better to honor their philosophy rather than themselves.

That Americans are "pleased" to explain things as they do might mean that they are somewhat superficial in how they regard themselves. This con-clusion is reinforced by the use here of "complacently." On the other hand, the author speaks of the Americans' resorting not to the "doctrine of inter-est well understood" but rather simply to "interest well understood." Does this hint that it is in their interest thus to explain themselves?

We are told that "almost all the acts of their life" are explained in this fashion. That is, virtually nothing is done except as it might contribute to their own well-being. Perhaps the most interesting question here is, why, if it should not be so, do Americans prefer to speak of themselves in this fashion? Is this because of the more "realistic" taste of modernity? Has it become unfashionable to display, or at least to admit to, high-mindedness? Is hardheadedness as much "feigned" as the "great abnegations" spoken of earlier? Is this in part due to the excesses of democratic rhetoric, which had (by the time this book was written) exploited noble sentiments for several generations in North America? Did the resistance to such rhetoric take two forms: the "realism" or "savvy" of the intelligent citizen and the stunning simplicity of literary craftsmen such as Mark Twain and Abraham Lincoln?[185]

Even so, one must wonder whether Americans in the author's time explained themselves almost exclusively by recourse to the doctrine of interest well understood. Did the people with whom the author talked in the United States express themselves thus? Or did he merely hear them thus, partly because of his own interests or predispositions? Somewhat revealing here may be his suggestion that Americans make sacrifices "to the good of the State." Is not this use of "State" highly suspect?[186] Would not Americans have spoken at this time of "community" or of "neighbors" or of "country"? Does not the use of "State" remind us that the author has a tendency, elsewhere as well as here, to put things in terms that he, as a Euro-pean, happens to understand?

Perhaps it is the author's own inclinations, both as the social scientist (or sociologist) that he is and as a European, that lead him to make as much as he does in this book of *The Federalist*. He says virtually nothing about the Declaration of Independence. But it is in the Declaration that much more is made of nobility: it is there that one hears echoes of Classical antiquity. The more interest-oriented *Federalist*—with its immediate appeals for ratification votes in a local contest—is much more instrumental, presumably serving thereby the grander purposes set forth in the Declaration.[187]

The author leaves us here in Paragraph 11 with two criticisms of the Americans. First, there are natural impulses that no doubt account for some American philanthropy.[188] In addition, to say that a people prefer "to honor their philosophy rather than themselves" is to suggest that they can hardly be said to philosophize.

But, then, we must wonder what philosophy means for the author. He virtually equates it, here and elsewhere, with something like ideology or august opinion. A related question is whether he recognizes *nature* as the source of more than impulses (or desires). Cannot nature, in its most refined and reflective form, lead to calm judgment and mature understanding? Perhaps the author's use here of "justice" is significant. Does this use point to a judgment that is to be made somewhat independent of consequences? Does it remind us of the attractions of virtue as something worthy for its own sake, not just for its utility?

Does the author, then, point to something more than the doctrine of interest well understood as the basis not only of his thought and judgment but also of what the Americans do? Are not Americans somewhere between the two tendencies toward which the author's French readers may be inclined, the reckless pursuit of glory by the thoughtless nobility and the determined pursuit of personal gain by the calculating bourgeoisie?

That the author himself prefers to be regarded as looking, at least in conducting *his* affairs, past the doctrine of interest well understood is suggested by the next paragraph:

> [12] *I might stop here and not attempt to judge that which I have described. The extreme difficulty of the subject would be my excuse. But I do not want to profit from it, and I prefer that my readers, seeing clearly my goal, should refuse to follow me than that I should leave them in suspense.*

The author, it seems, does not make the mistake that the Americans do: he does not speak only of interest moving *him* to act as *he* does. His interest (say, in serving his reputation or in making his book easy for readers) might seem to be served by stopping here rather than run the risk of so exposing his goal or so complicating his argument as to lose his would-be followers.

Of course, he seeks an effect by his book; he may even be considered to have an overall social-political purpose. The intended utility of his book in this respect is evident on its surface. But perhaps he also wants to be understood, at least by some. The truth about these matters and the beauty of that truth are there to be discerned by those who read carefully. Does he indicate as well that true virtue, including the virtue of wisdom, would be better than utility, especially for the great of soul? But can such virtue be counted on, especially if one has large-scale or long-term political purposes in view?[189] Does not the author, in the way he conducts himself here, attempt to reserve the best for himself?

Paragraph 11 shows the Americans being more altruistic (less concerned for their personal profit) than they admit; and Paragraph 12 shows the author being more altruistic (less concerned for his own profit) than other authors might be. Thus, both the author and the Americans look out for others, whatever the prevailing "philosophy" might be.[190] Does the author thereby suggest that whatever the utility of virtue—whatever the usefulness of the doctrine of interest well understood—virtue for its own sake (without regard to personal advantage in the ordinary sense) must be at the heart of a healthy and enduring community?

This book, we should remember, is not written primarily for Americans. Rather, the United States is used as part of the author's efforts to transform and guide Europeans, and especially his fellow citizens in France. Does he, as teacher-statesman, use the doctrine of utility to conduct his own community to habits and opinions that can make it as virtuous politically as the Americans are or are usefully said to be?

VI

We have seen, in the first half of this chapter of *Democracy in America* (Paragraphs 1–10), the development of the doctrine of interest well understood, particularly as it is put to work by Americans. We have been reminded, at the center of this chapter (in Paragraphs 11 and 12), of the underlying virtue (a disinterested virtue for its own sake) that can make this doctrine work properly, whatever may be said about it by its practitioners. We now go on, in the second half (Paragraphs 13–22), to develop the "goal" the author refers to in Paragraph 12. That is, the doctrine of interest well understood is examined in its statesmanlike applications, especially to European conditions.

Three sections remain to be touched upon in my commentary, sections in which there is far less said about the United States than in the first half of this chapter. The first remaining section is devoted to the consequences, good and bad, of the doctrine of interest well understood; the second, to the conditions that make acceptance of the doctrine necessary; the third, to the safeguards that must be resorted to once the doctrine is indeed relied upon.

First, then, in the fifth section of this chapter (made up of Paragraphs 13, 14, and 15) there are these observations:

> *[13] Interest well understood is not a lofty doctrine, but it is clear and sure. It does not seek to attain great objects; but it attains without too much effort all those it aims at. As it is within the reach of all intelligences, each can grasp it easily and can retain it without trouble. Accommodating itself marvelously to the weaknesses of men, it easily obtains a great empire, and it has no difficulty preserving it, because it turns personal interest against itself and uses, to direct the passions, the [same] goad that excites them.*

The references to "clear and sure" and to "the reach of all intelligences" once again remind us of Descartes. We are reminded as well of the Cartesian insistence upon modest but certain steps along a way that can eventually lead to great accomplishments, especially if one is not shackled by the past. Sights are to be lowered—perhaps that is to be regretted, but then the targets come within reach, and something is to be said for that. Machiavelli, for one, said much of what could be said here.[191]

This doctrine of interest well understood, since it is "within the reach of all intelligences," is easily grasped and retained. We are reminded of our observations about the popularity of doctrines that may not be correct—that, indeed, are suspect for their very popularity. The author himself had noticed earlier that "an idea [which is] false but clear and precise will always be more powerful in the world than an idea [which is] true but complex." And we have noticed, in our discussion of Paragraphs 11 and 12 (at the heart of this chapter), the extent to which the doctrine of interest well understood may depend upon a radically different approach to virtue from that of former times.

Loftiness is discounted—both in Paragraphs 1 and 2 and now here in Paragraph 13 (a second beginning?). But something of the lofty manages to slip back in, for is there not here also something for the great-souled statesman? Consider the invocations of the "marvelous" and of "a great empire." Something of Machiavelli may again be seen perhaps—and not least in the empire that the author of *Democracy in America* will himself achieve if he succeeds in transforming the moral and political sentiments of Europeans.

   The author counsels, like Machiavelli and Hobbes before him, that moralists should face up to the passions and hence limitations of human beings, making use of them rather than fighting them. This may perhaps best be seen, for its remarkable effects, in the economic life of a people when acquisitiveness is legitimated (as the free market does). (Whether the same approach can work in foreign policy and war, where honor and great personal sacrifice seem to mean much more, is touched upon in the following chapter of *Democracy in America*.)[192]

   The way spelled out in our chapter can indeed secure "all the [objects] it aims at." But cannot it lose sight of what it is truly after, of what (for instance) the pursuit of gain serves?[193] We can see in Paragraphs 14 and 15 what the doctrine of interest well understood does and does not secure. It is recognized that

> [14] *The doctrine of interest well understood does not produce great abnegations; but it suggests each day small sacrifices; by itself alone, it cannot make a man virtuous; but it forms a multitude of orderly, temperate, moderate, foresightful citizens, masters of themselves; and, if it does not conduct directly to virtue by the will, it insensibly brings it near by habituation.*

   Once again we are reminded that we are to turn away from the greatness that the aristocrats sought. What must be looked for now are not virtuous men but, rather, useful citizens. This approach, which both legitimates and redirects the lower passions, can transform most, if not all, of the inhabitants of a land into citizens—that is, into human beings working more or less together, in a reliable fashion, for the good of all, something that the aristocrats could never do or, at any rate, can no longer do.

   Who knows what can follow from these habits in regularity? These citizens might "insensibly" become virtuous, almost in spite of themselves. (Once again, "conduct" is used.) Whether one is truly virtuous in such circumstances remains a question.

   The prospect of success for the program implied in this chapter (if not in the work as a whole) leads to further suggestions about what is lost and gained:

> [15] *If the doctrine of interest well understood comes to dominate entirely the moral world, extraordinary virtues would no doubt become more rare. But I also think that then the coarser depravities would be less common. The doctrine of interest well understood perhaps prevents some men from mounting far above the ordinary level of humanity; but a great number of others who would fall below encounter it and catch hold of it. Consider some individuals, it debases them. Survey the species, it elevates it.*

We now see it conceded that men of extraordinary virtues have existed, perhaps still exist—and that they are vulnerable to the new way advocated by the author. Once the advantages of the new way have been shown
(as in Paragraph 14 and earlier), then this concession can be made, whereas it had been doubted at the outset of this chapter that "men were more
virtuous in aristocratic ages than in others" (Paragraph 2).

Since it might be questioned whether the loss of men of extraordinary
virtues should be accepted with equanimity, a further advantage of the new
way is at once suggested: "the coarser depravities would be less common."
True, some men would be prevented from "mounting far above the ordinary level of humanity," but "a great number of others who would [other-
wise] fall below" are propped up. Thus, a trade-off is indicated: individuals
might be debased, but the species would be elevated.

Is not, however, the use of "species" here curious? This seems to be a
scientific term, playing up the supposed malleability of the human race.
Perhaps we are meant to appreciate that the author senses that the new way
does, in certain aspects, turn away from the fully (or truly) human. Perhaps,
also, this fits in with the notion that the useful (or one's interest) sounds
more objective and verifiable and hence scientific (especially if it is seen
primarily in terms of economic interest) than virtue or goodness (which
can seem more "subjective" or a matter of taste). Of course, many of us in
this Country today can recognize what the elevation of the species that the
author speaks of means, when we compare our personal circumstances with
those "in the old country" of our immigrant parents, grandparents, or great-
grandparents.

Has the species been elevated? Certainly, there are many more human
beings supported now by the available resources, human beings who tend
to be healthier and to live longer than men of a couple of centuries ago.
But how have nobility and the quality of thought been affected? Does
mankind depend, somehow, on some great ones (such as Charles de
Gaulle), if it is to realize its full humanity? Does the elevation of the species
invoked here by the author make too much of peace and comfort?[194]

One must also wonder whether "the coarser depravities" have indeed
been made "less common." Perhaps this is true, in the sense that various
long-accepted depravities, in the form of callousness toward large-scale
economic exploitation, have come under general attack. But, on the other
hand, we must ask to what the unprecedented barbarities of the twentieth
century, beginning less than a hundred years after this book was written,
can be attributed. Did the great aspirations and pretenses of earlier centuries, as well as a more primitive technology, make the worst less likely in
those times?[195]

Does the author, in what he says about the elimination of the coarser depravities by the new way he advocates, underestimate the effects of modern technology and secrecy? (This means, among other things, that routine depravities can be carried out with fiendish thoroughness and yet can be concealed from public view and hence from any residual natural resistance to depravity.)[196] Such considerations are critical to any assessment of a book that makes so much of utility. That is, the practical effect of the new way is vital, since this is a way that is recommended not for its own sake but rather primarily for its consequences. Are, then, the "coarser depravities" indeed made "less common," something that had been put forth as compensation for the loss of the highest human types?

Has the eclipse of the highest human types, the men of extraordinary virtues, liberated the very worst to assert itself, and not only because the now concealed best were (among other things) best equipped to anticipate and to head off (perhaps even by great self-sacrifice) the worst? To what extent have the worst depravities come precisely because human beings remain open to greatness—because they have an innate taste for greatness, if not in themselves, at least in a few and in the community defined and inspired by those few? We are often reminded of the willingness, if not the eagerness, of some to pull down the high and mighty—and an egalitarian age all too often caters to envy. But perhaps we need to be reminded as well that there may be in mankind an innate openness to the sublime. Have not the most awful atrocities of the twentieth century been grounded partly in often mad efforts to supply mankind with substitutes for the obvious and enduring greatness that our new way of life has virtually eliminated? Has elimination of the appearance of such greatness also depreciated the standards in the light of which some things were considered great and others considered insane and despicable?

Aside from the question of depravities (to which we will return), there is the question of what happens to genius, both philosophic and artistic, when the new leveling prevails. Is not the fullest expression of genius compromised, and made less likely, when "some individuals" (that is, men of extraordinary virtues) are "debased"? Certainly there is a vast difference between the works of, say, Sophocles, Phideas, and Shakespeare, on the one hand, and the most widely acclaimed modern art, on the other. We are reminded of the question touched upon in Paragraph 11, which comes up again in Paragraph 16, of what philosophy means to this author.

We are obliged, then, to return to a question that the career of someone such as Abraham Lincoln can inspire: In what does mankind truly live—in raising the general level of the community at large, or in contemplating the peaks that only a few can reasonably hope to attain? Does the general recognition of distant peaks affect the moral tone of the community and affect also a people's sense of dignity and the meaning for them of life itself? Or can people be satisfied by the placid times to which a rough equality, in effect, aspires? Still, are not extraordinary virtues, including the intellectual virtues, the things that even the generality of mankind somehow lives for? Whatever the social and political consequences of such virtues, the human being comes to fulfillment thus—and mankind can, when properly instructed, take pride in the manifestation of extraordinary virtues just as a healthy family or community can take pride in the offspring or neighbor who rises far above his fellows.

One mark of the man of extraordinary virtues should be his ability to explain men such as himself in such a way as to make them acceptable. Is it not a sign of a people's limitations that they do not sense how critical a man or woman of extraordinary virtues (who should be distinguished from the "celebrity") can be for the vitality of the soul of mankind? Is not the author, even though not perhaps of the highest rank as a thinker himself, also somewhat vulnerable to the way of life he advocates? Certainly, one must question any way of life that can sometimes seem to rule out, almost on principle, the very best.

Paragraph 15, like Paragraph 8, can be considered a transition. The limitations of the doctrine of interest well understood have been touched upon here; its compensations, which are developed in the next section of this chapter, are anticipated.

VII

The sixth section (made up of Paragraphs 16–20) considers further what can be said on behalf of the doctrine of interest well understood. Perhaps no section of the chapter makes so much of the first person. Its first paragraph reads,

> *[16] I shall not fear to say that the doctrine of interest well understood seems to me, of all the philosophical theories, the one most appropriate to the needs of men of our time, and that I see in it the most powerful guarantee that remains to them against themselves. It is principally toward it then that the spirit of moralists of our time ought to be turned. Even though they may judge it to be imperfect, it still must be adopted as necessary.*

The author describes himself at the very outset of this paragraph as not fearful. In this he is like the bold American moralists referred to in Paragraph 4, not like the frightened European moralists of Paragraph 2. He is, that is, in tune with the time and its inclinations.

We here see again the problem of what philosophy means to the author (a problem that may be seen as well in Paragraphs 11 and 15). Philosophy, it seems, is something to be used—and this may be consistent with the greater interest the author may have in practice than in speculation. Is not this related to the down-to-earth approach displayed in Paragraph 13, with its (Cartesian?) invocation of the "clear and sure"?

Men "of our time," we are told, have special "needs." It may not matter how they got these needs; it is enough that they have them or, what may be the same in practice, that they believe they have them. Nothing is said about what should be done about these needs, such as changing them, except that they can usefully be turned against themselves. And for this the doctrine of interest well understood is eminently useful.

This doctrine, it is recognized, is imperfect. Yet it should be "adopted as necessary." Thus, the truth is respected here, at least to the extent of acknowledging that the doctrine, however useful, is defective. The truth is thus somehow preserved, at least for a while—but one must wonder how any doctrine can continue to be recognized as imperfect by anyone once it is generally accepted and turns out to be useful. Evidently, in order for this doctrine to be popular, it must not be *presented* as imperfect. The author's immediate readers, then, are not those who are likely to accept the doctrine without reservation.[197] Are his privileged readers to consider all this from a perspective that is somehow superior to that of those who do believe in the doctrine of interest well understood? Upon what does such a statesmanlike perspective depend? Nothing is said about that here. Rather, the author goes on to say something more about how Americans and Europeans differ in one critical respect, presumably because of the effect in the United States of the general acceptance of the doctrine of interest well understood:

> [17] I do not believe, on the whole, that there is more egoism among us than in America; the sole difference is that there it is illuminated and here it is not. Each American knows how to sacrifice a part of his particular interests to save the rest. We want to retain everything and often everything escapes us.

Europeans, it seems, are particularly in need of the moderating effects of the doctrine of interest well understood. That is because of the kind of egoism Europeans have. Egoism, the author explained six chapters before, "is a passionate and exaggerated love of self which leads a man to think of all things in terms of himself and to prefer himself to all." It "springs from a blind instinct." Individualism, on the other hand, "is based on misguided judgement rather than on depraved feeling"; it is "a calm and considered feeling which disposes each citizen to isolate himself from the mass of his fellows and withdraw into the circle of family and friends." Egoism, it seems, is associated more with the human being (is it almost natural?); individualism, more with the citizen—and it is the individualism of Americans, as citizens, from which this chapter takes its departure. Egoism, it also seems, is more of a problem with Europeans than it is with Americans, perhaps because Europeans remain, by and large, more private and more instinctive in their pursuits. (The concern here with egoism may help account for the considerable use of the first person in this section of our chapter from *Democracy in America*.)

Europeans are, with respect to their personal desires, less "illuminated" (or informed) than Americans. About what matters are Americans better informed? As to how egoistic all are? Or as to how to be effectively egoistic, especially by looking out somewhat for others? One way or another, Americans are sensible: they know how to give up a part to save the whole, whatever reasons they give. Has the legitimation of acquisitiveness in America made them less acquisitive? Are they thus on the way to that virtue, by gradual habituation, anticipated in Paragraph 14?

Europeans, on the other hand, the author suggests, are stupidly greedy. How bad they are, how much in need of correction, is evident in the next paragraph:

> [18] I only see around me people who seem to want to teach each day to their contemporaries, by their word and their example, that the useful is never dishonest. Shall I not discover finally some who undertake to make them comprehend how the honest can be useful?

People around him seem to want to teach the wrong thing: an act is moral, they seem to say, if it serves one's interest. That is, European moralists of his day try to rationalize, in terms of the honorable, the selfishness to which men are prone. Does such rationalization only create resentment among the exploited? On what basis were these arguments being made in the author's time? Was it being said that it is not wrong for a man to do what benefits him, but only "natural" to do so? Besides, it was perhaps added, only he can look out for himself. In this way, whatever natural regard one might have (à la Jean-Jacques Rousseau) for the welfare of others was disparaged, if not suppressed.

The author prefers to see the current teaching reversed. It should be insisted that it pays to be moral. No doubt, moral conduct can be useful. Is it always? Are there not instances when it is difficult to believe that one is

benefiting personally, in the ordinary sense of "benefit," from one's morality? Or should morality be vitally dependent upon prudence, a prudence
that makes much more of consequences than do everyday moral maxims?
That is, the right thing to do may often vary with the circumstances. Prudence does look to utility—but whose utility? Is not prudence consistent,
at least on rare occasions, with self-sacrifice?

Perhaps this is too sophisticated for the author's immediate purpose.
After all, it is a popular doctrine that is needed, one that is, or at least
appears to be, "clear and sure." The author seems to identify himself as one
of those who "undertake to make [people] comprehend how the honest
can be useful." Or is it really that he wants to persuade people to believe
that the honest is useful, not explain how it happens that it is? For, we
notice, it is not precisely spelled out here what the Americans believe that
they gain by giving up "a part of [their] particular interests" or how they
gain by acting morally toward others. What might happen would require a
case-by-case analysis to figure out—and that is not the author's concern
here. Rather, it is a general attitude that he wants to change: he wants people to begin to believe that it helps *them* to help their fellow citizens, for
whatever reason they do it. Perhaps he (as a responsible statesman) would
change his emphasis, and the rationale of his position, once Europeans
become so convinced by what he advocates that they act more like public-
spirited Americans. To begin to change Europeans, they must first be
brought to believe that one does the right thing toward others primarily
for one's own good, even though in fact it may be for the good of the
other. Of course, a better community and better fellow citizens, are thereby promoted—and so one does benefit, usually, by one's sacrifices.

French readers of these comments by Tocqueville on the relation of
the honest and the useful could well have been reminded of Montaigne's
essay, almost three centuries earlier, "On the Useful and the Honest."[198]
Tocqueville refers to Montaigne by name, for (I believe) the only time in
the entire book, in Paragraph 8 of this chapter; he now implicitly draws
upon him, here in Paragraph 18. An endorsement of Montaigne's approach
may be seen in Tocqueville's resistance to the emphasis in the teaching of
his own time upon the proposition that "the useful is never dishonest."
After all, Montaigne had virtually concluded his essay on this subject with
the sentence, "We poorly argue the honesty and beauty of an action from
its utility, and we commit a fallacy in thinking that everyone is obliged to
perform—and that it is honest to perform—an action merely because it is
useful." Again and again in his essay, Montaigne argues for the honest in lieu
of the useful, even though he recognizes that princes must sometimes violate their consciences in order to do what the common good (or general

utility) clearly requires. But private interest, he seems to insist, should not be permitted to sway one from proper conduct; that would hardly be worthy of, or becoming to, the true statesman.

It would take us too far afield on this occasion, however, to consider further what Montaigne says and how he questions the distinction in common usage between the useful and the honest. A full study of *Democracy in America* should consider this subtle essay by Montaigne; it is against this background (as well as that provided by Descartes and Rousseau) that Tocqueville speaks. Consider, for instance, the effects of shame (which is related to beauty?) and of conscience in Montaigne and what happens to these things in Tocqueville.

Perhaps Tocqueville meant to suggest that his entire book should be read in the light of Montaigne, another great "sociological" writer of the French school. And so, special reference may, in effect, be made by Tocqueville to the Montaigne essay on the useful and the honest. Montaigne does seem more elevated with respect to virtue than Tocqueville sometimes allows himself to appear in *Democracy in America*. But, one can suspect upon noticing correspondences between these two French authors' works, Tocqueville knew that Montaigne's public position on virtue was closer than was Tocqueville's to Classical models (even though Montaigne, too, departed from them). (Also, was not philosophy a more serious enterprise for Montaigne?) Tocqueville's public position and emphasis with respect to virtue and politics, he can be understood to have suggested, must appear (and hence be?) different from Montaigne's because times and circumstances have changed so much. We are thus reminded of how this subject might more fully be regarded.[199]

The author goes on, in the following paragraph, to remind us also of what has led to the changes in times and circumstances with which a statesman must reckon:

> *[19] There is no power on earth able to prevent the increasing equality of conditions from carrying the human spirit to seek out the useful, or from disposing each citizen to shrink into himself.*

No "power on earth" can prevent what is happening. Is it recognized that God may still do so, but He is not expected to do so? He, in any event, cannot be counted upon to intervene here. The author reconciles himself to the inevitable. Great historical forces are suggested. But could the excesses or debacle of triumphant equality lead to its subversion?

Should the worldwide inclination to equality be catered to, and used, or should it be resisted? Elsewhere in the book, there are indications that a rough justice is available from a dedication to equality which was not evident when liberty reigned, that very liberty which permits nobility and men of extraordinary virtues to manifest themselves. This opening to justice might make the author himself more inclined than others of his class to go along with, and to guide in a statesmanlike manner, the egalitarian revolution rather than to resist it. He is not heard to pray to God that this massive historical movement be reversed.

The key to this movement, we are told, is "the increasing equality of conditions." It seems that material conditions, not ideas, are considered by the author to be fundamental to this development, whatever he may say elsewhere about the primacy of the soul. But why have conditions changed? That is not explored here. Perhaps it cannot be, without sacrificing the notion that conditions are critical. That is, really to know why conditions have changed would be to challenge the (sociological?) opinion that conditions are dominant. Reason would thereby be considered somehow higher, if not sovereign, something that the author generally seems to doubt.

What does a dedication to equality mean in practice? We have noticed its opening to justice, especially when contrasted to regimes that find people confined in depressed stations generation after generation. This is an aspect of equality that Lincoln, for example, very much treasured in the American regime. Does equality tend to look to the useful, especially if traditional models and standards are repudiated? The useful in such circumstances is apt to be linked to the pleasant. One is encouraged to look out for oneself; or perhaps that turns out to be the only thing one is left with. It is not surprising, then, that each citizen becomes disposed "to shrink into himself," invoking ever more privacy, even while much is made of judging each man and woman on the basis of merit.

Each can see his merits equal to those of others, if only because (in the absence of authoritative standards) one naturally tends to consider one's own desires to be as worthy as those of others. (And as more and more material goods become generally available, appetites can be excited further.) It becomes fashionable to insist, "I'm as good as anyone else"— with the only sure and clear basis of one's claims to equal treatment being the fact of one's existence.[200] Thus, one can insist that one is as good as the next man, without having had to learn anything special or to act in any special way.

Besides, a usefulness keyed to pleasure is easier to "understand." The many can more easily believe that they comprehend what is going on, or at least where their interests lie, when utility is the key to choice. Nature, in any event, becomes suspect as a source of standards, even while it seems to legitimate the desires one happens to have. For one thing, if there should be standards of right and wrong recognized as evident from a study of nature, then it is likely that significant differences between human beings may also have to be recognized. Therefore, if one makes much of equality, one may tend (unless one is thoughtful) to rule out nature as a guide, insofar as nature works from differences between men. Invocations of nature are distrusted, for they have all too often been used to excuse unjust allocations among men.[201] Or, if nature is to be permitted to have a say, it should be only in the form of serving, as well as legitimating, whatever desires we happen to have. Thus, again, the pleasant is sovereign, which means a determined recourse to the useful.

The author sees two responses by men to prevailing egalitarian conditions. Either they will go out to seek the useful or they will shrink into themselves. Either way, they will try to serve themselves, or at least they will not submit to authority or to authoritative principles. So, he counsels, thoughtful men (that is, statesmen?) should make the moral seem useful. Thus, he closes this section of our chapter with this observation:

> *[20] It must then be expected that individual interest will become more than ever the principal, if not the unique, motive for the actions of man; but it remains to be learned how each man seeks his individual interest.*

Individual interest will be decisive. The critical question is what each man sees interest to be—that is, how he can be led to see his own interest. The author advocates in this chapter that each man should be led to see that his interest includes a considerable benevolence toward his fellow citizens.

The author does not say more about rightness for its own sake. Perhaps he is too much a modern, and not only in being "realistic," in shying away as he does from that recourse to nature that may be seen in invocations of natural right and in reliance upon the natural sociability of human beings.

VIII

The final section of this chapter (made up of Paragraphs 21 and 22) suggests the safeguards that must be resorted to now that equality is becoming triumphant and should the doctrine of interest be established.

First, the dangers that lie before mankind are dramatized:

> *[21] If citizens, in becoming equal, were to remain ignorant and coarse, it is difficult to foresee to what stupid excess their egoism will carry them, and it cannot be*

said in advance into what shameful miseries they would plunge themselves from
fear of sacrificing something of their well-being to the prosperity of their kind.

The author warns against stupid excesses and shameful miseries, especially if citizens remain "ignorant and coarse" Ignorance takes the form, it
seems, of a selfishness that is not tempered by the doctrine of interest well
understood. Here as elsewhere in this chapter, fear is a corrosive element in
society; this time it is "fear of sacrificing something of their well-being to
the prosperity of their kind."[202] We are reminded of the expectation voiced
in Paragraph 15 that "the coarser depravities would be less common" if the
doctrine of interest well understood should come "to dominate entirely the
moral world."

Ignorance and coarseness are seen as dangerous. And yet we now know
that perhaps the greatest systematic atrocities in recorded history came (in
our own time) in a highly cultivated country and under the leadership of
someone who challenged his people to make great sacrifices for the father-
land. Are not men apt to "plunge" most deeply when asked to sacrifice for
the most noble causes, especially if disciplined and elevated glimpses of the
truly great have been systematically denied them? That is, "debasing"
extends beyond the few great ones who are dragged down. Of course, those
who commit atrocities do not consider their victims to be their equals.
They may not even regard their victims as of the same species (or as "their
kind"). And so a thoroughgoing dedication to equality, in correcting such
opinions, can promote justice within a community. But, as I have suggested, equality can also be taken by all too many to relieve human beings of
any duty to submit to restraints imposed either by nature or by any who
are by nature superior.

Still, the author concludes this chapter by counseling what should be
done to make the equality-bound men of our day somewhat respectful of
the requirements of the community and of their fellow citizens:

> [22] *I do not believe that the doctrine of interest, as it is preached in America, is*
> *evident in all its parts; but it does contain a great number of truths so evident*
> *that it suffices to illuminate men for them to be seen. Illuminate them, then, at*
> *any cost, for the age of blind abnegations and of instinctive virtues already flees*
> *far from us, and I see approaching the time when liberty, the public peace and*
> *social order itself will not be able to exist without enlightenment.*

It is conceded here that the doctrine of interest is not "evident [or,
obvious] in all its parts." One is reminded, by way of contrast, of the Declaration of Independence, with its grounding in self-evident truths. But, the
author goes on to assure us, the doctrine "does contain a great number of

truths so evident" that one need only point them out in order for men at large to be persuaded.

This pointing out, this lighting up of what is there to be seen, is advocated. Such enlightenment does not seem to be genuine education; rather it is to be, as it has been in America, a kind of preaching.[203]

Can the enlightenment called for head off demagoguery and atrocities, to say nothing of a long-term decline? Demagogues, I have suggested, can appeal to the perhaps natural taste for sacrifice, for country, and for greatness—all of which tend to be neglected by the doctrine of interest well understood, which may rest ultimately upon the opinion that one does not really sacrifice anything when one acts morally, that what one does is for one's personal benefit as ordinarily understood, and that greatness is obsolete and otherwise unrealistic. We suspect that only citizens of democracies are apt to be able to apply systematically the doctrine of interest that the author advocates, if only because they alone have extensive choices in how they conduct themselves in social relations. Are democracies then most vulnerable to the permanent debasing effects of any doctrine that, however high-minded in its ultimate goals and in many of its consequences, places the emphasis in its method upon looking out for oneself?

What is the alternative to the doctrine of interest well understood? An old-fashioned answer looks to prudence (preferably a prudence instructed by political philosophy)—to prudence in statesmen who minister to a people properly trained with respect to "the duties of man," not just with respect to man's interests and rights. But "blind abnegations" and "instinctive virtues" seem to be ruled out by the author, whereas one might have hoped that one's leaders had been imbued with a spirit of appropriate sacrifice for the common good and that one's people had been so shaped that their virtues were deeply ingrained. Does the author, with the sense of sophisticated "realism" he promotes, make a thoughtful prudence (such as was evident among the Founders in the United States) more difficult to develop in leaders and to respond to by peoples, thereby making statesmanship less likely?

Our chapter from *Democracy in America* closes with a reminder of various goods that are threatened: "liberty, the public peace and social order." Liberty, it can be argued, makes nobility or excellence possible. It, perhaps more than the others—and more than equality as well—can be, as it were, an end in itself. Liberty is to be found as against the community, perhaps, but still *within* the community, at least if one regards the human being as a social animal. The natural sociability of man may be reflected in the reaffirmation here of public peace and social order. Do not these point to the community and not to one's own interest (however well understood), as primary in key respects? And is not a truly political approach required here, not an effort that seems to assure people that they are entitled, if not obliged, to look out first for themselves in their dealings with their fellow citizens? Certainly, political philosophy, not political sociology of the kind seen in *Democracy in America,* is needed to clarify what mankind needs and aspires to and what the place is, in a genuine political community, of human beings of extraordinary virtues. Perhaps this is also needed if we are to understand what is truly at the heart of the American regime and hence what it is that makes it work as well as it, in fact, does.

IX

We have seen, through an extended commentary upon one of its shorter chapters, that *Democracy in America* can be expected to repay detailed examination. Care in composition is evident throughout. Some of the things we have seen in examining the text of this chapter are evident as well in its title, "How the Americans Combat Individualism by the Doctrine of Interest Well Understood."

The author speaks here of combat (as in a related discussion four chapters before). This suggests that there is a battle going on—that the Americans have a mission, even a victory, in mind, perhaps even some notion of the common good that they want to see prevail. Without such an objective, the American effort would be but another purposeless skirmish, not part of a meaningful campaign.[204] Thus, the author seems to imply, Americans sense something higher for the sake of which a useful individualism should be curbed. What role do extraordinary men, "by their word and their example," play in reminding Americans of great goals? Our greatest "word," the Declaration of Independence, makes much of the place of prudence, and hence of statesmanship, in human affairs.[205]

Certainly it is difficult, if the doctrine of interest well understood is to be taken both as men ordinarily take it and as decisive in guiding American actions, to make sense of the great civil war in which magnificent passions were enlisted and to which incalculable sacrifices were made, that great war which, coming a generation after this book, could be called (not implausibly) the last great war among gentlemen. Perhaps, it can be added, the existence of slavery in the United States meant that early Americans should have emphasized as they did the principle of equality, if only to remind themselves continually that they could do no more than tolerate the dreadful institution they were saddled with—tolerate it until the opportunity came (albeit with great disregard for personal interest, as ordi narily understood) to rid themselves and their posterity of this affliction.[206]

Whether equality should continue to be made as much of as former-ly among us, now that circumstances have changed, depends upon pruden-tial political judgments of the highest order. And these in turn may depend in part upon the aristocratic critique of modern democracy which is implicit in the vocabulary and tone, if not in the argument, of our chapter from Tocqueville. (The endorsement by Thomas Jefferson and John Adams, a generation earlier, of a natural aristocracy should be remembered.) We are again reminded of the standards to which Americans must have looked in "combating" individualism or in determining what to emphasize and what to play down, both in their efforts to serve the common good and in the personal pursuit of happiness. I have suggested that the doctrine of interest well understood may help, when properly used, to guide both public opin-ion and private action. That is, it must rest, if it is to be used well, on a live-ly sense of right and wrong rooted either in nature or in a sacred tradition so firmly established as to seem natural. The author does not seem to appre-ciate the significance of the fact, which he reports elsewhere in his book, of the presence of treasured copies of Shakespeare and of the Bible in hum-ble dwellings all over the America he visited. Did not those works teach Americans not to insist only upon the utility of virtue but rather to prac-tice it for its own sake as well?[207]

What, finally, does Tocqueville do for that political philosophy upon which an enduring polity rests? He certainly draws on political philosophy, and yet, depending upon how he is read, he can be seen to undermine it— or, at least, he can make sound understanding more difficult for his succes-sors. How many of the difficulties implicit in his argument that I have sug-gested here did he himself recognize? Or was he, like a gifted artist, inspired to reveal more than he was conscious of? Did he, for example, counsel his more privileged readers not only as to how "insensibly" to lead the many to virtue but also as to how to attain for themselves and for others like themselves a noble grandeur by which still others might be enlightened, inspired, and perhaps even educated? To this end, should not much more be made of ideas and reasoning, and far less of mindless conditions and inevitable movements, as the fundamental causes of the soundest opinions and of the most celebrated actions of mankind? It is with such causes and such ends that the dedicated statesman must be preeminently concerned.[208]

I have suggested a few problems with Tocqueville's understanding of moral and political things and their sources. Need I add that this should not be taken as an attempt on my part to deny the extraordinary merits of a majestic oratorio on democracy which, in its inspired appeal, defies all critics?

7

John C. Calhoun and Slavery

We shall not shock anyone, we shall merely expose ourselves to
good-natured or at any rate harmless ridicule, if we profess ourselves inclined to the old-fashioned and simple opinion according to which Machiavelli was a teacher of evil.

—Leo Strauss

I

A law school teacher of mine, who served with defense counsel when fran-
tic officials succeeded in their disgraceful efforts (in 1953) to expedite the
Rosenberg atomic-espionage executions, recalled years later, "It was an
episode of governmental insanity." I am inclined, whenever I reflect upon
the decades that led up to the American Civil War, to make a similar assessment of the conduct of the extremists of that period, abolitionists and
secessionists alike.[209]

The eleventh volume of the papers of John C. Calhoun—issued mid-
point in the projected twenty-volume collection—shows Calhoun moving
from the position of a respected national politician to the messianic role he
would perform for the last twenty years of his life as the idolized spokesman
for the South. The public turning point in his career was his resignation as
Vice President of the United States (in December 1832) to become a Senator from South Carolina.

This book review, except its concluding section, has been previously published in *Modern Age,* Winter 1981, 106–11. (Original title: "The American Alcibiades?") It has also been published in 20 *Texas Tech Law Review* 722–32 (1989). The
book reviewed here is *The Papers of John C. Calhoun, 1829–1832,* vol. 11, ed. Clyde
N. Wilson (Columbia: University of South Carolina Press, 1978).

The epigraph is taken from Leo Strauss, *Thoughts on Machiavelli* (Glencoe, Ill.:
Free Press, 1958), 9.

Calhoun had by that time developed for his State the doctrine of Nullification (or, as he preferred to call it, Interposition). Only one refinement was needed to complete the intellectual armory of Southern extremists, and that was an insistence upon the "positive good" of slavery. This proposition Calhoun set forth in 1848, two years before his death (at age sixty-eight).

II

Calhoun has been called "surely one of the most intelligent men who ever lived."[210] The more one reads of this driven genius, however, the more his drive (or passion) becomes evident and the less his intelligence.

His passion was enlisted in the most extreme advocacy of the cause of States' Rights, but only after he had been tripped up on his way to the Presidency. Calhoun's political enemies (including, it seems, Martin Van Buren) were able to take advantage of his (and President Andrew Jackson's) sometimes exaggerated sense of honor to divert Calhoun from the Succession.[211]

Having lost the Presidency, for which he (as a prominent national figure since the War of 1812) had earned the right to be seriously considered, Calhoun became the foremost theoretician of South Carolinian fanaticism. It was either this, he came to feel, or reconcile his beloved State to the eventual repudiation of a way of life grounded upon slavery. In this rationalization of one's own as "sacred," Calhoun (as a modern) can be understood to have been a forerunner of Martin Heidegger, the Macbeth of philosophy.[212]

The public arguments (at least in these critical years, 1829–1832, when the final direction of Calhoun's career was set) were put in terms of constitutional rights not in terms of a defense of slavery. The Tariff Acts provided the occasion for the position taken at that time by South Carolina: a protective tariff was seen to place burdens upon the staple-exporting States (of the South) primarily for the benefit of the eventually more prosperous manufacturing States (of the North). The oppressiveness and even despotism of majority rule were condemned; repeated invocations of the minority's right to liberty were heard.[213]

And yet there is hardly an argument (whether social, moral-political, or economic) made by Calhoun and his associates on behalf of Southern grievances that did not apply with even greater force against what had been done for decades, if not centuries, to the minority of African descent in the South and elsewhere. Should not these eloquent, often self-righteous if not obsessed, Southern patriots have seen that the principles they paraded to justify their resistance to Congressional (and, later, Presidential) "tyranny" made a shambles of any justification for their own continued domination of Christianized slaves who could no longer be considered simply uncivilized?

Many of John Calhoun's protestations in the name of liberty could have easily been adapted to antislavery purposes by such abolitionists as the gifted Frederick Douglass—and this, as much as anything else, suggests the ultimate futility of Calhoun's position. Abraham Lincoln, for one, recognized well before the Civil War the profound inconsistency upon which the defense of slavery in the United States rested, just as he recognized the dangerous irresponsibility of all-too-human demands for immediate abolition.

III

American slavery, Lincoln could argue, was doomed at least from the time of the national dedication in 1776 to the "self-evident" truth that "all Men are created equal." But did the system of slavery have to be dismantled by means of war? Certainly, that had not been the expectation of the men of 1776 or 1787.

But mistakes were made. One of these mistakes may have been by President Jackson in not having arranged for Calhoun to succeed him. This particularly gifted South Carolinian should have been obliged, as he would have been as a national leader, to moderate his sectional passions and "principles." He should not have been left available to provide the cause of slavery the legitimation he did. Or, as the Athenians were advised about the irrepressible Alcibiades, "Best it is never to rear a lion in the city; but if he has been reared, it is best to humor him."[214]

A related mistake was made by Presidents and Congresses in exploiting protective tariffs without much regard for either the pocketbooks or the sensibilities of the South. Southerners again and again voiced the grievance that the economic interests of one section of the Union were being cynically sacrificed to those of another. Once the national public debt had been virtually discharged, it seemed to many in the South obvious bad faith for Congress to continue exacting a tariff which would produce so much revenue that how to dispose of the surplus would become a critical question. A generation of complaints about a discriminatory tariff accustomed the South, except in the face of a foreign enemy, to consider its interests distinct from those of the Country at large.

Should not Calhoun, as perhaps the most intelligent politician of his generation, have recognized the limitations of President Jackson as well as of the various spokesmen for sectional interests and have done their thinking for them? This would have meant, among other things, both different responses by him to the challenges to his honor and different approaches by him and others to the tariff grievances, to what stood behind those grievances, and to what lay ahead.

IV

That the slavery issue was indeed what ultimately stood behind the tariff grievances, giving them their staying power and corrosiveness, can be discerned here and there even in this eleventh volume of Calhoun's papers.

Articulate Southerners, in celebrating their way of life, "naturally" resorted to euphemisms (at least in this period) whenever they were obliged to refer to the institution of slavery upon which that way of life so much depended. Is it not likely that this reticence reflected a commendable uneasiness, rooted perhaps in a residual sense of natural right, about the institution with which they were saddled?[215]

In only one of the documents in this eleventh volume—in a letter of September 11, 1830, to a political intimate in Maryland—did Calhoun devote a few sentences to the underlying slavery issue of the period:

> The eye of the State [South Carolina] has thus been turned for relief [with respect to the Tariff] from the general to the State Government, and to the call of a [State] convention, as the best means, of devising a remedy, & which from present appearance, will be called by a large majority.
>
> If I really believed, that civil discord, revolution, or disunion would follow from the measures contemplated, I would not hesitate, devoted to our system of government as I am, to throw myself in the current with the view to arrest it at any hazard, but believing that the State, while she is struggling to preserve her reserved powers, is acting with devoted loyalty to the Union, no earthly consideration would induce me to do an act, or utter a sentiment, which would cast an imputation on her motives. Should the State ever look beyond her present object, to prevent a consolidation of all power in the General Government & thereby the loss of our liberty and Union, I trust no good citizen would better understand his duty to the Union or be more prompt to perform it, than myself; but of this there is not the least fear, unless the genl government should undertake to oppose force to Constitutional and peaceful remedies.
>
> I consider the Tariff act as the occasion, rather than the real cause

of the present unhappy state of things. The truth can no longer be disguised, that the peculiar domestick institution of the Southern States, and the consequent direction, which that and her soil and climate have given to her industry, has placed them in regard to taxation and appropriations in opposite relation to the majority of the Union, against the danger of which, if there be no protective power in the reserved rights of the States, they must in the end be forced to rebel, or submit it to have their paramount interests sacraficed, their domestick institutions subordinated by Colonization and other schemes, and themselves & children reduced to wretchedness. Thus situated, the denial of the right of the State to interpose constitutionally in the last resort, more alarms the thinking, than all other causes; and however strange it may appear, the more universally the State is condemned, and her right denied, the more resolute she is to assert her constitutional powers lest the neglect to assert should be considered a practical abandonment of them, under such circumstances.

I have written you fully, trusting to your discretion and tried friendship.[216]

V

On slavery itself, Calhoun simply did not think clearly enough, if he was truly able to think at all. He confined himself to protecting interests that not only resulted from an intensive use of slaves but also were dedicated to the indefinite continuation if not extension of slavery. Unless slavery could be shown to have been justified, if not even acclaimed as a continuing "positive good" for slaves and masters alike, he was clearly wrong.

This is not to deny that there were serious difficulties in the way of outright abolition of slavery during Calhoun's lifetime, difficulties that many today are not likely to appreciate.[217] But difficult as it no doubt would have been to eliminate slavery immediately, it should have been evident that it would be even more difficult (if not monstrous) to plan to continue it indefinitely. For one thing, the South would have become hopelessly callous on this issue. The somewhat opportunistic Henry Clay, with his compromises and reforms, may have had the sounder approach.

Vital to any serious attempt to deal properly with American slavery had to be the commonsensical recognition that it was truly evil. It was this recognition that Calhoun, unlike Clay, seems never to have been willing to make publicly—and, however intelligent Calhoun was, his course was not thoughtful. He thereby blinded himself to moral judgments that were obvious to a steadily growing number of decent men and women in his own time and that had been obvious as well to the leading Southerners of earlier generations whom he invoked for other purposes.

Whatever white Southerners were obliged to do about the emancipated Africans among them after 1865, could not they have done such things better before the devastation and bitterness of war, if they had been properly led? This, and the recognition that something had to be done to advance a truly defensible permanent solution, should have been apparent to Calhoun. If it should be said that he would have destroyed himself politically and would have been ineffectual as well if he had tried to moderate the Southern passion for the indefinite perpetuation and indeed expansion of slavery, it should be replied that what he did do can hardly be respected as "effective."

If Calhoun was truly incapable of changing the opinion of his countrymen, or of arresting their destructive course, then he would have been wiser to perceive the futility of politics in his time and devote himself to other pursuits. Instead, he betrayed his trust by permitting his considerable skills to be enlisted in support of a terrible injustice that his equally impassioned but far less talented countrymen were permitted to believe they need never face up to. Thus, he brought them to the brink of Secession for the sake of slavery, in the name of States' Rights, all the time protesting attachment to the Union and its Constitution.[218]

However much one recognizes the contributions that States' Rights have made, and continue to make, to the common good in this Country, it is difficult to find merit in Calhoun's Interposition. This doctrine, which treats the Constitution as if it were no more than a solemn treaty, permits any determined State to exercise, with respect to anything it happens to take seriously, a constitutional veto power over the legislative power of the national majority. Thus, South Carolina in 1832 voted to suspend the operations of the tariff laws within that State (unless overruled by three-fourths of the States), but President Jackson made it clear that he would have none of that!

Does not the Interposition doctrine assume that the unjust is necessarily unconstitutional? Would not this mean, as a practical matter, that government has no legitimate power to do either good or bad? In this and in other respects, Calhoun's Interposition doctrine is to be distinguished, on the one hand, from the freedom of speech protected by the First Amendment and, on the other hand, from the right of revolution invoked by the Declaration of Independence.

Indeed, the Southern recourse in 1861 to Secession made more sense than Calhoun's Interposition, though that recourse too was rendered dubious by the cause to which it was ultimately dedicated.[219]

VI

Magnanimity is vital in these matters. This virtue is consistent with sound moral judgment, as may be seen in General Ulysses S. Grant's appraisal of his defeated enemy, Robert E. Lee: "I felt [at Appomatox Court House] like anything rather than rejoicing at the downfall of a foe who had fought so long and valiantly, and had suffered so much for a cause, though that cause was, I believe, one of the worst for which a people ever fought, and one for which there was the least excuse."

Still another magnanimous, and yet just, assessment of Calhoun and his colleagues has been made in Lord Charnwood's life of Lincoln (emphasis added):

> In no other contest of history are those elements in human affairs on which tragic dramatists are prone to dwell so clearly marked as in the American Civil War. No unsophisticated person now, except in ignorance as to the cause of the war, can hesitate as to which side enlists his sympathy, or can regard the victory of the North otherwise than as the costly and imperfect triumph of the right. . . . The responsibility for the actual secession does not rest in an especial degree on any individual [Southern] leader. Secession began rather with the spontaneous movement of the whole community of South Carolina, and in the States which followed leading politicians expressed rather than inspired the general will. The guilt which any of us can venture to attribute for this action of a whole deluded society must rest on men like Calhoun, who in a previous generation, *while opinion in the South was still to some extent unformed,* stifled all thought of reform and gave the semblance of moral and intellectual justification to a system [which was] only susceptible of a historical excuse.[220]

An appropriate magnanimity may be seen as well in the remarks of Alan Paton, upon reviewing in the 1970s a novel that predicted the grim life that white South Africans would be obliged to endure if their harsh regime should continue to resist reform and therefore "have" to be overthrown: "[Can] cataclysm [be] avoided by deeds of love and generosity and courage and wisdom? Or is it beyond reason to expect rulers to do such deeds?"[221]

It is a prudent magnanimity—quite different from "governmental insanity"—of which Calhoun seems to have been incapable. And, partly because of him, so were the proud, often generous but yet crippled people whom he "led" to the brink of disaster.

VII

An immediate transition to the career and thought of Abraham Lincoln is provided by the further probing into the thought and career of John Calhoun offered us by Harry Jaffa. Mr. Jaffa is a scholar, perhaps more so than any other today, who is equipped to be particularly sensitive to the workings of the Calhoun soul. I have Mr. Jaffa's permission to conclude this chapter with three passages from Chapter 7 of the recently completed first volume of his treatise, *A New Birth of Freedom* (the sequel to his *Crisis of the House Divided*).

The importance for the South of the issue of the expansion of slavery into the Territories of the United States—an issue dramatized both by the decision in *Dred Scott* and by the emergence of the Republican Party—is recalled for us in this passage from the Jaffa book:

> To understand the sense in which the doctrines of Calhoun, on the one hand, and of Lincoln and the Founders on the other, are directly antithetical, we take a step back to [an earlier] crisis over slavery in the territories. That crisis was precipitated in 1846 when the Wilmot Proviso was introduced onto the floor of the House of Representatives. The Proviso declared that in any territory to be acquired from Mexico (whether by conquest or by purchase), slavery was to be forever prohibited. If the Proviso had become law no States formed from such territory could become slave States. The Proviso repeatedly passed the House [where Congressman Lincoln voted for it "about forty times"], but was as often defeated in the Senate. Calhoun saw then what Jefferson Davis and many others would also come to see—through Calhoun's eyes—namely, that without any more slave States, a succession of free States would eventually eliminate the Senate veto of antislavery legislation. And at some point the free States might possess the three-fourths majority to amend the Constitution to abolish slavery altogether without the consent of any slave State. Unless the slave States retained their veto of antislavery legislation in the Senate, the "numerical" majority would be able to ride roughshod over the "minority" interests of the slave States. Then the Constitution would no longer be able to protect those interests from the tyranny of the majority. For Calhoun, the essence of the Constitution consisted in the slave States' power to veto legislation hostile to their interests. The ending of that veto power would, in his understanding of constitutionalism, mean the end of constitutional government.

The doctrinal underpinnings of the Calhoun position are suggested by this passage from the Jaffa book:

> We saw in the [famous 1861] Cornerstone Speech that for Alexander Stephens it was a sufficient justification of slavery to say that it rested upon a scientific foundation, even though Stephens never even attempted to say in what that foundation consisted. It was therefore a sufficient refutation of the Founders' belief in the equality of the races to say that it had become anachronistic. Hence Calhoun did not really need to disprove the proposition "that all men are created equal." All he needed to say—as many since him have discovered—was that his political science was more scientific than what preceded it. The widespread and uncontradicted opinion that the non-human natural sciences are progressive had created a presumption in favor of the view that anything called science was progressive. This in turn had created a presumption in favor of any claim that represented itself as proceeding from progressive scientific thought. [In March 1861 Stephens told the South and the world that slavery was the "cornerstone of the Confederacy."]

Mr. Jaffa goes deeper still by suggesting how much of a modern Calhoun was in the way he dealt with the challenge of the Declaration of Independence:

> Although he treated the statement of principles in the Declaration of Independence as if it was superfluous, Calhoun knew that, in the eyes of the Continental Congress, it was nothing of the kind. in [his 1845] Oregon speech, he discharged his animus initially on the proposition in the Massachusetts Bill of Rights of 1780 "that all men are born free and equal." It was this, rather than the parallel assertion in the Declaration of Independence, that he called the "most false and dangerous of all political errors." Since the doctrine of equality was a commonplace of the state constitutions, his disparagement could not cast doubt upon Jefferson's assertion . . . that the Declaration was intended to be, and was taken to be, an expression of the American mind. Although Calhoun pretended that the doctrine of equality was an idiosyncrasy of Thomas Jefferson, he knew perfectly well that the Congress would never have accepted it into the text of the Declaration had it been that. He knew it was intended to provide the standard of judgment for the bill of particulars in the indictment of King and parliament. He knew that each item in the bill was meant to be seen as a particular violation of the rational principles of natural justice, whose premise was human equality. These principles—or some of them—may have been enshrined in provisions of the British constitution, but to the Continental Congress, it was not the British constitution that gave authority to the principles, but the

principles that gave authority to the constitution. But Calhoun, as an epigone of the historical school, thought he understood the Founders better than they understood themselves.

In this, as in so many other respects, he resembled Karl Marx, who thought that statements of principle, as in the Declaration of Independence, were "ideology," the rationalization of class interests. For Calhoun the scientific explanation of political behavior in [his posthumously published Disquisition on Government] had superseded the Lockean self-understanding of the Founders. Consequently, no matter how much credence the Founding Fathers placed in state-of-nature theory, Calhoun himself will not allow it any role in his understanding of the Founding. In this too he was like Marx, who brushed aside "ideals" professed in societies based upon the private ownership of the means of production. According to Marx, the meaning of these "ideals" was not to be found in the soundness or unsoundness of what was professed, but in the economic interests—whether consciously or unconsciously pursued—of the classes that benefited from them.

Does Mr. Jaffa, with his powerful theoretical capacity, attempt to understand Calhoun better than he understood himself—or, more to the point, better than someone such as Lincoln might have understood him? Lincoln, in any event, did recognize the substantial influence that the Southerners' tremendous investment in slaves (more than a billion dollars in the 1850s) had upon both their constitutional principles and their moral judgment. Or, as Lincoln observed in 1857, "the plainest print [whether in the Bible or in the Declaration of Independence?] cannot be read through a gold eagle. . . ." The prudence that John C. Calhoun, and Stephen A. Douglas after him, should have been guided by is offered in Christian terms and hence is a challenge to modern times and to modern realists in the opening paragraph (which has a Platonic cast to it) of Josef Pieper's book, *Prudence: The First Cardinal Virtue:*

> No dictum in traditional Christian doctrine strikes such a note of strangeness to the ears of contemporaries, even contemporary Christians, as this one: that the virtue of prudence is the mold and "mother" of all the other cardinal virtues, of justice, fortitude, and temperance. In other words, none but the prudent man can be just, brave, and temperate, and the good man is good in so far as he is prudent.

Should not Abraham Lincoln have been receptive to this approach to prudence, respectful as it is of an informed moral sense?

8

Southern Illinois's Abraham Lincoln

> But his muscular strength was great, and startling statistical tales
> are told of the weight he could lift and the force of his blows
> with a mallet or an axe. To a gentle and thoughtful boy with
> secret ambition in him such strength is a great gift, and in such
> surroundings most obviously so.
>
> —Lord Charnwood

I

I open this discussion in Southern Illinois with a confession, however presumptuous it may sound: I have long believed that we here in Illinois may be "naturally" better equipped than most people in this Country to understand the career, if not the thought, of Abraham Lincoln. And, it seems to me, there are facets of Lincoln's character and conduct to which the *Southern* Illinoisan may be particularly sensitive.

When one comes to Illinois in one's youth, as Lincoln did, one is not dependent upon the accident of one's place of birth for the attachment one develops to this State. Lincoln came to appreciate the State with which he matured after coming here from Indiana when he was twenty-one. (Lincoln was born in Kentucky in 1809; Illinois became a State nine years later.) I recall being able to notice things about Southern Illinois that its natives were not always able to notice—and this because I happened to have been born in St. Louis, not coming down here to live until I was in the fifth grade. (I lived here until I, as a seventeen-year-old, enlisted in the Army Air Corps. during the Second World War.) I even presume to believe that the Greek Orthodox community by which I was first shaped (in St.

This talk was given at Southern Illinois University, Carbondale, May 3, 1991.
The epigraph is taken from Lord Charnwood, *Abraham Lincoln* (New York.: Henry Holt, 1917), 8. See also the epigraph for Chapter 15 of this Collection.

Louis) helped equip me to look past the provincial side of Abraham Lincoln and to be particularly receptive to the nobility of his great ambition.[222]

II

I propose to talk about Southern Illinois's Abraham Lincoln by looking primarily at his years as a member of the General Assembly while that body was sitting at Vandalia (which is down here in Southern Illinois), before the State capital was moved north to Springfield in 1839. Lincoln is remembered for having helped engineer the move to Springfield, to which he himself moved in 1837 from the village of New Salem.

There may be something artificial about devoting myself here primarily to Lincoln's Vandalia career, but still it can be instructive to do so. For one thing, it permits us to examine Lincoln in the opening years of his political career. Also, it can show us what Southern Illinois is capable of, something which can be inspiring to Southern Illinois youth today who find themselves skeptical about traditional aspirations.

Illinois was the American future in Abraham Lincoln's youth. It was open and malleable; merit could be recognized, even though the spirit of equality was pervasive. The Northwest Territory, out of which Illinois had been formed, was (because of the Ordinance of 1787) antislavery from its inception, something that proved critical during the Civil War. This State supplied the Union with both its greatest political leader in Abraham Lincoln and its greatest military leader in Ulysses S. Grant.

We can begin our discussion of Lincoln's career at Vandalia by noticing the election manifesto he issued for his first campaign, which was in 1832. Lincoln failed to win election to the State legislature at that time, even though he was well enough regarded by those who knew him personally to secure 277 of 300 votes cast in his own precinct in New Salem. He was elected to the legislature two years later, in 1834, and reelected in 1836, 1838, and 1840. He was elected in 1846 to his one term in the U.S. House of Representatives, where it is said that he had a difficult time because of his principled opposition to the popular Mexican War.

The seriousness of the young Lincoln is evident in the opening paragraph of his first election manifesto addressed (at age twenty-three) to the People of Sangamon County:

> Fellow-Citizens: Having become a candidate for the honorable office of one of your representatives in the next General Assembly of this state, in accordance with an established custom, and the principles of true

republicanism, it becomes my duty to make known to you—the people whom I propose to represent—my sentiments with regard to local affairs.[223]

The "local affairs" he discusses include transportation, finance, usury, and education. Thus, he describes in detail what he has learned from working on the local waterways. Thus, also, he can say of education:

> For my part, I desire to see the time when education, and by its means, morality, sobriety, enterprise and industry, shall become much more general than at present.[224]

We can see here, as elsewhere in this manifesto, the moral focus that Lincoln routinely brought to public matters throughout his life, but without becoming either stodgy or self-righteous. Lincoln wanted to be, in everything he did, both right and successful.[225] It is important to see what ambition meant to him, something that is evident in this early manifesto, which includes these sentiments:

> Every man is said to have his peculiar ambitions. Whether it be true or not, I can say for one that I have no other so great as that of being truly esteemed of my fellow man, by rendering myself worthy of their esteem.[226]

We may well wonder, of course, whether too much is made here of public opinion—whether one is ever as self-sufficient as a mature human being can be if the esteem of the community is decisive for one's actions. Perhaps this is inevitable if someone of remarkable gifts dedicates himself to politics rather than to philosophy, however philosophical his political thinking may be.[227]

Dedication to politics seemed almost inevitable for the talented in so mobile and so striving a democracy as Illinois was in the 1830s. We can see from Lincoln's career how much his success depended upon an education that permitted him to see things as they were and to face issues squarely. The fact that Lincoln had altogether no more than one year of formal education should remind us that the key to a successful education need not be the material resources that happen to be available in a community. The level of political discourse in Illinois is testified to by the caliber of the Lincoln-Douglas debates of 1858, which were followed carefully by tens of thousands of citizens at a time. We may well wonder what reform in public habits and expectations would be needed for us to return to the caliber of education to which the people of Illinois were accustomed in the middle of the nineteenth century among those who were indeed educated.

III

We have been investigating the shaping of the political Lincoln. Supplementing, if not reinforcing, his underlying seriousness was his comic genius. He could always be counted on for a humorous touch, even sometimes when it was not called for. This was a youthful inclination, not unknown In Southern Illinois ever since, which he had to learn to curb.

Illustrative of Lincoln's touch is a suggestion he made when it was discovered by the General Assembly that its approval of an appointment to a county post had been premature. A member of the General Assembly introduced a resolution:

> That the nomination of Samuel McHatton, for County Surveyor of Schuyler county . . . be vacated for the reason that said office was not vacant at the time said nomination was made.[228]

This resolution drew this response from Lincoln:

> That if, as appeared to be the opinion of legal gentlemen, there was no danger of the new surveyor's ousting the old one so long as he persisted not to die—he would suggest the propriety of letting matters remain as they were, so that if the old surveyor should hereafter conclude to die, there would be a new one ready made without troubling the legislature.[229]

The resolution was tabled, in effect following Lincoln's suggestion.

Sometimes Lincoln's wit could be devastating. Thus, he could say of another member of the General Assembly who had presented himself as superior to Lincoln:

> In the course of what I shall have to say, whenever I shall have occasion to allude to that gentleman, I shall endeavor to adopt that kind of court language which I understand to be due to *decided superiority*. In one faculty, at least, there can be no dispute of the gentleman's superiority over me, and most other men; and that is, the faculty of entangling a subject, so that neither himself, or any other man, can find head or tail to it. Here he has introduced a resolution, embracing ninety-nine printed lines across common writing paper, and yet more than one half of his open-

ing speech has been made upon subjects about which there is not one word said in his resolution.[230]

Further on in this same speech, he could lambast politicians in this fashion:

> I make the assertion boldly, and without fear of contradiction, that no man, who does not hold an office, or does not aspire to one, has ever found any fault of the Bank. It has doubled the prices of the products of their farms, and filled their pockets with a sound circulating medium, and they are all well pleased with its operations. No, Sir, it is the politician who is the first to sound the alarm, (which, by the way, is a false one). It is he, [who,] by these unholy means, is endeavoring to blow up a storm that he may ride upon and direct. It is he, and he alone, that here proposes to spend thousands of the people's public treasure, for no other advantage to them, than to make valueless in their pockets the reward of their industry. Mr. Chairman, this movement is exclusively the work of politicians; a set of men who have interests aside from the interests of the people, and who, to say the most of them, are, taken as a mass, at least one long step removed from honest men. I say this with the greater freedom because, being a politician myself, none can regard it as personal.[231]

In short, politicians (as well as others) learned that Lincoln was not a safe man to cross. He became legendary for his stories, so much so that he was in demand as a storyteller. This talent could be most diverting as judges, lawyers, and their hangers-on rode circuit together (something that, it is said, Lincoln liked to do).

Lincoln became widely known in this State because of his exploits while practicing law on circuit. The population of his Illinois was then of a size that could be known by an enterprising citizen. Someone of talent, in turn, could be generally recognized.[232]

IV

We move now from the shaping and talents of Lincoln to his career as a legislator at Vandalia. The best account of his entire career in the State legislature is found in Paul Simon's book, *Lincoln's Preparation for Greatness: The Illinois Legislative Years.*[233]

Lincoln devoted considerable energy while at Vandalia to getting the capital moved to Springfield. (He was one of the notorious "Long Nine" banded together for this and other projects.) Not that Vandalia was not good for him—Paul Simon has said that Vandalia was a liberal education for

Lincoln—but Springfield seemed much more convenient and in other ways more promising for an ambitious young politician.[234]

Lincoln also busied himself at Vandalia with internal-improvements projects and with the Statewide and National politics of his party. (He was a Whig from 1834 until the formation of the Republican Party in the 1850s.) A speech he gave on the State Bank found him identifying himself with the poor against the manipulations of "capitalists."[235] He made in the same speech an appeal to law-abiding men.[236]

Lincoln's great speech of his Vandalia years, however, was made in Springfield, the famous Lyceum Speech of January 27, 1838, on the perpetuation of our political institutions. That speech makes a powerful argument for law-abidingness as a guard against the usurping tendencies to which the naturally talented are inclined. Edmund Wilson has seen this speech as prefiguring the temptations (or, better still, the challenge?) President Lincoln would himself face.[237] In Vandalia itself, Lincoln's most instructive statement may have been a protest he filed in the General Assembly with Daniel Stone, another member from Sangamon County.[238] We may never know how much of the language of this Protest that Lincoln was personally responsible for, but it was enough his to make him willing to be identified as a member of a minority of two on so sensitive an issue.

The General Assembly had received memorials from five States "relative to the existence of domestic slavery." A historian provides us this report:

> A joint select committee of both houses reported to the [Illinois] House [of Representatives] on January 12, 1837, deeply deploring "the unfortunate condition of our fellow men, whose lots are cast in thraldom in a land of liberty and peace," but holding that "the arm of the General Government has no power to strike their fetters from them," and spurning indignantly "an interference with the rights of property in other States." Following a diatribe against abolition societies, the committee recommended the adoption of the following resolutions:
>
> "Resolved by the General Assembly of the State of Illinois, That we highly disapprove of the formation of abolition societies, and of the doctrines promulgated by them.
>
> "Resolved, That the right of property in slaves, is sacred to the slave-holding States by the Federal Constitution, and that they cannot be deprived of that right without their consent.
>
> "Resolved, That the General Government cannot abolish slavery in the District of Columbia, against the consent of the citizens of said District without a manifest breach of good faith."[239]

The Stone-Lincoln response to the Committee Resolutions was "ordered to be spread on the journals":

Resolutions upon the subject of domestic slavery having passed both branches of the General Assembly at its present session, the undersigned hereby protest against the passage of the same.

They believe that the institution of slavery is founded on both injustice and bad policy; but that the promulgation of abolition doctrines tends rather to increase than to abate its evils.

They believe that the Congress of the United States has no power, under the constitution, to interfere with the institution of slavery in the different States.

They believe that the Congress of the United States has the power, under the constitution, to abolish slavery in the District of Columbia; but that that power ought not to be exercised unless at the request of the people of said District.

The difference between these opinions and those contained in the said resolutions, is their reason for entering this protest.[240]

There was indeed a "difference between these opinions and those contained in the . . . resolution." Thus, although the disturbing effect of "the promulgation of abolition doctrines" is recognized in the Stone-Lincoln Protest, there is not any diatribe against abolition societies. Further, the Protest expresses no reservations about the evils of slavery, nor is there any suggestion that the federal Constitution regards property in slaves as "sacred." Lincoln's connections with Southern Illinois—which could be then, as it still is today, somewhat Southern in its temperament and sympathies—permitted him to appreciate the dilemmas faced by decent slaveholders, even as he could insist that slavery was "founded on both injustice and bad policy."

The position to which the young Lincoln subscribes here, cautioning against abolition doctrines and recognizing the constitutional bargain that had been made with respect to both slavery and the Union, was to be the position he would stand for in his maturity as well—but with two important modifications.

He was later not as sure as he seemed to be in the 1837 Protest that Congress had no power "to interfere with the institution of slavery in the different States." During the debates with Stephen Douglas in 1858, for example, Lincoln claimed he had not determined whether Congress had power to regulate the interstate slave trade.[241]

Also, later on, Lincoln was to insist that Congress could and should restrict the spread of slavery to the Territories. Senator Douglas's 1854 Kansas–Nebraska bill acquiesced so much in the spread of slavery that it moved Lincoln, who was by then devoting himself primarily to a successful law practice, to reenter politics. He had been content to believe theretofore that the generally accepted national policies would suffice to contain slavery and eventually lead to its peaceful elimination even in the original slave-holding States.

Thus, critical to Lincoln's approach to slavery, anticipated in this 1837 Protest, is the opinion that the spread both of abolition doctrines and of slavery should be firmly discouraged if the Union was to continue, thereby permitting the United States to be someday the true land of liberty envisaged by its founders. Lincoln shows us, here and elsewhere, what the principled man of law is both limited by and capable of.

It was when Lincoln began to grapple seriously with the slavery issue that his deepest powers were enlisted. He could speak competently, and not uninterestingly, about other issues, such as State financial matters. But it is important to Lincoln's greatest success that he could and did devote his talents primarily to a vital issue.

We notice, in appreciating Lincoln's abilities and instincts as a politician, that this 1837 Protest, challenging the spirit of the General Assembly's antiabolitionist resolution, was not presented until "after other weighty legislation (notably the bill to remove the state capital from Vandalia to Springfield) had been safely passed."[242]

V

Also in need of being "safely passed," before Lincoln could really be and do what he was capable of, was what may be called his personal "legislation." For one thing, he had to settle, one way or another, the problem of marriage. His personal circumstances were such that his future did not look promising. We have a letter written by Lincoln from Vandalia to Mary Owens, who was evidently used to more physical comforts than she could reasonably expect upon marriage to Lincoln.[243] Lincoln sympathizes with her uncertainty as he spells out how unreliable he is, especially with his susceptibility to melancholy (which he refers to as hypo). Other letters to her, from Springfield, reinforce these concerns.[244]

But these financial and related concerns were probably not at the heart of the matter here. He had those difficulties because of what he did and did not care for. More critical was Lincoln's lack of ease in dealing with women, which was masked by his self-deprecating tone. It could also lead to the uncharitable letter about Mary Owens that he wrote to the wife of a friend of his.[245] Still, Lincoln could be kind to women. Not only did he dread doing any woman an injustice, but also he was an early advocate of permitting women to vote.[246]

Lincoln's remarkable apprehensiveness about marriage, probably not for the reasons he made explicit, was reflected in his erratic courtship of Mary Todd. She at least had the perspicacity to see that this awkward country lawyer held much more promise than the more polished men she was used to in Lexington, Kentucky.

Lincoln's torments about the prospects of marriage could perhaps be traced to a flaw in his psychic makeup. He may have been very much an American male of his day in this respect. (The way he discusses the perils of marriage in his letters seems to strike a responsive chord in his male correspondents.) Lincoln probably needed a wise man to counsel him as Socrates is said to have done when he was asked by a young man whether he should marry. The Socratic response to the young man was to this effect, "Whichever way you decide, you will be sorry."

Still, we venture to conclude, Lincoln probably did need a decent marriage to become fully what he could be. His love of circuit-riding may have permitted him to take marriage, at least with the somewhat difficult Mary Todd, in as strong a dose as he was capable of enduring.

VI

The personal problems I have referred to were grounded in Lincoln's passions, temperament, and peculiarities. The effort he had had to make in coming to terms with his own morbid inclinations (as may be seen in his Matthew Gentry poem)[247] probably helped equip him to appreciate what troubled other people and to sense how they could be appealed to. It usually helps, in dealing with others, to have come to know oneself. Lincoln learned, while still fairly young, that people tend to act correctly, and that a distorting element should be looked for when they do not.[248]

Thus, Lincoln may be seen dealing patiently with bad-tempered men, signing a pacifying letter to one of them (William Butler), "Your friend in spite of your ill-nature."[249] Earlier he had said that surely this friend did not believe a charge he had made against Lincoln.[250] Later he was to counsel this difficult man, "It is always magnanimous to recant whatever we may have said in passion; and when you and Baker shall have done this, I am sure there will no difficulty be left between you."[251] This follows immediately upon a description, in this letter to "Friend Butler," of the unsettling effects of having passion piled upon passion:

> Your letter enclosing one to Mr. Baker, was received on yesterday evening. There is no necessity for any bad feeling between Baker &

yourself. Your first letter to him was written while you were in a state of high excitement, and therefore ought not to have been construed as an emanation of deliberate malice. Unfortunately however it reached Baker while he was writing under a severe tooth-ache, and therefore he at that time was incapable of exercising that patience and reflection which the case required. The note he sent you was written while in that state of feeling, and for that reason I think you ought not to pay any serious regard to it.[252]

Further on in this letter he observes:

I write this without Bakers knowledge; and I do it because nothing would be more painful to me than to see a difficulty between two of my most particular friends.[253]

This is the sort of moderating counsel Lincoln could provide on the eve of his thirtieth birthday.[254]

Thus, again and again, Lincoln is both firm about what is right and wrong and tolerant of the failings of others. This may reflect the influence of biblical doctrine upon him, an influence that reaches its apotheosis in his Second Inaugural Address.[255] We can see that there is not for him any deep division between morality and politics, however practical he could be in his political career.[256]

One consequence of Lincoln's psychic development, which was already evident at Vandalia, was that he could hate slavery deeply without hating the slaveholder. He might even have said about the fevered Southern response to Northern abolitionist challenges, "Unfortunately they reached the South 'while [it] was writhing under a severe [soul-]ache.'" May not his magnanimity here be in part attributed to the influence upon him of Southern Illinois?

VII

I have sketched out the talents, character, and circumstances of one legislator at Vandalia who came to be the great man that he at least was capable of becoming. Did Lincoln have, in his youth, an awareness of his potentialities and, in his maturity, a recognition of his accomplishments? If he did not, must he not be considered inferior to the man who does know, in turn, both his potentialities and his accomplishments?

A justified self-confidence is vital in these matters. If one does know oneself, the esteem of one's fellows becomes unnecessary, except perhaps as an aid in executing one's political plans. Critical to genuine self-knowledge is that willingness (as Lincoln said at Vandalia) "to call things by their right names, no matter who [is] offended."[257]

And, Lincoln argues again and again, we must take experience seriously if we are to call things by their right names. The more practical side of Lincoln's reliance on experience may be seen in what he had to say, in the first session of the General Assembly at Springfield, about how to deal with an embezzler:

> By the Sub-Treasury System, the money is to lie month after month in the hands of individuals; larger amounts are to accumulate in the hands of the Receivers General, and some others, by perhaps ten to one, than ever accumulated in the hands of individuals before; yet during all this time, in relation to this great stake, the Secretary of the Treasury can comparatively know nothing. Reports, to be sure, he will have, but reports are often false, and always false when made by a knave to cloak his knavery. Long experience has shown, that nothing short of an actual demand of the money will expose an adroit peculator. Ask him for reports and he will give them to your heart's content; send agents to examine and count the money in his hands, and he will borrow of a friend, merely to be counted and then returned, a sufficient sum to make the sum square. Try what you will, it will all fail till you demand the money—then, and not till then, the truth will come.[258]

The more philosophical side of Lincoln's use of experience may be seen in another passage found earlier in this same speech:

> The experience of the past, I think, proves the truth of this. And here, inasmuch as I rely chiefly upon experience to establish it, let me ask, how is it that we know any thing—that any event will occur, that any combination of circumstances will produce a certain result—except by the analogies of past experience? What has once happened, will invariably happen again, when the same circumstances which combined to produce it, shall again combine in the same way. We all feel that we know that a blast of wind would extinguish the flame of the candle that stands by me. How do we know it? We have never seen this flame thus extinguished. We know it, because we have seen through all our lives, that a blast of wind extinguishes the flame of a candle whenever it is thrown fully upon it. Again, we all feel to know that we have to die. How? We have never died yet. We know it, because we know, or at least think we know, that of all the beings, just like ourselves, who have been coming into the world for six thousand years, not one is now living who was here two hundred years ago.[259]

This is, to be sure, not the kind of speculation one expects to hear in a legislature. (We notice in passing the adoption here, by Lincoln, of the then standard account of the date of the Creation believed to have been recorded in Genesis.)

If one follows Lincoln's lead by considering deeply the matters that happen to come one's way, one is apt not only to be more effective and hence useful but also to enjoy a more interesting life. The constraints of the mortality to which Lincoln alluded are thereby minimized, including that aspect of mortality evident in the role that chance plays in our lives. After all, Lincoln's career teaches—and perhaps teaches us here in Southern Illinois more than it does most people—that the self-respecting human being must take advantage of the opportunities that happen to come his way. Particularly to be guarded against as both demeaning and debilitating is the temptation either to blame others for one's troubles or to look to others for one's salvation. One helps oneself most effectively, perhaps, when one remains open to the truth, as may be seen in the assurance of Abraham Lincoln as his first election manifesto draws to an end:

> But, Fellow-Citizens, I shall conclude. Considering the great degree of modesty which should always attend youth, it is probable I have already been more presuming than becomes me. However, upon the subjects of which I have treated, I have spoken as I thought. I may be wrong in regard to any or all of them; but holding it a sound maxim, that it is better to be only sometimes right, than at all times wrong, so soon as I discover my opinions to be erroneous, I shall be ready to renounce them.[260]

9

The Poetry of Abraham Lincoln

> Here on our shores a woman died, Caieta,
> Nurse of Aeneas, and her name still guards
> Her resting-place with honor, if such glory
> Is comforting to dust.
>
> —Virgil

I

The severest trials to which human beings and human communities are subjected challenge them with respect to the very principles of their being. Lives both public and private can thus be put to the test in the most searching manner.

Such testing may be seen in two of Abraham Lincoln's utterances, one of them by the Springfield lawyer in 1846 (when he was in his middle thirties), the other by the President at Gettysburg in 1863. Lincoln's considerable influence upon us is in part due to the style he used to express himself, especially when that form aptly mirrored and hence reinforced his thought. The form in which Lincoln cast his thought was sometimes of so lyrical a quality that it can be regarded as poetic, so much so that the Gettysburg Address has been easy to commit to memory by generations of schoolchildren.

Lincoln's own taste in poetry developed significantly as he matured. He eventually became quite taken with poets as diverse as Shakespeare, Byron, and Burns. There are several reports by observers of him as President who testify to his great interest in, and remarkable grasp of, several of Shakespeare's tragedies.

This talk was given to the Friends of Literature, Chicago, February 9, 1991. The epigraph is taken from Virgil, *Aeneid,* VII, 1–4.

So sensitive was Lincoln to what the finest poets did that he became one of the greatest stylists in the English language. His style was shaped by and helped discipline a character naturally receptive to the principles that were central to his statesmanship, especially to his prudence.

II

However refined Lincoln's taste in poetry became, he retained to the end of his life considerable respect for an undistinguished poem that he had encountered as a young adult, "Oh, Why Should the Spirit of Mortal Be Proud?" This poem, which evidently touched the core of Lincoln's being, was written by a Scotsman, William Knox, who died in 1825 at the age of thirty-six.

Lincoln sent this poem to a Quincy, Illinois, lawyer and fellow Whig politician, Andrew Johnston, who then asked Lincoln about its author. Lincoln wrote to Johnston, in a letter of April 18, 1846:

> I have not your letter before me; but, from memory, I think you ask me who is the author of the piece I sent you, and that you do so ask as to indicate a slight suspicion that I myself am the author. Beyond all question, I am not the author. I would give all I am worth, and go in debt, to be able to write so fine a piece as I think that is. Neither do I know who is the author. I met it in a straggling form in a newspaper last summer, and I remember to have seen it once before, about fifteen years ago, and this is all I know about it.[261]

During his Presidency, Lincoln said to a visitor at the White House,

> There is a poem which has been a great favorite with me for years, which was first shown me when a young man by a friend, and which I afterwards saw and cut from a newspaper and learned by heart. I would give a good deal to know who wrote it, but I have never been able to ascertain.[262]

Then, we are told, "half closing his eyes, he repeated the verses."

The verses of Knox's poem, fourteen stanzas of four lines each, open and close with these words:

> Oh! why should the spirit of mortal be proud?
> Like a swift-flitting meteor, a fast-flying cloud,
> The flash of the lightning, a break of the wave,
> He passes from life to his rest in the grave.

. . . .

'Tis the wink of an eye, 'tis the draught of a breath,
From the blossom of health to the paleness of death,
From the gilded salon to the bier and the shroud,—
Oh, why should the spirit of mortal be proud?[263]

At the center of the poem, which is in much the same spirit throughout, are these lines:

So the multitude goes like the flower or the weed
That withers away to let others succeed,
So the multitude comes, even those we behold,
To repeat every tale that has often been told.[264]

The human condition dwelt upon in this poem evidently struck Lincoln as so finely presented that these lines became "a great favorite with [him] for years." Perhaps, indeed, having "so fine a piece" to express his sentiments, and to assure him that others shared them, may have helped make the dreary human condition bearable for a man of Lincoln's melancholy inclinations.

III

A key concern in the trials to which human beings are subject is how one comes to terms with one's limitations, with death usually regarded as the extreme case that colors all the others. This subject may be seen again and again in the Lincoln corpus, just as it is in the Knox poem, whose opening and closing stanzas emphasize how quickly the human being passes "from life to his rest in the grave."

The concern evident here could become particularly acute among the materialists and hedonists (or Hobbesians) that much in nineteenth-century Anglo-American life seems to have encouraged. This concern was probably heightened among those for whom Christian expectations with respect to an immortal life had begun to fade. Now we even have United States Supreme Court opinions in which self-preservation is given the highest rank.[265]

Americans in the first half of the nineteenth century were familiar enough with death. And in the West, which Illinois was then considered to be, death was quite frequent, accentuated by a high infant-mortality rate.

Lincoln himself had lost his mother when he was ten. One of his children died while he was still in Springfield; another died, at age twelve, in Washington. And, of course, the natural mortality rate of the day was capped, at midcentury, by a bloody war that ravaged the Country's finest men North and South for four years.

The first poem of his own composition that Lincoln sent to Johnston (in 1846) makes much of death, drawing upon a visit he had made two years before to the Indiana neighborhood (Gentryville) "in which [he] was raised, where [his] mother and only sister were buried, and from which [he] had been absent about fifteen years."[266] The ten-stanza poem opens,

> My childhood's home I see again,
> And sadden with the view;
> And still, as memory crowds my brain,
> There's pleasure in it too.

But Old Mortality asserts itself in the concluding stanzas:

> The friends I left that parting day,
> How changed, as time has sped!
> Young childhood grown, strong manhood gray;
> And half of all are dead.
>
> I hear the loved survivors tell
> How nought from death could save,
> Till every sound appears a knell,
> And every spot a grave.
>
> I range the fields with pensive tread,
> And pace the hollow rooms,
> And feel (companion of the dead)
> I'm living in the tombs.[267]

To feel that one is "living in the tombs" reflects, I suspect, the pervasive view of things to which Lincoln's temperament inclined him.[268]

Death, both in its private and in its public dimensions, is featured in the two poetical statements by Lincoln with which we are particularly concerned here. It is evident in both statements that there are things worse than death or pain. The first of Lincoln's poetical statements can even long for that "rest in the grave" which had seemed so oppressive in the Knox poem.

IV

I have suggested that the Knox poem provided, or at least reinforced, for Lincoln a way of dealing with the despair elicited by the circumstances of his life (a harsh and, at times, unpromising life), if not of life itself. A less disciplined—an angrier if not ferocious—response to one's circumstances is chronicled in the Lincoln poem to which we now turn. Here it is, along with the 1846 letter to Johnston describing it:

> Friend Johns[t]on: Springfield, Sept. 6th. 1846
>   You remember when I wrote you from Tremont last spring, sending you a little canto of what I called poetry, I promised to bore you with another some time. I now fulfil the promise. The subject of the present one is an insane man. His name is Matthew Gentry. He is three years older than I, and when we were boys we went to school together. He was rather a bright lad, and the son of the rich man of our very poor neighbourhood. At the age of nineteen he unaccountably became furiously mad, from which condition he gradually settled down into harmless insanity. When, as I told you in my other letter I visited my old home in the fall of 1844, I found him still lingering in this wretched condition. In my poetizing mood I could not forget the impressions his case made upon me. Here is the result—

> But here's an object more of dread
>   Than ought the grave contains—
> A human form with reason fled,
>   While wretched life remains.
>
> Poor Matthew! Once of genius bright,
>   A fortune-favored child—
> Now locked for aye, in mental night,
>   A haggard mad-man wild.
>
> Poor Matthew! I have ne'er forgot,
>   When first, with maddened will,
> Yourself you maimed, your father fought,
>   And mother strove to kill;
>
> When terror spread, and neighbours ran,
>   Your dange'rous strength to bind;
> And soon, a howling crazy man
>   Your limbs were fast confined.
>
> How then you strove and shrieked aloud,
>   Your bones and sinews bared;

And fiendish on the gazing crowd,
  With burning eye-balls glared—

And begged, and swore, and wept and prayed
  With maniac laughter joined—
How fearful were those signs displayed
  By pangs that killed thy mind!

And when at length, tho' drear and long,
  Time soothed thy fiercer woes,
How plaintively thy mournful song
  Upon the still night rose.

I've heard it oft, as if I dreamed,
  Far distant, sweet, and lone—
The funeral dirge, it ever seemed
  Of reason dead and gone.

To drink it's strains, I've stole away,
  All stealthily and still,
Ere yet the rising God of day
  Had streaked the Eastern hill.

Air held his breath; trees, with the spell,
  Seemed sorrowing angels round,
Whose swelling tears in dew-drops fell
  Upon the listening ground.

But this is past; and nought remains,
  That raised thee o'er the brute.
Thy piercing shrieks, and soothing strains,
  Are like, forever mute.

Now fare thee well—more thou the cause,
  Than subject now of woe.
All mental pangs, by time's kind laws,
  Hast lost the power to know.

O death! Thou awe-inspiring prince,
  That keepst the world in fear;
Why dost thou tear more blest ones hence,
  And leave him ling'ring here?

If I should ever send another, the subject will be a "Bear hunt."
Yours as ever   A. Lincoln[269]

The "Bear hunt" referred to in this letter is the third, and last, of the Lincoln poems of this period that we have. It is an exuberant account of a bear hunt in which much is made of how topsy-turvy the world of the bear hunt is (not without its applications to everyday life). The opening stanza reads,

> A wild-bear chase, didst never see?
> Then hast thou lived in vain.
> Thy richest bump of glorious glee,
> Lies desert in thy brain.[270]

Recourse to "glorious glee" is still another way of coming to terms with death, it seems.[271]

The first two Lincoln poems we have noticed were published anonymously by Johnston in the Quincy *Whig* for May 5, 1847. Johnston gave them as a main title, "The Return" (that is, to the Indiana village) and as subtitles "Part I—Reflection," "Part II—The Maniac."[272] Johnston evidently did not believe that the account of the bear hunt fit in with this pair, even as comic relief.[273]

However limited the lyrical quality of the lines of "The Maniac" may be, there is a clear description (which is characteristic of Lincoln) of what happened when, as we say, "something snapped" in Matthew Gentry, with the initial psychotic outburst followed by complete withdrawal.[274](This is common enough that there may even be some in this audience who have seen this sort of thing happen, something that today can be treated somewhat by medication and subsequent therapy.) What makes this sort of thing overwhelming is that it can erupt without any early signs that the layman is apt to notice.

That the narrator is still much moved, two decades later, testifies to the poet's own sensibilities and vulnerability. (There is not here the slightest trace of the somewhat callous glee at the struggle with the desperate animal in the bear-hunt poem.) We can see that, for Lincoln, the most profound challenge in the private realm comes in the form of the shattering (and then shuttering) of the rational element in the human being. He may see the conquest of death, or a kind of immortality, in reasoning well and in building on that. It is, then, not the loss of life, but rather the loss of reason that is truly to be mourned. To lose one's reason, as Poor Matthew did, is to die without being able either to rest oneself or to allow others truly to rest, however passive one becomes.

It is evident in the poem that there is something fierce, and perhaps unduly self-centered, in Poor Matthew that got woefully out of control.

Lincoln's Perpetuation Speech (the Lyceum Speech) of a decade before reveals the passion and ambition in the young lawyer. Lincoln's law partner observed that the ambitious Lincoln had in him a little engine that knew no rest.[275] Perhaps Poor Matthew seemed to be somewhat the same way, until *his* engine jumped its track—and for this warning of sorts Lincoln can be said to have retained a lifelong appreciation.[276]

V

Lincoln's greatest poetry, matched only perhaps in his Second Inaugural Address, may be seen in the Gettysburg Address, still another effort to come to term with death and graves.[277] It seems that after 1846, the year in which Lincoln won a seat in the House of Representatives for one term, he wrote no more rhymed poetry. But there is a curious connection, if I may be permitted a flight of poetic fancy myself, between his 1846 poems and the 1863 speech at Gettysburg: the Quincy lawyer, Andrew Johnston, who had gotten Lincoln's poems published in 1847, was the uncle of George E. Pickett of Virginia, who led the bloody and vain charge at Gettysburg. In fact, it is said, a former law partner of Lincoln's, if not Lincoln himself, had helped Pickett get his West Point appointment years before (Class of 1846!), preparing him thereby for his fateful service in the Confederate Army. It was indeed a small world in those days; perhaps it still is.[278]

The more serious connection between the 1846 poem and the 1863 speech may be seen, of course, in the effort to come to terms with what many would be inclined to lament as senseless losses. This is related to what must move everyone in the Gettysburg Address, where something enduring is reached for, if not grasped, beyond the everyday experience of unrelenting struggle and nigh universal destruction.

We can see that, for Lincoln, the most profound challenge in the public realm comes in the form of questioning the great self-evident truth recognized in the Declaration of Independence that "all Men are created equal." The nation, he tells us at Gettysburg, was conceived in liberty—and that initial exercise of liberty continues to find expression here, however much it may need to be transformed by "a new birth of freedom." That transformation depends upon the vindication of that equality principle which circumstances have evidently called into question: the principle had started as a "self-evident" truth, but it is now merely a "proposition," which suggests something in need of being established (or reestablished, perhaps on a firmer foundation than originally). The Gettysburg Address exhibits a distillation by Lincoln from a decade of wrestling with the issues he "settles" authoritatively in his speech. So compact is his thought that the speech can readily be put in poetic form.[279] Lincoln's mode of thought is characterized by, if I may be permitted a prosaic term, its efficiency, albeit a radical efficiency.

The horror of Poor Matthew, for Lincoln, was intensified by his recognition that everything (public as well as private) depends upon proper reasoning. The United States, he believes, represents the rational application of eternal principles to the circumstances of North America. His arguments are syllogistic as he works things out with rigor, a rigor that was influenced perhaps by his intense study of Euclid while he was in Congress (a rare diversion for a Congressman).

The men dealt with in the Gettysburg Address, unlike Poor Matthew, have an appropriate resting place. They can indeed rest: their lives and deaths can be said to make sense. To what extent does that depend upon their anonymity, an anonymity that abstracts from their particularities and hence from their personal failings and limitations? Not only are the dead unnamed, but so are the sides on which they fought. There is an equality in mortality that unites the dead, the living, and their posterity, as well as friends and enemies, in something greater and much more enduring than themselves. In these circumstances it does not even have to be noticed explicitly that slavery is repudiated.

How would such universal liberation bear upon the plight of Poor Matthew, who could still have been alive in 1863?[280]

VI

The remarkably practical cast of Lincoln's mind may be seen in his refusal to speculate about what caused Poor Matthew's breakdown. He said in the Johnston letter that at "the age of nineteen he unaccountably became furiously mad."[281] Lincoln does not speak of anything genetic, environmental (physical or familial), or divine as responsible: he simply does not know. He restricts himself to what he observes, including what he observes of the profound effect upon him of all that had happened both at the time of the first outburst and then years later. More dreadful than anything in the grave is "a human form with reason fled": this living corpse not only does not make sense but also seems to call order and hence sensibleness itself into question.

Today we would observe that the violent young man displays a great rage against "significant persons" around him, an eruption of homicidal passions, perhaps due to a sense of injustice nurtured for years. Both genetic and developmental factors would be looked to as accounting for this dramatic eruption. Thus, it would be said today, these things are never senseless; they have an explanation in terms of the experiences of an individual with particular genetic predispositions; they are not simply wild and meaningless episodes. Or, to sum up all this, we probably have here, in this eruption, a desperate effort to remedy what may have seemed to the young man an intolerable situation.[282]

Particularly revealing, perhaps, is what is reported by the narrator in the third stanza:

> Poor Matthew! I have ne'er forgot,
>   When first, with maddened will,
> Yourself you maimed, your father fought,
>   And mother strove to kill;

We are reminded, by this family-oriented outburst, of how much even intimate, instinct-driven human affairs depend upon the dictates of reason. We are reminded as well of how much of what is public, as well as of how much of our personal psychic development, depends upon the family, an association that can be shaken to its core by such an episode.

In this way, the most private of relations becomes very much a public concern. The narrator senses that this is, for the afflicted man, in his day and age, a permanent condition. He may be troubled by the sense as well that this is a condition into which all can be said to sink—a few abruptly, most of us gradually—however much the grave may conceal this mournful fact from view.

VII

Lincoln himself, we have been told, endured periodic paralyzing bouts of depression. He is spoken of as being subject to melancholia, which is associated with morbid thoughts, and spells of a profound sense of hopelessness. (The same has been said of Winston Churchill.) It would be instructive, as pointing up Lincoln's view of the matter, to have accounts of the Gentry case from others in the village in which the afflicted man lived and suffered.

Particularly impressive for Lincoln may have been the anger displayed in Matthew Gentry's initial outburst. It is appropriate that the term *mad* is several times drawn upon in the letter and poem, for it connotes both anger and insanity. But whatever resentment Lincoln himself had felt because of his circumstances and frustrations, he was able to overcome them, as may be seen, for example, in his Second Inaugural Address. His intelligence, indeed genius, may have been critical here.

Is it not almost certain, by the way, that there had been a history of revealing symptoms before the wild outburst in the Gentry family? Perhaps it fueled the violent resentment in Poor Matthew even more that those symptoms, or signs, had been ignored by the people who were thus being warned. Still, some telling message may have been conveyed to at least a few by this outburst and its consequences. For one thing, it may have helped Lincoln himself to see that nothing was to be gained, and much was to be lost, by permitting oneself to indulge the deep-seated inclinations of a dubious character that one might happen to have.

Certainly, Lincoln is haunted by the fate of the bright lad with whom he had gone to school. Did Lincoln ever recognize whatever parallel there may be between the two "poems" (by Knox and by Lincoln himself) at which I have glanced? At the least, Lincoln felt deeply about the fundamental issues in each case, issues that turned around the abandonment at a critical point of the reliance upon reason in matters both private and public.

VIII

The fury of an afflicted man and thereafter his unnatural passivity are described in the 1846 poem. The initial condition evoked terror. The permanent condition, evoking dread in its turn, seems even worse. Again and again, as we have seen, there is in the narrator an awareness of the critical role of reason in human affairs. The furious blows that had to be physically restrained at least offered the consolation of providing evidence of a mind still at work: he "begged, and swore, and wept and prayed / With maniac laughter joined." However, the pangs thus exhibited "killed [his] mind."

I have noticed, in Lincoln's refusal to speculate as to the causes of this breakdown, an instance in him (exhibited again and again in his political career) of that priceless capacity to know what one does not know. (On the other hand, he does speculate, from time to time, about the causes of slavery.) It is possible, however, that the narrator is mistaken in his observation, in the next-to-last stanza, that "All mental pangs, by time's kind laws, / Hast [thou] lost the power to know." The afflicted man may have continued to be aware of more, much more, than was generally recognized by those around him: in this condition, too, he may have been "saying" something to them. When Lincoln speaks of his "gradually settl[ing] down into harmless insanity," the perspective is that of the relieved bystanders, not that of the tormented man, who may continue to be somewhat aware of his miserable condition. We need not fault Lincoln for insensitivity here but merely notice the perhaps unavoidable limitations of the medicine of his times.[283]

I have also noticed that Lincoln was evidently haunted for decades by the plight of his former schoolmate. He tries to come to terms with his experience and memories through a poem, providing himself thereby salutary guidance in coming to terms as well with whatever passions he himself may have had that found affinities in the tormented soul of Matthew Gentry. And, we see in this poem, the neighbors vigorously combine to put down a young man's irrational assault upon family and community.

Much the same can be said about what the Gettysburg Address did, coming to terms as it did with great losses and confirming a determined communal resistance to the rule of the irrational in public affairs, however noble and awe-inspiring that irrational drive may have been in some respects.

IX

The grave is cheated in both of the poetic statements at which we have glanced on this occasion. In the first, that is to be lamented; in the second, it is to be celebrated. Things are somehow better, we are encouraged to believe, because of the great war: "a new birth of freedom," a freedom purged of deadly compromises, is anticipated. Even so, the United States today would be tamer, and otherwise less interesting and challenging, without the experience both of slavery and of the mighty struggle against it. We can be reminded thereby of intermittent threats to the principles of our regime, just as we are reminded that Poor Matthew's fate threatens us all, although not necessarily in so violent a form.[284]

However ennobling the Civil War may have been, it (like the instructive experience of Matthew Gentry) was not without enduring costs. For one thing, it required in the North an assertion of unprecedented Presidential power, an assertion that has come to haunt us down to this day. Thus, for example, if the originally intended constitutional relations had been respected, there would not have been in November 1990 those unilateral Presidential decisions that severely limited what Congress could do in January 1991 in deciding whether we should go to war in the Persian Gulf. Indeed, it can be said, some of the traditional liberties of the American people were abridged as a result of the "great civil war" that properly destroyed slavery. Among those liberties is the right of a self-governing people to have its representatives deliberate about the risks to which the young men and young women of the Country should be subjected.[285]

Be all this as it may, Lincoln can be said to have attained the peak in American poetic expression, at least in the realm of politics, in his address at Gettysburg, a peak to which he returned in his Second Inaugural Address. Why was he able to excel in his public but not in his private poetry?[286] The natural talent Lincoln had for each mode, public and private, may have been a factor in what he excelled at, as well as his personal interests (including ambition, the very ambition that can unhinge some men who do not know the uses to which it can properly be put).

Also, it was probably true for Lincoln, as it was then for most Americans, that training in conventional public speaking was better than training in that other form of public speaking known as poetry. Many distinguished public men, as well as considerable experience on the stump, could help shape the young man of talent into a fine orator. And, of course, there were great causes, both North and South, that could enlist the soul of the citizen seeking something exalted to which he could dedicate himself, reaffirming thereby the intrinsic dignity of that human existence threatened by the inevitable "funeral dirge."

10

The "House Divided" Speech

We all love great men; love, venerate and bow down submissive before great men: nay can we honestly bow down to anything else? Ah, does not every true man feel that he is himself made higher by doing reverence to what is really above him? No nobler or more blessed feeling dwells in man's heart.

—Thomas Carlyle

I

The opening and closing paragraphs of Harry Jaffa's challenging paper "The Speech That Changed the World" are these:

> Of all Abraham Lincoln's speeches, whether greater or lesser, the only one that can be said truly to have changed the course of history was delivered to the Republican State Convention in Springfield, Illinois, June 16, 1858. . . .
> [The] evisceration of "popular sovereignty" by Lincoln in the course of the joint debates [with Stephen A. Douglas] had its ultimate fruition in the Democratic National Convention that met in Charleston in April of 1860. When the majority in that convention, firmly committed to Douglas, refused to adopt a resolution in favor of a slave code for the territories, the seven states of the Deep South withdrew. These

This talk was given during the Lincoln–Douglas Debates Symposium, Ottawa, Illinois, August 28, 1993. (Original title: "On the Historic Significance of Abraham Lincoln's 'House Divided' Speech: For Harry V. Jaffa, Seventy-five and Still Counting.") The symposium was held in the Courthouse of the Illinois Appellate Court, Ottawa.

The epigraph is taken from Thomas Carlyle, *On Heroes, Hero Worship, and the Heroic in History* (Berkeley and Los Angeles: University of California Press, 1993), 14.

same seven states would secede from the Union before Lincoln's inauguration the following year. But it was secession from the Democratic Convention that was politically decisive. As Don Fehrenbacher has written, everyone knew that a South that would not accept Stephen A. Douglas as leader of the Democratic Party would never accept Abraham Lincoln as President of the United States. Yet the South was foolish in what it did. It actually looked at Douglas through the lenses Lincoln had kindly provided them in the debates, that followed the House Divided speech. Had they been wise they would have abandoned their demand for a slave code for territories like Kansas or Nebraska, where geography and a militant free soil movement made it unlikely that slavery could take root. They would have realized that if slavery was extended to Cuba, or elsewhere south of the border (as in the case of Texas) they would not have needed a federal slave code. They might then have elected a president who might have done everything both necessary and possible to guarantee the survival and success of slavery. Indeed, for all we know, slavery might be flourishing amongst us even now. That it does not, we have the House Divided speech to thank.[287]

The concluding sentences of the Jaffa paper oblige us to consider what we understand to be at the heart of the American regime. The paper itself, emanating from so thoughtful a scholar, is bound to have much in it that is sound and instructive. Even that which may not be sound is, because of the intelligence, learning, and imagination brought to bear upon his subject by its author, also likely to be instructive.

II

For all we know, Mr. Jaffa argues, "slavery might be flourishing amongst us even now" but for the "House Divided" Speech and what it and succeeding Lincoln speeches did to Douglas's political fortunes and hence to the power of the South. But this conjecture, I venture to suggest, tends to underestimate the power of the principles of the American regime. Not only that, but it also tends to underestimate the aversion to slavery in modernity, at least in the Western world, an aversion that drew upon a growing awareness in recent centuries of what is naturally wrong about chattel slavery.

   In addition, the Jaffa approach tends to overestimate the significance of Abraham Lincoln, however important he surely is. This approach does not, in my opinion, sufficiently appreciate how much and in what ways Lincoln was shaped by the United States. It is hard to imagine anyone of Lincoln's natural talents and sensibilities developing in other circumstances (that is, in other countries or in earlier times) his responses to efforts to perpetuate and expand the institutions of slavery. On the other hand, much of what Lincoln said, if not precisely the way he said it, drew upon thought that others shared and had in large part already expressed in this Country. Large numbers of his fellow citizens have been moved by Lincoln, but this is in part because he was able to draw upon the finest elements in the American soul in elevating the level of moral and political discourse in this Country.

It is a perennial question how much is to be made of the role in "history" of the individual, as distinguished from groups of men and women with special talents and experiences in particularly propitious circumstances.[288] (Such a gifted group was obviously in evidence in North America in the 1770s and 1780s.) I believe it underestimates the strength of the American regime to suppose that the antislavery cause might not have eventually prevailed in the United States if Abraham Lincoln had not been available to provide the memorable leadership that he did.[289]

III

The antislavery movement in the United States drew, as did Lincoln himself, upon the "created equal" principle recognized in the Declaration of Independence. The influence of the Declaration was not limited to the United States. On the other hand, the antislavery movement elsewhere, and most conspicuously in the British Empire, preceded the Declaration of Independence and continued much on its own, influenced in large part by Christian sentiments and the not-unrelated modern Enlightenment.

It can even be argued that American Independence delayed the abolition of slavery in all of North America, insulating as it did the former mainland colonies from the actions taken by the British Parliament to eliminate, first, the international slave trade and, then, slavery itself. The *Somerset* case recognized in 1772, with the authority of Lord Mansfield, that there was a strong presumption against slavery in the English-speaking world.[290] This antislavery development seems to have taken root in the British Empire well before the United States became known worldwide as the Country to which the poor and ambitious of Europe could go to make decent lives for themselves, an option that greatly enhanced the dignity of free labor and contributed, at least in the Western world, to an abhorrence of slavery.

The appeal of the antislavery movement in Great Britain is dramatized by the career of William Wilberforce. When Wilberforce died in 1833 he was, by the unanimous wish of Parliament, buried in Westminster Abbey. His coffin was followed through the streets of London by immense crowds.[291] His principal claim to fame was his decades-long campaign against the international slave trade, a cause in which he could bring together in Parliament such political rivals as William Pitt, Charles Fox, and Edmund Burke. Even so, it is obvious from a study of Wilberforce's career that he was (like Lincoln, a generation later?) more the instrument than the shaper of a great development.

The mighty battle in England in the late eighteenth century was over the African slave trade.[292] Once that battle was won, the abolition of all slavery in the remaining British colonies in North America followed in short order. Not that Europeans did not continue to exploit Africans in a variety of ways—an effort in which they could rely upon the help of all too many African tyrants, if not entire African tribes (a thesis John Wesley questioned)—but once Wilberforce and his colleagues had done their work, it was but a matter of time before the atrocities of slavery (and, later, of colonization) would be widely publicized and generally condemned.

IV

The political is very much concerned with one's own—with what may be accidentally one's own. This may be seen in how Harry Jaffa speaks of the United States and of his greatest hero (if not even his Moses) from childhood, Abraham Lincoln.[293] So great an emphasis is placed thereby upon one's own, which it may be salutary to regard as somehow deathless, that it becomes hard to notice how much one's own is dependent upon others.

One does not have to consider the American Civil War an "unnecessary war" in order to suspect that even an independent South, dedicated to slavery and able to expand southward, would eventually have had to come to terms with an aroused world opinion that had long condemned chattel slavery as barbaric. Has not so much been made of Lincoln around the world in part because he stood so well for just and humane principles that had always had an authority independent of anything said or done in the United States? It should be remembered that Canada did not need a Lincoln in order to become a reliable English-speaking refuge from slavery in North America.

Even if one posits, with Mr. Jaffa, successful Southern filibustering into Cuba, the Caribbean, and Latin America, what then? I suspect that an independent South would eventually have been crippled by its "successes," just as the Soviet Union was in Eastern Europe and in Cuba after the Second

World War. Even more important, young Southerners would have found it harder and harder to believe in the principles of their regime, especially when they learned (as their education and sophistication improved) what the most respectable parts of the world had long thought of the unjust institutions that the South continued to rely upon.[294]

An undue emphasis upon one's own may be seen in how the United States conducted the Cold War. It may also be seen in how we interpret what led to the collapse of the Soviet Union. We are now tempted to make far too much of our efforts and far too little of the internal contradictions of that regime. Of course, we played a significant part in checking the Soviet Union, but that was not all to the good, for we did not provide as well as we could have for a long period of transition for both them and us. How would we have conducted ourselves [I could ask in 1993] if we had all recognized a decade ago what was obvious to some long ago, that the Soviet military and economic threat to the West was grossly exaggerated?

I do not mean to suggest that the march to freedom has been inevitable for the human race. The twentieth century—in many ways, the American century—has had one highly repressive regime after another, of both the Right and the Left, to plague mankind with tyranny and slaughter on an unprecedented scale. But it is not only because of the United States that continuing barbarities have been widely recognized for what they arc, whether they be the practices of untouchability in India, or the massacres in Tibet (like those earlier in Cambodia), or the excesses on all sides in Central and South Africa. Does it not question the enduring validity of the natural-right position to suggest that barbarities will not eventually be recognized by civilized men and women for what they are?

V

Important as Lincoln was and still is, someone else—if an individual must be settled upon—might have been even more critical for the coming of the Civil War: John C. Calhoun of South Carolina. Not that the South could not have gone to the extremes it did if Calhoun had never lived; but it might have made a significant difference (with the South being led by men it trusted into a program of gradual compensated emancipation and, if need be, a program of training and resettlement of its slaves) if Calhoun had been salvaged for the National Cause (as perhaps he should have been) in the time of Andrew Jackson's Presidency.[295]

All this is not to deny that Lincoln remains of paramount importance, especially in the United States and for the education of Americans. This is in large part because of what he had to say, dramatizing and ennobling as he did a great and probably necessary struggle requiring huge sacrifices. Lincoln may also have been fortunate and hence permanently influential in his death, like Romulus, Moses, and Jesus before him and like John F. Kennedy and Martin Luther King Jr. after him.

That William Wilberforce, despite his great achievements, is now largely forgotten, even in England, may reflect in part the fact that he made no speeches that were bound to be remembered (however effective he was as an advocate at the time). The comprehensiveness of his success may also have contributed to the eclipse of his fame, especially since he was very much the instrument, rather then the cause, of a movement.

VI

The problems that we in this Country continue to confront, not least with respect to racial discrimination, require repeated recourse to first principles, and this makes Abraham Lincoln of continuing use and appeal. The American regime, illuminated by a traumatic Civil War following upon the glorious Revolutionary War, helped the world to see better the principles implied in the natural-law/natural-right and natural-rights developments that had been making their way in modernity.[296]

The United States, as a community, has always depended much more than, say, England upon explicit first principles. After all, that which makes us one, insofar as anything does, depends upon those principles: our *E pluribus unum* motto recognizes the diverse strands (and not only the States) that must constantly be woven together in this Country, generation after generation. An undue emphasis upon particular personages, as distinguished from the principles of the regime, may make the American Republic precarious in the way that republican Rome was when it depended as much as it did on someone such as Marcus Brutus to reverse the decline into Caesarism.[297]

The American reliance upon first principles is reflected in the importance here of constitutionalism, perhaps more so than anywhere else in the world. Related to this is that aspect of constitutional government exhibited in such extended deliberations as may be seen in the Lincoln–Douglas Debates of 1858. The first of those Debates was, as you all know, in the park across the street from this Courthouse.

Even more important perhaps than the men who took part in that Debate are several facts: the fact that such Debates were resorted to, the fact that vital issues were systematically discussed during those Debates, and the fact that such Debates made a difference both in the 1858 Senatorial contest here in Illinois and in the 1860 Presidential contest nationwide. It is in the spirit of the opening paragraph of the *Federalist,* seven decades earlier, that Senator Douglas could open the Debates here in Ottawa with these words:

> Ladies and gentlemen: I appear before you to-day for the purpose of discussing the leading political topics which now agitate the public mind. By an arrangement between Mr. Lincoln and myself, we are present here to-day for the purpose of having a joint discussion as the representatives of the two great political parties of the State and Union, upon the principles in issue between these parties and this vast concourse of people, shows the deep feeling which pervades the public mind in regard to the questions dividing us.[298]

Still another significant fact—one which is easy to overlook but which decisively exhibits the American dedication to the principle of equality—is that it had already come to be taken for granted by 1858 (even by Stephen Douglas, hardly a champion of equality) that women ("Ladies and gentlemen") have a rightful place in the political discourse shaping "the public mind." This, too, anticipates that "ultimate extinction" of slavery to which Lincoln looked. (Compare, in Plato's *Apology,* Socrates' repeated use of "Men of Athens." Douglas's inadequate response to the "House Divided" Speech is described in Section V of Chapter 11 of this Collection.)

We should take Lincoln at his word when he insists, again and again, that he was applying to the circumstances of his day the principles of the American regime, principles that had been stated so eloquently by Thomas Jefferson, among others. And Jefferson in his day, we remember, had insisted that he had, in his most celebrated statement (the first draft of the Declaration of Independence), "merely" expressed the thought of his fellow citizens.

VII

Lest it seem that there are fundamental differences between Professor Jaffa and me—something that would indeed be a sign of presumptuousness on the part of someone who has learned as much as I have from him—permit me to observe again that our differences (such as they are) can be considered differences merely with respect to emphasis. I would prefer to see more made of the American regime, and less of Abraham Lincoln, than he does. But in order to know our own regime better, we should appreciate fully the kind of men and women it can and does produce as needs arise and as opportunities present themselves.

We are helped toward that appreciation, which serves to help us know ourselves better and hence to do and be better, by what Harry Jaffa has done, for decades now, in putting Abraham Lincoln, a genuine American republican, on display before the spiritually impoverished Country we are in danger of becoming. Consider, for example, what is said in our Jaffa talk about the most memorable of the Lincoln speeches:

> The utterances that have come down to us, graven in bronze and in stone, like the Gettysburg Address and the Second Inaugural, are profound meditations on human experience. In the midst of the horrors of destruction and death, and amid the turmoil of the passions of war, they are designed to reconcile us to our fate by discerning the hand of God in events that might otherwise seem merely chaotic. Although these speeches arise out of particular events at particular times, they draw back the curtain of eternity and allow us, as time-bound mortals, to glimpse a divine purpose within a sorrow-filled present, and tell us how our lives, however brief, can nonetheless serve a deathless end.[299]

Any commentator who plumbs the depths of Abraham Lincoln's words generously shares with others the beauties of his own soul, thereby enriching the souls of his fellow students for decades to come.

11

The Lincoln–Douglas Debates

The first and most necessary topic in philosophy is the practical application of principles, such as, *We ought not to lie*; the second is that of demonstrations, such as, *Why it is that we ought not to lie*; the third, that which gives strength and logical connection to the other two, such as, *Why this is a demonstration*. For what is demonstration? What is a consequence? What a contradiction? What truth? What falsehood? The third point is then necessary on account of the second; and the second on account of the first. But the most necessary, and that whereon we ought to rest, is the first. But we do just the contrary. For we spend all our time on the third point and employ all our diligence about that, and entirely neglect the first. Therefore, at the same time that we lie, we are very ready to show how it is demonstrated that lying is wrong.

—Epictetus

I

The Lincoln–Douglas Debates in 1858 were not so long ago as they may seem—as I was reminded recently [in 1983] upon talking to a lady in one of my adult education classes at the University of Chicago. This lady, who is now in her sixties, recalls hearing, as a girl of twelve, her grandmother's telling how she, as a girl of twelve, had been taken by her grandmother in the family carriage into Ottawa to attend one of the series of Lincoln–Douglas debates. (Immediately at issue between these two debaters was a

---

This talk was given to the University of Chicago Chapter of the Intercollegiate Studies Institute, January 30, 1984. (Original title: "Liberal Education and Legal Education: Some Lessons from the Lincoln–Douglas Debates.") It has been previously published in 20 *Texas Tech Law Review* 732–53 (1989).

The epigraph is taken from Epictetus, *The Enchiridion,* sec. 51 (trans. Thomas W. Higginson).

seat in the Senate of the United States; eventually at issue was the Presidency and the fate of the Nation.) It was, the grandmother reported, a large and festive crowd in their best summer clothing that gathered, with picnic meals, for the three hours of speeches on that occasion. And, the grandmother also reported, "Nobody who was anybody was for Lincoln"—and by "anybody" the grandmother had meant especially those who owned property.

These recollections remind us that our Country is not so old that what the great men of its past said and did need be regarded as too distant to matter. In fact, the grandmother who took the twelve-year-old to the debates had an uncle who had signed the Declaration of Independence.

The best introduction to the Lincoln–Douglas debates, aside from the text of the debates themselves, is Harry V. Jaffa's *Crisis of the House Divided*.[300] Two quotations from his book are particularly useful for us on this occasion. The first is Professor Jaffa's observation, "The moral sense which condemned slavery naturally demanded a law preventing its extension and the demand for the law was simultaneously a demand for the preservation of that moral sense."[301] My second quotation from Mr. Jaffa's book is this: "Keeping slavery out, as Lincoln said repeatedly, was a thousand times easier than getting it out."[302]

Whether slavery *could* be kept out of the Territories (and hence out of future States) of the United States was one of the questions that the now notorious *Dred Scott* case (of 1857) spoke to.[303] It was there held that Congress could not constitutionally forbid the keeping of slaves in the Territories. Opposition to this *Dred Scott* doctrine was a major plank in the platform of the then newly constituted Republican Party.

I hope that what I have to say will provide sufficient details about the history of the period to permit you to follow my account. I also hope that what Lincoln and Douglas said, and the way they said it, will make apparent not only the quality of these Illinois debaters but also the quality of audiences capable of attentively following their speeches for hours at a time.

One cannot help but wonder, upon encountering such political discourse, what if anything can be done amongst us (in an age of supposed great communication) to begin to restore both our public speakers and their audiences to a level both worthy of our constitutional heritage and necessary for our political health.

II

At the heart of the long-standing constitutional and political controversy, of which the Lincoln–Douglas Debates of 1858 were a remarkable part, may have been a moral question that Stephen A. Douglas, both on principle and as a matter of expediency, resolutely refused to address. That question, Abraham Lincoln again and again insisted, was whether the institution of African slavery in the United States was just. All the provocative issues of the day—as to the status of the Fugitive Slave Act, or as to whether people of African descent could ever invoke the rights and privileges of citizens of the United States, or as to whether slavery could lawfully be excluded from the Territories of the Union (as the recently abrogated Missouri Compromise had partially done), or as to the role of the Supreme Court in settling these disputes, or as to what the basis was of the national association of States and hence of the means of their disassociation—all such issues, Lincoln argued, depended for their repeated agitation and for their proper resolution upon a determination of how the institution of slavery was to be regarded. And, Lincoln further argued, that determination in turn depended upon how the Declaration of Independence, and especially its dramatic insistence that all men are created equal, should be understood.

That the Declaration of Independence was authoritative in this Country Douglas and his supporters were not prepared to deny. But they did make less, as well as more, of the "all Men are created equal" language than did Lincoln and his supporters: more, in that Douglas insisted that no one who was entitled to the rights announced by the Declaration of Independence could conceivably be held in slavery; less, in that Douglas insisted that Africans were never intended to be among those entitled to those rights.

This *more* is intrinsically related to this *less*: since, in Douglas's opinion, no one covered by the Declaration of Independence could properly be enslaved, and since various signers of the Declaration obviously had continued to hold slaves, it was therefore evident that people of African descent were not considered to be among the "all Men" spoken of in the Declaration. It was decisive for Douglas that the authors of the Declaration had continued, after 1776, to conduct themselves as they had theretofore as owners of slaves. It was taken for granted by Douglas, as it was by Lincoln and by their vast audiences for these 1858 debates, that the signers of the Declaration were above reproach in their public life—and if so, Douglas argued, for them to have understood the Africans to be entitled to "Life, Liberty and the Pursuit of Happiness," even as they continued to hold them in slavery, would have been rank hypocrisy, unworthy of the great and honorable men that patriotic Americans generally acclaimed the Founding Fathers to have been.[304]

How, then, was the Fathers' conduct to be justified? Only by a sensible reading of the Declaration of Independence, Douglas argued, a reading which recognized that when its authors said "all Men," they meant no

more than men of European descent. Such a reading further recognized
that the government under the Constitution was "founded on the white
basis"—that is, by and for the benefit of white men, with Africans and
Asians possessing thereunder no rights that the white man was obliged to
respect.[305]

 This argument was made again and again by Douglas, and it was on
this basis that the Territories of the United States were to be developed,
leaving it to the people of European descent who settled there to determine whether they would have slavery among themselves and on what
terms.

 It is evident from the Lincoln–Douglas debates that Douglas himself
preferred to live in a State that did not permit slavery. It is also evident that
he wanted to see the Africans in this Country treated fairly. Thus, Douglas
could say during the first of the Debates (with an interpolation, here as
elsewhere, recorded from the audience):

> I do not hold that because the negro is our inferior that therefore he
> ought to be a slave. By no means can such a conclusion be drawn from
> what I have said. On the contrary, I hold that humanity and christiani-
> ty both require that the negro shall have and enjoy every right, every
> privilege, and every immunity consistent with the safety of the society
> in which he lives [That's so.] . . . On that point, I presume, there can be
> no diversity of opinion. You and I are bound to extend to our inferior
> and dependent being every right, every privilege, every facility and
> immunity consistent with the public good.[306]

But how slaves and emancipated slaves should be treated were for him,
on principle, matters of local option alone.[307] It was not for the Government of the United States, nor for the Union as a whole, to take a position
on slavery itself. It was neither right nor sensible for the United States to
do so—not right, in that (among other things) it would repudiate the constitutional bargain struck at Philadelphia in 1787 that left each State free to
go its own way in such matters; nor sensible, in that it would endanger
domestic tranquility and the Constitution of the Union itself to allow slavery to be exploited as a national issue. So concerned was Douglas to be
identified with a policy of calming down the agitation of this issue that he
did not dare state openly, no matter how often he was pressed to do so,
what may well have been his fond expectation: that leaving these matters
to unregulated immigration by Europeans, local initiatives, and economic
forces would eventually doom slavery in most of the Territories of the
United States, if not in the Old South as well.

 Critical to Douglas's position, it seems, was his opinion that a moral condemnation of slavery was highly offensive to conscientious Southerners, provoking them to doubt the good faith and the good will of the free States, which were then in the ascendancy in the Union. This meant disunion, if not war. So, Douglas believed, even the slavery-hating statesman was bound, if only as a matter of expediency, to take no public position on the morality of slavery.

But Douglas's position went even further than this, in that he (as we have seen) presented himself as defending the honor of the Framers of the Declaration of Independence (and especially of Thomas Jefferson) from the insult he saw in any interpretation of the Declaration that left the Framers exposed as "hypocrites." Rather, he insisted, the Framers (like Douglas himself, in emulation of them) made no public moral judgment about slavery. They (also like Douglas himself) left it to each State, if not also to each citizen, to deal with slavery as was thought best in the circumstances.

III

Lincoln, too, was prepared to concede that no interpretation of the Declaration of Independence was sound which required that the Framers be dishonored. He considered himself obliged to show that intelligent Americans who intended "all Men" to include Africans could nevertheless conscientiously continue to permit slavery, even to own slaves themselves and to return fugitive slaves.

Lincoln returned to this problem several times during the seven debates with Douglas and in the many other speeches he gave in the course of the 1858 campaign for the Senate in Illinois. (That campaign was directed at the election of the State legislature, which in turn would elect a Senator.) He refined the formulation of his position during these months, culminating perhaps in the following statement made in the Sixth Debate, which was held at Quincy on October 13:

> We have in this nation this element of domestic slavery. It is a matter of absolute certainty that it is a disturbing element. It is the opinion of all the great men who have expressed an opinion upon it, that it is a dangerous element. We keep up a controversy in regard to it. That controversy necessarily springs from difference of opinion, and if we can learn exactly—can reduce to the lowest elements—what the difference of opinion is, we perhaps shall be better prepared for discussing the different systems of policy that we would propose in regard to that disturbing element. I suggest that the difference of opinion, reduced to its lowest terms, is no other than the difference between the men who think

slavery a wrong and those who do not think it wrong. The Republican
party think it wrong—we think it a moral, a social and a political
wrong. We think it is a wrong not confining itself merely to the persons
or the States where it exists, but that it is a wrong in its tendency, to say
the least, that extends itself to the existence of the whole nation. Because
we think it wrong, we propose a course of policy that shall deal with it
as a wrong. We deal with it as with any other wrong, in so far as we can
prevent its growing any larger, and so deal with it that in the run of time
there may be some promise of an end to it.[308]

Lincoln made it clear that the proper national policy with respect to slavery looked to its eventual elimination as something intrinsically bad. That
must be understood, he seems to say, if the necessary compromises and sacrifices are to be identified and justified. Lest this solid reaffirmation of principle be misunderstood as an immediate declaration of war upon the
South—a declaration that would alarm Union men North and South as
provocative of secessionist sentiment—Lincoln went on to say:

We have a due regard to the actual presence of [slavery] amongst us and
the difficulties of getting rid of it in any satisfactory way, and all the constitutional obligations thrown about it. I suppose that in reference both
to its actual existence in the nation, and to our constitutional obligations, we have no right at all to disturb it in the States where it exists,
and we profess that we have no more inclination to disturb it than we
have the right to do it. We go further than that; we don't propose to disturb it where, in one instance, we think the Constitution would permit
us. We think the Constitution would permit us to disturb it in the District of Columbia. Still, we do not propose to do that, unless it should
be in terms which I don't suppose the nation is very likely soon to agree
to—the terms of making the emancipation gradual and compensating
the unwilling owners. Where we suppose we have the constitutional
right, we restrain ourselves in reference to the actual existence of the
institution and the difficulties thrown about it.[309]

Lincoln, having assured his audiences (which were not, by any means, limited to those there in Quincy that day), including those much concerned
about property rights generally, that he proposed nothing abrupt or
peremptory, he once again affirmed the principle that guided the policy of
his party with respect to the institution of slavery in the United States:

We also oppose [slavery] as an evil so far as it seeks to spread itself. We
insist on the policy that shall restrict it to its present limits. We don't suppose that in doing this we violate anything due to the actual presence

of the institution, or anything due to the constitutional guarantees thrown around it.[310]

Critical to the Lincoln approach was the assumption that an institution as important as slavery in shaping the moral tone and the social prospects, as well as to the worldwide standing, of the United States was something that the people of the entire Country should have a decisive say about—an authoritative say as to the terms of slavery's continued existence and of its eventual disposition.

Perhaps it would be useful, as a summing up of Republican policy before I go on with my own discussion of what Lincoln was advancing with respect to slavery, to recall a succinct statement on the very points discussed at length in the Quincy speech from which I have just quoted—a beautifully succinct statement by Lincoln from the Fifth Debate, which had been held in Galesburg, just one week before Quincy:

> Now, I confess myself as belonging to that class in the country who contemplate slavery as a moral, social and political evil, having due regard for its actual existence amongst us and the difficulties of getting rid of it in any satisfactory way, and to all the constitutional obligations which have been thrown about it; but, nevertheless, desire a policy that looks to the prevention of it as a wrong, and looks hopefully to the time when as a wrong it may come to an end. [Great applause.][311]

I know of no other statement by an American politician that compresses so well, in less than a hundred words, a complex policy requiring both determination and tact in its formulation and execution. There are two aspects of Lincoln's general argument on this subject of immediate interest to us.

First, Lincoln had to indicate that the Framers were in fact opposed to slavery, an institution that presented them with a detestable necessity with which they had to live but whose elimination they looked forward to. He repeatedly quoted their sentiments on slavery, critical (sometimes even anguished) sentiments that were reinforced by various measures designed to limit slavery in this Country—such measures as the pre-Constitution legislation of 1787 (reaffirmed by the First Congress in 1789) prohibiting the introduction of slavery into the Northwest Territory and the provision in the 1787 Constitution recognizing the power in Congress to prohibit altogether the international slave trade from 1808 on (which trade Congress did prohibit as early as it could). Lincoln also made much of the fact that the words "slave" and "slavery" were never used in the Constitution, reflecting (he said) the Framers' expectation that the institution would some day be eliminated, leaving behind no trace of its legitimacy in the Constitution itself.[312]

All this Lincoln took to reflect the fundamentally antislavery policy of the Founders. Certainly, he considered it useful for Americans to suppose that this had indeed been the Founders' policy, a supposition that did eighteenth-century statesmen the honor of regarding them as having had at least as sound a moral sense as nineteenth-century abolitionists. In these ways, then, Lincoln indicated that the Founding Fathers were in fact opposed to slavery.

Second, Lincoln himself defended a policy with respect to slavery (the policy of the Republican Party) that was in conformity with the better opinion in the Country since its foundation, a policy that had to contend with economic and other developments (including the invention of the cotton gin and the social consequences of such scares as the fierce 1791 Santo Domingo slave uprising)—developments that had come to make slavery more attractive and its elimination more threatening than they had appeared in 1787. Simply stated, this policy permitted slavery to continue in the States where it was then established by law even while it was resolutely forbidden any further expansion into the Territories of the United States. This policy, if carried out, meant that the National Government would be controlled in due time by the people of the States where slavery was not permitted, thereby liberating the Government to take measures to complete that elimination of slavery which its confinement (and consequent economic and political difficulties) had set in motion and which the moral sense of this long-standing policy clearly called for.

All this would mean a gradual elimination of slavery on the best possible terms (in the circumstances of this Country) for both the subjugated and the dominant races. This, Lincoln indicated, was truly the most just and the most practical, and hence the most moral, way of proceeding. No other opponent of slavery of that period could be as firm as Lincoln was in insisting upon slavery's eventual elimination even while he recognized the dilemmas faced by conscientious Southerners, of whom he could say that they were trapped by their circumstances. He could point out that if Northerners had slavery as pervasively established among them, they would be similarly trapped, and that if Southerners did not already have slavery, they certainly would not permit its introduction among them.

IV

What we see in all this is an indication of what (in Lincoln's judgment) prudence called for in the circumstances in which he found himself. Similarly, he had indicated (in a speech made the month before the Debates began) what prudence had called for in the circumstances in which the statesmen of the Constitutional Period had found themselves:

> It may be argued that there are certain conditions that make necessities and impose them upon us, and to the extent that a necessity is imposed upon a man he must submit to it. I think that was the condition in which we found ourselves when we established this government. We had slavery among us, we could not get our constitution unless we permitted them to remain in slavery, we could not secure the good we did secure if we grasped for more, and having by necessity submitted to that much, it does not destroy the principle that is the charter of our liberties [the Declaration of Independence]. Let that charter stand as our standard.[313]

Notice here his uses of "we," including in "We had slavery among us."

Then there is Lincoln's interpretation of the Declaration of Independence itself, made more than a year earlier, in which is exhibited further that high-minded combination of principle and practicality that we know as prudence:

> I think the authors of that notable instrument intended to include all men, but they did not mean to declare all men equal *in all respects*. They did not mean to say all men were equal in color, size, intellect, moral developments, or social capacity. They defined with tolerable distinctness, in what they did consider all men created equal—equal in "certain inalienable rights, among which are life, liberty, and the pursuit of happiness." This they said, and this meant. They did not mean to assert the obvious untruth, that all were then actually enjoying that equality, nor yet, that they were about to confer it immediately upon them. In fact they had no power to confer such a boon. They meant simply to declare the right, so that the *enforcement* of it might follow as fast as circumstances should permit.[314]

In these ways, then, Lincoln vindicated the prudence as well as the honor of the founding statesmen who were troubled by the institution of slavery, which they considered to have been originally forced upon them by Great Britain.[315] Does it not take a deep prudence to recognize and to appreciate prudence for what it is? But, someone might ask, what was there about Lincoln's policy, to say nothing of the policy of the Founding Fathers, which was truly prudent? That policy, it can be answered, was prudent in that it guided accommodations and national actions generally, always keeping in view the political objective desired, the eventual elimination of slavery; and

it did so in such a way as to ratify, and thereby continually encourage dedication to, property rights, constitutional government, and the moral standards
of the Country. On the other hand, to pursue such an objective covertly (as,
it can be granted, Douglas was perhaps doing) is to sacrifice something of
what one may achieve, in that the objective itself may be lost sight of and,
by some, even depreciated, along with the moral standards by which one
should be guided.

So, it can be said, Lincoln stated here a deeply prudential policy—and
he stated it in a sensible manner. Prudence applies also to the mode of saying things, not only to what is done and why. Among the considerations
prudently taken into account in the Republican policy of the 1850s were
both the "contract" entered into by the North and the disabilities labored
under by the South. One's mode of explaining oneself can be vital in such
matters. To speak prudently testifies to several facts—to the fact that language does matter, to the fact that judgment must be employed in dealing
with the passions as well as with the reasoning of mankind, and to the fact
that the sensibilities and aspirations of one's opponents are usually entitled
to respect. Prudence testifies as well to the recognition that in public life a
"universal feeling, whether well or ill-founded, can not be safely disregarded."[316] This Lincoln observed in the first of the Debates (at Ottawa). He
further observed, on that occasion, "In this and like communities, public
sentiment is everything. With public sentiment, nothing can fail; without it
nothing can succeed."[317] It is no accident then that the study of rhetoric
was traditionally recognized as essential to liberal education for public life
in a republic.

Lincoln's care in speech is reflected in the repeated complaint by Douglas that Lincoln was not a candid man. Thus Douglas could several times
ask, as he did in the second of the Debates (at Freeport), "Why cannot he
speak out and say what he is for and what he will do?"[318] By the time of
the sixth of the Debates (at Quincy), a frustrated Douglas could suggest that
Lincoln had "a fertile genius in devising language to conceal his
thoughts."[319] The context of this suggestion is illuminating: it was in the
course of Douglas's effort to get Lincoln to say whether he, if elected to the
Senate, would admit to the Union as a new State any Territory in which
the people had voted to permit slavery. Lincoln had, in the course of the
debates, replied in a most guarded manner to this question.[320] It was obvious that he and his most ardent supporters did not want to admit any new
slave States, but simply to say so would have gratuitously offended both
those who believed in playing by what they considered "the rules of the
game" and those who very much wanted a continent-wide republic, on
whatever terms.

Douglas himself could also be politic, of course: he would not have prospered as long as he did in Illinois and National politics if he could not be careful. He had the problem in 1858 not only of retaining his Illinois seat in the Senate of the United States, but of doing so on terms that would not make it impossible for him to secure enough Southern votes to be elected President in 1860. He succeeded in returning to the Senate, of course, but in order to do so he had to take positions that widened the already considerable split between Northern and Southern Democrats, thereby permitting the Republican Party to secure the Presidency in 1861.

Douglas was a man of great talent and, in the final analysis, a man with a genuine concern for the interests of his Country. But it is sadly indicative of the remarkable limitations of this remarkable man that despite considerable contact with Lincoln during a quarter of a century, he never seemed to appreciate how much more thoughtful Lincoln could be than anyone else he knew. All that Douglas could see in Lincoln's thoughtfulness were the elements of ambition and wiliness—both of which were there and in good measure. Did not Douglas, in noticing only what he did in Lincoln, reveal what mattered most to him, what he could notice? Are we not all tested by the responses we make, and fail to make, to manifestations around us of excellence?

V

Of course, the true greatness of Lincoln did not become fully manifest until he became President. Still, consider the sorts of things Douglas heard from him, even during that late summer and early fall of 1858 in Illinois. Consider, for example, how Lincoln could (in the first of the Debates, at Ottawa) accommodate himself to the considerable racial prejudice of his audience, thereby taking some of the sting out of the plausible insistence by Douglas that Lincoln really believed "that the negro was born his equal and yours, and that he was endowed with equality by the Almighty, and that no human law can deprive him of these rights which were guarantied to him by the Supreme ruler of the Universe."[321] Lincoln could accommodate himself to the racial prejudices of his audience even as he struck a blow for simple justice:

> Anything that argues me into [Judge Douglas's] idea of perfect social
> and political equality with the negro, is but a specious and fantastic
> arrangement of words, by which a man can prove a horse chestnut to

be a chestnut horse. [Laughter.] I will say here, while upon this subject, that I have no purpose directly or indirectly to interfere with the institution of slavery in the States where it exists. I believe I have no lawful right to do so, and I have no inclination to do so. I have no purpose to introduce political and social equality between the white and the black races. There is a physical difference between the two, which in my judgment will probably forever forbid their living together upon the footing of perfect equality, and inasmuch as it becomes a necessity that there must be a difference, I, as well as Judge Douglas, am in favor of the race to which I belong, having the superior position. I have never said anything to the contrary, but I hold that notwithstanding all this, there is no reason in the world why the negro is not entitled to all the natural rights enumerated in the Declaration of Independence, the right to life, liberty, and the pursuit of happiness. [Loud cheers.] I hold that he is as much entitled to these as the white man. I agree with Judge Douglas he is not my equal in many respects—certainly not in color, perhaps not in moral or intellectual endowment. But in the right to eat the bread, without the leave of anybody else, which his own hand earns, *he is my equal and the equal of Judge Douglas, and the equal of every living man.* [Great applause.]³²²

We should not be surprised, then, that Frederick Douglass, the former slave who was one of the most eloquent speakers of his day, could later say that Lincoln "was the first great man in the United States with whom [he] talked freely . . . who in no single instance reminded [him] . . . of the difference of color" between them.[323]

I continue with my inventory of the sorts of things Douglas did hear from Lincoln in 1858 that should have helped him to take a sounder measure of the man than he evidently did. Among the things Douglas heard was something Lincoln quoted from an 1854 speech of his, an observation by Lincoln that commented upon Douglas's insistence that he would not express any preference about the status of slavery in any Territory of the United States:

> This *declared* indifference, but as I must think, covert *real* zeal for the spread of slavery, I can not but hate. I hate it because of the monstrous injustice of slavery itself. I hate it because it deprives our republican example of its just influence in the world—enables the enemies of free institutions, with plausibility, to taunt us as hypocrites—causes the real friends of freedom to doubt our sincerity, and especially because it forces so many really good men amongst ourselves into an open war with the very fundamental principles of civil liberty—criticizing the Declaration of Independence, and insisting that there is no right principle of action but *self-interest*.[324]

Consider also the Socratic touches in the following argument, an argument which draws upon the fact that the much-better-known Douglas had (at the beginning of the Joint Debates) tried to get into Lincoln's and the audience's good graces by calling Lincoln a "kind, amiable, intelligent gentleman":

> If, in arraying [certain] evidence, I had stated anything which was false or erroneous, it needed but that Judge Douglas should point it out, and I would have taken it back with all the kindness in the world. I do not deal in that way. If I have brought forward anything not a fact, if he will point it out, it will not even ruffle me to take it back. But if he will not point out anything erroneous in the evidence, is it not rather for him to show, by a comparison of the evidence, that I have reasoned falsely, than to call the "kind, amiable, intelligent gentleman" a liar? [Cheers and laughter.] If I have reasoned to a false conclusion, it is the vocation of an able debater to show by argument that I have wandered to an erroneous conclusion.[325]

Consider, as well, Lincoln's insistence in the final debate, before an audience at Alton that had strong Southern sympathies:

> You may turn over everything in the Democractic [Party] policy from beginning to end, whether in the shape it takes on the statute book, in the shape it takes in the Dred Scott decision, in the shape it takes in conversation or the shape it takes in short maxim-like arguments—it everywhere carefully excludes the idea that there is anything wrong in [slavery].
>
> That is the real issue. That is the issue that will continue in this country when these poor tongues of Judge Douglas and myself shall be silent. It is the eternal struggle between these two principles—right and wrong—throughout the world. They are the two principles that have stood face to face from the beginning of time; and will ever continue to struggle.[326]

Finally, in this inventory of the sorts of things Lincoln had said which should have helped Douglas assess Lincoln properly, there is the opening paragraphs of Lincoln's "House Divided" Speech to the Republican State Convention in Springfield, June 16, 1858, a speech in which Lincoln examined (among other things) the consequences of a national policy (pushed by Douglas) opening up all the Territories to slavery. Lincoln had said:

> If we could first know *where* we are, and *whither* we are tending, we could better judge *what* to do, and *how* to do it.

We are now far into the *fifth* year, since a policy was initiated with the *avowed* object, and *confident* promise, of putting an end to slavery agitation.

Under the operation of that policy, that agitation has not only not ceased, but has *constantly augmented*.

In my opinion, it *will* not cease, until a *crisis* shall have been reached and passed.

"A house divided against itself cannot stand."

I believe this government cannot endure, permanently half *slave* and half *free*.

I do not expect the Union to be *dissolved*—I do not expect the house to *fall*—but I *do* expect it will cease to be divided.

It will become *all* one thing, or *all* the other.

Either the *opponents* of slavery, will arrest the further spread of it, and place it where the public mind shall rest in the belief that it is in the course of ultimate extinction; or its *advocates* will push it forward, till it shall become alike lawful in all the States, *old* as well as *new*—*North* as well as *South*.[327]

It is further indicative of the limitations of even so talented a politician as Douglas that he not only should not have appreciated the quality of this speech—a speech that anticipates (in these opening paragraphs) the political poet we see in the Gettysburg Address and in the Second Inaugural—but that he so misjudged it that he disdainfully quoted from these paragraphs in every one of the seven Debates with Lincoln in 1858. That is, he evidently believed that this remarkable statement exposed Lincoln as pretentious, reckless, and hence vulnerable to refutation and ridicule. In this, perhaps, Douglas may have revealed one considerable risk that a lawyer can run, the risk of becoming so adroit a technician that he is unable to be a master craftsman. There can be too much of the opportunist in such a man. (This is evident in the arguments Douglas resorted to, for the first time, in his final speech of the last Debate, when he knew Lincoln had no further reply available.)[328] So much then, at least for the moment, for the judgment of Douglas—and for the judgment of men of influence, then as well as now, who cannot recognize excellence in their midst.

VI

The judgment Lincoln displayed with respect to both the formulation of policy and the use of rhetoric depended upon a sound understanding—that is, upon a proper education for political purposes. (Whether someone may have that judgment as a result either of nature or of inspiration alone, not as a result of education, is a question we can leave for another occasion, noticing as we have that there was about Lincoln something of the political poet.)[329] A proper political education (under which is subsumed legal education) presupposes, among other things, that there are (as we have seen), enduring standards by which one may be guided even as one is being "practical."

One consequence of a proper education is that the doings of the community (in the form, say, of legislative enactments, constitutional declarations, and judicial decisions) can be reliably assessed. These assessments by the educated depend upon a natural-right teaching (or, if one prefers to consider these directives as critically influenced by revelation, a natural-law teaching).[330] Indeed, one can say, the question of the status of natural right is today the key issue in legal education and in jurisprudence, at least in this Country.[331]

Most legal scholars, I dare say, reject old-fashioned natural-right teachings "in theory," whatever they may personally do "in practice." This tends to lead, among their students if not among themselves, to either ruthlessness or sentimentality, sometimes even to both together. On the other hand, a moralistic approach that neglects prudence tends to encourage recklessness and hence its own kind of injustice (as in the case perhaps of many of the radical abolitionists in Lincoln's time). The principal alternative to a natural right–natural law approach is, especially among "practical" men who consider themselves "realists," something we now know as "positivism." For such men, the just and the unjust for a community depend, primarily, upon what lawgivers have ordained. In short, the just is the legal. This is substantially what Douglas stood for. It is appropriate that his last words in the memorable debates with Lincoln (during which debates he several times accused Lincoln of making war on the United States Supreme Court because of the *Dred Scott* decision)—Douglas's very last words (at Alton, October 15, 1858) were: "The only remedy and safety is that we shall stand by the constitution as our fathers made it, obey the laws as they are passed, while they stand the proper test and sustain the decisions of the Supreme Court and the constituted authorities."[332]

Of course, if one cannot properly look beyond the law in assessing the legal, there is the question of what it is that legislators, judges, and constitution-founders (as well as amenders of constitutions) can themselves look to in determining what the law should be. Related to this is the question of who the "constituted authorities" are, or should be, in various circumstances.

VII

It is well to be reminded here of the right of revolution, perhaps for our time (a time of determined tyrannies) the most critical self-evident truth in the Declaration of Independence. It bears repeating that to insist upon the right of revolution is implicitly to insist upon standards and ends, grounded in nature, that take precedence over what happens to be regarded at any particular moment as the law of the land. To deny that there are such enduring standards is to condemn oneself to an ultimately empty existence guided all too often by little more than self-interest keyed to personal gratification. It is such a set of standards to which one (almost instinctively?) resorts in condemning both Hitler's Germany and Stalin's Russia.

Lincoln, we have noticed, was obliged to make much of the Declaration of Independence. In this, too, there can be positivistic elements, unless one is careful to make more of the *teachings* of the instrument than of the fact that it embodies those teachings. That something more than even that instrument usually guided Lincoln is suggested by his reliance upon such teachers as the Bible, Shakespeare, and Euclid. He can be regarded as our best-educated President, as well as the finest lawyer who ever practiced in the State of Illinois.

The positivist depends more on deeds than on words—more, that is, on what chances to have been done by and to the community than on the ideas by which deeds are guided and justified. It is difficult, with such an approach, to avoid reliance upon material self-interest. Consider, for example, how Douglas accounted for the absence of slavery in Illinois: "We in Illinois tried slavery when a territory, and found it was not good for us in this climate, and with our surroundings, and hence we abolished it."[333] Douglas never referred in this context to such an influence as the Northwest Ordinance of 1787, which Lincoln even went so far as to see as an expression of Jefferson's interest in putting all American slavery in the course of ultimate extinction.[334] Nor did Douglas ever say publicly that freedom had been preferred to slavery in Illinois because it was simply better.

It is difficult, if material self-esteem is made much of, to regard the law as more than a neutral umpire, regulating conflicts between individuals and thereby leaving them free to pursue their private interests as they happen to please. (This does make for efficiency in the use of material resources.) Such an approach (of regarding the law primarily as an umpire) usually means, among other things, that morality cannot be legislated—and that even if it could be legislated, it should not be.

This position, which too is critical to the opinions of most legal scholars today, may also be found in Douglas's arguments. The community, he believes, should not be telling citizens what is good and bad; certainly, he insists, the Government of the United States should not be doing this for the State governments. Douglas goes so far as to say that it would be *despotic* of the Government of the United States to force the States without their consent to give up slavery, including the right of slaveholders to take their slaves with them into the Territories.[335] Douglas could invoke the cause of liberty (like Calhoun before him) even as he justified allowing some people (that is, slaveholders) to impose upon other people (that is, men and women of African descent) a far more severe despotism than anything that threatened the would-be slave owner who should be kept from continuing to enjoy property in human beings.

It is hard to believe that Douglas *listened* to what he himself was saying here. Of course, he must have assumed that Africans simply did not "count" in any balancing of equities in this matter. This is consistent with his reading of the Declaration of Independence, a reading that evidently regarded the Africans as not fully human. I notice in passing that his denunciation of the former slave Frederick Douglass, in the course of six of the seven Joint Debates with Lincoln, was a tacit acknowledgement that Africans were indeed capable of being regarded as human beings worthy of one's serious attention. Here, too, he did not really listen to what he was saying—and this can mean a kind of lying in the soul.

On the other hand, Jefferson had, long before, recognized that the grievances that white Americans had had against the British government were modest compared to those suffered by their slaves. And so Lincoln could say in the fifth of the Debates (at Galesburg):

> And I will remind Judge Douglas and this audience, that while Mr. Jefferson was the owner of slaves, as undoubtedly he was, in speaking upon this very subject, he used the strong language that "he trembled for his country when he remembered that God was just;" and I will offer the highest premium in my power to Judge Douglas if he will show that he, in all his life, ever uttered a sentiment at all akin to that of Jefferson.[336]

Consider, also, how Lincoln put Jefferson's sentiments in his Second Inaugural Address (in 1865):

> Fondly do we hope—fervently do we pray—that this mighty scourge of war may speedily pass away. Yet, if God wills that it continue, until all the wealth piled by the bond-man's two hundred and fifty years of unrequited toil shall be sunk, and until every drop of blood drawn with the lash, shall be paid by another drawn with the sword, as was said three

thousand years ago, so still it must be said "the judgments of the Lord, are true and righteous altogether."[337]

This is a far cry, indeed, from what Douglas had considered "despotism."

How far *should* one have gone—in the 1850s, say—in recognizing the rights due to the African slaves in this Country? Suppose one went as far as Lincoln did, including as he did the Africans among "all Men." Does it not follow, then, that the slaves themselves were entitled, in the words of the Declaration of Independence, "to alter or abolish"—that is, to resist and replace—any form of government that denied them their "unalienable Rights" to "Life, Liberty, and the Pursuit of Happiness"?

The answer to this question by a John Brown is clear: not only were the slaves entitled to revolt, but white sympathizers were entitled (if not even obliged) to help them do so. And so Brown led his dramatic raid upon Harper's Ferry in 1859. But this was not the kind of effort that a Lincoln could countenance. Indeed, it would have been political suicide for him to have acknowledged that rebellious slaves were merely attempting on that occasion to redeem the rights due them as human beings. Neither the sometimes virulent race prejudice of the day nor the desperate concern of many Unionists for law and order would permit such an acknowledgment. Consider, in this connection, how even the statesmen of our time who were most deeply opposed to the Soviet Union and its tyranny were obliged, in implementing that opposition, routinely to take into account the prospect of a nuclear holocaust in the event of all-out war.

We return to the question of the slaves' right of revolution in mid-nineteenth-century America. Here, too, prudence was called for—not only in what could be said by a politician to a Northern constituency very much concerned about domestic tranquility, about property rights, and about respect for the Constitution, but also in what might well have been said by any citizen to rebellious slaves and their sympathizers (and especially to the abolitionists). Did not the best hope for the African slaves, once they found themselves permanently in the United States, lie in a gradual political resolution of the slavery issue, one that permitted both the slaves and their masters to prepare for general emancipation and eventual citizenship? (Individual slaves, who could make their way to freedom in the North or in Canada, were special cases—and it was truly in everyone's interest that efforts be made to keep out of the sight of any sworn officer of the law those slaves able to make a run for freedom. I am reminded of what a Finnish border guard across from Vyborg answered me in July 1960 after we had crossed over from the Soviet Union: he and his colleagues would not turn back anyone fleeing from the Soviet Union unless the Russians knew that the highly vulnerable Finns had witnessed the escape. No doubt these guards recognized, as did the typical visitor to the Soviet Union in those days, that it was a quite repressive regime from which people naturally wanted to flee.)

The Republican policy, as Lincoln understood it, called for a determined national purpose, looking to the eventual extinction of slavery in this country—a purpose that should be firm and evident enough to induce even the Southern States to begin to plan sensibly for that eventuality. It was a policy guided by the moral and political principles enshrined in the Declaration of Independence—a policy that was intended to forestall the emergence several decades later of a regime much like that of South Africa during most of the twentieth century.

For better and for worse, that is, a full recognition of the rights of the African slaves depended upon a healthy political community in the United States, a community that was both moral and secure. Douglas insisted upon the right of white Americans to permanent safety; the abolitionists insisted upon the right of African slaves to immediate justice.

It takes someone who understands the limits as well as the uses of law—whether the law be an act of Congress, a decree by a court, or a Constitutional provision—to deal sensibly with the perennial (and not unnatural) conflict between self-interest and altruism. The law, to be effective, must take due account of the prosaic as well as of the exalted conditions for morality and for the common good.[338]

The First Inaugural Address

"Do you believe, Mr. Lincoln, that if the Republican Party
should elect a President they would be able to inaugurate him?"
"I reckon, friend, that if there are votes enough to elect a
Republican President, there'll be men enough to put him in."
—Anonymous

I

Abraham Lincoln's speech of March 4, 1861, is, of all our Presidential inaugural addresses, the most devoted to constitutional issues.[339] A new administration usually takes its constitutional powers for granted as its leader lays out its programs. But on this occasion the very existence of the underlying constitutional arrangements was in question.

Lincoln returned in the First Inaugural Address to several of the constitutional issues that had been examined, three years before, in the Lincoln-Douglas Debates in Illinois. Those issues had turned, in large part, around the soundness and consequences of the *Dred Scott* ruling by the United States Supreme Court in 1857.[340] The Debates inquiry, with respect to Congressional regulation of slavery in Territories, had included considerable discussion about the status and meaning of the Declaration of Independence.

Some ten thousand people gathered outside the unfinished Capitol building at noon on the fourth of March to watch Lincoln take the oath of office. The seven States of the Lower South had, by then, announced that

---

This talk was given at the Faculty Workshop, Loyola University of Chicago School of Law, April 22, 1997. (Original title: "Abraham Lincoln's First Inaugural Address and the Judiciary.")

The epigraph is taken from Carl Sandburg, *Abraham Lincoln: The War Years* (New York: Harcourt, Brace, 1939), 1: 4–5.

they were seceding from the Union, beginning with South Carolina on December 20, 1860, and continuing with Mississippi, Florida, Alabama, Georgia, Louisiana, and (only two days before) Texas.[341] Four more States (of the Upper South) were to join this attempted secession, making eleven in all: Virginia in April, Arkansas and North Carolina in May, and Tennessee in June. (It proved important in the war which followed that four other Slave States, also in the Upper South, were kept more or less loyal to the Union: Delaware, Kentucky, Maryland, and Missouri.) One big question, at the time of the Lincoln Inauguration, was whether Virginia would go the way of South Carolina and her sister Slave States. Lincoln himself had indicated, in pre-Inauguration negotiations, that he would be willing to trade Fort Sumter (in Charleston harbor) for Virginia.

Another big question had been whether Lincoln would be alive to take the oath of office. (He had been hidden from public view while passing through Baltimore on his way to Washington.) The Thirty-sixth Congress, which concluded its final session at 6 a.m. on Inauguration Day, had certified Lincoln's election on February 13. He would be, it had been pointed out, a minority President; but, Lincoln responded, he was not the first minority President—and, besides, he had gotten more votes than anyone else. (The new Congress, the Thirty-seventh, elected in November 1860, was not scheduled to assemble until December 1861. But, it was later learned, it would meet on July 4, pursuant to a call from President Lincoln, at which special session he laid out his programs and asked for retroactive validation of various measures he had taken on his own authority to preserve the Union. These were measures that his much troubled predecessor, James Buchanan, had evidently considered himself not permitted by the Constitution to use.[342]

Most of the Southern Slave States had come to be dominated by men who were convinced that a Republican Party administration would attempt to destroy slavery wherever it was found in the United States, even though the most that the Party's leaders had *said* was that they would not permit any further extension of slavery in the Territories.[343] But the more prescient leaders, South as well as North, recognized that if slavery could not grow, it would likely be suffocated as an institution. It was obvious, in any event, that the North was growing much faster than the South, both in population and in industrial strength, and that it would not be long before the South would have to submit to Northern control over the Union. Or so it was feared in the South, no matter what slavery-related assurances had been offered by Republican Party leaders since, as well as before, November 1860.

II

The understanding of the Constitution drawn upon by Lincoln in his First Inaugural Address, especially as he tried to reassure the South further with respect to slavery, addressed what can be expected in the constitutional system from the Judiciary (and especially the United States Supreme Court), from the President, from the Congress, and from the People.

The oath of office was to be administered on this occasion by the Chief Justice of the United States who had written the Opinion of the Court in *Dred Scott,* an opinion that had contributed to (or, at least, did not moderate) the crisis that the Country was facing. But however critical the Supreme Court had been theretofore, it would be largely set aside as the crisis deepened.

There are several references, at least by implication, to judicial proceedings in the Inaugural Address. In its Paragraph 8, there is (in the course of providing assurances to the South about implementing the Fugitive Slave Clause in the Constitution) an insistence upon "all the safeguards of liberty known to civilized and humane jurisprudence . . . so that a free man be not, in any case, surrendered as a slave."[344]

Assurances are given in Paragraph 7 of the Inaugural Address respecting the Fugitive Slave Clause, with further assurances in Paragraphs 21 and 25.[345] The courts, whether State or National, would presumably be used in the enforcement of fugitive-slave laws. Elsewhere, "constitutional controversies" could be referred to (Paragraph 22) and "constitutional checks, and limitations" (Paragraph 23).[346] No doubt, the courts could be expected to play a part in the resolution of these matters. But, it had long been obvious to thoughtful citizens, no court would be able to resolve what Lincoln (in Paragraph 25) called "the only substantial dispute" dividing the North and the South: "One section of the country believes slavery is right, and ought to be extended, while the other believes it is wrong, and ought not to be extended."[347] And, as I have indicated, many on both sides also believed that if slavery could not be "extended," it would eventually have to be given up. (What, for example, would be done, if extension was blocked, with the ever-growing surplus of slaves in the Old South? To emancipate a substantial number of them, it seems to have been feared, would jeopardize control over the rest of them.)

There were, bearing upon the extension-of-slavery issue, two questions that Lincoln introduced in this fashion in his First Inaugural Address (Paragraph 21):

May Congress prohibit slavery in the territories? The Constitution does not expressly say. *Must* Congress protect slavery in the territories? The Constitution does not expressly say.[348]

The Supreme Court was taken to have ruled in *Dred Scott* that Congress could not prohibit slavery in the Territories. Such prohibition was at the heart of the no-extension-of-slavery policy of the newly formed Republican Party. Stephen A. Douglas, in the Freeport Doctrine announced during the Lincoln-Douglas Debates in 1858, conceded that territorial governments could effectively prevent slavery by denying it police protection and supportive legislation.[349] Even though he had evidently been obliged to say something like this in accordance with his Popular Sovereignty position, in order to win reelection to the Senate from Illinois, this concession split the Democratic Party and may have cost Douglas's election to the Presidency in 1860.[350]

The Southerners who had refused to back Douglas in 1860 were determined to go even further than the Court had done in *Dred Scott,* insisting as they did that Congress and the courts had a duty to protect all legitimate property in the Territories, and that of course included slaves. Some Republicans (such as Lincoln in his "House Divided" Speech), on the other hand, were fearful that the Supreme Court had prepared the ground in *Dred Scott* for an even more devastating repudiation of the principles of the Declaration of Independence, a ruling that any citizen could take all of his legitimate movable property (including slaves) into any State of the Union. This difference of opinion can be said to have been at the heart of the Secession Crisis, a difference that ultimately rested upon the answers given to questions about the rightness of slavery.[351]

The Republican Party victory in the November 1860 Presidential election was the signal that Secessionist fire-eaters in the South, especially in South Carolina, had been waiting for. By January 26, 1861, six Southern State legislatures had passed bills such as that in South Carolina (December 20):"An Ordinance to dissolve the Union between the State of South Carolina and other States united with her under the compact entitled 'The Constitution of the United States of America.'"[352] All this cleared the way for the admission of Kansas to the Union, as the thirty-fourth State, on January 29, 1861. The admission of "bleeding Kansas" as a free State showed, as much as anything else, that the Southern Slave States had given up on the Union.[353]

In this and other ways, the *Dred Scott* Supreme Court had become irrelevant to the issues of the day. The coup de grace to judicial pretensions can be said to have been administered, at least for the time being, by Lincoln in his Inaugural Address when he said (in Paragraph 24):

> I do not forget the position assumed by some, that constitutional ques-
> tions are to be decided by the Supreme Court; nor do I deny that such
> decisions must be binding in any case, upon the parties to a suit, as to
> the object of that suit, while they are also entitled to very high respect
> and consideration, in all parallel cases, by all other departments of the
> government. And while it is obviously possible that such decision may
> be erroneous in any given case, still the evil effect following it, being
> limited to that particular case, with the chance that it may be over-ruled,
> and never become a precedent for other cases, can better be borne than
> could the evils of a different practice. At the same time the candid citi-
> zen must confess that if the policy of the government, upon vital ques-
> tions, affecting the whole people, is to be irrevocably fixed by decisions
> of the Supreme Court, the instant they are made, in ordinary litigation
> between parties, in personal actions, the people will have ceased, to be
> their own rulers, having, to that extent, practically resigned their gov-
> ernment, into the hands of that eminent tribunal. Nor is there, in this
> view, any assault upon the court, or the judges. It is a duty, from which
> they may not shrink, to decide cases properly brought before them; and
> it is no fault of theirs, if others seek to turn their decisions to political
> purposes.[354]

This had been substantially the position Lincoln had taken repeatedly on
Dred Scott during his 1858 debates with Douglas. Courts, he concedes, are
indispensable for deciding individual cases, and judicial rulings entered
there should be conclusive for the parties involved. But, he insists, such
determinations (whether or not erroneous) cannot be conclusive for the
Country at large: they should not be depended upon to settle serious political issues (or what he called "the policy of the government"). He argued,
in effect, that the Constitution need not be taken to mean whatever the
Supreme Court happens to say it does.

All this bears upon how judicial review should be regarded, especially since there is in the Constitution of 1787 neither any explicit provision
for judicial review of acts of Congress nor any provision that anticipates
the exercise of such power by the courts.[355] Although Lincoln does not
find it useful to say much more in the Inaugural Address about these matters than he does in Paragraph 24, the student of his argument can see
what is implicitly recognized: constitutional issues and political judgment
are likely to overlap or to be blended. It is difficult for judges not to be
influenced by "policy" considerations in making "constitutional" determinations. Is it not prudent, therefore, to rely more upon legislatures than
upon courts in dealing with such matters except when the propriety of

judicial proceedings (as in criminal trials) is itself the primary issue? Legislatures may properly weigh political concerns along with constitutional arguments. Put otherwise, it can be said that constitutional interpretation must often go hand-in-hand with political judgment.

Thus, Lincoln insisted that the Supreme Court cannot be so authoritative in these situations that the Congress must necessarily defer to it completely, whatever the respect that members of Congress should pay to the arguments offered by the judges. However much we still hear of the Supreme Court routinely passing judgment upon acts of Congress, has not the Lincoln position pretty much prevailed in practice since the early years of the New Deal?[356]

III

Critical to this issue of the place of the judiciary in the constitutional system is what can be understood about the natural characteristics of courts as compared to legislatures and magistrates.[357] *Nature* also has to be brought to bear upon what Lincoln identified as the fundamental question here, as to the rightness or wrongness of slavery. Nature bears as well upon the recognition of the political unit to which allegiance is ultimately owed.[358]

Was there indeed *a* country that they were talking about? Southerners made much of *compact* and of *confederation*. Lincoln, on the other hand, used *country* and *national* again and again in his Inaugural Address. (But he could also argue that a compact requires unanimous consent of all parties to it to be changed [Paragraph 12].[359] In the Gettysburg Address he would speak most solemnly of a *nation* having been *brought forth* on this continent in 1776, using language that suggests a natural birth.

Lincoln opens his First Inaugural Address by recognizing a custom—a custom "as old as the government itself"—the custom of delivering an address on such occasions.[360] By the middle of the address he can invoke memories that stretch back across decades (Paragraph 20).[361] By this time he has also made his audience familiar with the term *national,* which he will continue to use to the end of the address, along with *country, friends,* and *people* as if they are all the same, and naturally so—a single fraternal people, not the peoples of thirty-four different States.

That such talk makes a difference is testified to by the pains taken by the Confederate Constitutional Convention when, a week later, it issued its own constitution, changing as it did the opening lines of the Preamble to read, "We, the people of the Confederate States, each State acting in its sovereign and independent character, in order to form a permanent federal government."[362] There was to be no more "Yankee" talk among the Confederates either about a people somehow superior to the States or about "a more perfect Union."

However arbitrary a people's customs, like many other institutions, may be in their inauguration, they can begin in time to feel natural. This is why habits can be spoken of as second nature. It is upon this sense of things, promoted by almost a century of habituation (since at least 1774), that Lincoln draws in the lyrical final paragraph that he appends to his tightly reasoned, sometimes prosaic, and deliberately calming argument of this Address:

> I am loth to close. We are not enemies, but friends. We must not be enemies. Though passion may have strained, it must not break our bonds of affection. The mystic chords of memory, stretching from every battlefield, and patriot grave, to every living heart and hearthstone, all over this broad land, will yet swell the chorus of the Union, when again touched, as surely they will be, by the better angels of our nature.[363]

Deeply rooted ties are recalled as friendship, affection, memory, the graves of their patriotic ancestors, common battle-fields, this broad land, and the Union are invoked. Here, as earlier in Lincoln's First Inaugural Address, reinforcement is sought by the invocation of the divine (elsewhere in the Address explicitly, here implicitly with the references to "mystic" and "angels").[364] All this concludes with the word *nature,* reflecting as it does the instinct of patriots that there is something natural, as well as something divinely ordained, and hence right about the Country in whose cause citizens are asked to enlist.

13

The Fourth of July Message
to Congress

Mr. Lincoln, you say, was kind-hearted. In this, I fully agree. No man I ever knew was more so, but the same was true of Julius Caesar. All you have said of Mr. Lincoln's good qualities, and a great deal more on the same line, may be truly said of Caesar. He was certainly esteemed by many of the best men of his day for some of the highest qualities which dignify and ennoble human nature. He was a thorough scholar, a profound philosopher, an accomplished orator, and one of the most gifted, as well as polished writers of the age, in which he lived. . . .

> The case of Caesar illustrates to some extent my view both of the private character of Mr. Lincoln, and of his public acts. . . . I do not think that he intended to overthrow the Institutions of the country. I do not think he understood them or the tendencies of his acts upon them. The Union with him in sentiment, rose to the sublimity of a religious mysticism; while his ideas of its structure and formation in logic, rested upon nothing but the subtleties of a sophism! His many private virtues and excellencies of head and heart, I did esteem. . . . [W]e must discriminate between the man in private life, and the man in public office. . . . Power generally seems to change and transform the characters of those invested with it. Hence, the great necessity for "those chains" in the Constitution, to bind all Rulers and men in authority, spoken of by Mr. Jefferson.
>
> —Alexander H. Stephens

This talk was given in the First Friday Lecture Series, the University of Chicago, at the Chicago Cultural Center, Chicago, December 5, 1997.

The epigraph is taken from Alexander H. Stephens, *A Constitutional View of the Late War between the States* (Philadelphia: National Publishing, 1870), 2: 447–48. See note 386 below.

I

Abraham Lincoln, in his First Inaugural Address of March 4, 1861, attempted to calm down Unionists and Secessionists alike, hoping thereby to avert
disunion without war. He tried in various ways to reassure Southerners
who were apprehensive about the designs of a new administration and a
new Congress, both of which were expected to be more militantly antislavery than any theretofore in the history of the United States.[365]

By the time Lincoln was inaugurated, seven States of the Lower South
had enacted ordinances of secession.[366] He could still hope that reassur-
ances might keep Virginia loyal to the Union—and without Virginia the
movement for Southern Secession would be hopeless. With this in view,
Lincoln insisted that the Government of the United States would not strike
the first blow; it would not allow itself to appear the aggressor. South Carolina obliged him by being the first to open hostilities, firing upon Fort
Sumter in Charleston harbor on April 12.[367] But this was, it seems, all the
Secessionist element in Virginia needed to make its move. And with Virginia went half of the Upper South. It remained to be seen, in the Spring
of 1861, what the other half of the Upper South (Delaware, Maryland,
Kentucky, and Missouri) would do.[368]

Three days after the firing on Fort Sumter, which excited citizens
North and South, the President called a special session of Congress. The
date set, July 4, 1861, allowed the Lincoln administration two and a half
more months to implement a number of measures without having to deal
with Congress. Although Lincoln himself had had limited experience in
Washington, having served there for only one two-year term in the House
of Representatives (in 1847-1849), the men he had chosen for his Cabinet
were seasoned politicians with influential constituencies both in Washington and in their respective States.

In his Fourth of July Message, the President described what had been
happening since Inauguration Day, four months before, including the extraordinary measures to which his administration had resorted.[369] Some of
them he considered strictly legal; others were technically questionable,
however desperately needed, but not beyond the authority of Congress to
ratify retroactively. These were extraordinary times, he argued, and the Government's response had had to be so also. It is evident, from the way Lincoln made his case, that the Country was being asked to prepare for what
could be a long struggle. Additional measures, which only Congress could
provide, were recommended.[370]

Critical to the way that Lincoln proceeds is the impression he gives
that he wants to describe with care what he had done and why he had been

obliged to do it. Also critical is his emphasis upon a principle that had never had to be given such prominence before in the United States: nothing has been done, he argued, that was "beyond the constitutional competency of Congress"; that is, the power that had been exercised by his administration was available somewhere in the Government.[371] Along with this was the Government's reliance upon what has been called the war power, something that opened the way to such radical measures (a year and a half later) as the Emancipation Proclamation.

II

Care may be seen as well in how other things are talked about in this Fourth of July Message. After observing how much benefit had been conferred upon ordinary people by the United States Government, Lincoln asks,

> Whoever, in any section, proposes to abandon such a government, would do well to consider, in deference to what principle it is, that he does it—what better he is likely to get in its stead—whether the substitute will give, or be intended to give, so much good to the people?[372]

He, as a longtime champion of the Declaration of Independence, then warns:

> There are some foreshadowings on this subject. Our adversaries have adopted some Declarations of Independence; in which, unlike the good old one penned by Jefferson, they omit the words "all men are created equal." Why?[373]

His warning continues:

> They have adopted a temporary national constitution, in the preamble of which, unlike our good old one, signed by Washington, they omit "We, the People," and substitute "We, the deputies of the sovereign and independent States." Why? Why this deliberate pressing out of view, the rights of men, and the authority of the people?

He is accurate in what he says about the *temporary* constitution adopted six months before by the States attempting to secede: "We the People" was omitted on that occasion, but it was restored in the permanent constitution (approved in Montgomery, Alabama, shortly after Lincoln was inaugurated in March 1861).[374]

That restoration may have testified to the hold that the "We the People" language had in the South and elsewhere, however accidental may have been its original formulation in the Constitution of 1787.[375] Even so, the restoration of "We the People" was not effected without qualification, for it was at once indicated by the Confederates that reference was being made, not to any national people (not even to the people of the South), but rather to the people of "each State acting in its sovereign and independent character." This qualification is reinforced by what is done in the Confederate Constitution with the Ninth and Tenth Amendments: the Ninth Amendment's "retained by the people" becomes "retained by the people of the several States"; the Tenth Amendment's "reserved to the States, respectively, or to the people" becomes "reserved to the States, respectively, or to the people thereof."[376]

The significance of "We the People" is pointed up by Lincoln's next statement in his Fourth of July Message:

> This is essentially a people's contest. On the side of the Union, it is a struggle for maintaining in the world that form and substance of government whose leading object is to elevate the condition of men; to lift artificial weights from all shoulders, to clear the paths of laudable pursuit for all, to afford all an unfettered start and a fair chance in the race of life. Yielding to partial and temporary departures from necessity, this is the leading object of the Government for whose existence we contend.[377]

The status of "the people" is reflected in the fact that wartime elections have always been held in this Country, even in the course of a devastating civil war. Compare Great Britain, for instance, where elections to the House of Commons may be suspended during a major war, however important Parliament remains. This is related to Lincoln's repeated insistence upon "time, discussion, and the ballot box" and upon not allowing bullets to be substituted for ballots.[378] Lincoln himself was prepared to surrender power if he lost the 1864 election.[379]

The completely unacceptable transgression by the Confederates was their attempt to set aside the will of the people, constitutionally expressed in 1860 in a fair election. But however much Lincoln insisted upon the authority of the will of the people, properly registered, he could ally himself, as we have seen, with aristocrats such as Jefferson and Washington. It did not hurt his argument that these men were Southerners.

III

It can be instructive to consider all of the changes made by the Confederates when they adapted the United States Constitution of 1787 to their purposes. We must settle, by way of illustration on this occasion, for the following adaptations made in the 1787 Preamble:

> We the People of the [United] *Confederate* States, *each State acting in its sovereign and independent character,* in order to form a [more perfect Union] *permanent federal government,* establish Justice, insure domestic Tranquility, [provide for the common defence, promote the general Welfare,] and secure the Blessings of Liberty to ourselves and our Posterity—*invoking the favor and guidance of Almighty God*—do ordain and establish this Constitution for the [United] *Confederate* States of America.[380]

(The bracketed words in the 1787 Preamble, set forth here, were stricken by the Confederates in drafting their 1861 Preamble. Changes in capitalization are not noted here. The italicized words were added to the 1861 Confederate Constitution.)

We have already noticed how "We the People" was qualified along States' Rights lines.[381] The reference to the "sovereign and independent character" of the States echoes the Articles of Confederation. Southerners were thus carrying to an extreme that invocation of States' Rights that other States and sections of the Country had seen fit to make much of from time to time since 1789, when *their* grievances had become acute.[382]

Of course, "United" became "Confederate," suggesting more of a league than an amalgamation, if not a consolidation, of States. Along these lines was the abandonment of "a more perfect Union"—but the times were ominous, with a serious struggle threatening, and something more than a temporary alliance would be needed as the object of sacrifice, and so the Confederates did have to speak of "a permanent federal government."

The divisions with respect to slavery that contributed to the Civil War were anticipated by the divisions in the United States with respect to the tariff. Southerners had protested for at least two generations that the tariff was being used to encourage Northern manufactures at the expense of Southern agriculture. This grievance is addressed in the body of the Confederate Constitution, which placed severe restrictions upon what the Confederate government could do to finance internal improvements and promote manufactures.[383] Such restrictions are anticipated by the removal from the constitution, beginning with the Preamble, of any power in the federal government of the Confederacy to promote the general welfare.

The common defense is also removed from the Preamble, although it is retained in Article I, Section 8 (where the second reference to the general welfare is removed).[384] Perhaps retention of "common defence" in the Preamble was regarded as encouraging a general power; perhaps, that is, it was believed that it would be safer to hedge in the common-defense power by providing a limiting context for it in the body of the Constitution. Southern apprehensions were not without substance here, for it was upon the common-defense power—what we call the war power—that Lincoln drew as authorizing his Emancipation Proclamation.[385]

We have seen how "We the People" was qualified in the Preamble, with the people keyed to States, not to any multi-State body. Perhaps compensation of sorts, for the Confederates, was the addition to the Preamble of a concern for "the favor and guidance of Almighty God," an authority surely not limited by State borders. It was not in the South alone that God came to be made so much of—compared, for example, to what was said in the Constitutional Convention of 1787 and what is said (or rather is not said) in the document framed by that convention. Lincoln spoke more and more about God as the war took its awful toll, culminating in the theology of his Second Inaugural Address.

IV

Vital to Lincoln's position in his Fourth of July Message is his insistence that *sophistry* must be guarded against.[386] Solid reasoning, grounded in a sound political morality, is essential for effective government—and sophistry is *seeming* reasoning.

Lincoln discerns sophistry in the Southern reliance upon the "magical omnipotence of 'State rights.'"[387] He insists, here and elsewhere, that the States never had any existence independent of the United States. He also insists, as we have seen, upon a careful use of words. The Southerners are identified as "adversaries," "insurrectionists," "rebels," and so on; their association is spoken of as "the so-called Confederate States." Indeed, there are a half-dozen uses of "so-called," including "the so-called Border States," which are (Lincoln insists) really the Middle States.[388] Such care in his language may be seen throughout the war, even though he slips occasionally into the common usage, "Border States."[389] At times, Lincoln could even refer to some of the Southerners as "traitorous," especially those rebel leaders who had been officers in the Army of the United States or members of Congress.[390]

Perhaps the supreme sophistry was exhibited by those Southerners who attacked Lincoln for not remaining fettered by the Constitution in trying to suppress insurgents who repudiated altogether their obligations under the same Constitution.[391] Even so, Lincoln did insist upon going through the form of getting Congressional ratification for his extraordinary measures. A respect for forms can help shape law-abidingness and can promote confidence in the self-restraint of anyone who has to wield vast powers in an unprecedented emergency.

V

Does not systematic recourse to sophistry, whatever it may say about the general level of education, testify to a people's moral sense? Lincoln recognized that the Southerners' moral sense had to be catered to by their leaders: they could not justify rebellion but only the more mechanical, legalistic term, *secession*.[392]

Lincoln draws upon the moral sense in his arguments about the financial obligations on which the South is defaulting by its attempted secession. He makes far more of this than we would expect in comparable circumstances today. In this he may be very much a lawyer aware of the balance sheet.[393]

The moral sense is also evident in the importance of public opinion in a regime such as that found in the United States.[394] This is related to how the right of revolution should be regarded. Good reasons have to be alleged in order for a people to be justified in exercising this invaluable right. The Declaration of Independence provides a model here, listing as it does a number of grievances along with the principles that are relied upon. That is, desire is not enough, nor is resentment or anger.[395]

What, it may well be asked, did the South really want? The best case to be made for it is perhaps in terms of self-determination. But, unfortunately, the *self* involved here was in large part defined by a defense of, if not a reliance upon, slavery. It is hard to believe it was anything else but their respective opinions about slavery that accounted for the deep cleavage between North and South.[396]

Southerners did see themselves as defending their liberty. Their Preamble could retain "the Blessings of Liberty" among the ends of government. But this makes sense (at least in modern times) only if their system pointed to, or at least permitted, the eventual abolition of slavery—and this the Southerners of the 1860s, unlike their more thoughtful ancestors of the 1770s and 1780s, were not prepared to concede.[397]

VI

A reliance upon words, which sophistry undermines (as may be seen today in how our language is cheapened by incessant and shameless advertising), is counted upon in a sound political order. It is related to the importance of the oaths taken by those in public service.[398]

The conscientious public servant is obliged to rise above his personality. Lincoln, in his Fourth of July Message, rarely speaks of himself in the first person singular—and when he does, it is to speak of what he *believes,*[399] thereby exhibiting himself as personally limited, however firm and sure he is about the duties and prerogatives of the Executive and the Government.

The steady reasoning that is needed, in place of sophistry, depends upon sound principles—as well as upon an *appearance* of both steady reasoning and sound principles. Lincoln, after all, is a man who rose to the Presidency primarily because of his speeches—not because of political organization or party service and the like (although these were not neglected). His reliance upon reasoning is related to the emphasis he placed upon "time, discussion, and the ballot box." It is this that shows up as ill-conceived much of the talk one hears about Lincoln as a dictator.[400]

To a surprising extent, how the war was seen and conducted depended upon how Lincoln spoke about it, particularly in his Inaugural Addresses, his Fourth of July Message, and the Gettysburg Address. Also important were his four annual messages to Congress, made each December.[401] Much of each of the annual messages was devoted to the problems dealt with by the various departments of the Government, with each Cabinet officer evidently supplying material for the message. Then Lincoln would rise above these pedestrian, however necessary, concerns by reporting how the great struggle looked *this* year.

His speeches, in Congress and out, were important for focusing the attention and energies of the people. But his words could not have been as effective as they were if there had not been a deeply rooted passion for the Union among the people at large, a passion that found spontaneous expression in the nationwide response to the firing upon Fort Sumter in April 1861.

Lincoln considered the people (and certainly not the judiciary) as the ultimate human judge of his actions, a people that had been shaped by the regime and that had experienced its great benefits. Throughout the war he deferred, at least in form, to the Congress, as the immediate agents of the people.[402] (See Section IV[iv] of Chapter 14 of this Collection.)

VII

Lincoln, in the opening months of the war, urged a massive effort by Unionists, expecting thereby to make it a short conflict. Perhaps it would have been much shorter than it was if his predecessor had acted with much more confidence and vigor between November 1860 and March 1861.[403] Perhaps it was fortunate, considering all that was *not* done then by the Government, that Washington did not fall to the rebels in the opening months of the great struggle.

Both sides, it seems, expected a much shorter war than they got. What would have happened if the war's devastation had been anticipated? Lincoln insisted, as we have seen, that ordinary people, aware of the benefits of their Union, were prepared to fight for it. Perhaps their dedication grew as their investment in sacrifices mounted.

One of the consequences of the equality principle made so much more of in the North than in the South was the elevation in the North of the status of labor. There, perhaps much more than in the South, the Country could be spoken of as the land of opportunity.[404] This contributed significantly to the military, as well as to the industrial, strength of the North, since that is where the steady flow of immigrants went, replacing at once many of those lost in the war.[405]

We have several times noticed the Southern emphasis upon the liberty that they were defending from Northern tyranny. The exalted status of personal liberty in the United States is testified to by how bitterly Lincoln's suspensions from time to time of the writ of habeas corpus were responded to both North and South. Particularly resented, it seems, was that the suspension had been by the President rather than by Congress. Although the Constitution can plausibly be read as recognizing Congress as the branch to which the power of suspension is entrusted, there is considerable merit to Lincoln's extended argument that the Framers could not have intended that so vital an emergency power depended for its exercise upon whether Congress happened to be in session. Even so, he asked for a retroactive ratification by Congress of what he had done as well as for an empowerment of future suspensions.[406]

One can see in the sensitivity about the status of the writ of habeas corpus something of that American resistance to authority that finds such measures as gun controls so threatening to many (albeit not a majority) of our fellow citizens today. Even Chief Justice Taney, who had insisted upon the liberty of slaveholders in *Dred Scott,* got into the act here, lecturing the President at length (in a Maryland case) about the unconstitutionality of *his,* rather than the Congress's, suspension of the writ of habeas corpus.[407]

Lincoln ignored him, just as he ignored most of the newspapers in the
Country who attacked him and his administration throughout the war in
the bitterest terms.[408]

Lincoln attempted in his First Inaugural Address to assure the South
that the traditional constitutional relations among the States could be
restored once hostilities ceased. The South, it was hoped, would be encouraged thereby to end its rebellion immediately. Lincoln also held out this
prospect in his Fourth of July Message. But it is obvious, as one reviews the
President's major speeches, that the longer the war continued, the greater
the risks were that the Southern States (and all other States as well) would
not be able to return to their original station within the Union.

The longer the war continued, that is, the more the fundamental differences between North and South called for permanent resolution. The
longer the war lasted, the more it came to be recognized that it was really
about slavery. One of the last acts by the Thirty-sixth Congress, shortly
before Lincoln's inauguration, was to attempt to reassure the South by
approving for submission to the States of a constitutional amendment to
this effect:

> No amendment shall be made to the Constitution which will authorize
> or give to Congress the power to abolish or interfere, within any State,
> with the domestic institutions thereof, including that of persons held to
> labor or service by the laws of said State.[409]

This proposed amendment never made its way into the United States
Constitution. It was evidently too late for such assurances. But its equiva-
lent, and much more, may be found in the Confederate Constitution, with
the added touch that the Southerners of 1861 were willing, if not eager, to
do what the Framers of 1787 had been ashamed to do: the framers of 1861
referred explicitly to slavery in their constitution.[410]

The proposed amendment of 1861, if ratified, would have been the
Thirteenth Amendment to the United States Constitution. The longer the
war went on, the more likely it became that the Thirteenth Amendment
would be instead one altogether abolishing slavery everywhere in the
United States.

VIII

Lincoln had recognized in his First Inaugural Address that the only substantial difference between North and South in the circumstances of the

1860s was with respect to the status of slavery. That recognition may be seen also in his Second Inaugural Address.

In his Fourth of July Message, however, Lincoln barely alludes to slavery as a factor to be considered. Some critics, then as well as since, criticized him bitterly for making so much of preserving the Union and so little of abolishing slavery. Pro-slavery Southerners, however, knew better: they feared that the rise to power of the Republican Party meant the decline and eventual elimination of slavery throughout the Country. It is evident, in one ordinance of secession after another, that Lincoln was recognized in the South to be an implacable enemy of slavery.[411]

Lincoln recognized, in turn, that vital to Union prospects was keeping the Middle States of Delaware, Maryland, Kentucky, and Missouri from seceding. And to this end, in the first year of the war, the less said by Republicans about slavery, the better. Besides, racial prejudice was such in the North (as we have noticed) that many more loyal citizens could be expected to make sacrifices to preserve the Union than to abolish slavery.

We can see, in how guarded Lincoln was about slavery in his Fourth of July Message, the kinds of compromises with respect to slavery made by the Founders back in 1776 to 1789. In 1861, as in 1787, other matters had to be dealt with, including the development and perpetuation of a Country that would eventually make slavery impossible.[412]

Lincoln moved carefully here, waiting until all the loyal States in the Upper South were secure. A year later, by the Fourth of July of 1862, he was already working on the Emancipation Proclamation that he would publicly anticipate in September 1862, a measure designed to help put down the rebellion by striking at the core of Southern strength, both materially and spiritually.

IX

That Lincoln could discipline himself, in his only Fourth of July speech as President, not to speak more than he did about slavery should have put others, friends and foes alike, on notice as to what kind of man they were dealing with. After all, he had set the Fourth of July as the date for the special session of Congress that he had called.

It was generally known how much he had made of the Declaration of Independence for at least a decade, culminating in what he said when he visited Independence Hall on his way to his inauguration.[413] Again and again, he recognizes the importance of 1776, not least in the dating of the origins of the Nation in the opening words, two years later, of the Gettysburg Address.

Lincoln, in his profound opposition to slavery, depended upon his own ability to avoid being enslaved by prejudices and catch-phrases.[414] It is this ability that permitted him to use his Constitutional powers so broadly without showing disrespect for the Constitution.

Still, Lincoln would have had his fellow citizens understand that not all crises are like a civil war and that not all Presidents need be entrusted with extraordinary powers. Fundamental to his approach here is his Fourth of July observation that "when an end is lawful and obligatory, the indispensable means to it, are also lawful, and obligatory." Both his reasoning powers and his moral sense are exhibited in his insistence on that occasion that "nothing should ever be implied as law, which leads to unjust, or absurd consequences."[415]

Perhaps most important of the lessons to be learned from Abraham Lincoln—more important even than what he said on any particular occasion—was his informed assurance that there are enduring standards of the heart and of the mind by which the *absurd* and the *unjust* can be seen and judged for what they are.[416]

14

The Emancipation Proclamation

A word fitly spoken is like apples of gold in pictures of silver.

—Solomon

I

The greatest tribute ever paid to the Constitution of 1787 since the founding period may have been in 1861 by the framers of a constitution for the Confederate States of America. Their 1861 constitution is, with some revealing changes, patterned on the 1787 model.[417] Another great tribute—but one that was *not* perverse in some of its implications—was the measured response by Abraham Lincoln to the Great Rebellion. His Emancipation Proclamation was revealing of his constitutional understanding and political judgment, even as it opened the way to substantial political developments and constitutional amendments for more than a century thereafter.[418]

There are, in responses to men singled out for our attention as Lincoln is, two tendencies among articulate citizens. One tendency is virtually to deify them as people somehow outside and above the Constitution. The other is to denigrate them, even (as in the case of Lincoln) to dismiss them as "racists," "dictators," and the like. Thus, one writer observed:

This talk was given at K. A. M. Isaiah Israel Congregation, Chicago, April 14, 1974, and then in expanded forms at the Center for the Study of Democratic Institutions, Santa Barbara, California, June 19, 1974, and at the First West Coast Conference on Constitutional Law, Los Angeles, September 17–18, 1977. It has been previously published in George Anastaplo, *The Amendments to the Constitution* (Baltimore: Johns Hopkins University Press, 1995), 135–67, 431–37. See also Ronald K. L. Collins, ed., *Constitutional Government in America* (Durham, N.C.: Carolina Academic Press, 1980), 421–26; George Anastaplo, *The Artist as Thinker: From Shakespeare to Joyce* (Athens: Ohio University Press, 1983), 279–83.

The epigraph is taken from Proverbs 25:11.

However admirable the character of the American Constitution, it [is not] the most admirable expression of the regime. The Constitution is the highest American thing, only if one tries to understand the high in the light of the low. It is high because men are not angels, and because we do not have angels to govern us. Its strength lies in its ability to connect the interest of the man with the duty of the place. But the Constitution, in deference to man's nonangelic nature, made certain compromises with slavery. And partly because of those compromises, it dissolved in the presence of a great crisis. The man—or the character of the man—who bore the nation through that crisis, seem[s] to me . . . the highest thing in the American regime.[419]

Thus, also, another writer (in the *Chicago Tribune,* taking issue with an editorial therein on President Lincoln) observed:

A close look at Lincoln, the Civil War, slavery, and the political, social, and economic movements and moral climate of that era convinces me that Lincoln should not be credited with freeing the slaves. Rather he was clearly forced by his critics and the urgencies of war to end chattel slavery or go down in defeat. No thinking person objects to Lincoln's adept use of the art of compromise. What I, as a black descendant of slaves, cannot escape is the fact that he also used that talent to delay as long as he could the recognition of a black human as something other than a piece of property.

This columnist added:

[Lincoln's] insistence that a slave was a property first and a person second resulted in the great Lincoln plan: the freeing of slaves thru (1) Southern state initiative (slavery forever); (2) government payment for slaves to be freed; (3) gradual emancipation (to be complete around the year 1900); (4) government aid to slave states suffering from loss of slaves (more sympathy for the criminal than for the victim); and (5) colonization of blacks out of the United States. To those unsung heroes who didn't permit Lincoln to "push thru his program," this one descendant of slaves belatedly thanks you.[420]

A defense of Lincoln, by the *Tribune* editorial referred to in the column just quoted, had argued that Lincoln's attitudes and policies should not be judged by "today's standards."[421] Such a defense, however, misses the point. Does it not imply that we know better than Lincoln did what should have been done, that our consciences or our understanding or our feelings are somehow superior to his?

It is not only we who believe ourselves in a superior position. Many, perhaps most, of Lincoln's fellow citizens believed at one time or another that their judgments and consciences were also better than his. (At times, all they would give him credit for was a rough honesty, or sincerity.) Even his Secretary of State, William H. Seward, could observe in 1862 of Lincoln's Emancipation Proclamation policy: "[W]e show our sympathy with slavery by emancipating slaves where we cannot reach them, and holding them in bondage where we can set them free."[422]

But a more prudent assessment of that policy than may be found in most of the writings of either our contemporaries or Lincoln's is suggested by an oration delivered by Frederick Douglass on April 14, 1876, "on the occasion of the unveiling of the Freedmen's Monument [in Washington, D.C.] in memory of Abraham Lincoln." The distinguished former slave argued :

> I have said that President Lincoln was a white man, and shared the prejudices common to his countrymen toward the colored race. Looking back to his times and to the condition of his country, we are compelled to admit that this unfriendly feeling on his part may be safely set down as one element of his wonderful success in organizing the loyal American people for the tremendous conflict before them, and bringing them safely through that conflict. His great mission was to accomplish two things: first, to save his country from dismemberment and ruin; and, second, to free his country from the great crime of slavery. To do one or the other, or both, he must have the earnest sympathy and the powerful co-operation of his loyal fellow-countrymen. Without this primary and essential condition to success his efforts must have been vain and utterly fruitless. *Had he put the abolition of slavery before the salvation of the Union, he would have inevitably driven from him a powerful class of the American people and rendered resistance to rebellion impossible.* Viewed from the genuine abolition ground, Mr. Lincoln seemed tardy, cold, dull, and indifferent; but measuring him by the sentiment of his country, a sentiment he was bound as a statesman to consult, he was swift, zealous, radical, and determined. Though Mr. Lincoln shared the prejudices of his white fellow-countrymen against the negro, it is hardly necessary to say that in his heart of hearts he loathed and hated slavery."[423] (Emphasis added.)

Douglass quotes at this point Lincoln's letter of April 4, 1864, "I am naturally anti-slavery. If slavery is not wrong, nothing is wrong. I can not remember when I did not so think, and feel."[424] Whether Lincoln was, in fact, "prejudiced" would depend, first, on what one means by this term; second, on what all the causes were of African slavery; and, third, on what the effects were upon the slaves of their bondage.

Earlier in his 1876 oration, Douglass made an observation about his immediate response to the Emancipation Proclamation, an observation that can provide our point of departure both in considering that Presidential decree and in assessing Lincoln's political judgment:

> Can any colored man, or any white man friendly to the freedom of all men, ever forget the night which followed the first day of January, 1863, when the world was to see if Abraham Lincoln would prove to be as good as his word [pledged the preceding September 22]? I shall never forget that memorable night, when in a distant city I waited and watched at a public meeting, with three thousand others not less anxious than myself, for the word of deliverance which we have heard read today. Nor shall I ever forget the outbursts of joy and thanksgiving that rent the air when the lightning [the telegraph] brought to us the emancipation proclamation. In that happy hour we forgot all delay, and forgot all tardiness, forgot that the President had bribed the rebels to lay down their arms by a promise to withhold the bolt which would smite the slave-system with destruction; and we were thenceforward willing to allow the President all the latitude of time, phraseology, *and every honorable device that statesmanship might require* for the achievement of a great and beneficent measure of liberty and progress.[425] (Emphasis added.)

II

It is Lincoln's statesmanship, as exhibited in the Emancipation Proclamation, with which we will be concerned here. In order to understand what happened in 1862 and 1863 and why, we must remind ourselves of the circumstances in which the Proclamation was issued. The first part, the Preliminary Proclamation, was issued September 22, 1862; the second part, the Final Proclamation, was issued January 1, 1863.

The general setting was, of course, the Civil War, the prosecution of which President Lincoln understood as primarily an effort, in accordance with his constitutional duty, to save the Union from unjustified dismemberment. Thus, he observed (in a statement of August 22, 1862, just one month before his issuance of the Preliminary Proclamation—a statement that angers some of his antislavery critics down to our day):

> I would save the Union. I would save it the shortest way under the Constitution. The sooner the national authority can be restored; the nearer the Union will be "the Union as it was." If there be those who would not save the Union, unless they could at the same time *save* slavery, I do

not agree with them. If there be those who would not save the Union unless they could at the same time *destroy* slavery, I do not agree with them. My paramount object in this struggle *is* to save the Union, and is *not* either to save or to destroy slavery. If I could save the Union without freeing *any* slave I would do it, and if I could save it by freeing *all* the slaves I would do it; and if I could save it by freeing some and leaving others alone I would also do that. What I do about slavery, and the colored race, I do because I believe it helps to save the Union; and what I forbear, I forbear because I do *not* believe it would help to save the Union. I shall do *less* whenever I shall believe what I am doing hurts the cause, and I shall do *more* whenever I shall believe doing more will help the cause.[426]

Lincoln concluded this statement—an open letter to Horace Greeley—with the assurance, "I intend no modification of my oft-expressed personal wish that all men every where could be free."[427] It should be noticed that Lincoln's flexibility, in his effort to save the Union, did not include a willingness to *enslave* anyone for that end. He observed in December 1864:

I repeat the declaration made a year ago, that "while I remain in my present position I shall not attempt to retract or modify the emancipation proclamation, nor shall I return to slavery any person who is free by the terms of that proclamation, or by any of the Acts of Congress." If the people should, by whatever mode or means, make it an Executive duty to re-enslave such persons, another, and not I, must be their instrument to perform it.[428]

This suggests the limits of what Lincoln was willing to do or to say in the service of "statesmanship."

That is, he was not willing to enslave or to reenslave anyone, even though he was willing to live with slavery. But we should be clear what "living with slavery" meant for him (and, it seems, for the Republican Party). It meant that the Union would be preserved, a Union in which slavery would be permitted to continue in those Southern States where it happened to exist at the time Lincoln became President. He did not mean to touch it there but neither did he mean to let it expand into any new territory. Thus, he was a "Free-Soil Man," not an "Abolitionist." But he also believed that if slavery *could* be contained, it would wither away—and in such a way as to leave both former slaves and former masters in the best possible condition for living with one another as free men. In the meantime, a South that continued to remain part of the Union could not help but be moderated by Northern opinion and National power in what it did to Africans, both at home and abroad.

The more radical Abolitionists insisted, "No union with slaveholders." It has been noticed that "[t]he extreme abolitionists, in the supposed purity of their principles, would have abandoned the four million slaves to their fate."[429] The alternative to them, of preserving the Union but destroying slavery, depended upon a successful war effort—and that, it was generally believed, depended upon a united effort on the part of the diverse factions loyal to the Union.

Among those factions were not only the abolitionists—Lincoln figured, no doubt, that they had nowhere else to go—but also Northerners who did not have strong opinions about slavery (but who did care about the Union and its Constitution) and Middle States-men who retained both slaves and loyalty to the Union. These men of the Middle States were not, despite their slavery institutions, simply bad men; nor, for that matter, were the Southerners generally. Lincoln recognized that slavery was essentially a national affliction, that (for the most part) those who were burdened by it would have long since gotten rid of it if they could have seen a way to do so that was both economically and socially feasible.

In this respect, Lincoln appreciated the Country's long past and looked ahead to its even longer future. He recognized why one section of the Country was slave and another was free. He had long hoped so to contain and thereby begin to ease out slavery as to make it possible for two races (both emancipated from the curse of slavery) to live thereafter, whether together or separated, in the best possible way. What was called for, he saw, was neither sentimental moralizing nor bitter recrimination. He was obliged, in any event, so to conduct the war as not to lose the support of the many men in both the Northern and the Middle States who were, at best, indifferent about slavery. He believed, in short, that the goal for which the maximum support could be gathered was that of preserving the Union. Thus, "fighting the war was always secondary to keeping alive the political coalition willing to fight the war."[430]

Once great sacrifices had been made, more could be ventured in explaining how matters truly stood. Once, that is, considerable Northern and Middle States blood had been shed on behalf of the Union, it was possible to direct the attention of the Country to slavery itself. "Slavery was what the rebel states were fighting for, and slavery enabled them to fight for slavery."[431] It had long been recognized by the laws of war that one could deprive an enemy of any property that helped keep him in the field. One could even appropriate such property for one's own use. The slaves were useful, perhaps even essential, property for the Southern war effort. It was on this basis, then, that Lincoln could eventually mobilize Union men to move against Southern slavery, to ally themselves in effect with the freedom-seeking slaves held by the rebels.

The Emancipation Proclamation was thus a military fulfillment of the prophecy with which, we can recall, Lincoln had opened his 1858 "House Divided" Speech:

> "A house divided against itself cannot stand."
> I believe this government cannot endure, permanently half *slave* and half *free.*
> I do not expect the Union to be *dissolved*—I do not expect the house to *fall*—but I do expect it will cease to be divided.
> It will become *all* one thing or *all* the other.
> Either the *opponents* of slavery, will arrest the further spread of it, and place it where the public mind shall rest in the belief that it is in course of ultimate extinction; or its *advocates* will push it forward, till it shall become alike lawful in *all* the States, *old* as well as *new*—*North* as well as *South.*[432]

III

Much of what I have said thus far should be generally familiar. Too much originality in such matters would be suspect, just as it usually should be in Constitutional interpretation. No doubt some may be inclined to question the assessment I have been tacitly making of Lincoln's judgment. That assessment is, to state it plainly, that Lincoln seems most impressive in his surefootedness: he never seemed to err in the principles brought to bear upon the major moves he made in response to the South once he assumed the Presidency.

The mistakes he did make were due not to inadequate principles or to faulty judgment but rather to mistaken information, and in circumstances where he had to rely upon what was told him. Throughout the war, he was remarkably adept, knowing both what he should want and what he was doing. He was, that is, a model of prudential judgment, or at least as fine a practitioner of it as we have perhaps had in government in this Country.

I can best illustrate what I mean—what prudence means in action, and especially in war circumstances (and a civil war, at that, where passions run particularly deep)—by examining in some detail the terms of the two documents that comprise the Emancipation Proclamation. By so doing, we can see once again what the Civil War meant and how it progressed, for the history of that war seems distilled in these documents. Perhaps even more important in the context of this study of Lincoln's constitutionalism, we can see how first-class practical reason works, the kind of reason evident in the Declaration of Independence, the Constitution of 1787, and (it can be said) the Bill of Rights.

The Emancipation Proclamation, unlike the Declaration of Independence and the Constitution, was in a sense the work of one man, and hence of one mind. It was carefully thought out by Lincoln, with only a few suggestions by his Cabinet added after he revealed to them what he proposed to do. It is, we will see, both bold in its conception and disciplined in its execution, the lawyer's art in its perfection. It is also, I suggest, more "American" than either the Declaration or the Constitution, in that its author had been fully shaped by the regime established after 1776.[433]

There are in our effort to grasp what Lincoln did both a challenge and an opportunity. There is the opportunity of fully asserting ourselves as citizens, in that we can, at least for the moment, walk with someone who thought as deeply as any American statesman has about the character, the aspirations, and perhaps the deficiencies of our regime. There is also a challenge, in that we are obliged to strive for a degree of seriousness to which we are no longer accustomed. We have come to rely in our discussions of political things upon the exposés and the superficialities of journalism and upon the abnormalities and irrationalities of psychology—so much so that it is difficult to avoid either irrelevance or sensationalism. We have to make an effort, therefore, to understand the Emancipation Proclamation. But, then, was not the Proclamation issued for the likes of us?

Lincoln challenges us to think; he challenges us to reconstruct the thinking he devoted to the problems he faced. We know that he devoted many hours to the text of the Emancipation Proclamation, especially to the preliminary statement of September 22, 1862. If we are able to work out what he took into account, and why, we can then be assured that we begin to understand the Civil War as an eminently political man did.

To take seriously a statesman's carefully expressed thought is, after all, the best tribute we can pay to him. Such an attempt at the most noble imitation is worthy of our greatest efforts if we are to understand who we are, what we aspire to, and why.

IV

It is said that Lincoln issued no statement or argument to support the Emancipation Proclamation. "He let the paper go forth for whatever it might do."[434] But this is not to say that he never discussed it, for in a preparatory Cabinet meeting he "proceeded to read his Emancipation Proclamation, making remarks on the several parts as he went on, and showing that he had fully considered the whole subject, in all the lights under which it has been presented to him." The discussion of the Proclamation on that occasion, we are told, included "the constitutional question, the war power, the expediency, and the effect of the movement."[435]

It is that discussion in Lincoln's Cabinet which we can, in effect, recreate. We turn first to an examination of the Preliminary Proclamation of September 22, 1862, whose entire text (along with the entire text of the Final Proclamation of January 1, 1863) is set forth in italics in the course of this commentary.[436]

i

> *I, Abraham Lincoln, President of the United States of America, and Commander-in-chief of the Army and Navy thereof, do hereby proclaim and declare that hereafter, as heretofore, the war will be prosecuted for the object of practically restoring the constitutional relation between the United States, and each of the states, and the people thereof, in which states that relation is, or may be suspended, or disturbed.*

This is the first of Lincoln's proclamations as President that opens thus with his name and titles.[437] It is as if he intends to assert from the outset that this statement is especially his doing, that it emanates from his very being—and, insofar as he is a thinking being and this is well thought out, that is so.

This is only the second of his proclamations in which his title as Commander in Chief of the armed forces of the Country is invoked. Such invocation was not customary in Presidential proclamations.[438] We notice in passing the precision in his language: "proclaim and declare that hereafter, as heretofore." Such precision encourages us to expect that what he says throughout may profitably be read with care.

The insistence at the outset upon his status as Commander in Chief anticipates his insistence throughout upon this action as a legitimate war measure. He probably thought then what he was to say a year later (August 26, 1863) to a critic of the Proclamation:

> I think the constitution invests its commander-in-chief, with the law of war, in time of war. The most that can be said, if so much, is, that slaves are property. Is there—has there ever been—any question that by the law of war, property, both of enemies and friends, may be taken when

needed? And is it not needed whenever taking it, helps us, or hurts the enemy? Armies, the world over, destroy enemies' property when they can not use it; and even destroy their own to keep it from the enemy. Civilized belligerents do all in their power to help themselves, or hurt the enemy, except a few things regarded as barbarous or cruel. Among the exceptions are the massacre of vanquished foes, and non-combatants, male and female.[439]

We see in this opening paragraph of the Preliminary Proclamation an insistence as well upon the purpose of this war, that of restoring the constitutional relations among the States. An antislavery crusade from the outset of the Lincoln administration would have been widely regarded as far more questionable than an effort to save the Union—and that was, in many quarters, questionable enough. We should remember that even today more citizens in this Country are in favor of "law and order" than are in favor of "racial justice" or "military justice" or "class justice."

For most citizens, justice is what the law prescribes. They cannot be depended on habitually to accept much more than that or even to want much more than that. Would "much more than that" be for them an unwelcome freedom? Does not Lincoln's approach recognize the limits of public opinion? Does it not recognize that respect for law is more "knowable" and hence reliable than respect for justice?

But, one is obliged to ask, are there not various kinds of constitutions (or master laws)? Should this one have been established in the first place? That is, should the bargain ever have been made, that "constitutional relation" which permitted the States to retain extensive if not exclusive jurisdiction over slaves? Was that bargain so immoral that it should never have been expected to hold? Still, what would have happened if the Southern States had been allowed to depart in peace, whether in 1787 or 1861? Had not the Union by 1861 served better the "Free States," leaving them in a stronger position relative to the "Slave States" than they had been in the beginning?

Granted that the Union is to be preserved, upon what terms can that best be done? Cannot people more readily be led to see that their interest is better served by a stable constitutional regime (by orderly government, a continent-wide market, an absence of threatening neighbors) than by a completely free regime (especially when the freedom yet to be sacrificed for is that of others, not obviously their own)? On the other hand, once a crusade for freedom *is* launched, it is much more difficult to control: passions are much more likely to rage unchecked, whereas constitutionalism has a sense of restraint built into it.[440]

Besides, blatantly to attack slavery *is* to attack property rights and perhaps even the principle of property. Where is the stopping point once one starts down that path? Today, slaveholders; tomorrow, the wealthy? And the day after, anyone of talent or distinction? Is it not sensed by men and women of affairs that property depends somewhat on the arbitrary, on the accidental, on peculiarly local circumstances? Does it not also depend, at least in part, on the bargains that happen to be made from time to time?

Lincoln must insist on the object of "restoring the constitutional relation" as critical, especially in light of what he is about to do. Cannot he effectively do what he is about to do partly because he *has* insisted heretofore on the proper constitutional relation, on constitutional technicalities and niceties?[441] Does one adhere scrupulously to a constitution and the law (as generally understood) in order to be able to rise above them at the propitious moment, thereby leading one's people to a higher or more solid constitutional plateau than they are accustomed to?

We notice the emphasis upon restoration. Things will go back to what they were—except of course for the opinion that some had held that secession was constitutionally proper. But full restoration will be impossible once that particular opinion is disavowed, for the status of slavery will never be the same again. A refounding is thus anticipated, something that is celebrated in the Gettysburg Address. Still, the closest the South can now come to having the original Constitutional relation restored is by quickly acceding to the terms of the Preliminary Proclamation, thereby not "permitting" Lincoln to declare *any* slaves emancipated at this time.

We should notice as well that it is not only the South that threatens the Constitutional regime. Thaddeus Stevens, one of the radical abolitionist leaders in Congress, had proclaimed that there was no longer any Constitution and reported that he was weary of hearing the "never-ending gabble about the sacredness of the Constitution."[442]

Finally, we notice that the "constitutional relation" has not been destroyed; rather, it has been "suspended, or disturbed" in some States—and it is there that immediate restoration is called for. Self-preservation calls for such restoration—that self-preservation which we shall later on see to be so critical a guide for human action.

Much more can be said about this first paragraph. But we have said enough to permit us to pass on to the subsequent paragraphs.

ii

That it is my purpose, upon the next meeting of Congress to again recommend the adoption of a practical measure tendering pecuniary aid to the free acceptance or rejection of all slave-states, so called, the people whereof may not then be in

*rebellion against the United States, and which states, may then have voluntarily
adopted, or thereafter may voluntarily adopt, immediate, or gradual abolishment
of slavery within their respective limits; and that the effort to colonize persons of
African descent, with their consent, upon this continent, or elsewhere, with the
previously obtained consent of the Governments existing there, will be continued.*

Having laid in his opening paragraph the groundwork—that is, to
paraphrase, "We are determined to restore the authoritative constitutional
relation"—Lincoln can then indicate what would be an improvement consistent with such restored constitutional relation: compensated emancipation by nonrebellious slaveholders. This offer is extended, it seems, to all
Slave States, "so called," those now in rebellion and those that had never
been in rebellion against the United States. It was unlikely that the rebellious States would be won over, but what about the other Slave States, the
loyal Middle States? They would not be directly affected by the impending
proclamation, but was there not for them here, as there had been the preceding March, the suggestion that they would do better to "sell" their slaves
now to the United States than to be deprived of them later upon the collapse of their ever more vulnerable systems of slavery?

Is not at least a useful appearance of fairness achieved by Lincoln's
offer to pay for what he considered himself empowered, if not even obliged, to take? Does not this reinforce the Lincolnian position that it is not the
slaveholder, but slavery, which is the critical problem here, that it is not punishment or political and social reform but rather a reaffirmed Union that
he is after? If it is to be a Union in which the traditional role of the States
is respected, it is up to the States "voluntarily" to adopt a program of abolishment of slavery.

Does he use "abolishment" rather than "abolition" in order to soften
what he is asking for? That is, *abolition* may still have been seen, in its
abruptness, as far too radical, even by many antislavery Northerners.
Besides, Lincoln cannot abolish the institutions of slavery in any State: he
can only emancipate certain people in certain places at a certain time. Abolition (as it had come to be spoken of in the preceding decades) required a
more comprehensive change of a permanent legislative character than any
President was constitutionally capable of making on his own authority.

The reference to "gradual abolishment" recognizes not only concerns
among the public at large about the danger of precipitate action but those
of Lincoln as well. What was to be done with the millions of people "of
African descent" if they should be suddenly cut loose from their accustomed moorings in this Country? Would they thereafter be exploited even
more than they had long been? Would they constitute a danger to the com-

munity at large? Could they be expected to know what to do with themselves? The difficulties seen then in any program of wholesale emancipation remain to a considerable extent in American race relations down to this day. Was time needed, then as now, to effect a proper transition? Or, failing that, should the removal of most (if not all) Africans from this Country be planned, for their own good as well as that of the Caucasians? Did Lincoln have to explore alternatives in this way, if only to indicate that he understood what many of his countrymen, North and South, were concerned about? By so indicating, did he not make it more likely that the public would eventually accept whatever he decided upon and offered as the least objectionable way of achieving the desired end? If he had failed to appreciate alternative positions, he probably would not have been trusted the way that he came to be.

But to "appreciate" is not necessarily to agree; it is, rather, to grasp why another might make the mistakes he is making. Slavery was, to say the least, a mistake, not only a moral mistake but (perhaps even more important for the future of the regime) a constitutional mistake. Was not American constitutionalism, with its rule of law and its dependence upon substantial equality, bound eventually to undermine slavery or to be undermined by it? Was not slavery somehow hostile to the principles of the American regime? The Slave States depended upon the law-abidingness of the Free States—upon the respect of Free States for such Constitutional arrangements as the Fugitive Slave Clause—in order to be protected in an institution that was, in a sense, lawless.

Finally, we notice the double emphasis upon the necessity for consent: the consent of those to be colonized, the consent of those governments that would receive the colonists. This, along with the deference to voluntariness on the part of the Slave States, points up once again the vulnerability of slavery in any regime in which consent of the governed is made as much of as it has always been in ours.[443]

iii

That on the first day of January in the year of our Lord, one thousand eight hundred and sixty-three, all persons held as slaves within any state, or designated part of a state, the people whereof shall then be in rebellion against the United States shall be then, thenceforward, and forever free; and the executive government of the United States, including the military and naval authority thereof, will recognize and maintain the freedom of such persons, and will do no act or acts to repress such persons, or any of them, in any efforts they may make for their actual freedom.

One offer has just been made, that of compensated emancipation. Now comes another offer to this effect: "You can keep your slaves, if you wish, so long as you return to your allegiance." This once again emphasizes that Lincoln seeks to preserve the Union, not to destroy slavery. One hundred days are provided rebellious slaveholders in which to take advantage of this offer. Some in the North, if not also others abroad, still needed to be assured that Southern property and the American Constitution were being dealt with fairly.

"All persons held as slaves": does not this formulation permit the inference that they are not truly slaves? One who is called a slave may be no more than someone held as a slave, perhaps as a prisoner of war. May he merely be regarded as a slave? Is not slavery as practiced in North America at that time only conventional slavery, with its conventions arbitrarily guided by color differences and based primarily upon force? Yet, even if slavery originated in injustice, it might have compounded the original injustice to have tried to free all slaves at once or to have freed them one way rather than another.

Notice that Lincoln can command only the response of the "executive government of the United States." The Courts and Congress act independently. We can see in the second paragraph of the Preliminary Proclamation that it is Congress, not the Executive, which can provide the "pecuniary aid" Lincoln speaks of there.

Notice also that freedom comes in two stages, so to speak: recognized freedom and actual freedom. Recognized freedom is what comes to someone from the sayings and actions of others; actual freedom depends more upon one's own efforts. It should go without saying that not everyone who is recognized to be free is actually free. Men who have lived for generations in slavery may need generations of purgation and training before they become actually free—as the Israelites' forty years in the desert suggest.

iv

That the executive will, on the first day of January aforesaid, by proclamation, designate the States, and parts of states, if any, in which the people thereof respectively, shall then be in rebellion against the United States; and the fact that any state, or the people thereof shall, on that day be, in good faith represented in the Congress of the United States, by members chosen thereto, at elections wherein a majority of the qualified voters of such state shall have participated, shall, in the absence of strong countervailing testimony, be deemed conclusive evidence that such state and the people thereof, are not then in rebellion against the United States.

A promise is made as to what Lincoln will do on January 1: designate the States, or parts of States, if any, in which the people thereof shall then be in rebellion. Is not that to be the principal purpose of that January 1 proclamation? What follows from such designation will have already been indicated in this September 22 proclamation. Little more needs to be added on January 1: the emancipation then will even have the effect of a promise fulfilled. That revolutionary step will be living up to a bargain already struck. There is about this sequence a psychological master-stroke.

By thus pointing ahead, Lincoln succeeded in shifting attention to an occasion that was itself expected and even demanded by a kind of contract. (The designation required for that day was, for the most part, perfunctory. Most of the States designated could have been designated by anyone; as we shall see, they in effect designated themselves.) Lincoln succeeded so well in shifting attention to the expected measure (on January 1) from the extraordinary measure (of September 22) that the January 1 statement (which is, except for its concluding language, more pedestrian) has become the one that is remembered and reproduced in anthologies, more so than the earlier one that had truly been decisive.

Notice Lincoln's precise use of "if any"—"the States, and parts of states, if any." After all, an offer has been made; it must not be assumed in advance that it will be rejected by anyone. To do so would be virtually to admit that it is a mere form (as was seen a half-century later, for example, in the world-shaking July 1914 ultimatum delivered by Austria-Hungary to the defiant Serbians). It would, besides, deny the rationality and hence the humanity of those in rebellion. They must be considered as, in principle, open to argument. They remain American citizens, whatever they may happen to believe.

Notice, also, that the decisive indication that a State is not in rebellion is its good-faith representation in the Congress. Lincoln says, in effect, "If you wish to avoid the harsh effects of this necessary military measure, exercise your rights as free men; send representatives of your choice to Congress; return to your seats in the national legislature and resume the duty and power you have always had there to help run the Country." Does not this approach acknowledge the fundamentally republican character of the Country, a character to which the military power is ultimately subservient? We need not concern ourselves here with whether Congress would have immediately accepted such representatives from the States that had been in rebellion for almost two years. It suffices to notice that republican standards were apparently relied upon even in those trying times.

Notice, finally, that Lincoln in effect cedes to rebellious States the power to decide for themselves whether they are again to be in good standing. "[I]n the absence of strong countervailing testimony," their recourse to Congressional elections will "be deemed conclusive evidence" that they "are not then in rebellion against the United States." Is there not something generous about this also? Indeed, does not generosity pervade the Proclamation, the generosity of a truly magnanimous man who can be both shrewd and knowing about the usefulness as well as the limitations of generosity?

v

That attention is hereby called to an act of Congress entitled "An act to make an additional Article of War" approved March 13, 1862, and which act is in the words and figure following:

> *Be it enacted by the Senate and House of Representatives of the United States of America in Congress assembled, That hereafter the following shall be promulgated as an additional article of war for the government of the army of the United States, and shall be obeyed and observed as such:*
>
> *Article——. All officers or persons in the military or naval service of the United States are prohibited from employing any of the forces under their respective commands for the purpose of returning fugitives from service or labor, who may have escaped from any persons to whom such service or labor is claimed to be due, and any officer who shall be found guilty by a court-martial of violating this article shall be dismissed from the service.*
>
> *Sec. 2. And be it further enacted, That this act shall take effect from and after its passage.*

Also [attention is hereby called] to the ninth and tenth sections of an act entitled "An Act to suppress Insurrection, to punish Treason and Rebellion, to seize and confiscate property of rebels, and for other purposes," approved July 17, 1862, and which sections are in the words and figures following:

> *Sec. 9. And be it further enacted, That all slaves of persons who shall hereafter be engaged in rebellion against the government of the United States, or who shall in any way give aid or comfort thereto, escaping from such persons and taking refuge within the lines of the army; and all slaves captured from such persons or deserted by them and coming under the control of the government of the United States; and all slaves of such persons found on [or] being within any place occupied by rebel forces and afterwards occupied by the forces of the United States, shall be deemed captives of war, and shall be forever free of their servitude and not again held as slaves.*
>
> *Sec. 10. And be it further enacted, That no slave escaping into any State, Territory, or the District of Columbia, from any other State, shall be*

delivered up, or in any way impeded or hindered of his liberty, except for crime, or some offence against the laws, unless the person claiming said fugitive shall first make oath that the person to whom the labor or service of such fugitive is alleged to be due is his lawful owner, and has not borne arms against the United States in the present rebellion, nor in any way given aid and comfort thereto; and no person engaged in the military or naval service of the United States shall, under any pretence whatever, assume to decide on the validity of the claim of any person to the service or labor of any other person, or surrender up any such person to the claimant, on pain of being dismissed from the service.

And I do hereby enjoin upon and order all persons engaged in the military and naval service of the United States to observe, obey, and enforce, within their respective spheres of service, the act, and sections above recited.[444]

This passage draws attention to two acts of Congress: one prohibits military officers from returning certain fugitive slaves, and the other (in the sections quoted from it) declares certain fugitive slaves free and places restrictions upon the return of certain other fugitive slaves to their masters. The passage thereafter orders "all persons engaged in the military and naval service of the United States to observe, obey, and enforce, within their respective spheres of service, the act, and sections above recited."

What is all this doing in here? Perhaps it is partly to suggest that what Lincoln is now doing is not without Congressional precedent. This passage may address the more conservative Unionists. They are assured that all this is not simply executive usurpation on the President's part, that there may even be some Congressional guidance for what the President is doing. Perhaps, also, it is partly to counter the hostility of abolitionists who would not like an emancipation decree framed in so qualified and so partial a manner as this one is. Such singleminded critics are reminded that at least the notorious Fugitive Slave Clause of the Constitution has been in effect suspended, permitting "*captives* of war" to become "forever *free*," an intriguing juxtaposition of terms that Lincoln surely appreciated.

In addition, there are other hints. The first act that Lincoln calls attention to is reproduced in its entirety, including the superfluous enacting clause (the title of the act, also given, would have sufficed) and the immediate-effect clause. But only two sections of the second act are called to our attention, in marked (and intended?) contrast to what was done with the first act. Does Lincoln thereby tacitly repudiate the other sections of the second act?

We cannot, on this occasion, explore this question. It suffices to notice that several of the sections of the second act that Lincoln does not mention here are quite harsh, authorizing death sentences and comprehensive confiscation of all property. That harsh spirit is foreign to what Lincoln is interested in establishing in the Proclamation. Property in slaves is to be confiscated, so to speak; but, after all, free human beings will thereby come into being.

The emphasis here is upon fugitive slaves. Does not this suggest who may be able to take advantage at once of the Proclamation—those who flee from rebel territory? Is not an implicit invitation issued? This anticipates and to some extent deals with the complaint that the Proclamation emancipates only where the Union army is not.

Finally, we cannot help but notice that the language of Congress is less precise, less carefully thought out, than Lincoln's. Is this intended to show the reader that Lincoln is truly more worthy of being taken seriously? In any event, the Proclamation will free all slaves within the designated areas, regardless of whether their masters are able or willing to "make oath" about their constant loyalty to the United States—and no matter what compensation they may happen either to be entitled to or to be in a position to collect.

vi

And the executive will in due time recommend that all citizens of the United States who shall have remained loyal thereto throughout the rebellion, shall (upon the restoration of the constitutional relation between the United States, and their respective states, and people, if that relation shall have been suspended or disturbed) be compensated for all losses by acts of the United States, including the loss of slaves.

Once again, we see that the demands of war are not to be permitted to obscure permanently either the desire or the duty to see justice done. Certainly, loyalty must be noticed and, if possible, rewarded. And, it has to be said, the United States should recognize that there has existed up to now an acknowledged property interest in slaves that must still be taken account of. Does this remark (the closing one among the substantive paragraphs of the Preliminary Proclamation) appeal to the apprehensive Middle States Unionists, just as the preceding passage incorporating the acts of Congress appealed in large part to impatient Abolitionists? Do we once again see that Lincoln must keep quite divergent, but vitally necessary, horses yoked together if the war chariot is to advance?

vii

In witness whereof, I have hereunto set my hand, and caused the seal of the United States to be affixed.

This is the standard testamentary statement for such proclamations. We will return to it at the end of the Final Proclamation.

viii

Done at the City of Washington, this twenty second day of September, in the year of our Lord, one thousand eight hundred and sixty two, and of the Independence of the United States, the eighty seventh.

The eighty-seventh year hearkens back to 1776 and the Declaration of Independence. It is that "eighty seventh," reminding as well of both the Northwest Ordinance and the Constitution, which Lincoln will transform into "four score and seven" in November of 1863 at Gettysburg.

Why September 22? Lincoln had planned to issue this Preliminary Proclamation some weeks earlier (in fact, in July). But he had been dissuaded by Seward's argument that he should at least wait until the Union forces won another victory rather than make the proclamation seem an act of desperation—for it had been a time of one defeat after another. Then there came the "victory" of Antietam, in the middle of September 1862—and, a few days later, the Emancipation Proclamation.[445]

Did Lincoln choose an interval of one hundred days so that the final proclamation would fall on New Year's Day, a day of rebirth and rededication?

ix

There is, in the handwritten original of the Preliminary Proclamation of September 22, 1862, the repetition of "sixty two," in this fashion: "in the year of our Lord, one thousand, eight hundred and sixty two, and sixty two, and of the Independence of the United States the eighty seventh." This passage is in the handwriting of a clerk.[446]

Here, for the only time in this commentary upon the text of the Emancipation Proclamation, I venture to move from what Lincoln thought and intended, to what may have been "unconscious" (and hence "inspired"?). This inadvertent repetition by a clerk of "sixty two" suggests that he, at least, made much of the date—as if to emphasize, "It is late 1862, not early 1861. We Loyalists have tried for a year and a half to put down this dreadful rebellion with conventional measures. We can now proceed in good faith to a measure that we have had to be cautious in using, not only because it challenges long-standing constitutional arrangements (after all, it is a constitution we are defending) but also because it conforms to and gratifies the deepest desires of those of us who have always hated slavery. It *is* 1862!"

I must leave further poetic probings of the unconscious (or of the providential?) to others. Still, one can wonder whether Lincoln himself ever noticed this slip of the pen and, if so, what he (a master psychologist) thought of it.

We turn now to the Final Proclamation (of January 1, 1863). Much of what might be said about the parts of this proclamation has already been said in my review of the Preliminary Proclamation. We can therefore be brief.

x

Whereas, on the twentysecond day of September, in the year of our Lord one thousand eight hundred and sixty two, a proclamation was issued by the President of the United States, containing, among other things, the following, towit:

> *"That on the first day of January, in the year of our Lord one thousand eight hundred and sixty-three, all persons held as slaves within any State or designated part of a State, the people whereof shall then be in rebellion against the United States, shall be then, thenceforward, and forever free; and the Executive Government of the United States, including the military and naval authority thereof, will recognize and maintain the freedom of such persons, and will do no act or acts to repress such persons, or any of them, in any efforts they may make for their actual freedom.*
>
> *"That the Executive will, on the first day of January aforesaid, by proclamation, designate the States and parts of States, if any, in which the people thereof, respectively, shall then be in rebellion against the United States; and the fact that any State, or the people thereof, shall on that day be, in good faith, represented in the Congress of the United States by members chosen thereto at elections wherein a majority of the qualified voters of such State shall have participated, shall, in the absence of strong countervailing testimony, be deemed conclusive evidence that such State, and the people thereof, are not then in rebellion against the United States."*

A solemn version of the date of the Preliminary Proclamation is given, that version used in the final paragraph of that proclamation. We recall that when the dates were given for Acts of Congress in that first proclamation, simpler versions of their dates were given (that is, "March 13, 1862," "July 17, 1862"). Is a proclamation somehow of greater dignity than an act of Congress? Does the Presidency, properly employed, tend to have a greater dignity than the Congress? Is this one reason why a Presidential proclamation about Southern slaves means more, and has a greater effect, than Congressional enactments? Does the Commander in Chief of the armed forces in time of war tend to seem the decisive ruler of a country, especially when the war is a civil war—for that makes war comprehensive?

These questions lead us to notice that there is nothing said about Congress in the Final Proclamation. Lincoln quoted at length from Congress in the Preliminary Proclamation; here he quotes only from himself. Both Congress and the States take second place in the constitutional drama now being enacted. They have served their purpose, they have had their chance—and now the President must get on with conducting the war to save the Union.

We also notice that nothing is said about compensation for voluntary emancipation; nor is anything said about compensation for loss of slaves by loyal slaveowners. Both of these had been proposed, as promised, to Congress. But nothing substantial had come from the proposals. (Later, the Fourteenth Amendment would forbid such compensation by any government in the United States.) The emphasis is now upon this emancipation and its consequences.

A new stage has been reached in the war—but a stage that, it can be argued, developed constitutionally as well as naturally from the preceding stage. This proclamation gets right down to business. There are no frills or offers or alternatives, but rather a judgment set forth in prosaic yet somehow solemn terms.

xi

Now, therefore I, Abraham Lincoln, President of the United States, by virtue of the power in me vested as Commander-in-Chief, of the Army and Navy of the United States in time of actual armed rebellion against authority and government of the United States, and as a fit and necessary war measure for suppressing said rebellion, do, on this first day of January, in the year of our Lord one thousand eight hundred and sixty three, and in accordance with my purpose so to do publicly proclaimed for the full period of one hundred days, from the day first above mentioned, order and designate as the States and parts of States wherein the people thereof respectively, are this day in rebellion against the United States, the following, to wit:

Arkansas, Texas, Louisiana, (except the Parishes of St. Bernard, Plaquemines, Jefferson, St. Johns, St. Charles, St. James, Ascension, Assumption, Terrebonne, Lafourche, St. Mary, St. Martin, and Orleans, including the City of New Orleans) Mississippi, Alabama, Florida, Georgia, South-Carolina, North-Carolina, and Virginia, (except the fortyeight counties designated as West Virginia, and also the counties of Berkley, Accomac, Northampton, Elizabeth-City, York, Princess Ann, and Norfolk, including the cities of Norfolk & Portsmouth); and which excepted parts are, for the present, left precisely as if this proclamation were not issued.

Lincoln's status of Commander in Chief is again emphasized and is reinforced by the references to "time of actual armed rebellion" and "fit and necessary war measure". A solemn version of the date is again relied on as Lincoln draws in this decree upon the full majesty of the language as well as upon the full force of the war power.

But the war power is properly to be employed for a specified purpose. It must be used discriminatingly, if constitutional government is truly to be defended. This is recognized by the exceptions Lincoln insisted upon making, in the application of his proclamation, for those parishes in Louisiana and those counties in Virginia where Union forces were already in control. Might not Lincoln also have thought that such exceptions made his policy seem discriminating and hence contributed to its effectiveness?

Secretary of the Treasury Salmon P. Chase argued against such exceptions and kept after the President thereafter to extend the Emancipation Proclamation to all of Virginia and Louisiana. Lincoln replied to him on September 2, 1863:

> Knowing your great anxiety that the emancipation proclamation shall now be applied to certain parts of Virginia and Louisiana which were exempted from it last January, I state briefly what appear to me to be difficulties in the way of such a step. The original proclamation has no constitutional or legal justification, except as a military measure. The exemptions were made because the military necessity did not apply to the exempted localities. Nor does that necessity apply to them now any more than it did then. If I take the step must I not do so, without the argument of military necessity, and so, without any argument, except the one that I think the measure politically expedient, and morally right? Would I not thus give up all footing upon constitution or law? Would I not thus be in the boundless field of absolutism? Could this pass unnoticed, or unresisted? Could it fail to be perceived that without any further stretch, I might do the same in Delaware, Maryland, Kentucky, Tennessee, and Missouri; and even change any law in any State?[447]

Notice the words "Could this pass unnoticed?" "Could it fail to be perceived . . . ?" It is important for constitutional government what the people of the Country understand their officers to be doing and on what authority. It is also important that the people be trained to expect the basis of governmental authority to be evident, even when extraordinary measures have to be resorted to.

Yet, we might ask, in what sense *are* the "excepted parts . . . left precisely as if this proclamation were not issued"? Should it not have been evident to all—was it not evident to (and perhaps even intended by) Lincoln—that if the proclamation was effective with respect to the States and parts of States listed, then the system of slavery would collapse not only in the rebellious States but also in the loyal Middle States (about which Lincoln always had to be concerned) and in the "excepted" counties and parishes of Virginia and Louisiana?

The emancipation of so massive a body of slaves made slavery itself quite vulnerable in the Country at large. Such slavery as then existed in North America could find intelligent defenders in this Country only if virtually all members of the slaves' race were subjected to slavery. If a significant number were free, and could develop themselves as free and responsible residents here, an argument based upon the supposed natural basis for African slavery would no longer be tenable. Slavery could not survive, in a regime such as ours, if it clearly rested as much as it would have had to rest (after the Emancipation Proclamation) upon obvious accidents of geography and history. The moral basis of slavery would have been undermined insofar as everyday morality rests in large part upon the customary and the uniform.

Consider finally, in this passage, how the States are listed: they are not alphabetical; nor in the order of admission to the Union; nor in order of secession. Rather, Lincoln begins with the only landlocked state among them (Arkansas), and then moves along the coast of the continent, starting with the State farthest away from him (Texas) and coming closer and closer to Washington (ending with Virginia). It is as if he sweeps them all in to himself. (States are listed differently in other proclamations.) Lincoln displays here a methodical and yet imaginative turn of mind, a combination familiar to us in poets.

In this way, too, we should be reassured to notice, he avoids "the boundless field of absolutism." This means that we can safely think about what he is doing, for then we are thinking about thinking rather than trying to think about that which is irrational or accidental and hence not truly knowable.

xii

And by virtue of the power, and for the purpose aforesaid, I do order and declare that all persons held as slaves within said designated States, and parts of States, are, and henceforward shall be free; and that the Executive government of the United States, including the military and naval authorities thereof, will recognize and maintain the freedom of said persons.

We see here brought to completion what had been promised on September 22. We again see that Lincoln's formal control is limited to "the Executive government of the United States." Most of what one might say about this paragraph has already been anticipated in this commentary.

But what about "order and declare"? Perhaps he understands that he can order only some things, that he can merely express a strong preference or hope with respect to other things. Consider other pairs of terms in this paragraph: "are, and henceforward shall be free"; "recognize and maintain the freedom of said persons". Does he order such persons to be free now? Does he order such freedom to be recognized now? He can do that, perhaps. But he cannot order that such freedom exist "henceforward" or that it be maintained. Will not that depend upon future governments and future circumstances, perhaps ultimately upon the judgment and will of the American people, including the freed slaves and their descendants?

I note in passing that "maintain" had been put into the Preliminary Proclamation at the suggestion of a cabinet member; but Lincoln had misgivings about it. He was reluctant, he indicated, to promise something he did not know he could perform. He retained "maintain" here but perhaps not without hinting at his reservations.

xiii

And I hereby enjoin upon the people so declared to be free to abstain from all violence, unless in necessary self-defense; and I recommend to them that, in all cases when allowed, they labor faithfully for reasonable wages.

We see here one great problem of the future, a problem that continues to this day. In dealing with the freed people, Lincoln recognizes what he can and cannot say. He can, as President, enjoin them to "abstain from all violence." That is what the law ordains. But he cannot enjoin them to work. If they are truly free men, they must decide that on their own. Here he can only recommend. They can be urged to work faithfully; their prospective employers are implicitly instructed to pay them reasonable wages. Emancipation is one thing; preparation for self-government is quite another—for that takes time and such willingness as Lincoln himself had both to face up to facts and to restrain himself. What can be proclaimed, therefore, is neither virtue nor genuine freedom but, at best, the removal of chains and a provision of opportunities. Education and training, as well as experience, must thereafter do their part.

Are not the serious problems with immediate comprehensive abolition reflected in the virtually complete silence about what is to become of the emancipated slaves? Is it sensible to expect them to manage at once on their own like other free men? Is not this why Lincoln had argued again and again for gradual, compensated emancipation, a mode of emancipation that could both motivate and empower masters to provide a proper transition for their slaves into a free life? Such a mode would have had the minimum of bitterness and of general poverty (due to the passions and ravages of war) to contend with.

Violence on the part of freed slaves is forbidden. Lincoln is speaking here to longstanding fears among slaveowners of bloody slave rebellions, fears which Middle States Unionists as well as Northern humanitarians shared. If such violence had broken out on a large scale, the Union cause might have been discredited. The old concerns of slaveholders and the repressive measures in the South might have then appeared justified. Still, violence is understood to be permitted to the freed slaves for "necessary self-defense." Is this a law of nature? Would it be self-defense to use force against the master who wants to retain his emancipated slave?

We see in this "necessary self-defense" an echo of the "necessary war measure" Lincoln had declared himself obliged to resort to in defense of the Union. Indeed, self-defense had promoted and permitted the original compromises with slavery in 1776 and 1787—that is, the defense of the several States, threatened by European powers and by continual war among themselves.

xiv

And I further declare and make known, that such persons of suitable condition, will be received into the armed service of the United States to garrison forts, positions, stations, and other places, and to man vessels of all sorts in said service.

This sentence is quietly stated; the use of "declare and make known" almost suggests he is reporting something rather than ordering something—reporting something that is happening, that is bound to happen. The military uses to which freed slaves may be put are not immediately, or obviously, combative. Lincoln still has to think of Southern fears and Northern prejudices, both of which can lead to actions harmful either to the slaves or to Lincoln's government. There would be something shocking, perhaps even unnatural, many must have felt, in former slaves fighting against their former masters. This was a development that took some time getting used to, but it eventually came about on a significant scale.

Southerners themselves were finally reduced to freeing slaves who would serve in their army. This too testified to Lincoln's policy as a genuine war measure, a war measure that helped make chattel slavery thereafter untenable among Americans.

xv

And upon this act, sincerely believed to be an act of justice, warranted by the Constitution, upon military necessity, I invoke the considerate judgment of mankind, and the gracious favor of Almighty God.

This is perhaps the most complicated sentence in the two stages of the Proclamation. We must settle on this occasion for only a few preliminary observations about it. Interpretation is made even more difficult when one understands these words to have been supplied (for the most part?) by a member of the Cabinet, not by Lincoln himself. If that should be so, what appears to be complexity may only be confusion.

Still, a few questions may be in order: "this act" is considered to be "warranted by the Constitution, upon military necessity." Is it done because it is warranted? Or it is done for some other reason, and the power to do so is provided by "military necessity"? An "act of justice" is pointed to as somehow involved here. Is this the true purpose? Or is it understood that a respect for justice is itself good military strategy? Notice that it is regarded as certainly a "military necessity" but that it is only "sincerely believed" to be "an act of justice." Is the truth about justice sometimes far harder to arrive at than truth about military strategy? The President had delayed a long time in doing this. He had had to decide what the right thing to do was, and that depended not only upon military strategy, natural right, and political circumstances, but also upon his Constitutional powers, duties, and limitations.

The "considerate judgment of mankind" reminds us of the Declaration of Independence's "Opinions of Mankind" and "a candid World." Mankind has "judgment"; Almighty God has "gracious favor." It is not for human beings to assess what moves God or, indeed, to determine whether God moves at all. They, it seems, must do what they think right, and then hope or pray for the best. The references to both mankind and God serve to remind the citizen that immediate, personal concerns should not be permitted to usurp in us the proper, one might say the constitutional, role of the truly human, the justly divine.

xvi

In witness whereof, I have hereunto set my hand and caused the seal of the United States to be affixed.

It is said that the issuance of the Emancipation Proclamation was delayed on New Year's Day because when it came to be signed that morning, it was discovered that another formal testamentary paragraph, one appropriate for another kind of proclamation, had been used in the place of this one in the official copy. It had to be sent back to the State Department to be redone. (It is this, along with a reception Lincoln had had to attend for much of the day, that contributed to the delay indicated in one of the passages I have quoted from Frederick Douglass. Compare the earlier inadvertent use of "sixty two.")

We can see even here, in constitutional matters as in worship, the importance of forms, of appearances, and perhaps of chance.

xvii

Done at the City of Washington, this first day of January, in the year of our Lord one thousand eight hundred and sixty three, and of the Independence of the United States of America the eighty-seventh.

Nothing more (in addition to what has been said about the conclusion of the Preliminary Proclamation) needs to be said about this concluding sentence, except perhaps to notice that it *is* in the City of Washington that the decisive declaration against slavery was issued, that system of servitude which even the slaveholders of Washington's generation, including Washington himself, can be said to have looked forward to ending in a responsible manner as the Republic matured.

A responsible examination of the Emancipation Proclamation suggests that if Lincoln, as Washington's legitimate successor, could have constitutionally "save[d] the Union" either by "sav[ing] slavery" or by "destroy[ing] slavery," he would have preferred to do so by taking advantage of this opportunity to destroy slavery. Indeed, to preserve the Union on Lincoln's terms was, even without the Emancipation Proclamation, to destroy slavery—and this the Southern Secessionists had known for years.

V

Three topics remain to be discussed—but not at length—in this commentary. I will suggest the sorts of things that need to be considered.

There is needed, first, a consideration of the effects of the Emancipation Proclamation. One should note first and foremost that it did work—in that it promoted the flight of slaves from the South, in that it undermined not only the economy but also the moral standing of the

South both at home and in Europe, and in that it contributed a significant military force of freed slaves to the North. We have seen that, in order for such a policy to work, timing was critical. Also critical was that the President should have had a clear notion of standards and goals. This means that his ultimate considerations drew upon prudence and justice more than upon liberty or equality or natural rights (as these are generally understood).

As the Union army moved South, thereafter, it "naturally" left freed slaves in its wake. This had, it seems, a great moral effect upon what the North was doing and what it was seen to be doing. For example, the Proclamation began to emancipate Lincoln himself and people like him, as well as the Constitution itself and the very idea of republican government, from the burden of slavery.

We can see as well that ideas do matter in political life. One might even say that only ideas matter for long. That which we now call "symbolic" can be very important. One should, in considering such matters, begin with the fact that the Proclamation was at once regarded as important. Only the Thirteenth Amendment, abolishing all slavery in the United States (proposed by Congress early in 1865 and ratified by the States later that year), produced as enthusiastic a response from the antislavery people as the Proclamation had done. To be regarded as important is, in political matters, to be at least somewhat important.

It should be evident to us, upon thinking about the Proclamation and its effect, how critical the opinion of the public is for law and, in turn, how critical law is for morality and for civilization. Above all, it should be evident to us how critical it is to know what one is (and is not) doing—as well as to know what one cannot or should not do.

It should also be evident to us that the Proclamation and the war effort it served have had questionable effects as well. The ascendancy of Executive power in the United States was made eminently respectable because of the Civil War; the substantial separation of powers was undermined, as were the States; the war power was magnified; and the notion of "total war" was made respectable.

Should not a political man of Lincoln's understanding and temperament now devote himself to redefining, for our changed circumstances, what is now appropriate in our constitutional relations? Would not Lincoln himself insist today that practical (but not necessarily constitutional) reforms, some of a far-reaching character, should be made if we are to address ourselves sensibly and safely to the new (as well as to the age-old) challenges that confront us?

VI

That is one topic which should be developed. I have already touched upon my second remaining topic in this commentary—that which addresses itself to what we can learn, of a more general nature, from our study of the Emancipation Proclamation.

We again see, of course, what prudence can mean in a particular situation—and hence what prudence itself means. One must adjust to one's materials, including the prejudices and limitations of one's community. Such adjustment often includes settling for less than the best. But the most useful adjustment is not possible unless one knows what the very best would be. We can also sense, upon the study of the doings of prudent men and women, how important chance is in human affairs—and hence how limited we often are in what we can do, even when we know what should be done.

We should notice as well, and guard against, that fashionable opinion which dismisses what is reasonable and deliberate as cold-blooded and calculating. It is important, however, if one is to be most effective as a reasonable, deliberate, and deliberating human being, to seem other than cold-blooded and calculating—that is, it is important to be a good politician. Once again we are reminded of the importance in political things of appearances, of a healthy respect for the opinions (and hence the errors as well as the sound intuition) of mankind.

Certainly, self-righteousness should always be held in check, but not always a show of indignation. Still, indignation even in a good cause should be carefully watched. Consider, for example, the famous abolitionist William Lloyd Garrison's 1831 promise:

> I will be as harsh as truth, and as uncompromising as justice. On this subject I do not wish to think, or to speak, or write, with moderation. No! No! Tell a man whose house is on fire to give a moderate alarm; tell him to moderately rescue his wife from the hand of the ravisher; tell the mother to gradually extricate her babe from the fire into which it has fallen;—but urge me not to use moderation in a cause like the present. I am in earnest—I will not equivocate—I will not excuse—I will not retreat a single inch—AND I WILL BE HEARD.[448]

Such passion may be useful, even necessary, if great evils are to be corrected, but only if a Lincoln should become available to supervise what finally happens and to deal prudently with others (zealous friends and sincere enemies alike) with a remarkable, even godlike, magnanimity.

VII

Now, to my final topic for the future, which I preface with three quotations which can serve to illuminate as well this commentary on the Emancipation Proclamation.

The first quotation is from the New Testament. "Behold, I send you forth as sheep in the midst of wolves: be ye therefore wise as serpents, and harmless as doves."[449]

The second is from Stephen A. Douglas who (it will be recalled) said of Lincoln, in the course of their celebrated Illinois debates in 1858, that he "has a fertile genius in devising language to conceal his thoughts."[450]

The third is from Lincoln himself who (it will also be recalled) once observed, "I am very little inclined on any occasion to say anything unless I hope to produce some good by it."[451]

Artemus Ward was evidently Lincoln's favorite humorist during the Civil War. Thus, we are told,

> The President's reading of the humorist's story, "High-Handed Outrage at Utica" to his cabinet before presenting them with the Emancipation Proclamation [of September 22, 1862] is well known. "With the fearful strain that is upon me night and day," said Lincoln, "if I did not laugh I should die, and you need this medicine as much as I do."[452]

There may be even more to this famous episode than has heretofore been recognized, except perhaps by Lincoln himself. Why was that particular story selected by him for this occasion? The story Lincoln read to his Cabinet *is* amusing. But notice, also, that it is about a great traitor, perhaps indeed the greatest traitor who has ever lived. This traitor is dealt with soundly, if irrationally, in the story.[453]

Consider the title: "High-Handed Outrage at Utica." Utica was the famous African city that allied itself to republican Rome in the mighty struggle against Carthage. Did not Lincoln intend to gather to the cause of the American Republic an African power (the "persons of African descent" dealt with in the Emancipation Proclamation) against the threatening Carthage represented by the South?

But perhaps he recognized that there was in his own action something questionable, something dubious, even high-handed and outrageous—at least there would be in appearance, especially if he did not handle it properly. Thus, he saw himself as others saw him, or as others might see him, and laughed at himself.

This would be, of course, most subtle, and far higher humor than anything Artemus Ward was ever capable of. But if Lincoln was so subtle, so detached, should not that really make us take notice? It points up the deliberateness, the self-conscious artistry, the coolness of Lincoln. This is, indeed, startling self-criticism, which he would share with his most perceptive observers. Or should what I am now drawing upon be dismissed as mere chance and hence unsound speculation? So be it—for those who would have it so.

In any event, we are obliged to emphasize, even more than we have already, that Lincoln must have known what he was doing, including what impression he needed to make.[454] This citizen is truly a remarkable prodigy of the American constitutional regime. He is, in this sense at least, subordinate to the constitutional regime. Should not these observations induce us to return to the Emancipation Proclamation and to take it, as well as the Declaration of Independence and the Constitution that it both draws upon and serves, even more seriously than we have? We have examined little more than the Proclamation's surface—but in doing so, we have been reminded that the surface, the appearances of things, can be critical for responsible political action, however inconclusive appearances may ultimately be. We are encouraged here, in pursuing the dialogue that this Collection (and especially its banks of notes) represents, upon recalling an observation by Leo Strauss in the introduction to his *Thoughts on Machiavelli:*

> There is no surer protection against the understanding of anything than taking for granted or otherwise despising the obvious and the surface. The problem inherent in the surface of things, and only in the surface of things, is the heart of things.

The words one uses—and the words one keeps to oneself—contribute to the appearances of things and hence to one's effects. In this sense, a word fitly spoken is indeed like apples of gold in settings of silver.[455]

15

The Gettysburg Address

[Abraham] Lincoln, who regarded lawlessness and slavery as twin evils, could say of John Brown's [October 1859 Harper's Ferry] raid: "That affair, in its philosophy, corresponds with the many attempts related in history at the assassination of kings and emperors. An enthusiast broods over the oppression of a people till he fancies himself commissioned by Heaven to liberate them. He ventures the attempt, which ends in little else than his own execution. . . ." [William H.] Seward, it must be recorded, spoke far more sympathetically of [John Brown] than Lincoln; and far more justly, for there is a flaw somewhere in this example, as his chief biographer reports it, of "Mr. Lincoln's common-sense judgment." John Brown had at least left to every healthy-minded Northern boy a memory worth much in the coming years of war and, one hopes, ever after. He had well deserved to be the subject of a song which, whatever may be its technical merits as literature, does stir. [Ralph Waldo] Emerson took the same view of [John Brown] as the song writer.

—Lord Charnwood

I

A discussion of the constitutionalism that is vital for Abraham Lincoln's thought would not be complete without at least an attempt to suggest

This talk was given at the Hillel Foundation Jewish Student Center, the University of Chicago, March 3, 1963. (Original title: "The Gettysburg Address: America's Political Religion.") It has been previously published in *Abraham Lincoln, the Gettysburg Address, and American Constitutionalism,* ed. Leo Paul S. de Alvarez (Irving, Texas: University of Dallas Press, 1976), 113–25, 151–70.

The epigraph is taken from Lord Charnwood, *Abraham Lincoln* (New York: Henry Holt, 1917), 152. See also the epigraph for Chapter 8 of this Collection. See as well note 533 below.

how the true statesman may legitimately employ the forum available to him to shape, or reshape, the institutions of his Country so as to contribute to their perpetuation. Such a leader need not "hold and enjoy any Office of honor, Trust or Profit under the United States." In fact, his effectiveness in office may depend, in part, upon how well he has (before assuming any office) prepared himself, his fellow citizens, and his colleagues to recognize and confront the fundamental rather than the transient issues of their time.

The perpetuation of our political institutions was the task to which Abraham Lincoln, a devoted grandson of the Revolution, can be said to have dedicated himself from the days of his youth in Springfield—he was not yet thirty when he spoke on this subject to the Young Men's Lyceum[456]—until the hour of his assassination on Good Friday, in the year 1865. The most effective perpetuation, it can also be said, can amount to a new founding. Such a founding can remind a people of what was required for the original establishment of its constitution and of what is called for by the meaning (or end) of the country and people that the constitution was designed to serve.

Lincoln's 1837 Springfield Lyceum Speech, it will be remembered, discerned a threat to American political institutions in the rise of what he referred to as the "mobocratic spirit" that was then being exhibited in extralegal attacks upon life and property. This lawlessness on the part of mobs, and the insecurity and disgust that it creates, would, he warned, undermine the attachment of the best citizens to their government and give an opportunity to men of sufficient talent and ambition to overthrow republican institutions.[457]

The threats to American political institutions were particularly critical at that time, Lincoln argued, because the former supports of the regime were disappearing. The passions and memories of the Revolution were fading with the rapidly disappearing heroes of that war; furthermore, there was no longer available the opportunity for individual success and glory that the men of the Revolution had had to induce *them* to support the regime.

Men of the loftiest genius and greatest ambition—men who belong "to the family of the lion, or the tribe of the eagle"—would no doubt arise, and it was only natural, he thought, that such men (including the likes of John C. Calhoun and John Brown?) would thirst for distinction, for far more distinction than could be offered by "a seat in Congress, a gubernatorial or a presidential chair."[458]

"Towering genius," he warned, "disdains a beaten path. It seeks regions hitherto unexplored. It sees *no distinction* in adding story to story, upon the monuments of fame, erected to the memory of others."[459] Such a man, he indicated, is essentially lawless—or, rather, he hearkens only to the law of his nature, not to that reflected in any constitution or regime. When this kind of man arises, Lincoln counseled, "it will require the people to be united with each other, attached to the government and laws, and generally intelligent, to successfully frustrate his designs."[460]

Thus, such a man evidently disdains the law-abiding. But since he is one and the people are many, he can be restrained, if the people are united by being conscientiously law-abiding themselves. The mobocratic spirit undermines this attachment of the people. Lincoln urged, therefore, that "reverence for the laws" should "become the *political religion* of the nation."[461] He identified, in the concluding passage of this speech, the problem confronting the founders of such a political religion:

> Passion has helped us; but can do so no more. It will in future be our enemy. Reason, cold, calculating, unimpassioned reason, must furnish all the materials for our future support and defense. Let those materials be moulded into *general intelligence, sound morality,* and, in particular, *a reverence for the constitution and laws.* . . .[462]

Reason, not passion, was to provide the critical support for the regime. Passions threatened the institutions—the passions of the mob (of men who want to secure justice outside the law) and the passions of the exceptional man (of the man who can likewise be said to want to secure justice outside the law)—and it was to reason that Lincoln looked for the proper training of the people to defend themselves against the ill effects of folly and of apathy. But, as he indicated elsewhere, reason might well use the passions to buttress its position.

Whether the Civil War resulted from the kind of insatiable ambition that the young Lincoln warned against can remain for the philosophical historian to ponder. That war can be understood as merely the final stage of a rise of the mobocratic spirit that would prepare the ground for "an Alexander, a Caesar, or a Napoleon." Is it not evident, in any event, that President Lincoln (in his effort to preserve and perpetuate the Union under the Constitution) deliberately and skillfully trained and molded the people he was leading?

The Gettysburg Address remains the most distinctive distillation of Lincoln's "political religion."[463] We return to it, then, as still another introduction not only to his thought but also to the problems addressed and, in turn, inevitably created by that thought. By so doing, we illustrate even as we examine the role of the statesman among us, as well as the role and limits among us of genuine Constitutionalism.[464]

II

It is more than a century now [I could first say in March 1963] since Lincoln delivered in 1863 his address dedicating a military cemetery near a Pennsylvania town. But it is not much more than a century—and we have talked to men who were alive then. Yet, it seems much, much longer than a century. Indeed, it can be argued that his statement was intended to have from the outset the grandeur and venerability that we usually associate with such "ancient" constitutional documents as the Declaration of Independence and the Constitution of the United States.

The lyrical compactness of the Gettysburg Address, its sense of authority, and its sublimity make it seem a pronouncement out of an even more distant past than its venerable American predecessors. It is delivered to us from a great height in intellect, time, and moral stature. Indeed, it resembles in its solemnity and pithiness the Lord's Prayer. And like that prayer, it begins with an invocation of the paternal and concludes with a vision of the ever after.[465]

The language seems deliberately archaic, particularly in the opening section, which is itself devoted to the past: "Four score and seven years" makes the interval since the founding of the Country seem longer than it really is, much more so than "eighty-seven years" or even "three generations" would have sounded. The language is not only archaic but (here as elsewhere) even Biblical in its connotations.[466]

We are further reminded of the Biblical in the chronology which is attributed to the life of the Country. The fathers ever so long ago brought forth on a new continent a new nation: one might be tempted to think of the Creation account in Genesis; certainly, one is meant to think of Moses and the companions who also went to a new continent, ever so long ago, and founded (or, at least, refounded) a new nation, a nation of and for a particular people.[467]

The new nation on this continent became the wonder of the world, if only for its unique aspirations. The goal is not reached, however, when the holy land, this hallowed ground, is occupied. The new nation—will it not, if it should be true to itself, always remain essentially "new"?—has within it a deadly division. Demands arise for its perfection, for the elimination of that which has been heretofore an ugly but necessary compromise with the temporal, with the here and now. The here and now must be taken fully into account, but it must also be transcended. One is reminded of the crisis in Israel that culminated, as the Christian views it, in the ministry of Jesus, a bloodstained ministry that embraces all mankind.

The crisis leads to struggle and to death—and from this death, new life comes, "a new birth of freedom"—but a life, now that there is a rebirth, which is superior to its predecessors, if only in that it has become perpetual. Who, then, would deny that it is ultimately good that all this struggle and suffering came? Death and resurrection—and eternal redemption: there is culmination in a life that is expanded beyond limit.

The structure of the sentences Lincoln employed in sketching this development reflects and reinforces the content. The sentences get generally shorter and shorter, down to, "It is altogether fitting and proper that we should do this." We reach the dedication for which they had gathered, having moved "down" from the continent to a nation on that continent to a battlefield in that nation to a portion of that field.

Then the movement is reversed; from here to the end, there is an expansion in sentence lengths, heralded by, "But, in a larger sense." The sentences get longer and longer—as does the dedication of the Country, which had theretofore contracted—and the scope of vision becomes larger: he moves from a "portion of that field" to "the earth." The time with which he deals also expands, moving from "four score and seven years" and the contest over whether this government "can long endure" to the recitation of deeds that will never be forgotten and to the expression of the determination that this government "not perish from the earth." This sense of expansion is reinforced by the final sentence, the last of ten, which contains almost one-third of the entire address. This sentence, which marches steadily along to the drumbeat of a high proportion of one- and two-syllable words, runs on and on, as if forever.

What might be established upon purgation of the crippling and perhaps fatal compromise surpasses as the infinite does the finite all that has gone before.[468]

III

A new nation was established—"brought forth" by males, it should be noted[469]—but more than a nation is founded. For unlike other nations (one can ignore the neighbors to the north and south on the same continent, for they are not essentially new), this nation is uniquely constituted: it is "conceived in Liberty, and dedicated to the proposition that all men are created equal."

But liberty has come to be abused: some presume to make ever more of the liberty to keep others slaves.[470] They have come, that is, to claim the liberty to preserve indefinitely the institution of slavery by extending it to ever new territory, with the result that the principle of equality has been decisively challenged if not repudiated. What had been announced in the Declaration of Independence as a "self-evident" truth, "that all Men are created equal," is now, at best, but a "proposition," something that must be tested if it is to be maintained.[471]

The test is, at least for the moment, that of battle—and it may not be essentially peculiar to this nation. No names are mentioned, no dates; what is happening here and now could happen anywhere, anytime; it is of universal significance. But what is determined here may be decisive not only now but, it seems, always, not only here but everywhere.

It is equality, particularly, that is threatened. And in the course of its defense, all are here made equals: friends and enemies, all the living—perhaps the immediate dead alone are temporarily of superior worth. In a sense, even the fathers are placed on the same level as ourselves, since we can do now what they did once; perhaps we can do even more. Furthermore, the activities of the common man are ennobled: the anonymous soldiers, volunteer and conscript, friend and enemy, living and dead, share in the great endeavor with us, those present and those to come. We notice also that he does not speak of "crusade" or even of "mission," but rather of "work" and of "task": the commonplace is elevated in this reaffirmation of equality.

But equality cannot be left, as it is said by some of its partisans to have been left in the Declaration of Independence, without qualification: objections must be met and limitations recognized, if there is to be a sensible dedication to equality. Liberty, too—that liberty for which the vanquished in the Civil War can also be said to have fought—must be redefined. Liberty is qualified by the necessity of recognizing the principle of equality; it becomes "freedom," a word connoting more perhaps of restraint and reflection than does "liberty." Thus, liberty is transformed into a newly born freedom, a freedom that may be seen as somehow subordinated to the cause of responsible popular government.[472]

We return to the development of equality. It, too, is transformed into, or at least culminates in, "government of the people, by the people, for the people." This suggests the total dedication to popular government, to a regime that recognizes in this manner the political relevance of the equality of all men.[473] Equality, thus perfected or at least transformed in its Trinitarian garb, becomes politically defensible. This equality, coupled with an essentially subordinated liberty, can even become permanent. Republican institutions, thus somehow transformed, can be perpetual.

Men begin by wondering about the durability of their uniquely constituted regime. This one, properly tested—for the magnitude of the sacrifices seems to drive and permit partisans to make the necessary qualifications of the conflicting principles that were originally proposed at their fullest—this regime, then, properly tested (that is, tempered, as well), will endure forever. And thus the struggle will not have been in vain.[474] The limitations of the political are transcended: the kingdom of God (perhaps for the first time?) is brought forth on this earth.

IV

This prophetic, perhaps even messianic, statement opens with an emphasis on the deed. We have been reminded both of the Creation of Genesis and of the Exodus. This emphasis on the deed, however, is but an appearance, for is it not the word that marks the true beginning? The "four score and seven years" go back to 1776 and the Declaration of Independence, from which this, as well as the "created equal," language is drawn.

The deeds would be seen, one might say, in the Revolution itself, which began in 1775 (if not earlier) and continued until 1783; or the deeds are seen, in a sense, in the Constitution ordained and established in 1787 to 1789. But 1776 is indicated as the decisive date for bringing forth the new nation—and with this designation there is foreclosed a constitutional controversy that had racked the republic for decades. A *nation,* not a union—the word "union" is not used (just as "nation" is not used for the United States in the Constitution—was formed in 1776. That nation is older than the Constitution; it is a nation that can somehow be said to be one—and, of course, separation and dissolution of that nation would be unnatural as well as impious.

The word constitutes the beginning. Yet, the self-effacing statesman notes, "The world will little note, nor long remember what we say here, but it can never forget what they did here." We, of course, know better; but perhaps he did, too. He remembered what was said in 1776. But did others? Had the deeds of the Revolution been remembered but its words forgotten? Are fresh words needed every generation or two? However that may be, this was but one of many battles of the war—in fact, it was three battles—in some ways inconclusive. Yet this is the battle that is remembered—but primarily because of the word that has become associated with it and that has helped make it what we take it to be, the turning point of the war.

Still, the deeds of men are extolled. They are unsurpassable, at least as measures of devotion and sacrifice. But even these unforgettable deeds will have been in vain if continued effort is not made. However great the deeds up to now have been—the deeds both of the fathers and of the brave men living and dead who struggled here—they can be lost forever.

The first of the deeds to follow immediately upon those that have gone before consists of the dedication of this field. The dead must be properly buried. But the dead are left to bury the dead: "we can not dedicate—we can not consecrate—we can not hallow—this ground." We cannot, we will not, perform the duty we came to do.[475] The dead are left to themselves, as are, one might even say, the fathers who have gone before.

Another task, a greater task, awaits us, awaits those who share in the words that are delivered. A new nation is brought forth, one that first came to light in "ancient" words but that can now be realized to a degree impossible for its predecessor. It is the role of the political poet—a poet who knows that "heard melodies are sweet, but those unheard are sweeter"—it is this poet's work to make that word manifest. Do we move from fallible fathers to a father whose word can be universal and whose regime is unlimited? This dedication he seems to conceive to be his duty. But we have seen him unable to perform one duty. The devotion and sacrifices of many are required for effective dedication, and the many continually change. Does he bring forth a goal that is both realistic and illusory—realistic in that it can enlist the efforts of worldwide multitudes but illusory (and hence deceptive) in that it is doomed (as a mortal thing) to eventual disappointment?

V

The primacy of the word is, as we have seen, implied by Lincoln's thought. And yet, but for the support of many deeds, many unsung and even many unknown deeds, words are without effect. It is painful for us to imagine how the Declaration of Independence and the Gettysburg Address would be regarded today had their authors gone down in defeat.[476] But, on the other hand, victories alone do not ensure undying glory; they must be explained, extolled, and utilized.

Deeds depend upon circumstances. Words are much more flexible: the eternal city, like the best regime, can be enshrined in words. One who makes much of words may even ignore the particular, the concrete. But the Declaration of Independence recognizes limitations: no single form of government is advocated. That is, there can be circumstances when any particular form of government might be harmful and undesirable. It is hard to imagine the authors of the Declaration speaking of any one form of government as enduring forever or even for as long as the earth remains.

But the claim may not have been made that the form of government of which Lincoln speaks will always be present on the earth. Rather, one might suggest, it is only said that the possibility of its reincarnation will always exist once it has been tested and found adequate. The memory of it as successful will endure, and so it will remain continually available, continually attractive to people who will again and again establish it *when and where conditions permit*. On the other hand, the failure of the test now could discredit "forever" this form of government.

But is the Gettysburg Address *this* restrained? Do not the passions of war usually make prudence and selective restraint less attractive to a suffering people than they would be in ordinary times? The tenor and effect of Lincoln's argument point to a single form of government that can be made permanent and, by extension, available to (if not even the best for) all peoples.[477] Does not such single-mindedness lose sight of the ends of government and of the limitations imposed by those ends?

There may be, in the Gettysburg Address, except for what is implied in the reference to "fitting and proper," no invocation of standards outside or above the very regime that is to be perpetuated. Perhaps there cannot be. Perhaps that would constitute a limitation upon that all-inclusive popular sovereignty seen in "of the people, by the people, for the people." The only test suggested—aside, perhaps, from the deference that seems to be paid to the permanent public or world opinion—is that of endurance. Nobility is seen in terms of sacrifice; the principal virtue—but of course this is a time of war—is courage. Nothing is said explicitly of human excellence generally or of beauty.[478]

Still, both nobility and beauty are exhibited in the flowering that is Abraham Lincoln. Perhaps he can be seen as the peak of the regime he seeks to perpetuate, at least in his time and before that regime is transformed. For there had been in that regime an element that seems to have been eclipsed by the Civil War, an element that could be regarded as aristocratic. This is evident not only in our constitutional documents but also in the men who produced them. There is implied by that element, which may be seen in its more material manifestation in the beauty and grace of Jefferson's Monticello, a regard for excellence for its own sake. The writings of Lincoln, on the other hand, as well as what is generally known of his life, strike a curiously utilitarian—a sublimely utilitarian—note. Would not politics, rather than philosophy, be in his view the highest pursuit of the human being?[479]

This utilitarian note seems related to the egalitarian inclination of Lincoln's political thought. That inclination, with its reflection of Christian influences, may be responsible for what can be noticed about the ambiguous status of human excellence under this regime. It must be doubted whether the highest human excellence can be nurtured in a people as a whole, however much a popular regime recognizes an aspect of justice that the confident aristocrat may tend to overlook or, at least, to slight.

VI

Our regime, it has been said, can be made perpetual; the essentially political may thereby be transcended. Men will sacrifice for such a regime, especially men who have been nourished (in a Christian era) on a yearning for immortality. But does not the refusal to recognize limitations conceal dangers? Does not, for example, the dedication to the recognition of equality—as distinguished from the conception in liberty—lead to an insistence upon unqualified popular government and, in principle, upon eventual unquestioning conformity to whatever the people may happen to decree, especially through *their* government?[480]

This is not to suggest that Lincoln should not, in the circumstances in which he found the Country, have thrown his weight on the side of equality; the case of equality is, at its roots, the case for social justice. The struggle for equality among us seems to have been successful. Thus, for example, one can, not unreasonably, observe today that the critical racial problem in this country has been (for at least two generations now) placed "in the course of ultimate extinction." The general, as well as the better, public opinion on this issue seems to be deepening and is reinforced by the effective law.[481]

But, on the other hand, liberty may have become more dubious than it has ever been. It is perhaps intrinsically more fragile than equality, since the people at large can more readily see the stake they have in equality and the institutions (including the economic institutions) in which a dedication to equality is expressed. One encounters in the twentieth century more and more complaints about the dangers of liberty, about its limitations, about its self-contradictions. This is reflected as well in the move among us toward the consolidation of a comforting General Government and in the distrust, at least among the more sophisticated, of local self-government. Thus, does there not continue to this day something valid in the claim that was heard in Lincoln's day, that the South is the champion of American liberty?[482]

Even so, those among us who belittle liberty do not seem to recognize that in a regime such as ours, where equality is vital and perhaps unavoidable, liberty provides an opportunity as well as an incentive for excellence.[483] Lincoln's recognition of this can be said to have been testified to by the care he took to preserve the liberties of citizens even in the midst of clear, present, and overwhelming dangers to constitutional government. It can even be seen, in his First Inaugural Address (delivered at the outset of a terrible rebellion). It can be seen in his reaffirmation there of the right of revolution, that most challenging doctrine of the Declaration of Independence, a doctrine that acknowledges the right and the duty of the human being to look beyond any particular government (including a popularly elected government) to standards above all regimes and all governments.

It may well be that the right of revolution, properly qualified, should be for us today, especially in a century of totalitarian governments and despotic "mass movements," the particular affirmation of the Declaration of Independence as appropriate to our immediate concerns as the "created equal" affirmation was to Lincoln's; for, as I have suggested on more than one occasion, the right of revolution looks ultimately to a standard of human excellence and hence to nature.[484] This contemporary cause on behalf of natural right may call for the articulate sacrifice and dedication that Lincoln's did. Effective dedication depends upon a return to an understanding not only of the fundamentals of this regime but also of the nature of men and hence of all regimes. We must return, that is, not only to the Founding Fathers, but also to *their* teachers.[485]

VII

Traditional political thought emphasized the dependence of the commonweal upon religious support for the moral and even political virtue of the citizen body. This awareness is reflected in the 1846 handbill by Lincoln in which he replied ever so cautiously to the charges of infidelity made against him in the course of a Congressional election campaign:

> I do not think I could myself, be brought to support a man for office, whom I knew to be an open enemy of, and scoffer at, religion. Leaving the higher matter of eternal consequences, between him and his Maker, I still do not think any man has the right thus to insult the feelings, and injure the morals, of the community in which he may live.[486]

Lincoln accepted under the Constitution the practical necessity for separation between the Church and the General Government. Thus, we find him, as President, insisting on more than one occasion, in directives to the military governors of occupied rebel territory:

> The U.S. government must not . . . undertake to run the churches. When an individual, in a church or out of it, becomes dangerous to the public interest, he must be checked; but let the churches, as such take care of

themselves. It will not do for the U.S. to appoint Trustees, Supervisors, or other agents for the churches.[487]

And again, to a complaining citizen,

> I have never interfered, nor thought of interfering as to who shall or shall not preach in any church; nor have I knowingly, or believingly, tolerated any one else to so interfere by my authority. If any one is so interfering, by color of my authority, I would like to have it specifically made known to me. . . . I will not have control of any church on any side.[488]

But Lincoln never lost sight of the reliance that government places upon the religious sentiment of its people. Even more vital—and this is seen in several of his proclamations as well as in the Gettysburg Address and the Second Inaugural Address—religious passions may be needed to provide the transcendent supports that the essentially temporal and temporary political enterprise seems to require. This is especially so in a continent-wide popular government, where glory cannot be depended upon either to sustain or to restrain mass action and where political tradition may be sapped by egalitarian doctrines.

The excellent man must guide and shape. He is among the relatively few who can give an enduring grace and meaning to the deeds and even the aspirations of human beings. Lincoln did so by taking the materials at hand and devoting them to a restatement, and hence a refounding, of the American creed. Perhaps because of its aristocratic accents and its historical associations, he seems to have seen the Declaration of Independence as somewhat compromised in his time. Its doctrines, especially what he regarded as its most immediately vital doctrine with respect to equality, had to be adapted to his circumstances and then reinforced by the use of the religious fervor and imagery that the authors of the Declaration had not seen it as possible or fit or necessary to use.[489]

The Declaration of Independence does invoke divinity—but it is not simply the God of Israel or the God of the Christians. Instead, we have noticed that there is to be found in the Declaration the molding of God to political institutions; the divine order of the universe conforms to the Trinitarian separation of powers of eighteenth-century American political thought.[490] Lincoln, on the other hand, recruited the God of the Bible for a great struggle. This is reflected in the Gettysburg Address even in his "under God" underpinning to the final resolve, the great oath that the embattled American people is, in effect, to take. In his thought, in fact, the political history of the nation is seen as somehow conforming to, if not duplicating and perhaps even replacing, the spiritual or divine history of the world.

One can wonder about the circumstances that permitted and entitled Lincoln to employ the imagery and draw upon the passions he did. A century earlier such an endeavor might have been regarded by some as blasphemous and by others as sentimental and irrelevant; a century after him, it would have been dismissed as either affected or anachronistic. The religious devotion of his people, while still strong, was already weakening:[491] not too strong to resent an exploitation of religious sentiment for political purposes; not too weak to make such a dedication of religious sentiment ineffective. In any event, the passions aroused by the terrible fratricidal struggle proved to be such as to permit, perhaps even to compel, the public identification of the entire experience with the Passion.[492]

Some students of politics have warned that the development in a people of a lively taste for personal immortality robs the temporal, the political, of its significance; that is, man is diverted from a proper regard for his present human condition to a concern for rewards that despise the worldly and the temporal.[493] Did Lincoln, on the other hand, help make religion, and particularly American Christianity, this-worldly, by subtly identifying it with the political enterprise made manifest in the Constitution? Does such a blending, if successful, contribute eventually to the undermining among a people of the sublime sentiments upon which the patriotic poet relies?[494]

Even so, what else should one expect of political life but that the very triumphs of a people are likely to generate crises among their posterity? Perhaps this is yet another way of saying that it is most difficult, if not virtually impossible, in the large-scale affairs of this world, really to know what one is doing.

16

The Second Inaugural Address

> And having thus chosen our course, without guile, and with
> pure purpose, let us renew our trust in God, and go forward
> without fear and with manly hearts.
>
> —Abraham Lincoln

I

The relation of religion to politics is critical to an understanding of Abraham Lincoln's Second Inaugural Address. Aspects of that Address, which are bound to be anticipated in any review of the First Inaugural Address, the Fourth of July Message to Congress, the Emancipation Proclamation, and the Gettysburg Address, can be further illuminated for us by considering, in the light of current issues, how sensitive subjects may be dealt with by conscientious leaders. "Hate speech" is one form that provocative talk takes among us these days. Radically different in spirit from hate speech are the concluding lines of Abraham Lincoln's Second Inaugural Address of March 4, 1865:

> With malice toward none; with charity for all; with firmness in the
> right, as God gives us to see the right, let us strive on to finish the work
> we are in; to bind up the nation's wounds; to care for him who shall have
> borne the battle, and for his widow, and his orphan—to do all which
> may achieve and cherish a just and lasting peace, among ourselves, and
> with all nations.

This talk was given to the Cliff Dwellers, Chicago, Illinois, June 17, 1997.
(Original title: "Lessons on Hate Speech from Abraham Lincoln.")

The epigraph is taken from *The Collected Works of Abraham Lincoln,* ed. Roy P.
Basler (New Brunswick, N.J.: Rutgers University Press, 1953), 4: 441 (Washington,
D.C.; July 4, 1861).

Hate speech, instead of binding up wounds, inflicts, exposes, and reopens them. But we know from experience how risky it can be to try to censor provocative talk among us. Such talk, however disturbing and even outrageous it can be, may sometimes be needed if there is to be the kind of discussion of issues and characters upon which an effective political life depends in a republic. We also know, however, how much our productive discourse about public affairs depends upon orderly processes and disciplined talk. Irregularities have to be kept in check if the body politic is to benefit from wide-ranging and, to some extent, uninhibited discussion of the issues that matter.

Guides such as *Robert's Rules of Order* are useful, if not essential, for reliable public discourse. These guides include restraints upon offensive speech. Hate-speech codes, such as may be found on college campuses these days, also aim to curb offensiveness.[495]

Hate speech is usually considered the kind of talk that disparages traits in others which are natural, or virtually natural, and hence difficult if not impossible for a person to change. Such speech is apt to be regarded as unfair. These traits include one's race (or color or ethnicity) and one's religion (which, usually being inherited, also tends to be how one is born).

II

Reliance upon hate-speech codes for the sake of domestic tranquility is not without serious difficulties, however commendable their purpose. It can be difficult, for example, to distinguish the *offensive* from the *controversial*. For one thing, it can be difficult to avoid *sounding* offensive when one is obliged to examine anyone's cherished preconceptions and policies.

Thus, the response provoked from the community at large can be fierce if one dares to challenge the conventions, and especially the pieties, of one's day. Even though there are formal free-speech protections to which we are accustomed in this Country, a high price may be exacted (covertly and quietly, if not openly and loudly) whenever someone appears to be impious. The critical issues here tend to be, at least among us, political and social rather than constitutional and legal.

It is difficult, if not impossible (and is usually undesirable), to immunize anyone against the unofficial sanctions that the community may impose. This is especially so in any community, such as ours, where public opinion is dominant. The conscientious citizen may have to pay a stiff price for insisting upon what he believes to be the truth—or for presuming to press a serious inquiry about sensitive matters.[496]

It can be a serious political problem what is to be done about the pieties of one's day. It can be risky, that is, either to challenge directly or to leave completely alone those opinions and practices that people love or venerate without measure.

III

The risks both of attacking and of indulging others may be seen in how Abraham Lincoln dealt with the problem of the relation of religion to politics early and late in his career.

Consider, for example, the charge of infidelity brought against Lincoln by an opponent during the 1846 contest for a seat in the House of Representatives in the Thirtieth Congress. It is evident from the way Lincoln responds, in his handbill of July 31, 1846, that he had been believed by some to have been "an open scoffer at Christianity."[497]

An ambitious politician—Lincoln was then thirty-seven years old—could hardly allow such a charge, if persistent, to go unanswered, especially if he should not be known as a regular churchgoer. Lincoln, in his handbill, dealt with infidelity charges as honorably as possible in his circumstances. (One can speculate about what he was not willing to say on his own behalf. For example, he evidently did not want to affirm critical, specifically Christian doctrines, however conclusive that may have been as a defense.)

One's truthfulness and sincerity may not suffice in such matters. Lincoln recognized that one should take into account, in what one says, the sensibilities of others. Thus, he recognized that no man "has the right ... to insult the feelings" of the community by being "an open enemy of, and scoffer at, religion." He recognized as well that whatever the validity of any particular religion may or may not be, its subversion can "injure the morals" of the community. Certainly, he cannot stand "on principle" and say nothing.[498]

IV

Is not one consequence of a regime such as ours, in which both liberty and equality are made much of, the tendency to regard all peaceable religious associations as immune from social as well as governmental regulation? This can make it difficult to subject a cult's "religious" opinions to rigorous examination by outsiders. In his handbill, Lincoln seems to recognize a considerable leeway for denominational differences.

Even so, he must have known that people can believe dangerously foolish things about religion. That is, aberrations were known to him comparable to what we hear from some quarters today about alien abductions and governmental tyranny, leading now and then to such insane actions as the Oklahoma City bombing and the Heaven's Gate suicides. Lincoln could have known, for example, of the ferocious human sacrifices, on a grand scale, that had been required by the Aztec religion.[499]

Lincoln implies in his handbill that if a set of opinions (whether or not labeled "religious") should be harmful to the morals of the community, they should not be immune from criticism. Some doctrines, it would seem, *should* be scoffed at. The most serious threat may be posed by any doctrine that insists there are no enduring standards of good and bad. Such a doctrine, which can deny also both the right and the ability of government to identify and promote morality, cuts at the roots of community vitality.[500]

V

Whatever Lincoln thought, or considered prudent to say publicly, about prevailing Biblical doctrines, he did believe and say that other prevailing (also deeply held) opinions were wrong and ill-fated—particularly those promoting the extension of slavery. Apologists for slavery, especially men who wished to extend the institution, had to be scoffed at, even if theological opinions were used by some to justify (if not to require) the enslavement of inferior races. (John Wesley, for one, condemned such talk.) President Lincoln, in his Fourth of July Message to Congress, warned against permitting "rebellion" to be sugarcoated. Slavery too, he believed, should not be permitted disguises that concealed its awfulness, even though it had become virtually the "religion" of some in the South. Still, because of his circumstances, he said little about slavery in his Fourth of July Message.

The President, in his First Inaugural Address, identified differences about the morality as well as about the possible extension of slavery as being at the core of the impending civil war. He usually managed, however, to be more temperate and charitable in his attacks upon slavery than were some of his allies.[501] Four years later, in his Second Inaugural Address, Lincoln again identified the Southern interest in slavery as "somehow the cause of the war:"

> To strengthen, perpetuate, and extend this [slavery] interest was the object for which the insurgents would rend the Union, even by war; while the government claimed no right to do more than to restrict the territorial enlargement of it.[502]

The Government, in seeking to preserve the Union, had aroused patriotic passions enlisted in a just cause. A dangerous enemy was identified and ultimately shown to be grounded in slavery, which Unionists had been taught to hate to the tune of hundreds of thousands of casualties.

VI

By the time of Lincoln's Second Inaugural Address, the Secessionist Cause was well on its way to total defeat and slavery was well on its way to nationwide abolition. The President, who would be assassinated six weeks later, prepared to shift the stance of the Country from war to peace, from hate to charity.[503]

This shift required that the people at large, in the North as well as in the South, should be encouraged to see that their great struggle had not been in vain. Care had to be taken lest it come to be believed that the war had served no good end; both government and patriotism would thereby be called into question.[504]

The Lincoln of the 1846 handbill confessed to having been inclined in his youth "to believe in what . . . is called the 'Doctrine of Necessity.'" In his Second Inaugural Address, Lincoln makes use of a more mature version of that doctrine by suggesting the expiation required for long-standing offenses of both the North and the South with respect to slavery:

> Fondly do we hope—fervently do we pray—that this mighty scourge of war may speedily pass away. Yet, if God wills that it continue, until all the wealth piled by the bond-man's two hundred and fifty years of unrequited toil shall be sunk, and until every drop of blood drawn with the lash, shall be paid by another drawn with the sword, as was said three thousand years ago, so still it must be said "the judgments of the Lord, are true and righteous altogether."[505]

Lincoln, even as he cautioned against judging others lest one be judged oneself, stood by his opinion that there was something deeply wrong with chattel slavery, an opinion that can be consistent with the recognition that the descendants of slaves in this Country may be better off (if not even better people) than their counterparts in Africa today.[506]

Whatever reservations Lincoln may have had about Christian doctrines, one can see in the Second Inaugural Address, from its opening words, how steeped his thought and language were in Biblical thought. (This may be seen in the Gettysburg Address as well.) If President Lincoln had lived to write his memoirs (as General Grant did), would he have tried to explain how he had determined that the Divine intervened in human affairs on various occasions?

VII

Critical to Lincoln's understanding of affairs both human and divine can be said to have been the belief that all actions *aim* at the good. This bore upon how both a vanquished South and the emancipated slaves were to be treated by the Government of the United States once the war was over.

Christian influences upon Lincoln may be seen here also. He, in prescribing a post-war policy toward the South, insisted that the sin and not the sinner should be hated. In addition, the Northern victors were asked to *believe* what they had fought for throughout the war, that the South had never "really" seceded—and that, therefore, the people of the South were entitled to help govern the Country pursuant to a Constitution purged thereafter of its toleration of slavery.

Fraternal feelings between North and South had to be revived. Preservation of the Union had been insisted upon—and with that preservation came ever greater sanctification of the United States as a *nation,* something seen in the opening lines of the Gettysburg Address and in the closing lines of the Second Inaugural Address. (In neither address is any distinction made between the sacrifices North and South.)

The hatred-arousing speech and the killing that had been required for war must now be put aside; genuine reconciliation is required if the Union is truly to be saved. Lincoln teaches us again and again that the best remedy against hating is to try to see what can be said for the other side, an effort that can open the way to uncovering common ground. Both the vanquished and the emancipated have to be urged to take advantage of the opportunities available to them, however painful their grievances and however limited their opportunities may happen to be from time to time.

The substantial, not complete, success of both sectional and racial reconciliation may be seen in the respect with which national military service, as well as Abraham Lincoln himself, has long been regarded in the South. It is seen also in the deepening repudiation of racial segregation among the descendants of Confederates. This is a vindication of the insistence by eminent Southerners, in the late eighteenth century, that slavery was a curse that no sensible people would bring upon themselves if they were free to choose.[507] That is, Southern whites have come to see that they too had been enslaved by the bonds of African slavery that they had inherited from their Colonial ancestors, a system that still has disturbing aftershocks to be dealt with in this republic. Those aftershocks include the hateful things sometimes said as well as done by desperate partisans on all sides, partisans who (it may be prudent to believe) are also trying to do the right thing, however much in need of restraint they may sometimes be.

17

Abraham Lincoln's Legacies

[An Old Man:] Mr. President, I'm from up in York state where we believe that God Almighty and Abraham Lincoln are going to save this country!
[The President:] My friend, you're half right.
—Anonymous

I

Both liberals and conservatives, in the South as well as in the North, inherit legacies from Abraham Lincoln. Much of what has been said about Lincoln can be recapitulated by briefly surveying those legacies.

Liberals readily notice what Lincoln said and did for the cause of equality. This is reflected in the President's words of July 4, 1861:

> This is essentially a People's contest. On the side of the Union, it is a struggle for maintaining in the world, that form, and substance of government, whose leading object is, to elevate the condition of men—to lift artificial weights from all shoulders—to clear the paths of laudable pursuit for all—to afford all, an unfettered start, and a fair chance, in the race of life.[508]

He immediately adds, in recognition of the compromises that had had to be made in 1776 and 1787 with slavery interests, "Yielding to partial, and temporary departures, from necessity, this is the leading object of government

---

This talk was given at the Illinois Political Science Association Annual Convention, Springfield, Illinois, November 19, 1988. (Original title: "Abraham Lincoln's Conservative Legacy.")

The epigraph is taken from Orrin B. Hatch, "Avoidance of Constitutional Conflict," 48 *University of Pittsburgh Law Review* 1025 (1987).

for whose existence we contend."[509] Such yielding to necessity, in which timeliness can very much matter, is related to the appeal of conservatism to the prudent mind.

The liberal legacy of so thoughtful a leader as Lincoln is grounded in enduring standards and in a Constitution framed and administered so as to advance the implementation of those standards for all mankind.

II

Conservatives should appreciate that the sources for Lincoln of the enduring standards to which he was dedicated included the authors he read, and read with great care. Among these were Shakespeare, Euclid, and Blackstone.

He deepened, with the help of Shakespeare, his grasp of human *nature,* even as he elevated his mastery of the English language. Euclid sharpened his ability both to identify the truths capable of demonstration and to understand what that means. And Blackstone broadened his everyday knowledge of the moral principles and of the law by which the American people had long conducted themselves.[510] Underpinning all of this, for Lincoln and even more perhaps for most of his contemporaries, was the Bible.

The lives described by Plutarch also served to educate Americans in the early decades of the Republic. The significance of conservatism for an enduring regime was indicated by what Plutarch's Lycurgus had to do to preserve the way of life he wanted to see established. The importance of language could be seen in the use Lycurgus made of the songs of Thales. It could be seen even in what Plutarch says of Lycurgus's banishment from Sparta of "all strangers who would not give a very good reason for their coming thither." Lycurgus did not want to give outsiders an opportunity to "introduce something contrary to good manners":

> With strange people, strange words must be admitted; these novelties produce novelties in thought; and on these follow views and feelings, whose discordant character destroys the harmony of the state. [Lycurgus] was as careful to save his city from the infection of foreign bad habits, as men usually are to prevent the introduction of a pestilence.[511]

III

A lively concern for conservation may also be seen in Lincoln, even in the young Lincoln. He was only twenty-nine years old when he delivered, here in Springfield, his Lyceum Speech, "On the Perpetuation of Our Political Institutions." He warned on that occasion that despotism would come if the then-mounting lawlessness was permitted to run unchecked in the United States.[512]

In addition, Lincoln was a man of the law—and quite successful at it. That required, among other things, a respect for precedent, tradition, and the enduring standards upon which the law depends and which it attempts to serve.

His concern for preservation eventually found expression in the efforts he led to induce the South to respect constitutional limitations and determinations, especially the results of a free election. The right of revolution is conceded by Lincoln in his First Inaugural Address. But the exercise of even that undeniable right of a people, he insisted, must be assessed in the light of enduring standards.[513]

His First Inaugural Address, delivered as one State after another was attempting to withdraw from the Union, opened and closed with emphases on the ancestral. Much is made of the collective memories of the American people, those memories of great men and great deeds that should make this people want to remain united.

But the last word in the First Inaugural is *nature,* in the invocation of "the better angels of our nature." Is it not to nature that we must look for the ultimate grounding of such enduring standards that human reason can discover, that nature to which conservatives look in defending the old way, that nature to which liberals look in advocating reforms whenever the old way happens to lead the community astray?[514]

IV

Lincoln's conservatism is evident in his use of language. This may best be seen perhaps in his Fourth of July Message to Congress—at a time, that is, when it had become apparent that the efforts anticipated four months before in the First Inaugural Address for averting civil war had failed.

Much of the Fourth of July Message is devoted to an examination of the efforts made by the disunionists to lead their States out of the Union.[515] These efforts Lincoln can repeatedly describe as sophistry; he can subject their uses of language to searching analysis. The leaders in disunion are called "movers"; they play upon the passions of their people, as they mislead them against their own interests. A philosophical issue is, for Lincoln, at the core of the controversy: the sophistic principle of Secession, he insists, means either anarchy or despotism.

His description of what the disunionist leaders have resorted to is testimony to the native good senses of the people of the South, the majority of whom, he reports, were not in favor of Secession, except perhaps in South Carolina. The general Southern respect for both natural justice and an enlightened self-interest was such as to require their disunionist leaders to deceive them into permitting the hasty, ill-considered actions that Secession represented.

It is always sobering to recognize how much our political discourse has declined since Lincoln's day. Even more impressive, perhaps, than the competency of his arguments is the evident capacity of the audiences to which such arguments could be confidently addressed.

V

The Union could not be preserved, Lincoln seems to have believed, if the integrity of the language was not defended. Again and again in his Fourth of July Message to Congress he uses the term *so-called:* "the seceded States, so called"; "the so-called 'Confederate States'"; "the border States, so called." Thus he can elaborate, "the border States, so called—in fact, the middle states": that is, for him to recognize the term *border States* would be to concede a separation between the states, and this he stoutly refused to do. Something that is called "armed neutrality" in those Middle States is, he says, really disunion.[516]

Secession, Lincoln argues, is "rebellion . . . sugar-coated," and this confection has drugged the public mind into accepting public deeds it would not otherwise have accepted.[517] Thus, he insists upon calling the separationist efforts by what he considers their correct names: *rebellion, insurrection,* and even *treason.* The fine people of the South, he also insists, would never have gone along with their more impassioned leaders if their language had not first been debauched.

The importance of words, Lincoln argues, may be seen as well in how the disunionists have changed the Preamble to the Constitution in preparing their own temporary national constitution: "We the People" became, at least for a while, "We, the deputies of the sovereign and independent States." Even more significant, perhaps, are the changes in the newly fashioned Southern declarations of independence "in which, unlike the good old one, penned by Jefferson, they omit the words 'all men are created equal.'"[518]

Lincoln, it should also be noted, did some shifting in emphasis of his own. Thus, on July 4, 1861, he makes much more of the "*Federal* Union" in the first half of his speech, and much more of the "*National* Union" and of "country" in the second half. This shift is carried even further in the Gettysburg Address, where his dating of the origins of the community, called a *nation* (no longer merely a *union*), carries it back to 1776 and the Declaration of Independence. His use of "brought forth" at Gettysburg suggests also the natural rather than the compactual origins of the nation, something that is ratified, so to speak, by the Biblical language in which he clothes this restatement of our constitutional creed.

VI

Lincoln's conservative legacy stands as a barrier against that massive assault by positivism, value-free social science, legal realism, existentialism, and relativism to which intellectuals have been routinely subjected in the twentieth century.

We can see in the career of Lincoln, both as President and as a political man (such as in the Lincoln–Douglas Debates), the importance of *argument* for serious political discourse, argument that begins from and protects the language of a people. The contemporary atrocity of political campaigning through television, culminating perhaps in the toleration among us of twenty-second "sound bites," should be apparent upon considering the Lincolnian (or at least the nineteenth-century) alternative.[519]

We are reminded by Lincoln's willingness to concede the *principle* of the right of revolution, even in the face of a massive rebellion, of the ways in which that right ultimately depends upon, and serves to instruct us about, the vitality of moral absolutes and the sovereignty of nature in any sound ordering of human affairs.

VII

A proper respect for language, which we must especially depend upon conservatives to stand for, permits us to take the Constitution seriously, even as we depend upon liberals to question the unfair arrangements about which we may be complacent. Only if the integrity of language is insisted upon can the Constitution be read in the way that a well-crafted book should be read.

Of course, there is a problem in how we generally read books these days. This bears upon what is needed for the appropriate education of citizens in a republic. Lincoln concluded his First Inaugural Address with reliance upon the virtue and vigilance of the American people. The centuries-old constitutional system we have inherited cannot long continue to serve the common good if the public mind is indeed debauched.

Citizens, when called to the Presidency, often grow in that office. But it is instructive to notice how well-developed the mind of Lincoln was before he took office, as may be seen in the thoughtfulness of his first inaugural address and, a few months later, of his Fourth of July Message to Congress.[520]

It is remarkable how well educated someone *could* be coming out of Southern Illinois at a time when the material resources devoted to education were appallingly meager compared to those available today. But, then, material resources are merely instrumental in such matters—and this Lincoln knew as he mobilized, for the great struggle ahead, not only the young men and the wealth of the American people, but even more the language in and through which the energy of that people was liberated and the political heritage of that people was conserved.

Epilogue

Since we see that every polis is some kind of association [koinonia] and every association is constituted for the sake of some good (for all men do everything they do for the sake of what seems to be good), it is clear that while all associations aim at some good, there is one which is most authoritative of all and comprehends all the others and does so in the highest degree and aims at the good which is most authoritative of all. This is the one called polis, the political association.

—Aristotle

I

I have long acknowledged that those of us who embrace both Plato's *Apology of Socrates* and the Declaration of Independence attempt to combine two somewhat diverse, perhaps even conflicting, approaches to the governance of human affairs.[521] With the end of the Civil War the newer way (with its suspicions of "aristocracy") was firmly established in the United States, if not generally in the modern world. Perhaps much the same can also be said about the end of the Cold War, for it too has glorified "the American Way."

We are obliged, if we are truly to understand both Abraham Lincoln and ourselves, not to lose sight of whatever may remain valid in the older way. Among the matters that should continue to be taken seriously are old questions about the status of nature and about whether there are enduring principles, accessible to human reason on its own, with respect to prudential determinations of right and wrong in matters both personal and political.[522]

This Epilogue includes material from a talk given at Mortimer J. Adler's Paideia Principals Conference, Aspen Institute for Humanistic Studies, Aspen, Colorado, August 14, 1986. (Original title: "Aristotle on Slavery.") It has been previously published in 20 *Texas Tech Law Review* 691–96 (1989).

The epigraph is taken from Aristotle, *Politics,* opening passage (Laurence Burns translation).

It can be instructive, in the light of Abraham Lincoln's career, to remind ourselves of how slavery, which is now almost universally condemned (and for good reason), could once be explained, if not defended, by thoughtful commentators. With this reminder we can conclude, if only for the time being, our own thoughts on Abraham Lincoln.

Slavery figures prominently not only in ancient communities but also at the outset of the seminal political teaching of Aristotle, a teaching that has had a profound influence upon Western social thought. Apologists for slavery in Great Britain and the United States, for example, were aware of (even though they might not have understood) the Aristotelian discussion of slavery.

When one probes into that discussion of slavery, one discovers in it a recourse to, and an understanding of, nature which are largely missing from sophisticated political discourse today. If only for this reason, the Aristotelian discussion is very much worth our recollection.

II

Slavery comes to view in Aristotle when the origins and constitution of the polis are discerned.[523] He presents the polis as the mature and healthy association, that stage of political development and material accumulation which can seem most in accord with human nature.

Wherever Aristotle looked among human associations, he evidently saw slavery. It could appear almost as much a part of communities as the family. Both family and slavery obviously served vital needs of community—the need for the procreation and nurturing of children, and the need for the prosperous development of the association.

Slavery, however, poses questions that the family does not. It is when Aristotle turns to the discussion of slavery that the first distinction between *nature* and *law* (or *convention*) emerges in his *Politics*. He had recognized the polis itself as a natural growth. As men gathered in primitive and then in more sophisticated communities, they established special relations both with women and with outsiders. The women became wives (neither mere sexual objects nor full partners); the outsiders among them tended to become serfs if not slaves (neither out-and-out enemies nor fellow citizens). A thoughtful student of the polis has to take both the marital relation and the master–slave relation into account.

It is far easier to condemn slavery if the polis is *not* regarded as natural. That is, it is far easier to dismiss all slavery as illegitimate if the human being is not recognized as a political animal, if he is considered an "individual" who is ultimately independent of society.[524] The ready dismissals in our time of Aristotle's concern with slavery may reflect a general depreciation of the status of nature in public discourse (including in political science).

All this is not to suggest that slavery should be defended among us. But it is to suggest that the arguments for, or at least about, slavery should be taken more seriously than they are apt to be today. It should be noticed, lest we become self-righteous in our contemplation of ancient slavery, that Aristotle makes his arguments in response to a vigorous attack (which he reports) upon the established slavery of his day. In fact, we must wonder whether the institution of slavery was accompanied "even then" by significant sustained condemnation of it, if only by a few, as always unjust.

III

Is it not prudent to assume that the ancient Greeks, who produced the greatest works of philosophy and perhaps of literature in the West, were at least as intelligent and high-minded as we are?

What did they see when they examined the political life of their time? Whatever one may believe or say generally about the human species (such as that "all Men are created equal"), one cannot help but notice socially relevant differences among people. Several of those differences have political significance, so much so that it is usually recognized, including among us, that some people are better equipped to rule than are others. (Thus, I recently heard one African-American cyclist say to another, as they passed me on the Chicago Lake Shore bicycle path, "But then when you put dumb persons in charge, they do dumb things.")

Who will rule, and on what terms, depends in large part, of course, upon the regime (with its history, its constitution and laws, and its economic and other circumstances). Whether slavery will be permitted and precisely what it consists of depend, in turn, upon the law of the land. (This Aristotelian recognition dominates Lord Mansfield's opinions in the *Somerset* case two millennia later. That case is discussed in the Prologue to this Collection.) Aristotle assumes, for example, that there are better and worse ways for the master to conduct himself with his slaves.

But, it seems, the critical practical issue with slavery is not so much who will rule but rather who will be ruled. Can those who are to be ruled as slaves, and especially those who are to be permanently ruled, be reliably identified?

IV

It is clear to Aristotle that permanent rule over others in the capacity of slaves can be justified only in the case of natural slaves. Who are they? What, if anything, are they good for?

Vital to reliable identification of the natural slave is the expectation that he and perhaps his master will be better off because of their association than either of them is likely to be on his own. It would seem, therefore, that there is something inherently defective about the natural slave. But he is not so defective as to be utterly helpless, and hence useless, just as he is not constituted to be as useful as free, self-reliant human beings are apt to be.

It we should report to Aristotle that we know of no human beings who would be better off under the rule of a master, he might suggest that our circumstances may be such that no natural slaves can be reliably identified or justly managed among us. He might well add the caution that we should not neglect something presupposed not only by natural slavishness but also, and even more important, by sound politics—that the intellect should be primary, that reason should rule over bodily elements and over most if not all of the passions. That is, he would caution us against repudiating nature along with belief in natural slavery.

Natural differences among men, Aristotle says, begin to become evident at birth. Even so, he does not suggest that slaves are naturally bred from slaves. Rather, he can be taken as recognizing that the son of a slave may be equipped to be a master—and that the son of a master may be fit only to be a slave. This is hardly a doctrine that the typical slaveholder is likely to cherish.[525]

V

We turn now, with Aristotle, from the relatively few who are naturally slavish to most of the slaves found in the typical slaveholding community. These slaves, along with the institution of slavery, should be called into question for the thoughtful reader by Aristotle's analysis of the natural slave.

Most enslaved people, Aristotle recognizes, come from war, especially when victors enslave prisoners whom they might otherwise kill. Included among these wars are hunting expeditions for slaves. These expeditions, he hints at the very end of his discussion of slavery, are simply unjust. Ordinary wars may also be unjust, of course—and when they are, a question may be raised about the propriety of permanently enslaving the resulting prisoners.

The slave, it should not be forgotten, can always purchase his freedom by death—by refusing to surrender when defeated in battle or by committing suicide (or by starving himself to death) if he should happen to be captured. The slave, therefore, is usually someone who prefers life at the cost of servitude. He may be quite sensible in making this choice, however degraded his life may be in some respects, at least for a while.[526]

Such a trade-off may be a form of ransom or a form of reparations, designations with which we are much more likely to be comfortable. What the victors are truly entitled to depends in part upon their merits. The victors even in an unjust war usually exhibit some virtue (or excellence), the trait at least of superior power (which can depend upon discipline, strategy, luck, etc.).

Thus, even here, Aristotle suggests, there is likely to be some natural basis for enslavement. He thereby recognizes the unsentimental truth ratified by nature that, generally speaking, it is usually better to be strong than weak, it is usually better to be lucky than unlucky, it is usually better to win than to lose.

To this extent, then, Aristotle acknowledges the justice that there may be in the large-scale conventional slavery of his day.

VI

It must at once be added that this justice is most limited. Certainly, any recourse to war in order to secure an ample supply of slaves cannot help but expose the dubious foundations of conventional slavery. Besides, as Aristotle notices, the fortunes of war are such that good men are all too often enslaved.[527]

That good men were enslaved in Aristotle's time was most likely to be noticed when Greeks enslaved Greeks. And so the Greeks came to believe, as Aristotle indicates, that barbarians were far preferable to Greeks as slaves.[528] This seems to have been a tacit deference by them to the promptings of nature: the strangeness of barbarians, especially with respect to language, must have made it easier to avoid facing up to the fact that human beings were all too often enslaved who were no more destined by nature for slavery than were their masters.[529]

Aristotle leaves it to us to make explicit one argument against even natural slavery which can be said to be implicit in his recognition that most conventional slavery was, at best, dubious. The distinction between the relatively rare natural slave and the multitude of conventional slaves is likely to be lost sight of because of the selfish interests of any ruling class. This can lead to the thoughtless or even cynical defense of unjust enslavements, or at least to the permanent political subjugation of a large part of the population (as had happened in Sparta).

This kind of selfishness, when it is noticed, can lead to the prudent conclusion that any sustained recognition in public of natural slavery is politically irrelevant if not pernicious, whatever its intrinsic validity.[530]

VII

Aristotle in his tough-mindedness would have us notice, if only in passing, that conventional slavery has itself permitted in communities enduring salutary developments that might not have been possible otherwise.

Of course, modern technology can make recourse to the atrocity of slavery far less tempting. But one must still wonder what slavery (that is, generations of productive slaves) contributed to the leisure that freed a few for the arts and philosophy (including the natural sciences) and freed even more men and women for serious politics and other community service, thereby permitting the refinement of civilization (including the development of a liberating technology). We are reminded of the aristocratic challenges to modern democracy implicit in our chapter from Tocqueville.

These observations can remind us also of the dark side of the foundations of great enterprises. (The relation between justice and expediency could well be explored here.)[531] All this can mean, among other things, that even conventional slavery (with its callous imposition of what Lincoln called "artificial weights") may have something beneficial about it, so much so as to make it seem called for (or at least permitted) by nature in limited circumstances.[532]

Thus, slavery well used can even contribute to the emergence of the recognition that "all Men are created equal," a recognition that dramatizes the ultimate questionability of slavery itself. The culmination of civilization with respect to our subject is Aristotle's deceptively casual observation that of course no one would assert that someone not meriting enslavement ought ever to be a slave. In this manner, does he not call into question (rather guardedly, as befits a noncitizen residing permanently in Athens) the no doubt useful slavery of his day, once again affirming thereby the authority of nature in human affairs?

These observations suggest fundamental questions, not least about the nature of nature. These questions may appear to many to have been foreclosed, for better and for worse, by that political redemption of the United States that the career of Abraham Lincoln so nobly advanced.[533]

Notes

Prologue

1. See the text at note 451 below. See also notes 267, 450, and 479 (end) below, and the text at note 319 below. See as well George Anastaplo, *The American Moralist: On Law, Ethics, and Government* (Athens: Ohio University Press, 1992), 213; George Anastaplo *The Constitutionalist: Notes on the First Amendment* (Dallas: Southern Methodist University Press, 1971), 89, 499. Consider also note 420 below (on "colonization of blacks" talk). Consider as well the text at notes 423 and 425 below; note 476 below.

In considering what Abraham Lincoln could reasonably have expected from the words he uttered and why, it is hard to overestimate the role, in shaping American public opinion in his time, of the development in the United States both of the telegraph and of the newspapers relying on the telegraph. The telegraph also permitted constant supervision from Washington of military operations every where in the Country. All this was critical during a struggle that depended as much as the Civil War did upon a clash of fundamental arguments. See the text at note 425 below. See also note 17 below (on the Magnetic Ocean Telegraph). It remains to be appreciated how much the Soviet Union was subverted (and China is yet to be subverted?) by the development of the worldwide communications network. See note 81 below.

Which, if any, of Lincoln's addresses may be considered works that can stand alone? Is that an apolitical, if not even an antipolitical, criterion? See Martin Heidegger, *Schelling's Treatise on the Essence of Human Freedom,* trans. Joan Stambaugh (Athens: Ohio University Press, 1985), 3 ("between lectures and a finished self-contained work there is not only a difference of degree, but an essential difference"). Even so, it is believed on good authority that

> the writings of Aristotle that we possess as wholes are school texts that, with the possible exception of the *Nicomachean Ethics,* seem never to have been meant for publication. The title that we have with the *Physics* describes it as a "course of listening." The likeliest conjecture is that these works originated as oral discourses by Aristotle, written down by students, corrected by Aristotle, and eventually assembled into longer connected arguments. (Joe Sachs, trans., *Aristotle's "Physics"* [New Brunswick, N.J.: Rutgers University Press, 1995], 1–2) (emphasis added).

Lincoln, too, seems to have been very careful about the texts of his discourses that he released for publication. See also note 485 (end) below. See, on Martin Heidegger and John C. Calhoun (who is perhaps the most ominous counterpart thus far to Abraham Lincoln in American political thought), the text at note 212 below; note 464 below. See, on Calhoun, Chap. 7 of this Collection.

Martin Heidegger began a 1936 lecture course by observing, "[Friedrich W.] Schelling discusses the essence of human freedom in a treatise bearing the title: *Philosophical Inquiries into the Nature of Human Freedom and Matters Concerned Therewith.*" After noticing that this treatise first appeared in 1809, Heidegger records other notable events of sorts of that year:

> Eighteen hundred and nine: Napoleon ruled, that means here, he oppressed and abused Germany. Ever since 1806 the *Reich* did not even have a nominal existence. . . .
>
> Eighteen hundred and nine: Goethe became sixty years old. *Faust,* part one, had just appeared. Five years earlier, in 1804, Kant had died at the age of eighty. Four years before, 1805, Schiller was snatched away before his time. In 1809 Napoleon suffered his first serious defeat in the battle of Aspern. . . .
>
> In 1809 Wilhelm von Humboldt became the Prussian minister of culture and worked on the founding of the University of Berlin for which the writings of Fichte and Schleiermacher prepared the way. That same year the royal court returned to Berlin from Königsberg. The following year Queen Luise died. Next year Heinrich von Kleist, the poet who was long driven by the dark plan of getting rid of Napoleon by force, shot himself at Wannsee—Napoleon, whom Goethe admired as a great "phenomenon of nature," whom Hegel called the "world soul" as he saw him ride through the city after the battle of Jena, and about whom the old Blücher said, "Let him do what he wants, he is a stupid fellow." Meanwhile, Hardenberg, the diplomat, became the Prussian chancellor of state. He kept the growing Prussian-German revolt from attacking prematurely.
>
> All these new men, however—quite different from each other and idiosyncratic in their manner—were in agreement as to what they wanted. What they wanted is expressed in that word of exhortation that circulated among them: they called the new Prussian state the "state of intelligence," that is, of the Spirit. The soldier Scharnhorst demanded more and more insistently courage above all in the case of war, but in the case of peace—knowledge, more knowledge, and culture. Culture meant at that time essential knowledge which shaped all of the fundamental positions of historical existence, that knowledge which is the presupposition of every great will.
>
> The profound untruth of those words that Napoleon had spoken to Goethe in Erfut was soon to come to light: Politics is fate: No, Spirit is fate and fate is Spirit. The essence of Spirit, however, is freedom.
>
> Schelling's treatise on freedom was published in 1809. It is his

> greatest accomplishment and at the same time was one of the most pro-
> found works of German, thus of Western, philosophy. (Heidegger,
> *Schelling's Treatise,* 1–2.)

It probably never occurred to Heidegger or to any of his preliminary readers and editors, in reviewing this inventory of significant 1809 events, to notice that Abraham Lincoln was born that year. I have suggested elsewhere that Heidegger, in his survey of ancient philosophy, skips the career of Socrates. This may help explain, or at least illuminate, Heidegger's lamentable conduct in the 1930s. See Anastaplo, *The Constitutionalist,* 438–39; George Anastaplo, *The American Moralist: On Law, Ethics, and Government* (Athens: Ohio University Press, 1992), 154–60. Heidegger, in his survey of the modern development of freedom, skips the career of Abraham Lincoln. This may reflect the fact that *freedom* is somehow different on the Continent from what it is in the Anglo-American tradition: it is on the Continent less political and less constitutional, being more concerned with Freedom of the Will, Necessity, and the Spirit. Thus, the British seem more open to Abraham Lincoln, as is testified to by the statue of him, not far from the statue of Winston S. Churchill, in front of their Houses of Parliament. This Collection is being published upon the 190th anniversary of Lincoln's birth.

The reader is urged, as with my other publications, to begin by reading the text of this Collection without reference to its notes. See note 473 (beginning) below. More than one-third of the space devoted to notes in this Collection is found in Chaps. 1 and 15 (on the Declaration of Independence and the Gettysburg Address). These two chapters, the texts of which are the oldest in this Collection, introduced issues and themes that I have depended upon and returned to for a third of a century, with the intention (as occasions permitted) of crafting the pieces that would make up this Collection. This is especially so with respect to the Gettysburg Address notes developed for the original publication of that 1963 talk. See, e.g., note 492 below, with its critique of Lincoln and his partisans, among whom I should be numbered. (It can be considered providential that the number of that note echoes the date of Columbus's opening up of the New World for the Old. See, on the lessons of Christopher Columbus, George Anastaplo, "Law, Education, and Legal Education," 36 *Brandeis Law Journal* [1999], parts 4 and 9.)

2. See, on *Dred Scott v. Sandford* (60 U.S. [19 How.] 393 [1857]), Chap. 11 of this Collection. See also notes 85, 86 below. (The decision in *Dred Scott* was announced on March 6, 1857, two days after James Buchanan was inaugurated as President. See, on how judicial decisions should be regarded, the text at note 354 below.) I have discussed at length, as occasions permitted, most of Abraham Lincoln's major talks. (See the Abraham Lincoln entry in the index.) An important omission is the Cooper Institute Address of February 27, 1860, which I touch upon here and there. That talk, which considers matters dealt with in other Lincoln talks that I do discuss (such as the "House Divided" Speech), is usefully described in Richard H. Cox, ed., *Four Pillars of Constitutionalism: The Organic Laws of the United States* (Amherst, N.Y.: Prometheus Books, 1998), 49 f. See also note 303 below, and the text at note 312 below. See as well notes 393 and 430 below. (Mr. Cox suggests that it is "the most extraordinary campaign speech ever uttered in America.")

See, on how high a place Abraham Lincoln should have in the pantheon of American constitutional heroes, Chap.10 of this Collection. See also note 492 below.

3. *Somerset v. Stewart*, 98 Eng. Rep. 499 (K.B. 1772). See George Anastaplo, *The Amendments to the Constitution: A Commentary* (Baltimore: Johns Hopkins University Press, 1995), 341 f. The greatest slavery-related litigation since *Dred Scott* can be usefully said to be *Brown v. Board of Education,* 347 U.S. 483 (1954). See, e.g., the text at note 92 below. See also the text at note 290 below.

4. *Somerset v. Stewart,* 499. See, for what this case suggests about the proper scope of *habeas corpus* actions, George Anastaplo, "On Freedom: Explorations," 17 *Oklahoma City University Law Review* 465, 717 (1992). See, on habeas corpus, Anastaplo, *The Constitutionalist,* 814.

5. See William M. Wiecek, "*Somerset,* Lord Mansfield, and the Legitimacy of Slavery in the Anglo-American World," 42 *University of Chicago Law Review* 86, 128 f, 132 f, 137 f. (1974).

6. See the text at notes 423–25 below. See also note 156 below. Compare Benjamin Franklin's failure to appreciate the implications of *Somerset.* See Wiecek, "Legitimacy of Slavery," 88, 108. See, for Martin Luther King Jr.'s characterization of Lincoln as "vacillating," note 123 below. See, on Magna Carta, note 80 below.

7. See *Somerset v. Stewart,* 509. President Lincoln, too, regularly had to take into account, in developing policies, the considerable investment in slaves that Southerners had been permitted by law to depend upon. In such matters the *just* and the *noble* may not be fully coterminous. See, e.g., Anastaplo, *The Constitutionalist,* 651, 798–99; George Anastaplo, *The Thinker as Artist: From Homer to Plato & Aristotle* (Athens: Ohio University Press, 1997), 182; note 523 below (the instructive *Titus Flamininus* episode). See also notes 63, 167, 443, 466, 479, and 485 below. See as well note 137 below, and the text at note 239 below.

Extensive materials about slavery are provided in my two-volume collection, *Liberty, Equality, and Modern Constitutionalism: A Source Book* (Newburyport, Mass.: Focus Publishing/R. Pullins, 1999). The authors of these materials include Aristotle, John C. Calhoun, Frederick Douglass, Hugo Grotius, Andrew Jackson, Lord Mansfield, John Milton, Thurgood Marshall, John Stuart Mill, Jean-Jacques Rousseau, Alexander H. Stephens, John Wesley, and of course Abraham Lincoln. The slavery issue can continue to help us examine aspects of both liberty and equality. Critical here can be the question of whether, and, if so, how, either of these can be an end in itself.

8. See Wiecek, "Legitimacy of Slavery," 108. See also note 532 below.

9. See, e.g., ibid., 115.

10. See *Somerset v. Stewart,* 509. See, for President Lincoln's argument to the same effect, the text at note 354 below. See also note 357 below.

11. William Shakespeare, *Julius Caesar,* III, i, 114.

12. *Somerset v. Stewart,* 510. See Anastaplo, *Amendments to the Constitution,* 344. See also note 220 below.

13. *The Case of James Sommersett,* 20 *Howell's State Trials* 1, 26 (1772). On the British emancipation of slaves in the West Indies, see note 17 below. See, on the consequences in England and elsewhere of Jewish legal disabilities, Thomas

Babington Macaulay, *Selected Writings* (Chicago: University of Chicago Press, 1972), 190–91. Compare, on the status of Jews in the United States, ibid., 187.

Chapter 1. The Declaration of Independence: An Introduction

14. The Declaration of Independence opens the first volume (at pp. 1–3) of *The Public Statutes at Large of the United States of America,* printed in 1845 by authority of Congress. (It is followed by the Articles of Confederation [at pp. 4–9] and the Constitution of 1787 [at pp. 10–20].) The original spelling and capitalization of the Declaration are used in the text of this Collection. The Northwest Ordinance is also included among "the organic laws of the United States." See, e.g., George Anastaplo, *The Constitution of 1787: A Commentary* (Baltimore: Johns Hopkins University Press, 1989), 235, 239–44.

It is pointed out by Richard Cox (*Four Pillars of Constitutionalism: The Organic Laws of the United States* [Amherst, N.Y.: Prometheus Books, 1998], 14–15) that anyone who has access to the latest edition of the United States Code (1994)

> will readily discover that the very first section of *The Code* is titled "The Organic Laws of the United States of America." He will also readily discover that this section contains four fundamental documents: (1) *The Declaration of Independence—1776.* It is the organic law which states the principles of natural right, denominated as self-evident truths, justifying the thirteen states' uniting for the revolutionary overthrow of the rule of England. (2) *The Articles of Confederation—1777.* It is the organic law which first binds the newly independent states together and which states the principles of government of what is repeatedly called a "perpetual union." (3) *Ordinance of 1787: The Northwest Territorial Government.* It is the organic law which states the principles of government for the vast territory in what we now call the upper Midwest, principles among which, most notably, is an explicit prohibition, rooted in the principles of the Declaration of Independence, against the introduction of slavery into all that area of the burgeoning republic. (4) *Constitution of the United States of America—1787.* It is the organic law which states the purposes of "We the People of the United States" and the frame of government which they have ordained and established in the Constitution.

See, on the Northwest Ordinance, Chap. 3 of this Collection. See, on the inclusion of the Ordinance among "the organic laws of the United States," note 91 below. See, on the Articles of Confederation, George Anastaplo, "The Constitution at Two Hundred: Explorations," 22 *Texas Tech Law Review* 967, 1083 f. (1991); Anastaplo, *Constitution of 1787,* 331.

15. John Adams, *Works,* ed. C. F. Adams (Boston: Little, Brown, 1850), 2: 512. See Carl L. Becker, *The Declaration of Independence* (New York: Vintage Books, 1942), 28 f.

16. Thomas Jefferson, *Works,* ed. P. L. Ford (New York: G. P. Putnam's Sons, 1892), 10: 343. Scholars, upon examining various sources of the document, lay particular stress on the Virginia Bill of Rights and John Locke's *Second Treatise of Government.* See, e.g., William F. Dana, "The Declaration of Independence," 13 *Harvard Law Review* 319 (1900). See, on Aristotle and slavery, the Epilogue to this Collection.

17. Ralph W. Emerson, *Works,* ed. Edward W. Emerson (New York: Houghton, Mifflin, 1903), 11: 316. Here is Emerson's account of these "acts of great scope" (11: 315–16):

> Every step in the history of political liberty is a sally of the human mind into the untried Future, and has the interest of genius, and is fruitful in heroic anecdotes. Liberty is a slow fruit. It comes, like religion, for short periods, and in rare conditions, as if awaiting a culture of the race which shall make it organic and permanent. Such moments of expansion in modern history were the Confession of Augsburg, the plantation of America, the English Commonwealth of 1648, the Declaration of American Independence in 1776, the British emancipation of slaves in the West Indies, the passage of the Reform Bill, the repeal of the Corn-Laws, the Magnetic Ocean Telegraph, though yet imperfect, the passage of the Homestead Bill in the last Congress, and now, eminently, President Lincoln's Proclamation on the twenty-second of September.

See, on Emerson and the Emancipation Proclamation, note 448 below. See, on the significance of the telegraph, note 1 above. See, on the British emancipation of slaves, Sec. VII of the Prologue to this Collection.

18. Daniel Webster, *Works* (Boston: Little, Brown, 1869), 1: 127. Webster's speech "A Discourse in Commemoration of the Lives and Services of John Adams and Thomas Jefferson," delivered in Faneuil Hall, Boston, August 2, 1826, presents a useful political appreciation of the Declaration of Independence and of the men of the Revolution. See Webster, *Works,* 1: 113–50. Compare Emerson, *Works,* 11: 201–5.

19. The resolution introduced in the Continental Congress on June 7, 1776, evidently by Richard Henry Lee of Virginia, provided:

> That these United Colonies are, and of right ought to be, free and independent States, that they are absolved from all allegiance to the British Crown, and that all political connection between them and the State of Great Britain is, and ought to be, totally dissolved.
>
> That it is expedient forthwith to take the most effectual measures for forming foreign Alliances.

That a plan of confederation be prepared and transmitted to the respective Colonies for their consideration and approbation. (*Journals of the Continental Congress* [Library of Congress edition, 1906], 5: 425.)

20. John Bouvier, *Law Dictionary,* 5th ed. (Philadelphia: 1855), 1: 382.
21. William A. Jowitt, *Dictionary of English Law* (London: Sweet & Maxwell, 1959), 1: 586.
22. Henry Hallam, *Constitutional History of England* (New York: A. C. Armstrong, 1893), 2: 317. See, for the text of the 1689 Bill of Rights, Anastaplo, *Amendments to the Constitution,* 263. See as well the text at note 90 below.
23. See, for declarations by early American Congresses, Anastaplo, *Amendments to the Constitution,* 269–80.
24. Thucydides, *The Peloponnesian War,* 2: 35. (The translation used here is by Thomas Hobbes.) See also Leo Strauss, *Natural Right and History* (Chicago: University of Chicago Press, 1953), 1.
25. Consider, e.g., the reference in the Declaration to "the merciless Indian Savages." See George Anastaplo, "'Racism,' Political Correctness, and Constitutional Law: A Law School Case Study," 42 *South Dakota Law Review* 108, 113 (1997); George Anastaplo, "'McCarthyism,' the Cold War, and Their Aftermath," 43 *South Dakota Law Review* 103 (1998). See also George Anastaplo, "An Introduction to North American Indian Thought," 1993 *The Great Ideas Today* 252 (1993). See as well the text at note 90 below; notes 305 and 439 below.
26. Abraham Lincoln, in his Ottawa speech of August 21, 1858, invoked considerations of justice in his application of the Declaration of Independence to relations between "the white and the black races":

There is a physical difference between the two [races], which in my judgment, will probably forever forbid their living together upon the footing of perfect equality, and inasmuch as it becomes a necessity that there must be a difference, I, as well as Judge Douglas, am in favor of the race to which I belong having the superior position. I have never said anything to the contrary, but I hold that notwithstanding all this, there is no reason in the world why the negro is not entitled to all the natural rights enumerated in the Declaration of Independence, the right to life, liberty and the pursuit of happiness. [Loud cheers.] I hold that he is as much entitled to these as the white man. I agree with Judge Douglas he is not my equal in many respects—certainly not in color, perhaps not in moral or intellectual endowment. But in the right to eat the bread, without leave of anybody else, which his own hand earns, *he is my equal and the equal of Judge Douglas, and the equal of every living man.* [Great applause.] (Abraham Lincoln, *Collected Works,* ed. Roy P. Basler [New Brunswick, N.J.: Rutgers University Press, 1953], 3: 16) (emphasis in the original)

See, for a longer quotation from this passage, the text at note 322 below. See, for a valuable discussion of Lincoln as *the* champion of the Declaration of Independence, as well as of Lincoln's thought generally, Harry V. Jaffa, *Crisis of the House Divided: An Interpretation of the Issues in the Lincoln-Douglas Debates* (Garden City, N.Y.: Doubleday, 1959). See also notes 210, 237, 456, 466, and 492 below. See, as well the text at note 300 below, and Chap. 10 of this Collection. See, for a vigorous critique of Mr. Jaffa by a determined legal positivist who (like Robert H. Bork, William H. Rehnquist, Antonin E. Scalia, and Roger B. Taney?) can somehow remain a political conservative, Lino A. Graglia, "Jaffa's Quarrel with Bork: Religious Belief Masquerading as Constitutional Argument," 4 *Southern California Interdisciplinary Law Journal* 705 (1995). Fundamental to the Graglia position, as we think about Abraham Lincoln, is the suggestion that the 1860 Republican Party platform was "created in an attempt to justify *an illegal or extra-legal act,* the North's waging war on the South to prevent its withdrawal from the Union." (Ibid., p. 709. Emphasis added.) Compare Harry V. Jaffa, "Graglia's Quarrel with God: Atheism and Nihilism Masquerading as Constitutional Argument," 4 *Southern California Interdisciplinary Law Journal* 715 (1995). See also the text at notes 37 and 45 below. See as well notes 108, 389, 391, 397, 455, and 470 below. Compare also the text at note 521 below. See, on positivists ancient and modern, note 140 below. See, also, George Anastaplo, "Bork on Bork," 84 *Northwestern University Law Review* 1142 (1990). See as well notes 151 and 154 below; Secs. VI and VII of Chap. 11 of this Collection. See, on sophistry, Sec. IV of Chap. 13 of this Collection. See, for a different kind of critique of Mr. Jaffa, George Anastaplo, "Prophets and Heretics," *Modern Age,* Summer 1979, 314–17; note 492 below.

27. See Lincoln, *Collected Works,* 2: 406 (Springfield speech of June 26, 1857). Lincoln could also refer on that occasion to "our once glorious Declaration." .

28. See, on *prudence,* George Anastaplo, *Human Being and Citizen: Essays on Virtue, Freedom, and the Common Good* (Chicago: Swallow Press, 1975), 329; George Anastaplo, *The Artist as Thinker: From Shakespeare to Joyce* (Athens: Ohio University Press, 1983), 496; Anastaplo, *American Moralist,* 618. See also the text at notes 46, 95, 143, and 533 below. See as well notes 205, 211, 212, 214, 216, 316, 477, 485, and 492 below.

29. See Plato, *Republic* 414D–415D. There is in the Declaration of Independence, as in Plato's works, tension between "mankind" and "one people." See also notes 53, 58, 59, and 529 below. See as well the text at note 521 below.

30. See, on the Emancipation Proclamation and the Gettysburg Address, Chaps. 14 and 15 of this Collection. See, on the Thirteenth, Fourteenth, and Fifteenth Amendments, Anastaplo, *Amendments to the Constitution,* 168 f.

31. Lincoln, *Collected Works,* 2: 405–6 (Springfield speech of June 26, 1857).

32. Ibid., 2: 406. William F. Dana argued that the Declaration of Independence was adopted "with no intention of conferring suffrage upon the negro, and probably with none of freeing him." In support of this proposition, which is essentially one of the revisionist arguments of the *Dred Scott* case, Dana quotes several passages from Lincoln but neglects to come to grips with his Springfield speech of June 26, 1857 from which I quote here. See Dana, "Declaration of Independence," 329–30.

See, on the uses of history and the pitfalls of revisionism, my discussion of

Leonard W. Levy's *Legacy of Suppression* (Cambridge: Harvard University Press, Belknap Press, 1960) in *Human Being and Citizen,* 33. Compare Leonard W. Levy, *Emergence of a Free Press* (New York: Oxford University Press, 1985), xii–xiii, xiv n. 11; George Anastaplo, "Freedom of Speech and the First Amendment: Explorations," 21 *Texas Tech Law Review* 1941, 2016 (1990). See, for Lincoln's use of history, the passage quoted in the text at note 49 below. See also note 50 below.

33. See, e.g., *Brown v. Board of Education,* 494 n.11 (1954). See also George Anastaplo, ed., *Liberty, Equality and Modern Constitutionalism: A Source Book* (Newburyport, Mass.: Focus Publishing, 1999), vol. 2, sec. 10.9 ("Moral Relativism and the United States Supreme Court").

34. *Dennis v. United States,* 341 U.S. 494, 508 (1951). See note 36 below. See, on the Declaration and its "self-evident lie," note 492 (beginning) below.

35. It is assumed, that is, that government is very much to be desired. See Anastaplo, *Human Being and Citizen,* 203; Anastaplo, *American Moralist,* 537. See, on invocations of the right of revolution today, notes 38, 94, 201, and 297 below.

36. See, for President Lincoln's recognition of the right of revolution, Chaps. 12 and 13 of this Collection. See also note 484 below.

37. See Thomas Aquinas, *Treatise on Law,* Q. 94, A. 2. See also note 26 above.

38. See George Anastaplo, "The Declaration of Independence," 9 *St. Louis University Law Journal* 390, 399 n. 20 (1965); Anastaplo, *The Constitutionalist,* 384–89. See also George Anastaplo, "What Is Still Wrong . . . ?" 35 *DePaul Law Review* 551 (1986). The reader is reminded that the terms and the tone of many of the passages in the text and notes of this Collection reflect the concerns and vocabulary of the time when the chapters of this Collection were originally prepared. The lecture drawn upon in Chap. 1, for example, was delivered on Abraham Lincoln's birthday in 1961. See, e.g., notes 47, 201, and 297 below.

39. See George Anastaplo, "Natural Law or Natural Right?" 38 *Loyola of New Orleans Law Review* 915 (1993) (to be incorporated in George Anastaplo, *Campus Hate-Speech Codes, Natural Right, and Twentieth Century Atrocities* [Lewiston, N.Y.: Edwin Mellen, forthcoming]) (1st ed., 1997). See also notes 58, 78, and 201 below; the text at notes 150, 215, 296, 330, and 514 below. See as well notes 172 and 208 below; and the Epilogue to this Collection. See, on *nature* and the *nation,* Sec. III of Chap. 12 of this Collection.

40. See Richard Hooker, *Ecclesiastical Polity* (1593), 1:, 16 (1, 5–6). See, for the qualified right of revolution recognized in Chapter 61 of Magna Carta, Anastaplo, *Amendments to the Constitution,* 253–55, 413–14 n. 105, 461. See, on Magna Carta, Anastaplo, "On Freedom," 481 f. See also notes 64 and 80 below.

41. Self-indulgence can take the form also of radical individualism, as may be seen in the cult among us of gun ownership: "Charlton Heston, a spokesman for the National Rifle Association, delivered a blistering defense of gun ownership, insisting that the Constitution's Second Amendment, which refers to the 'right of the people to keep and bear arms,' was the 'most vital' of all the amendments and was 'more essential' than the First Amendment, which guarantees freedom of religion and of the press." *New York Times,* September 12, 1997, p. A2. See also the full-page advertisement signed by Mr. Heston, *New York Times,* May 4, 1998, p. A11. Compare Richard Moran, review of John R. Lott Jr., *More Guns, Less*

Crime: Understanding Crime and Gun-Control Laws, Chicago Tribune, August 16, 1998, sec. 14, p. 6; Anastaplo, *Amendments to the Constitution,* 61–65; notes 147 and 408 below. Compare also a *Chicago Tribune* editorial on the shootings that we have made much more likely in our schools, which includes these observations (May 24, 1998, sec. 1, p. 20):

> There is no shortage of theories about what is going on here. Some are patently self-serving, such as the National Rifle Association's knee-jerk explanation that existing gun laws are more than adequate and merely need to be enforced. It has been this kind of NRA rot, spread by political influence-buying, that has allowed this nation to be flooded with almost as many guns (220 million) as citizens.

Compare as well Garry Wills, "Awash in Guns," Universal Press Syndicate, August 4, 1998, which includes this vignette from accounts of Russell Weston's assault upon the Capitol in Washington on July 24, 1998:

> There is a certain grim appropriateness in the spot where Weston was shot, the office of [a Congressman who] is a darling of the National Rifle Association. [This Congressman] not only protects long guns and handguns, but also voted to repeal the ban on assault weapons. Police organizations have described those as hunting guns for hunting policemen. [He] does not care. The more guns, the better.
>
> [This Congressman] was looking at the wrong end of the gun in the Capitol, so he locked himself in his bathroom while Weston killed policemen. The hunt was on, but [he] seemed to have no stomach for it when it came so close to him. Only a lack of imagination prevents [this Congressman] from seeing the results of his sponsorship of the gun culture when it plays itself out in other places, streets and alleys distant from his office.

See note 408 below. See, for reservations about Mr. Wills's constitutional jurisprudence, Anastaplo, "Prophets and Heretics," 314, 317.

42. See, e.g., Anastaplo, *Amendments to the Constitution,* 369 f.

43. U. S. Grant, *Personal Memoirs* (New York: Charles L. Webster, 1894), 130–31. See Anastaplo, *Amendments to the Constitution,* x, 386. See also note 482 below.

44. The following passage, rejected by the Continental Congress, was in the Jefferson original of the Declaration of Independence:

> He has incited treasonable insurrections of our fellow-citizens, with the allurements of forfeiture and confiscation of our property. He has waged cruel war against human nature itself, violating its most sacred rights of life and liberty in the persons of a distant people who never offended him, captivating and carrying them into slavery in another hemisphere, or to incur miserable death in their transportation thither. This piratical warfare, the opprobrium of INFIDEL powers, is the warfare of the

CHRISTIAN King of Great Britain. Determined to keep open a market where MEN should be bought and sold, he has prostituted his negative for suppressing every legislative attempt to prohibit or to restrain this execrable commerce. And that this assemblage of horrors might want no fact of distinguished die, he is now exciting those very people to rise in arms among us, and to purchase that liberty of which he has deprived them, by murdering the people on whom he has obtruded them: thus paying off former crimes against the LIBERTIES of one people with crimes which he urges them to commit against the LIVES of another.

See the text at note 315 below. See, for a discussion of the problems implied here (with special emphasis upon the well-known horrors of the international slave trade), Sec. IV of Chap. 4 of this Collection. See, also, Cox, *Four Pillars of Constitutionalism,* 41; Becker, *Declaration of Independence,* 212 f. See, for the observations about slavery in Jefferson's *Notes on the State of Virginia* (1781–1785), Anastaplo, "'Racism,' Political Correctness, and Constitutional Law," 120–21. See also the text at notes 109 and 507 below. See as well note 25 above, notes 72, 73, and 527 below.

45. See Chaps. 13, 15, and 16 of this Collection. In the Declaration of Independence it is accounted "pretended Legislation" (and still another grievance) to "tak[e] away our Charters, abolish our most valuable Laws, and alter fundamentally the Forms of our Governments." See note 26 above.

46. See the text at note 28 above. See also the text at note 162 below. See, on plebiscites and the like, note 447 below.

47. See, for earlier versions of these observations, Anastaplo, "Declaration of Independence," 404–6; Anastaplo, *Constitution of 1787,* 21–22, 308 n. 16. See also the text at notes 473 and 490 below.

48. See, e.g., Lincoln, *Collected Works,* 1: 108, 112 (Speech of January 27, 1838). Jefferson's attitude toward organized religion is implied in the passage quoted in note 44 above. See also Anastaplo, *Amendments to the Constitution,* 120; note 490 below. See as well note 497 below, and the text at note 498 below.

49. Lincoln, *Collected Works,* 6: 319–20(July 7, 1863).

50. See Chaps. 15 and 16 of this Collection. See also George Anastaplo, "Church and State: Explorations," 19 *Loyola University of Chicago Law Journal* 61, 86 f. (1987). See as well note 212 below.

51. Thucydides, *Peloponnesian War,* 2: 43.

52. *The Adams-Jefferson Letters,* ed. Lester J. Cappon (New York: Clarion Books, Simon & Schuster, 1971), 391. See Anastaplo, *Amendments to the Constitution,* 107 f. It might even be argued that death itself can be avoided by so explaining and hence understanding oneself that the best part of oneself becomes assimilated to the eternal ideas. See note 59 below. See, on a perhaps excessive (if not even a morbid) concern with mortality, note 286 below. See also Anastaplo, *Human Being and Citizen,* 214 f.

Chapter 2. The Declaration of Independence:
On Rights and Duties

53. Jefferson, it should again be noted, recognized (with references to Aristotle and Cicero) his reliance on Classical writers in drafting the Declaration of Independence. See the text at note 16 above. See, for introductions to two Platonic dialogues, George Anastaplo, *Human Being and Citizen: Essays on Virtue, Freedom, and the Common Good* (Chicago: Swallow Press, 1975), 8, 203. See also George Anastaplo, *The Thinker as Artist: From Homer to Plato & Aristotle* (Athens: Ohio University Press, 1997). See as well the Epilogue to this Collection.

54. Compare, on Eastern European prospects today, George Anastaplo, *The American Moralist: On Law, Ethics, and Government* (Athens: Ohio University Press, 1992), 537.

55. Compare Plutarch, *Lycurgus.* See, for the significance of traditional piety (and of its deterioration) among the Spartans, Xenophon, *Hellenica,* esp. 2.2.19–20; 3.2.21–26; 3.3.1–11; 4.3.13–14; 4.4.12; 4.7.2–7; 4.8.36–39; 5.1.29–30; 5.3.27–4.1; 7.1.29–32; 7.4.32.

56. See Aristotle, *Nicomachean Ethics,* 1.8–9; 10.9. See also the epigraph to Chap. 2 of this Collection. See, on Aristotle's *Ethics,* Anastaplo, *Thinker as Artist,* 318 f. See also note 163 below.

57. See Anastaplo, *Human Being and Citizen,* 46, 74. See also note 63 below.

58. See, on nature, Anastaplo, *American Moralist,* 716; George Anastaplo, "Teaching, Nature, and the Moral Virtues," 1997 *The Great Ideas Today* 23 f. (1997). See also the text at notes 358 and 364, below. See as well note 392 below.

59. See, on the Idea of the Good, Anastaplo, *Thinker as Artist,* 303 f.

60. It is striking how much Southern slaveholders invoked liberty in their opposition to the Unionists. See, e.g., Chap. 13 of this Collection, beginning with its epigraph. See also notes 26 and 41 above and the text at notes 93, 213, 335, 472, and 482 below. See as well notes 220, 339, 389, 391, 397, 470, and 529. The Southern appetite for liberty, which is related in this case to a heightened sense of honor among a traditionally well-armed people, may be reflected in the "scandalously high homicide rates" in the United States, which have been said to be "Southern in origin." See Fox Butterfield, "Why America's Murder Rate Is So High," *New York Times,* July 26, 1998, sec. 4, p. 1. See also Letters, *New York Times,* July 28, 1998, p. A18. During the fifty years prior to independence, thousands of "criminals" were transported from England to the Southern colonies. Is the baronies-littered South, in its proneness to violence, the American Sicily? See the text at note 174 below. See also the text at note 525 below. See as well note 533 below.

See, on the reluctance of Southern Secessionists in 1861 to invoke the socially dangerous right of revolution, note 484 below.

61. See, on affirmative action, George Anastaplo, "The O. J. Simpson Case Revisited," 28 *Loyola University of Chicago Law Journal* 461, 489, 498 (1997). See also note 25 above and the text at note 92 below.

62. See the text at note 42 above.

63. See, for arguments supporting the abolition of broadcast television in

the United States, Anastaplo, *American Moralist,* 245. See also notes 81, 221, and 514 below. See as well note 511 below. See, on political heresy and the limits on freedom of expression, note 492 (beginning) below. See, on the tension between the noble and the just, Anastaplo, *Thinker as Artist,* 133, 182 f. See also note 7 above. See, on couching American principles in terms of self-interest, Chap. 6 of this Collection.

64. See, on the right of revolution, Secs. III and IV of Chap. 1, Sec. IV of Chap. 2, and Secs. IV and V of Chap. 13 of this Collection. See also note 40 above and notes 219, 484, and 513 below.

65. See, on freedom of speech, George Anastaplo, *The Amendments to the Constitution: A Commentary* (Baltimore: Johns Hopkins University Press, 1995), 52–54, 458–509. See also my article on censorship in the post-1984 printings of the 15th ed. of the *Encyclopaedia Britannica.* See as well note 1 above and note 492 (beginning) below. See, on *rights* versus *duties,* note 220 below. Is this another way of distinguishing *moderns* from *ancients?* See note 521 below.

Chapter 3. The Northwest Ordinance

66. Ohio was admitted to the Union as a State in 1803; Indiana, in 1816; Illinois, in 1818; Michigan, in 1837; and Wisconsin, in 1848. Part of Minnesota, which was admitted in 1858, was also in the Northwest Territory. See note 353 below.

The text of the Northwest Ordinance may be found in, among other places, George Anastaplo, *The Constitution of 1787: A Commentary* (Baltimore: Johns Hopkins University Press, 1989), 258. See ibid., 236. See also Richard H. Cox, ed., *Four Pillars of Constitutionalism: The Organic Laws of the United States* (Amherst, N.Y.: Prometheus Books, 1998), 97 f. Particularly instructive about the Northwest Ordinance, its origins and consequences, is a text prepared in 1937 by the Northwest Territory Celebration Commission, Marietta, Ohio, *History of the Ordinance of 1787 and the Old Northwest Territory.* See also note 14 above. See, on the common law in the Northwest Territory, Chap. 5 of this Collection.

Useful accounts of the various States' claims to Western lands, of the cessions of such claims to the United States, and of Congressional development of the Territories may be found in Merrill Jensen, *The Articles of Confederation* (Madison: University of Wisconsin Press, 1940) and in Andrew C. McLaughlin, *The Confederation and the Constitution.* (New York: Harper, 1905). "[We can] see how much the Americans accomplished in the eventful years from 1774 to 1788: they won their independence from Britain, began with astounding courage and zeal the occupation of the 'western world,' worked out the principles of territorial organization, and, almost without knowing it themselves, prepared the outlines of a system which assured the facile extension of their power from the Atlantic coast across the continent." McLaughlin, *Confederation and Constitution,* 137. See note 78 below.

67. The Northwest Ordinance was enacted in the closing years of the old Congress under the Articles of Confederation. On August 7, 1789, the Ordinance was recognized by the First Congress under the Constitution of 1787 by a statute

that "adapt[ed] the [Ordinance] to the present Constitution." See Anastaplo, *Constitution of 1787,* 265 n. See also notes 77, 78 and 88 below.

68. The Constitution of 1787, we have noticed, was written by the Federal Convention in Philadelphia during the same summer that the Northwest Ordinance was enacted by the Continental Congress in New York. *Federalist No. 38,* in support of the Constitution of 1787, said this about the Western territory of the United States:

> It is now no longer a point of speculation and hope that the Western territory is a mine of vast wealth to the United States. . . . We may calculate, therefore, that a rich and fertile country, of an area equal to the inhabited extent of the United States, will soon become a national stock. Congress have assumed [under the Articles of Confederation] the administration of this stock. They have begun to render it productive. Congress have undertaken to do more: they have proceeded to form new States, to erect temporary governments, to appoint officers for them, and to prescribe the conditions on which such States shall be admitted into the Confederacy. All this has been done; and done without the least colour of constitutional authority. Yet no blame has been whispered; no alarm has been sounded.

69. Daniel Webster, *Works* (Boston: Little, Brown, 1869), 2: 263. See also C. B. Galbreath, "The Ordinance of 1787: Its Origin and Authorship," *Ohio Archaeological and Historical Publications* 33: 129–30 (1924).

70. Ibid., 128, 170, 143; *History of the Ordinance of 1787,* 16. "The Ordinance of 1787 belongs with the Declaration of Independence and the Constitution. It is one of the three title deeds of American constitutional liberty." *Old South Leaflets,* vol. 1, no. 13, 11 (George F. Hoar). See note 91 below.

71. See note 69 above. Far less has been made of the fugitive-slave proviso required by some Southern delegates to Congress (something that came to be required in the Constitution of 1787 as well): "Provided always, that any person escaping into the [Northwest Territory], from whom labor or service is lawfully claimed in any one of the original states, such fugitive may be lawfully reclaimed and conveyed to the person claiming his *or her* labor or service as aforesaid." (Emphasis added.) This kind of guarantee for the slaveholder was familiar enough—but not the *national* and hence astonishing insistence that any vast territory of the United States should be kept forever free of slavery. See notes 79, 85, and 116 below. See also note 156 below. (Is this, by the way, the first American constitutional document in which the equality of the sexes is recognized, however perversely?)

72. It is said that Jefferson had come very close, in one of the predecessors to the Ordinance of 1787 (the Ordinance of 1784), to securing a prohibition of slavery in *all* of the territories of the United States beyond the original thirteen States. This was to have taken effect in 1801. See Galbreath, "Ordinance of 1787," 117–21, 131, 133, 144–45; McLaughlin, *Confederation and Constitution,* 114–17; note 73 below. Must not Jefferson have sensed that a prohibition upon the spread

of slavery, *if it could have been enforced,* would probably have meant the gradual and peaceful elimination of slavery even in the Old South? See Sec.VII of the Prologue to this Collection; note 85 below.

73. Thus, Col.Timothy Pickering (a Revolutionary War soldier interested in Western settlements), in endorsing what Jefferson had tried to do about slavery in the Territories (note 72 above), said in a 1785 letter, "I hardly have the patience to write on a subject in which what is right is so obvious and so just, and what is wrong is so derogatory to Americans above all men, so inhuman and iniquitous in itself." Jay A. Barrett, *Evolution of the Ordinance of 1787* (New York: G. P. Putnam's Sons, 1891), 29. See note 44 above, the text at note 507 below.

The anticipation of new States on an equal footing with the original States, profound in its implications, went back for some years. See McLaughlin, *Confederation and Constitution,* 110–11, 115.

74. "The [Northwest] Ordinance was a great state paper. It is true that, even had it not been framed, slavery could probably not have gained a permanent footing in the northwest. But it prevented the introduction of slavery in early years when settlers were moving into the region, it assured the development of the northwestern states unembarrassed by the slavery issue, and, not less important than all else, *it stated a principle and established a precedent."* Ibid., 122 (emphasis added). See also the text at note 287 below. Lincoln, on the other hand, did believe (as we have seen) that, but for the Ordinance, slavery would have gained "a permanent footing" in the Northwest. See the Lincoln quotation at the head of Chap. 3 of this Collection. Consider also the unsuccessful efforts in 1802 by William Henry Harrison, as governor of the Indiana Territory, to suspend the prohibition in the Ordinance so as to be able to introduce slavery into the Territory. See William F. Poole, *The Ordinance of 1787, and Dr. Manasseh Cutler as an Agent in Its Formation* (Cambridge, Mass.: Welch, Bigelow, 1876), 5–6. Lincoln always recognized that it is much harder to eliminate slavery once established than it is to exclude it. The same can be said of tobacco, television, and other drugs. See, e.g., the text at note 302 below.

75. Galbreath, "Ordinance of 1787," 166–67. The reference here to "cheap labor" reminds us of how the institution of slavery tended to discourage the immigration of free laborers into the Slave States. See the text at note 80 below. See also Sec.VII of Chap. 3 of this Collection; the text at note 101 below; note 405 below. See, on geography and slavery, the text at note 287 below.

76. See, on the differences between "idealists" and "materialists," George Anastaplo, *The Artist as Thinker: From Shakespeare to Joyce* (Athens: Ohio University Press, 1983), 284; George Anastaplo, *The Thinker as Artist: From Homer to Plato & Aristotle* (Athens: Ohio University Press, 1997), 303. See also notes 108 and 338 below. See as well notes 189 and 531 below.

77. The designation of these parts is mine. Part 1 includes Sec. 1; Part 2 includes Sec. 2; Part 3 includes Secs. 3–13; Part 4 includes Sec. 14. The original section numbers were dropped by the First Congress in 1789. See note 67 above.

78. Part 5 was dropped by the First Congress in 1789: it was no longer needed. See note 67 above. Part 4 is introduced by, "It is hereby ordained *and declared"* (emphasis added). It is appropriate that "the fundamental principles of civil and religious liberty" should have been considered to have been declared, not simply

ordained: that is, the framers of the Northwest Ordinance were stating some of the long-established, if not natural and unalienable, rights of mankind. See note 39 above. Is it not also appropriate that the authorship of the ordinance should be as uncertain as it still is? That is, should not the Ordinance be considered the product of a deliberative body that was expressing the enduring good sense and moral judgment of the American community? See note 66 (end) above. See, on the 1791 Bill of Rights as "declared," George Anastaplo, *The Amendments to the Constitution: A Commentary* (Baltimore: Johns Hopkins University Press, 1995), 41–42, 326. See also the text at note 153 below.

79. The slavery prohibition was tacked on, so to speak, when it suddenly appeared that the Southern delegates in the Continental Congress would be willing to accept it, provided a fugitive-slave provision was added as well. See note 71 above.

80. Is not Henry Thoreau, for example, merely an extreme version of a common American type? Of course, both the Northwest Ordinance and Henry Thoreau recognized the need for proper development of character but with an emphasis upon local (if not even personal) control of that development. See, on Thoreau, George Anastaplo, *Human Being and Citizen: Essays on Virtue, Freedom, and the Common Good* (Chicago: Swallow Press, 1975), 203; note 529 below. See, for the text of Magna Carta, Anastaplo, *Amendments to the Constitution*, 239, 244 f. See also note 40 above. See, on the civic-minded channeling of private desire, Chap. 6 of this Collection.

81. This can lead to a volatile public opinion, which can be made even worse by the mass media. A major influence here remains television, which (I presume to say again) a sensible people who know their interests and understand their powers would simply abolish. See note 63 above, notes 221 and 494 below. See also note 1 above.

82. See Galbreath, "Ordinance of 1787," 163; McLaughlin, *Confederation and Constitution,* 120; Jensen, *Articles of Confederation*, 354–58. Consider how much fuss was made in Illinois about the inauguration in 1969 of a 2.5 percent income tax, compared to the considerably larger income-tax exactions that are much more readily accepted when levied by the United States Government. See Taylor Pensoneau, *Governor Richard Ogilvie: In the Interest of the State* (Carbondale: Southern Illinois University, 1997), 29 f, 95, 263.

83. This contracts guarantee has been thought by some to be as important as the slavery prohibition, especially since it served as the principal forerunner of a similar provision in the Constitution of 1787. See Galbreath, "Ordinance of 1787," 136, 143; Barrett, *Evolution of the Ordinance of 1787,* 63–64; *History of the Ordinance of 1787*, 27. But, it should be noticed, the guarantee in the Ordinance extends only to "private contracts, or engagements, bona fide and without fraud previously formed," whereas the guarantee in the Constitution of 1787 is not explicitly limited to contracts "previously formed." See, on the possible implications of this difference, William W. Crosskey, *Politics and the Constitution in the History of the United States* (Chicago: University of Chicago Press, 1953), 352 ("The True Meaning of the Contracts Clause"); note 209 below. See also Anastaplo, *Constitution of 1787,* 70, 174, 313 n.47.

84. Do not the intestate provisions reflect an opinion about family life—about what are the best, perhaps the natural, lines of division of property? It is clear, by the way, that division is indeed called for among the surviving children, not primogeniture. "Thus did the law regarding the descent of property become purely republican." Barrett, *Evolution of the Ordinance of 1787,* 58. See also *History of the Ordinance of 1787,* 82.

85. A slavery-confinement policy is essentially the policy that Lincoln's Republican Party came to stand for, one based on the expectation that a slave economy that could not expand would eventually wither away. See notes 71 and 72 above. On the other hand, some interested parties considered the Northwest Ordinance to have tacitly permitted slavery to be introduced in any territories not directly governed by the Ordinance. See Richard B. Morris, *Witness at the Creation* (New York: New American Library, 1985), 183; McLaughlin, *Confederation and Constitution,* 192.

See, on the less organized (more "natural"?) movement of settlers, with their slaves, into the Southwestern territories, ibid., 28. See also Sec. VII of the Prologue to this Collection.

86. Publius, in the *Federalist No. 38* passage quoted in note 68 above, suggests that it is prudent to give the new Congress the constitutional authority to do what should be done and would be done anyway by sensible men, just as the Continental Congress had acted as it did (without formal authority?) with respect to the Northwest Territory. Whether the Constitution of 1787 gave Congress the power to do with the Territories what the Continental Congress tried to do with the Northwest Ordinance is considered in the *Dred Scott* case (1857). See Chap. 11 of this Collection.

87. See *History of the Ordinance of 1787,* 28, 29; McLaughlin, *Confederation and Constitution,* 112, 129–30; James C. Welling, "The States'-Rights Conflict over the Public Lands," in *Papers of the American Historical Association,* vol. 3 (1887–1888): Allan Nevins, *The American States during and after the Revolution* (New York: Macmillan, 1924), 592. When the post-1789 Southern States "seceded" in 1860 and 1861, they went with the Confederacy, which they must have somehow or other regarded (retroactively?) as the source of *their* being. See Chap. 15 of this Collection.

88. The Continental Congress, pursuant to the Northwest Ordinance, appointed the governor and other officers for the Territory. The First Congress in 1789, upon adapting the Northwest Ordinance to the Constitution of 1787, assigned this appointive power to the President. See note 67 above.

89. See *History of the Ordinance of 1787,* 46–48.

90. Is there not here a recognition that there is a basis for just allocations of property independent of positive law? Or are the Indian rights that are referred to dependent solely upon treaty obligations? See note 305 below.

91. See Lincoln, *Collected Works,* 1: 382; Chap. 16 of this Collection. See also Anastaplo, *Human Being and Citizen,* 51. See as well note 492 (beginning) below.

The formal inclusion of the Northwest Ordinance among "the organic laws of the United States" evidently did not take place until 1878. See Cox, *Four Pillars of Constitutionalism,* 29 f. See also notes 14 and 70 above. Is this inclusion a ratification, in effect, of the destruction of slavery by the Civil War, serving also thereby as a tribute to Abraham Lincoln, who had made so much of the Northwest Ordinance?

Chapter 4. Slavery and the Federal Convention of 1787

92. 347 U.S. 483 (1954). See note 3 above. See also the text at note 33 above. See as well note 25 above, note 526 below. See, on slavery always being with us, note 529 below.

93. See note 60 above.

94. See, e.g., George Anastaplo, "One's Character Is One's Fate?" 35 *DePaul Law Review* 624, 627 (1986); George Anastaplo, *The American Moralist: On Law, Ethics, and Government* (Athens: Ohio University Press, 1992), 399.

95. See note 28 above; the text at note 143 below.

96. See, e.g., Staunton Lynd, *Class Conflict, Slavery, and the United States Constitution* (Indianapolis: Bobbs Merrill, 1967), 154.

97. Max Farrand, ed., *The Records of the Federal Convention* (New Haven: Yale University Press, 1937), 2: 371. This speaker, Charles Pinckney, was a cousin of General Charles Cotesworth Pinckney, another delegate from South Carolina. See, on slavery in antiquity, the Epilogue to this Collection.

98. Ibid.,1: 438. See also ibid.,1: 165, 465, 512.

99. Ibid.,1: 318.

100. Ibid., 2: 364.

101. Ibid., 2: 221–22.

102. Ibid., 2: 223.

103. See, e.g., ibid., 2: 371.

104. See, for this prohibition, the text at note 71 above.

105. See Farrand, *Records,* 2: 443. See, on Madison's *Notes,* note 118 below.

106. Farrand, *Records,* 2: 453–54.

107. Ibid., 2: 601–2.

108. Ibid., 2: 628. The Madisonian observation stands as a challenge to those "realists" who insist upon separating the *legal* from the *moral.* See note 76 above, note 531 below.

109. Ibid., 2: 220, 370. See note 44 above.

110. Ibid., 2: 415.

111. See ibid., 2: 559, 602, 629–31.

112. See ibid., 2: 95, 364–65, 371–72. Compare ibid., 2: 374–75.

113. See ibid., 2: 220, 364.

114. Eight of those twenty years were added on August 25, 1787. See ibid., 2: 414–15. It has been estimated that some additional 250,000 slaves were illegally imported between 1808 and 1860. See note 44 above. See, on limits in the conduct of war, the text at note 439 below.

115. See, on the extensive powers of the national government provided for in the Constitution of 1787, William W. Crosskey, *Politics and the Constitution in the History of the United States* (Chicago: University of Chicago Press, 1953); George

Anastaplo, *The Constitution of 1787: A Commentary* (Baltimore: Johns Hopkins University Press, 1989); George Anastaplo, "*In re* Antonin Scalia," 28 *Perspectives in Political Science* 22 (Winter 1999). See also note 85 above, note 151 below.

116. See *Encyclopedia of the American Constitution* (New York: Macmillan, 1986), 3: 148, 4: 1690–91.

Laurence Tribe is quoted as having said, "Slavery is the only economic arrangement our Constitution has ever specifically endorsed, and Prohibition the only social policy it has ever expressly sought to implement." C. Herman Pritchett, "Why Risk a Constitutional Convention?" *Center Magazine,* March 1980, 14, 21. But compare the following report in *Newsweek,* May 25, 1987, 65: "Dr. Benjamin Rush, [an eighteenth-century] progressive, went so far as to state that this [1808] clause made the Constitution an antislavery document." Consider as well the "social policy" set forth in the Thirteenth, Fourteenth, and Fifteenth Amendments. See note 76 above, note 156 below. See also the Prologue to this Collection. See, on the Eighteenth Amendment and Prohibition, George Anastaplo, *The Amendments to the Constitution: A Commentary* (Baltimore: Johns Hopkins University Press, 1995), 195 f, 457. See, on Mr. Pritchett, the dedication for George Anastaplo, *Campus Hate-Speech Codes, Natural Right, and Twentieth Century Atrocities* (Lewiston, N.Y.: Edwin Mellen Press, forthcoming).

117. Albert I. Beveridge, *The Life of John Marshall* (Boston: Houghton Mifflin Co., 1919), 4: 475, 477. Consider also Lincoln's distinction, much later, between the slave owner and the slave trader. See, e.g., George Anastaplo *The Constitutionalist: Notes on the First Amendment* (Dallas: Southern Methodist University Press, 1971), 553 n. 133; note 7 above.

The United States may also have the distinction of having produced the most humane account of an ordinary slave. Consider my letter to the editor, as published in the *Chicago Sun-Times,* April 18, 1984, 48:

> I read with interest your recent editorial on the efforts of a teacher at a Springfield High School to ban the book *The Adventures of Huckleberry Finn.*
>
> That there should be a controversy about the use of this book in our schools suggests the superficiality of much current discussion of serious literature. There are few characters in an American novel presented with the sympathy and the respect extended by Mark Twain to his runaway slave. Indeed, this presentation is a profound condemnation, in effect, of the institution of slavery—and a celebration of what the human spirit is capable of even in the most trying circumstances.
>
> The typical reader of the book should end up less of a racist than he might otherwise be. One must wonder whether those who condemn its use in our schools have truly read it.

I am not responsible for the rather puzzling caption supplied by the *Chicago Sun-Times* editor, "Twain respected Tom." See, on this novel, George Anastaplo, *The Artist as Thinker: From Shakespeare to Joyce* (Athens: Ohio University Press, 1983), 179.

118. See, e.g., Farrand, *Records,* 1: 561, 588; 2: 220–22. All quotations in this

Collection from Farrand's *Records* are taken from James Madison's *Notes of Debates in the Federal Convention of 1787*. I sometimes make minor adjustments in spelling or punctuation. See, for who "counted" in aristocratic times, Sec. II of Chap. 6 of this Collection.

119. See, e.g., ibid., 1: 583.

120. See ibid., 1: 201, 562. See also ibid., 1: 229.

121. See, e.g., ibid., 1: 580–81, 587–88.

122. See, e.g., ibid., 1: 196; 2: 4–5, 182–83.

123. See, e.g., ibid., 1: 594–95, 597.

124. See, e.g., ibid., 1: 561. Compare ibid., 2: 415.

125. See, e.g., ibid., 2: 417 (James Madison). See also notes 137 and 215 below.

126. See, e.g., ibid., 2: 374.

127. Compare ibid., 2: 371.

128. See, e.g., ibid., 1: 484–87, 542, 591–93, 596. See also ibid., 2: 221–22.

129. Ibid., 2: 415–16.

130. Ibid., 2: 369–70 (emphasis added). See also ibid., 2: 371. Were Connecticut ships then engaged in the international slave trade?

131. See, e.g., ibid., 1: 585–86, 595, 604–5; 2: 111, 305.

132. See, e.g., ibid., 1: 397–98.

133. See, e.g. ibid., 1: 321, 405–6, 421. Compare ibid., 1: 342.

134. See, e.g., ibid., 1: 486, 601–2; 2: 9–10.

135. See, e.g., ibid., 2: 305–6.

136. See Chaps. 12–16 of this Collection.

137. See, e.g., Farrand, *Records,* 1: 594 (Edmund Randolph): "He urged strenuously that express security ought to be provided for including slaves in the ratio of Representation. He lamented that such a species of property existed. But as it did exist the holders of it would require this security." See the text at note 507 below. See also note 7 above.

138. See, e.g., ibid., 1: 595–96; 2: 6, 10–11.

139. See the text at notes 107–8 above.

140. Ibid., 2: 628. See, on Madison's *Notes,* note 118 above. Modern positivists and ancient sophists (such as Plato's Thrasymachus) would find Madison's argument here hard to understand. See note 26 above. See as well the text at note 145 below; notes 151 and 154 below.

141. See, on John C. Calhoun, Chap. 7 of this Collection, especially the text at note 220 below. See also note 286 below.

142. See, on post–Civil War America, Henry Adams, *Democracy.* Northerners were led astray by avarice after the Civil War in somewhat the way Southerners had been after the invention of the cotton gin. See, on "the proneness of prosperity to breed tyrants," the text at note 32 above.

143. See George Anastaplo, "Clausewitz and Intelligence" (a 1986 Defense Intelligence College talk), 16 *Teaching Political Science* 77, 81 (1989) (part of a symposium on intelligence organized by Richard G. Stevens).

Chapter 5. The Common Law
and the Organization of Government

144. See, for the text of the Northwest Ordinance, note 66 above. That ordinance is introduced in Chap. 3 of this Collection. See, on the common law, George Anastaplo, "Nature and Convention in Blackstone's *Commentaries,*" 22 *Legal Studies Forum* 161 (1998).

145. See, on the 1945–1946 Nuremberg Trial, George Anastaplo, "On Trial: Explorations," 22 *Loyola University of Chicago Law Journal* 765, 977 (1991). See also note 504 below, the text at note 196 below.

146. *Axtell's Case* (All the Judges of England, 1660. Reported J. Kel. 13). See George Anastaplo *The Constitutionalist: Notes on the First Amendment* (Dallas: Southern Methodist University Press, 1971), 475.

147. See, on the status of property among us, Anastaplo, *The Constitutionalist,* 213–17. This may be related to how many among us feel about guns. See note 41 above, and note 402 below.

148. See George Anastaplo, *The Constitution of 1787: A Commentary* (Baltimore: Johns Hopkins University Press, 1989), 265.

149. *Encyclopedia of the American Constitution,* 1: 332.

150. See note 39 above, and note 155 below.

151. See, e.g., the exchange I had with Justice Antonin Scalia as recorded in *Blackacre* (Loyola University of Chicago School of Law), April 22, 1997, May 6, 1997; note 115 above. See, for an exchange with B. F. Skinner George Anastaplo, *Human Being and Citizen: Essays on Virtue, Freedom, and the Common Good* (Chicago: Swallow Press, 1975), 87, 282–83. See also John Otrompke, "No lawyer, Anastaplo resorts to common sense in rebuttal of Scalia," *Bar News* (Illinois State Bar Association), September 2, 1997, 14. See as well notes 26 and 140 above. See, on the distortions prompted by self-interest, note 142 above. See also Chap. 6 of this Collection; Secs. VI and VII of Chap. 11 of this Collection.

152. See, e.g. *Huidekoper's Lessee v. Douglass,* 3 Cranch (U.S.) 1 (1805). See also William W. Crosskey, *Politics and the Constitution in the History of the United States* (Chicago: University of Chicago Press, 1953), 719 f.

153. See, e.g., George Anastaplo, *The Amendments to the Constitution: A Commentary* (Baltimore: Johns Hopkins University Press, 1995), 92 f.; note 78 above.

154. *Black & White Taxicab Co. v. Brown & Yellow Taxicab Co.,* 276 U.S. 518, 533–34 (1928). See also *Erie Railroad Co. v. Tompkins,* 304 U.S. 64, 73 f.(1938). Scholars are not apt to appreciate these days the profound implications of one of the sentences just quoted from Justice Holmes: "If there were such a transcendental body of law outside of any particular State but obligatory within it unless and until changed by statute, the courts of the United States might be right in using their independent judgment as to what it was." Unfortunately, Justice Holmes did not quit while he was still ahead, for he then goes on to assert, "But there is no such body of law."

155. See William T. Braithwaite, "The Common Law and the Judicial Power: An Introduction to *Swift–Erie,*" in *Law and Philosophy,* ed. John A. Murley, William

T. Braithwaite, and Robert L. Stone (Athens: Ohio University Press, 1992), 2: 774; Anastaplo, *Constitution of 1787*, 128–37; note 39 above, the text at note 171 below. *Erie* overruled *Swift v. Tyson,* 41 U.S. (16 Pet.) 1 (1842). (Justice Story's opinion in *Swift v. Tyson* is drawn upon in the epigraph for Chap. 5 of this Collection.) See notes 356 and 392 below. See also note 495 below.

156. "I hold that the Federal Government was never, in its essence, anything but an anti-slavery Government." Frederick Douglass, *Papers,* ed. John W. Blassingame (New Haven: Yale University Press, 1979), 3: 596 (July 6, 1863). Does Douglass go too far in what he says here, but in a salutary way? See George Anastaplo, "'Racism,' Political Correctness, and Constitutional Law: A Law School Case Study," 42 *South Dakota Law Review* 108, 113 (1997), 119; note 25 above. See also notes 71 and 116 above. See, for the fundamental antipathy to slavery in Anglo-American law, the discussion of *Somerset v. Stewart* (1772) in the Prologue to this Collection. Compare, for the discussion of slavery in antiquity, the Epilogue to this Collection.

Chapter 6. Alexis de Tocqueville
on Democracy in America

157. Alexis de Tocqueville, *Democracy in America*, ed. J.-P. Mayer (New York: Doubleday, 1969), 9.

158. See, e.g., ibid., 61 f, 584 f.

159. See notes 199 and 203 below.

160. The most useful introduction to the book of which I know is Marvin Zetterbaum's Tocqueville chapter in *History of Political Philosophy*, ed. Leo Strauss and Joseph Cropsey, 3d ed. (Chicago: University of Chicago Press, 1987). See also note 206 below.

161. This is aside from the question of whether a community needs, for its own good, some accumulation of wealth in it, wealth that can be put to cultural and political as well as economic and productive uses. See, on slavery and an initial accumulation of capital, the Epilogue to this Collection. See, on culture, note 1 above.

162. See, on God being usefully depicted in some respects as manlike, the text at note 47 above. See also George Anastaplo, *The American Moralist: On Law, Ethics, and Government* (Athens: Ohio University Press, 1992), 139. Compare, as to who counts in democratic times, Sec. V of Chap. 4 of this Collection.

163. See, on how Aristotle and Kant seem to differ here, Anastaplo, *American Moralist,* 20 f, 27 f. See also note 56 above. See as well Donald Meiklejohn, Book Review, *Ethics,* January 1980, 296–300.

164. See the introduction to *Democracy in America* for indications of the causes of this centuries-old development. Providence itself is not ruled out as a factor. See note 206 below.

165. The most useful introduction to Descartes of which I know is Richard Kennington's chapter in *History of Political Philosophy,* ed. Leo Strauss and Joseph

Cropsey, 3d ed. (Chicago: University of Chicago Press, 1987.). See also Anastaplo, *American Moralist,* 83 f. See as well Anastaplo, "Beginnings," 1998 *The Great Ideas Today* part 3 (1998). (The complete version of this article is appended to Anastaplo, "Law and Literature and the Bible: Explorations," 23 *Oklahoma City University Law Review* 787 [1998].)

166. It seems to be indicated that the times referred to in Paragraph 1 were "aristocratic," which may again point more to the Christian, largely Feudal, centuries preceding the present era than to Classical antiquity.

167. It is not merely a coincidence that the same word *(kalon)* could be used in ancient Greek to designate both the *noble* and the *beautiful*. See, e.g., Leo Strauss, *Liberalism Ancient and Modern* (New York: Basic Books, 1968), 8. See also note 7 above.

168. One can be reminded of the Senate of the Roman Republic. See, e.g., George Anastaplo, *The Thinker as Artist: From Homer to Plato & Aristotle* (Athens: Ohio University Press, 1997)., 361 f.

169. See, e.g., George Anastaplo, "Teaching, Nature, and the Moral Virtues," 1997 *The Great Ideas Today* 4 f., 23 f. (1997). See also note 178 below.

170. See, for discussions of Joan of Arc and Thomas More, George Anastaplo, "On Trial: Explorations," 22 *Loyola University of Chicago Law Journal* 919 f., 950 f. (1991).

171. See the text at note 155 above.

172. See, on the Good, the True, and the Beautiful, George Anastaplo, *The Artist as Thinker: From Shakespeare to Joyce* (Athens: Ohio University Press, 1983), 275 f. See also note 208 below. See as well note 39 above, notes 443 and 527 below.

173. Thus, the largest class in the best city of Plato's *Republic* remains interested, for the most part, in a life of production and consumption.

174. The author recognizes again and again in *Democracy in America* the primacy of the soul over the body.

175. Consider his "Discours de la méthode *pour bien conduire* sa raison et chercher la vérité dans les sciences" (emphasis added).

176. One is reminded somewhat of Cephalus's impression of justice, in the first book of Plato's *Republic*. We will return to this word *honest,* its antecedents, and its implications when we consider Para. 18 of this chapter of *Democracy in America.*

177. After all, Socrates recognizes in the second book of Plato's *Republic* that it is difficult to show that justice, which is often (whatever else it may be) obviously another's good, is also always in the interest of the just man—and it takes a very long argument to establish whatever *is* established along these lines. See Harry V. Jaffa, *Original Intent and the Framers of the Constitution* (Washington, D.C.: Regnery Gateway, 1994), 199 f., 352 f. See also David Hume, *An Inquiry Concerning the Principles of Morals,* Conclusion, Part 2 ("Treating vice with the greatest candor and making it all possible concessions, we must acknowledge that there is not, in any instance, the smallest pretext for giving it the preference above virtue with a view to self-interest, except, perhaps, in the case of justice, where a man, taking things in a certain light, may often seem to be a loser by his integrity.") See, on the term *integrity,* George Anastaplo, Book Review, 1996 *The Great Ideas Today* 464 (1996).

178. Leo Strauss has observed, "All good men whom I know, have taught me

that we do not commit a grievous error if we make it our purpose to be as good as possible." Hugh S. Moorhead, ed., *The Meaning of Life* (Chicago: Chicago Review Press, 1988), 188. See also note 169 above.

179. Montaigne, *Essays,* I, 44.

180. I leave it to those who know Montaigne well to help us here.

181. Otho, Cato, Augustus, and Marius.

182. See, e.g., Plato, *Apology* 40D. See also George Anastaplo, *Human Being and Citizen: Essays on Virtue, Freedom, and the Common Good* (Chicago: Swallow Press, 1975), 239 n. 30, 214 f.

183. Does the reference to "a long time ago," in introducing Montaigne, reflect Tocqueville's awareness that he is obliged to depart in the circumstances in which he happens to find himself from fine old teachers and teachings still attractive to him personally?

184. See, e.g., Anastaplo, *American Moralist,* 15. See, on what the American Founders got from Montesquieu; George Anastaplo, "On Freedom: Explorations," 17 *Oklahoma City University Law Review* 490 f. (1992).

185. See, on Mark Twain, Anastaplo, *Artist as Thinker,* 179 f.; note 117 above.

186. I do not believe that Americans at this time would have been apt to use "State" except to refer to one of the States of the United States. See, e.g., the text at note 216 below. Compare, however, the end of the Declaration of Independence.

187. Tocqueville's reading of the Constitution itself is deeply flawed, however instructive it surely is. Thus, despite his respect for the principle of equality, his constitutional interpretation is sometimes closer in critical respects to John Calhoun than to Abraham Lincoln. I am reminded of how other eminently useful critics of American institutions, such as Alexander Solzhenitsyn in our own time, can simply be off the mark. See, on *The Federalist,* George Anastaplo, "The Constitution at Two Hundred: Explorations," 22 *Texas Tech Law Review* 967, 1042 (1991).

188. One is reminded of what Jean-Jacques Rousseau said, almost a century earlier, about the natural inclination of members of a species to sympathize with one another. One is also reminded of what Aristotle had to say about the natural sociability of human beings.

189. This seems critical to Thomas Hobbes's approach to these matters: the best is too rare to be counted on. See, for a useful introduction to Hobbes, Laurence Berns's chapter in *History of Political Philosophy,* ed. Leo Strauss and Joseph Cropsey, 3d ed. (Chicago: University of Chicago Press, 1987). See also note 76 above.

190. The well-known story about Abraham Lincoln's rescuing the desperate sow stuck in the mud—and this despite the radical "self-interest" and "necessity" arguments he had just been making—is instructive here. See note 259 below. See also note 468 (end) below. See, for Lincoln's opposition to the insistence "that there is no right principle of action but *self-interest*," the text at note 324 below. See also the text at note 338 below.

191. See, e.g., the chapter on Machiavelli in *History of Political Philosophy,* ed. Leo Strauss and Joseph Cropsey, 3d ed. (Chicago: University of Chicago Press, 1987). See also the epigraph for Chap. 7 of this Collection.

192. "How the Americans apply the doctrine of interest well understood in the matter of religion." See note 203 below.

193. See, on this point in Charles Dickens's *Christmas Carol,* Anastaplo, *Artist as Thinker,* 123 f.

194. The protests of Friedrich Nietzsche may be heard here. See, for learned reservations about Nietzsche, J. Harvey Lomax, translator's introduction to *Nietzsche's Philosophy of the Eternal Recurrence of the Same,* by Karl Löwith (Berkeley and Los Angeles: University of California Press, 1997), xxvii–xxviii.

195. On the other hand, democratic aspirations, which contributed to the removal of Czar and Kaiser, may have been partly responsible (Winston Churchill has argued) for twentieth-century barbarities.

196. See, e.g., Anastaplo, "On Trial," 977 f. Consider as well the systematic nonpolitical depravity depicted in Gera-Lind Kolarik, *Freed to Kill* (Chicago: Chicago Review Press, 1990).

197. See Plato, *Republic* 414D ff.

198. See Montaigne, *Essays,* III, i.

199. Possible additional support for the suggestion that the Montaigne essay bears looking into if one is to understand what Tocqueville is driving at may be developed along these lines: There are worthy of note in the table of contents of *Democracy in America* some ninety-five units (if one includes the author's introduction and the separate conclusion to the first volume, conveniently omitting the appendices and the obviously expendable "advertisement" that prefaces each of the two volumes). And, it so happens, the critical Montaigne essay on the useful and the honest, which I suggest is somehow commented on in the central chapter of *Democracy in America,* itself happens to be the ninety-fifth essay in Montaigne's collection of essays. (Montaigne's essays seem to have been in the order in which we now have them since at least 1588. That is, ours seems to be the form of the essay that Tocqueville had also.) See note 203 below.

200. Is this a perversion of Descartes's approach? See, on the enthronement of privacy, George Anastaplo, "The Public Interest in Privacy," 26 *DePaul Law Review* 767 (1977). Consider also George Anastaplo, "'Private' Gambling and Public Morality," in *Representative American Speeches, 1996–1997,* ed. Calvin M. Logue and Jean Deltart (New York: H. W. Wilson, 1997), 126; Anastaplo, *Human Being and Citizen,* 119 f. (on obscenity, still another artificially stimulated addiction).

201. This may help account for Justice Hugo L. Black's suspicion of "natural law" arguments. See George Anastaplo, "Mr. Justice Black, His Generous Common Sense, and the Bar Admission Cases," 9 *Southwestern University Law Review* 977, 1025 n. 66 (1977). See also notes 38 and 39 above, and the Epilogue to this Collection. Compare *Lochner v. New York,* 198 U.S. 45 (1905).

202. See Paragraph 2. Compare Paragraphs 4 and 16.

203. The chapter following in the Tocqueville book, to which I have already referred, describes "how the Americans apply the doctrine of interest well understood in the matter of religion." That is, religion, properly explained and employed, can serve useful social purposes. *That* chapter is the central *unit* of the ninety-five or possibly ninety-six units (see the two-paragraph preface to part 4 of vol. 2) in this book. The "universe" of chapters, from which I have worked in this discussion,

seems to me both "purer" and more productive. See the text at note 159 above. See also note 199 above.

204. See, on Matthew Arnold's "Dover Beach," Anastaplo, *Artist as Thinker,* 150. See also the Matthew Arnold epigraph at the beginning of this Collection.

205. See, on prudence and the Declaration of Independence, Sec. IV of Part 1 of this Collection. See, for the Declaration of the Rights of Man and Citizen (the French counterpart perhaps to the Declaration of Independence), George Anastaplo, *The Amendments to the Constitution: A Commentary* (Baltimore: Johns Hopkins University Press, 1995), 398–400.

206. See, on Lincoln's "hard nut to crack," the text at note 32 above. My critique of Tocqueville (as well as my discussions of the Declaration of Independence) has been offered, in large part, from what I take to be a Lincolnian perspective. This critique can usefully be supplemented by an observation made by Leo Strauss upon opening his Spring 1966 course on Plato's *Meno* at the University of Chicago:

> Tocqueville in his famous book on democracy in America seems to say, at least at first glance, that the case for democracy is in itself not stronger than the case for aristocracy. Democracy has its particular virtues and vices and so has aristocracy. But, Tocqueville continues, Providence has decided in favor of democracy. Practically there is no longer a choice. We have to make the best of democracy; we cannot have a romantic longing for aristocracy. Now what Tocqueville understands by Providence is now called by most people who speak in these terms, History, with a capital "H." History has decided in favor of democracy.

See also note 160 above. See as well note 489 below.

207. See, e.g., George Anastaplo, *The Constitution of 1787: A Commentary* (Baltimore: Johns Hopkins University Press, 1989), 75 f. See also George Anastaplo, "Private Rights and Public Law: The Founders' Perspective," in *Original Intent and the Framers of the Constitution,* ed. Harry V. Jaffa (Washington, D.C.: Regnery Gateway, 1994), 209; note 521 below.

208. See, on the Idea of the Good, Anastaplo, *Thinker as Artist,* 303 f. See also note 172 above. See as well note 39 above, note 476 below. See, on Lincoln and the status of self-interest, the text at note 324 below.

Chapter 7. John C. Calhoun and Slavery

209. See, e.g., George Anastaplo *The Constitutionalist: Notes on the First Amendment* (Dallas: Southern Methodist University Press, 1971), 239–53. Consider, for Lord Charnwood's phrase "a whole deluded society," the text at note 220 below.

The law school teacher quoted from here is Malcolm P. Sharp of the University of Chicago Law School. See, on Mr. Sharp, George Anastaplo, "Malcolm P. Sharp and the Spirit of '76," *University of Chicago Law Alumni Journal,* Summer 1975, 18–24 (reprinted in 121 *Congressional Record* 40241 [12 December 1975];

inserted by Patsy T. Mink); George Anastaplo, "Mr. Crosskey, the American Constitution, and the Natures of Things," 15 *Loyola University of Chicago Law Journal* 181, 216 n. 2 (1984). George Anastaplo, "Lessons for the Student of Law: The Oklahoma Lectures," 20 *Oklahoma City University Law Review* 19, 133 f. (1995). See also note 83 above.

See, on the Rosenberg case, Anastaplo, *The Constitutionalist,* 632–39; George Anastaplo, "On Trial: Explorations," 22 *Loyola University of Chicago Law Journal* 994 f. (1991); "George Anastaplo, "The Occasions of Freedom of Speech," 5 *Political Science Reviewer* 383 (1975); George Anastaplo, "Freedom of Speech and the First Amendment: Explorations," 21 *Texas Tech Law Review* 1941, 2046 f. (1990).

See, on "governmental insanity" and the First World War, Anastaplo, *The Constitutionalist,* 784–85; notes 221 and 504 below. See also George Anastaplo, "Did Anyone 'in Charge' Know What He Was Doing? Thoughts on the Thirty Years' War of the Twentieth Century," in *A Weekend with the Great War,* ed. Steven Weingartner (Shippensburg, Pa.: White Mane Publishing, 1996), 3 (to be incorporated in George Anastaplo, *Campus Hate-Speech Codes, Natural Right, and Twentieth-Century Atrocities* [Lewiston, N.Y.: Edwin Mellen Press, forthcoming]) ; notes 492 and 504 below.

210. Harry V. Jaffa, *How to Think about the American Revolution* (Durham: Carolina Academic Press, 1978), 18. See also Ralph Lerner, "Calhoun's New Science of Politics," 57 *American Political Science Review* 918 (1963). Mr. Jaffa's sequel to his remarkable treatise, *Crisis of the House Divided: An Interpretation of the Issues in the Lincoln–Douglas Debates* (Garden City, N.Y.: Doubleday, 1959), provides a valuable restatement of Calhoun's arguments. (Three passages from the manuscript of this sequel, *A New Birth of Freedom,* are quoted, with Mr. Jaffa's permission, in Sec. VII of Chap. 7 of this Collection.) See, on Mr. Jaffa's always challenging work, George Anastaplo, *Human Being and Citizen: Essays on Virtue, Freedom, and the Common Good* (Chicago: Swallow Press, 1975), 476–79; George Anastaplo, "Prophets and Heretics," *Modern Age,* Summer 1979, 374 f.; Chap. 7 of this Collection; note 26 above, notes 237 and 492 below. See also Jaffa, *Original Intent,* 167 f., 359 f.

211. This is how the Seminole War controversy and the Peggy Eaton affair, dealt with at length in the volume of the Calhoun papers being reviewed, can be understood. Former President James Monroe gave Calhoun advice of moderation that was not acted upon. See Clyde N. Wilson, ed., *The Papers of John C. Calhoun* (Columbia: University of South Carolina Press, 1978), 11: 167. See, on prudence, note 28 above.

212. See George Anastaplo, "Jacob Klein of St. John's College," *Newsletter,* Politics Department, University of Dallas, Spring 1979, 1, 5–6; Anastaplo, *The Constitutionalist,* 738–39. (See, for a Calhounian anticipation of Heideggerian *resoluteness,* the text at note 216 below. See also note 1 above.) The decline of the South in pre–Civil War America may be seen in the subservience of Virginian prudence to South Carolina hotheads. It is not insignificant that Calhoun's last speech was read for him in the Senate by one of the Senators from Virginia.

Is it not devotion to one's own as "sacred" which contributes to the insistence that so deeply rooted an affliction as slavery is really a "positive good"? (One can be reminded of the Serbs today.) See Lincoln, *Collected Works* 3: 549 n. 38. See also the text at note 507 below. Is there in Calhoun's doctrines a distortion of that reliance upon the sacred seen in the Declaration of Independence? See Sec. VI of Chap. 1 of this Collection. See also Sec. VII of Chap. 7 of this Collection.

213. See note 60 above. Former President John Quincy Adams evidently recognized the merits of Southern grievances with respect to the tariff. See Wilson, ed., *Papers of Calhoun*, 11: 543–44. Compare note 478 below. But a Georgian (Tomlinson Fort) wrote Calhoun in 1831: "We feel but one evil; the low price of cotton. This some may attribute to the tariff of 1828. By far the greater [number believe] it arises from the competition of half the world in the production of this article. How the consumption has so far kept pace with the enormous production is the standing wonder of our times." Ibid., 11: 411. (See note 396 below. See also note 219 below.) Even so, may not free trade and a market economy, if properly explained and used, minimize recourse to, and the effects of, selfish politics?

214. Aristophanes, *The Frogs,* 1432–33. See, for Lincoln's recognition of this problem in his Perpetuation Speech (January 27, 1838), *Collected Works,* 1: 114.

Senator John L. McClellan (of Arkansas) once had occasion to say to his former Senatorial ally, Lyndon B. Johnson (of Texas), "I appreciate your calling me and I know you have problems and you're going to do a lot of things I wouldn't do— unless I was President." Doris Kearns, *Lyndon Johnson and the American Dream* (New York: Harper & Row, 1976), 184. Consider also Governor George C. Wallace's observation, upon leaving office (only to return later), that he felt it is good that Southern racial segregation is gone: "It will be best if things are never back the way they were in the good old days. It's better like it is now." *Chicago Sun-Times,* December 8, 1978, 25. See also the text at note 507 below; note 443 below. I have long thought that the excesses of the McCarthy Period, with their destructive effects on foreign policy (for example, in China and hence Indochina), might well have been avoided if the Republican Party could have recovered the Presidency in 1948. See, on the McCarthy Period, George Anastaplo, "On Freedom: Explorations," 17 *Oklahoma City University Law Review* 518 f. (1992). Among our failures with respect to Vietnam was our disregard of the centuries of animosity between the Vietnamese and the Chinese. See note 532 below.

See, for a South Carolinian, contemporary with John C. Calhoun, who was less of a "lion" and much more prudent than Calhoun about the slavery question and States' Rights, James Louis Carson, *Life, Letters and Speeches of James Louis Petigru* (Washington, D.C.: W. H. Lowdermilk, 1920). See also George Anastaplo, "We the People: The Rulers and the Ruled," 1987 *The Great Ideas Today* 71–72 n. 13 (1987); note 295 below.

215. Thus, Calhoun could refer to slavery as "our peculiar domestick institution," "their great and peculiar agricultural capital," "the peculiar nature of the labor and production of this, and the other suffering States." Wilson, *Papers of Calhoun,* 11: 270, 429, 676. Compare Lincoln's understanding of why slavery is not explicitly spoken of in the Constitution (August 31, 1858): "We have no idea of interfering with [slavery] in any manner. I am standing up to our bargain for its maintenance where it lawfully exists. Our fathers restricted its spread and stopped the importation of negroes, with the hope that it would remain in a dormant condition till the people saw fit to emancipate the negroes. There is no allusion to slav-

ery in the constitution—and Madison says it was omitted that future generations might not know such a thing ever existed—and that the constitution might yet be a 'national charter of freedom.' And [Congressman Laurence M.] Keitt of [South Carolina] once admitted that nobody ever thought it would exist to this day." Lincoln, *Collected Works,* 3: 77–78. See also George Anastaplo, "Slavery and the Constitution: Explorations," 19 *Texas Tech Law Review* 677 (1989): 681 f.; the text at note 125 above; the text at notes 311 and 312 below; note 430 below. See, on natural right, note 39 above.

216. Wilson, ed., *Papers of Calhoun,* 11: 228–29 (a letter to Virgil Maxcy). It should be noticed that I try to preserve Calhoun's spelling throughout, and this without the use of *sic, canceled,* and *interlined.* See, on Heideggerian *resoluteness,* note 212 above. A section (originally Sec. II) of the book review upon which Chap. 7 of this Collection is based included the following suggestions about the editorial handling of the somewhat erratic Calhoun materials:

> The Calhoun collection of which this volume [Volume 11] is a part represents an impressive effort to publish everything reduced to writing by the great South Carolinian. It is supplemented by many of the letters written to him, as well as by other materials such as transcripts of Congressional exchanges involving Calhoun.
>
> This particular volume, like its predecessors, is so edited and annotated as to permit the reader easily to keep track of the hundreds of documents laid before him. Anyone with the dimmest recollection of the history of the period should be able, from this volume alone, to get a reliable introduction to what happened at this critical stage in the life of the Republic.
>
> The quality of this collection is fairly indicated by the appraisal of an early volume by the *Times Literary Supplement* (as reproduced on the dust jacket of this eleventh volume): "The great enterprise of publishing the Calhoun papers moves majestically on and the standards of near perfection achieved in the first three volumes . . . are maintained in the current instalment." This work, except for supplementary volumes whenever new materials are discovered, should "never" have to be done again.
>
> My principal reservation here is with the liberal use by the editors of such designations as *"sic,"* "canceled," and "interlined." Calhoun's quite erratic spelling could have been noticed at the beginning of each volume. Thereupon we (like his original readers) could have been left (without the benefit of *sic's* and the like) to shift for ourselves. That is, I prefer to see almost all of his letters presented as he allowed them to leave his hand.
>
> If cancellations and interlineations must be preserved for posterity, and in the text rather than indicated in an appendix, this could better have been better done by the use of discreet symbols placed immediately before or after the words to be removed or inserted. In this way, the practiced reader could read straight through, incorporating whatever is

necessary to complete each sentence. As it is now, many passages are exasperatingly difficult to read.

217.   See, e.g., Alexis de Tocqueville's sympathetic recognition of the problems confronting the South, *Democracy in America*, ed. J.-P. Mayer (New York: Doubleday, 1969), 360. See also Anastaplo, *Human Being and Citizen*, 175 f. Were Southerners trapped in slavery somewhat as we sometimes have seemed to be trapped in preparations for nuclear and biological war? See, e.g., Brian Hall, "Overkill Is Not Dead," *New York Times Magazine*, March 15, 1998, 42; Ted Gup, "The Doomsday Blueprints," *Time*, August 10, 1992, 32. See also note 221 below.

218.   Compare, e.g., Plato, *Apology* 31C–33A. See, on Henry Clay, Lord Charnwood, *Abraham Lincoln* (Garden City: Garden City Publishing, 1917), 41–42, 99–102, 122–23. See, on Sam Houston's political self-sacrifice, Anastaplo, "Lessons for the Student of Law," 163. See also note 286 below. See, on what can properly be said for States' Rights, Anastaplo, *The Constitutionalist*, 171 f. See also note 367 below.

219.   It does not seem to me that it was States' Rights that Calhoun really argued for but rather Sectional Interests (with the sections to be defined by chance passions from time to time?). Sections (unlike States), it should be remembered, are not recognized by the Constitution. Calhoun purported to draw, for his Interposition doctrines, upon the Virginia and Kentucky Resolutions (of 1798–1800). See, for indications of Daniel Webster's response to such use of the Founders, Anastaplo, *The Constitutionalist*, 728; George Anastaplo, "American Constitutionalism and the Virtue of Prudence," in *Abraham Lincoln, The Gettysburg Address, and American Constitutionalism*, ed. Leo Paul S. de Alvarez (Irving, Texas: University of Dallas Press, 1976), 106 f.

Tomlinson Fort pointed out (continuing the passage in the letter to Calhoun quoted in note 213 above), "None know better than we do the unjust operation of the tariff of '28. To frame laws operating equally on a vast empire, with interests so diversified as ours is impossible. To object to a majority passing laws to favor their own interests is to object to our system altogether. An improvement allowing the minority to govern, would last only long enough for the promulgation of laws enacted by them." Wilson, *Papers of Calhoun*, 11: 411.

In any event, Calhoun observed (evidently in a letter of 1831 which does not seem to be extant in its original form), "Nullification is not my word. I never use it. I always say 'State interposition.' My purpose is a suspensive veto to compel the installing, the highest tribunal, provided by the Constitution, to decide on the point in dispute. I do not wish to destroy the Union! I only wish to make it honest! The Union is too strong to break! Nothing can break it—but the Slavery question, if *that* can! If a Convention of the States were called, and *it* should decide, that the protective policy is constitutional, what then? *Then give it up!*" Ibid., 11: 533. But is there any indication in the Constitution that whenever any State chooses to insist upon a serious question, "the point in dispute" must be decided by calling "a Convention of the States?" Is this "honesty"—or is it the original "Polish joke"? See Lerner, "Calhoun's New Science of Politics, " 927 n. 39 (on Calhoun's endorsement of the Polish *liberum veto*). See, on Calhoun, State Interposition, and the right of revolution, George Anastaplo, *The Constitution of 1787: A Commentary* (Baltimore: Johns Hopkins University Press, 1989), 225 f. See also the text at note 295 below. See, on Southern Secessionists and the right of revolution, note 484 below. The provisions for amendments in Art. V of the Constitution prescribe what the States may do (and by implication what they may not do?) to make fundamental changes.

220. Charnwood, *Abraham Lincoln*, 181–82. See, for the quotation from a magnanimous Commanding General Grant (U. S. Grant, *Personal Memoirs* [New York: Charles L. Webster, 1894], 629–30), note 482 below. See, for a useful account of the sacrifices that *should* be made on behalf of a truly oppressed people, Martin Gilbert, *Exile and Return: The Struggle for a Jewish Homeland* (Philadelphia: J. P. Lippincott, 1978). See also Anastaplo, *Human Being and Citizen*, 155 f.; "The O. J. Simpson Case Revisited," 481 f.

See, for how Calhoun continues to mold his fellow Carolinians, Richard M. Weaver, *Life without Prejudice and Other Essays* (Chicago: Henry Regnery, 1965), 162–63 (a Weaver passage is among the epigraphs for this Collection):

> It took the study of John Calhoun to wake me up to a realization that a constitution is and should be primarily a negative document. A constitution—and we may think primarily of the Constitution of the United States in this connection—is more to be revered for what it prohibits than for what it authorizes. A constitution is a series of "thou shalt nots" to the government specifying the ways in which the liberties of individuals and of groups are *not* to be invaded. A constitution is a protection against that kind of arbitrary interference to which government left to itself is prone. It is right therefore to refer to our Constitution as a charter of liberties through its negative provisions, and it is no accident that in our day the friends of liberty have been pleaders for constitutional government.

See also note 60 above. Compare note 532 below. Compare also note 35 above. Does this approach make too much of *rights* at the expense of *duties*? See Chap. 2 of this Collection. The Calhounian concern about the "arbitrary interference to which government itself is prone" was somehow insensitive to that extreme form of governmental arbitrariness and hence tyranny that chattel slavery represented. See, for Lord Mansfield's old-fashioned condemnation of slavery, the text at note 12 above. See also the text at notes 335 and 447 below.

221. The Paton review is quoted on the dust jacket of Karel Schoeman, *Promised Land* (New York: Summit Books, 1978). See also Anastaplo, "Slavery and the Constitution," 780 f.

Other cataclysms, closer to home, require our attention. One is the virtually unlimited "abortion on demand" available in this Country since 1973. Another is the callousness we can sometimes exhibit toward the prospect of large-scale nuclear war. Still another is the general unconcern about what we are permitting to be done to the national character (and to the rearing of future "lions") by television and much of the press. See, e.g., Anastaplo, *Human Being and Citizen*, 46 f., 74 f.,

117 f.; George Anastaplo, *The American Moralist: On Law, Ethics, and Government* (Athens: Ohio University Press, 1992), 245 f.; George Anastaplo, "Getting Set for the End," *Chicago Sun-Times, Book Week,* June 26, 1977, 8 (in which I include this counsel: "Proliferation of nuclear arms among the smaller nations should be sternly discouraged. Also to be discouraged, with an almost religious fervor, is any use in battle of any nuclear weapons by anybody in the foreseeable future. Such recourse should be regarded much as we do the cannibalism to which people have resorted in desperate circumstances."). See also notes 63, 81, and 217 above, note 511 below.

Chapter 8. Southern Illinois's Abraham Lincoln

222.   There was for me something "personal" in thinking about Lincoln on this occasion. This was reinforced by my decision to dedicate this 1991 Carbondale talk to the memory of June Fulkerson, a distinguished alumna of Southern Illinois University who had died the preceding October. June and I were in high school together at Carterville (some ten miles from Carbondale), where her father, Elbert Fulkerson, was the principal. (He was a tall man who was himself somewhat Lincolnesque in appearance. See, on Mr. Fulkerson, George Anastaplo, "A New Look at an Old Lesson," *Chicago Tribune,* June 12, 1976, sec. 1, p. 10. See also George Anastaplo, "Samplings," 27 *Political Science Reviewer* 349–62 [1998].) June Fulkerson got her B.A. from Southern in 1948 and her M.A. in 1954. She became thereafter one of the best high school teachers in Illinois, serving most of her career at New Trier High School, where she was one of the "stars" of a very good faculty.

I find it instructive, in thinking about Abraham Lincoln's career, to contemplate the life and circumstances of so driven a Southern Illinoisan as June Fulkerson. She, like him, could be "melancholy," not least because of a marital relationship. (It is a curious coincidence, which did not occur to me until after I had announced the dedication of this 1991 talk, that both Lincoln and she married a difficult Todd.) June, again like Lincoln, strove for the best despite various personal (including psychological) difficulties: the best depended, for both of them, on a respect for language and a grounding in old-fashioned standards of right and wrong.

That my high school friend was not destined to use fully her considerable natural talents points up the remarkableness of what Lincoln achieved despite the much greater burdens he had to bear. One can see in these matters the role of chance, including the associates one happens to have at critical moments in one's life. June was fortunate at the end of her life, when things become most difficult for her, to be able to return to Southern Illinois, where her sister, Merle (another distinguished graduate of Southern Illinois University who also became a fine high school teacher), could help take care of her.

The intense lifelong determination of someone as talented as June Fulkerson to serve her community can remind us of what Southern Illinois, with its strong sense of community ties, may have meant to, and done for, Abraham Lincoln.

David Riesman has observed that "Southern Illinois University at Carbondale [is] a very interesting university in about as unpromising a college town as there could be." Wilfred M. McClay, "The State of American Higher Education: A Conversation with David Riesman," *Academic Questions,* Winter 1994–1995, 15. I attended Southern Illinois University for a few months in 1947 before entering the College of the University of Chicago. Compare George Anastaplo, "The University of Chicago," *Academic Questions,* Spring 1998, 44; "'McCarthyism,' the Cold War, and Their Aftermath," 120 f.

223. Lincoln, *Collected Works*, 1: 5 (March 9, 1832). See also ibid., 1: 48, 57. Consider as well the deference to custom in the opening lines of Lincoln's First Inaugural Address. See Chap. 12 of this Collection.

224. Ibid., 1: 8.

225. See, e.g., ibid., 1: 145, on taxing the rich, who have few votes anyway.

226. Ibid., 1: 8.

227. See, on the limits of honor, Aristotle, *Nicomachean Ethics*, 1: 1. Aristotle argues that what one should want is to be truly worthy of the esteem of the sensible people to whom one is known. See, on Edmund Burke's somewhat questionable determination not to be bound by his constituents, George Anastaplo. "Lessons for the Student of Law: The Oklahoma Lectures," 20 *Oklahoma City University Law Review* 19, 133 f. (1995).

228. Lincoln, *Collected Works,* 1: I, 31 n. 1.

229. Ibid., 1: I, 31 (January 6, 1835). See toward the end of note 533 below. See also note 479 below.

230. Ibid., 1: I, 62 (January 11, 1837).

231. Ibid., 1: I, 65–66. See also, on capitalists and their ways, ibid., 1: I, 64. See as well See as well Carl Sandburg, *Abraham Lincoln: The Prairie Years* (New York: Harcourt Brace, 1926), 1: I, 192 (the George Forquer story).

232. The population of the United States was 15 million in 1839. See Lincoln, *Collected Works,* 1: 161. Illinois had 40,258 people when it was admitted to the Union as a State in 1818. It had 159,443 people in 1830 and 851,430 in 1850.

233. Paul Simon, *Lincoln's Preparation for Greatness: The Illinois Legislative Years* (Norman: University of Oklahoma, 1965; reprint, University of Illinois Press, 1989). Mr. Simon himself had a distinguished career both in the Illinois General Assembly and in the Congress of the United States.

234. See ibid., 32–33.

235. Lincoln, *Collected Works*, 1: 63–64.

236. See ibid., 1: 67.

237. The best discussion of this remarkable speech (Lincoln, *Collected Works,* 1: 108) is that found in Harry V. Jaffa, *Crisis of the House Divided: An Interpretation of the Issues in the Lincoln–Douglas Debates* (Garden City, N.Y.: Doubleday, 1959). See notes 26 and 210 above, note 492 below, and the text at notes 268 and 512 below.

238. See Lincoln, *Collected Works*, 1: 74–76.

239. Ibid., 1: 75 n.2. See note 7 above.

240. Ibid., 1: 74–75. See, for another effort to cool off passions, Lincoln's First Inaugural Address, which is discussed in Chap. 12 of this Collection. See note 533 below.

241. It should be noticed that the Commerce Clause, in Art. I, Sec. 8, of the Constitution, was believed from the beginning to empower Congress to regulate the *international* slave trade. So why not, it could be wondered, the *"interstate"* slave trade as well? See, e.g., Lincoln, *Collected Works,* 2: 254–55; Sec. III of Chap. 11 of this Collection. See also George Anastaplo, *The Constitution of 1787: A Commentary* (Baltimore: Johns Hopkins University Press, 1989), 64–65; *"In re* Antonin Scalia" (notes 115, 151 above). See as well the text at note 309 below.

242. Lincoln, *Complete Works,* 1: 75–76 n. 2.

243. Carl Sandburg describes Mary Owens as "the daughter of a rich farmer in Green County, Kentucky." *The Prairie Years,* 1: 201.

244. See Lincoln, *Collected Works,* 1: 78, 94.

245. See ibid., 1: 117 f.

246. See ibid., 1: 48, 94. It remains to be determined, John Simon of Southern Illinois University argues, how much truth there is to the Ann Rutledge legend and what effect, if any, her life and, perhaps even more, her death had upon Lincoln. See, e.g., Lord Charnwood, *Abraham Lincoln* (Garden City: Garden City Publishing, 1917), 78–80.

247. See Lincoln, *Complete Works,* 1: 366 f. See also Chap. 9 of this Collection.

248. See, e.g., ibid., 1: 66.

249. Ibid., 1: 140 (January 26, 1839).

250. See ibid., 1: 139.

251. Ibid., 1: 141 (February 1, 1839).

252. Ibid., 1: 141.

253. Ibid., 1: 141.

254. Compare, however, his dismissal of William L. D. Ewing as worthless. Ibid., 1: 143. Thus critical to Lincoln's being were the principles of the American regime and his ability to size up the men and women he might enlist to defend and apply those principles. See, on the mature Lincoln as peacemaker, the Randall quotation in note 533 below.

255. See, e.g., Chap. 16 of this Collection. See, for Lincoln's lack of tolerance for political heresy, note 492 (beginning) below.

256. Was Lincoln more explicit in his references during this period to Biblical and religious matters than he was to be later, at least until the Civil War affected his language? See, e.g., the text at note 259 below. See also Charnwood, *Abraham Lincoln,* e.g., 76–77, 439–41; notes 491 and 492 below. See as well note 497 below.

257. Lincoln, *Collected Works,* 1: 134 (January 17, 1839).

258. Ibid., 1: 168–69 (December 26, 1839).

259. Ibid., 1:. 165–66. See, on Lincoln and the "Doctrine of Necessity," Sec. VI of Chap. 16 of this Collection. See also note 190 above, the text at note 313 below. See as well note 497 below.

260. Lincoln, *Collected Works,* 1: 8 (March 9, 1832). See, on taking charge of one's affairs, George Anastaplo, "'Racism,' Political Correctness, and Constitutional Law: A Law School Case Study," 42 *South Dakota Law Review* 118 f., 122, 127 f., 135 f. (1997). See also Sec. IX of Chap. 4 of this Collection.

Chapter 9. The Poetry of Abraham Lincoln

261. Lincoln, *Collected Works,* 1: 377–78.

262. Osborn H. Oldroyd, *The Poets' Lincoln* (Boston: Chapple Publishing, 1915), ix.

263. Ibid., ix, xi.

264. Ibid., x.

265. See, e.g., George Anastaplo, *The American Moralist: On Law, Ethics, and Government* (Athens: Ohio University Press, 1992), 154.

266. Lincoln, *Complete Works,* 1: 378 (April 18, 1846).

267. Ibid., 1: 379. See, for a longer poem that seems to have been turned into two poems, ibid., 1: 366–70. This can remind us of how much Lincoln, unencumbered by footnotes, reworked his materials throughout his life. See the text at note 1 above. It can be said of Lincoln that he read little but thought much. See, e.g., Lord Charnwood, *Abraham Lincoln* (Garden City: Garden City Publishing, 1917), 10, 103, 132. See also the text at note 319 below.

It can be said of Lincoln as well that he, in the way he accounted for the Civil War in his great Presidential speeches (see the text at note 401 below), served as Homer to his own Odysseus. See, on the eminently prudential Odysseus as storyteller, George Anastaplo, *The Thinker as Artist: From Homer to Plato & Aristotle* (Athens: Ohio University Press, 1997), 27 f.

268. Is *glory* a remedy? See, on Lincoln's Perpetuation Speech, note 237 above.

269. Lincoln, *Collected Works,* 1: 384–86. See, for an earlier version of this poem, ibid., 1: 368–70; note 267 above. See also note 275 below. Lincoln had misspelled his addressee's name as "Johnson" on this occasion. See note 278 below. See as well Lewis A. Warren, *Lincoln's Youth: Indiana Years, Seven to Twenty-one, 1816–1830* (Indianapolis: Indiana Historical Society, 1991), 134, 174–75, 245–47.

270. Ibid., 1: 386.

271. Compare, for example, the need to deal with the Masque of Death at the center of Cervantes's *Don Quixote.* See "Death and Art in Cervantes's *Don Quixote,*" in George Anastaplo, "Lawyers, First Principles, and Contemporary Challenges: Explorations," 19 *Northern Illinois University Law Review,* part 11 (1999). Consider also the discussion of the right to burial at the very center of Hugo Grotius's massive *Law of War and Peace.* Consider as well Socrates' argument, at the end of Plato's *Symposium,* that the same man might be capable of writing both comedy and tragedy. See note 475 below.

272. See Lincoln, *Collected Works,* 1: 392.

273. All that we know about these poems comes from Lincoln's correspondence with Johnston covering a period of a year and a day. See Paul M. Angle and Earl Scheck Miers, *Poetry and Prose by A Lincoln* (Kingsport, Tenn.: Kingsport Press, 1956), 11. See, on Andrew Johnston, Lincoln, *Complete Works,* 1: 367.

274. This "snapping" has been diagnosed as a case of catatonic schizophrenia. See note 282 below. There may not be enough evidence available for a definitive diagnosis. This could have been a manic episode (psychotic, but not schizophrenic) that led to a depressive psychosis.

275. "That man who thinks Lincoln calmly sat down and gathered his robes

about him, waiting for the people to call him, has a very erroneous knowledge of Lincoln. He was always calculating, and always planning ahead. His ambition was a little engine that knew no rest. The vicissitudes of a political campaign brought into play all his tact and management and developed to its fullest extent his latent industry." William H. Herndon and Jesse W. Weik, *Herndon's Life of Lincoln* (1889; repr. Cleveland: World Publishing, 1942), 304 (Chap. 12). See, on the ambition and the remarkable secretiveness of Lincoln, Emanuel Hertz, ed., *The Hidden Lincoln: From the Letters and Papers of William H. Herndon* (New York: Viking Press, 1938), 86–91 (letter of November 24, 1882), 200–202 (letter of August 22, 1887). See also the text at note 319 and 400 below; notes 450 and 492 below. See, for a facsimile of Lincoln's handwritten version of his poem about Matthew Gentry, ibid., 447–53. See the text at note 269 above.

276. If one's reasoning is sound, should not passion be brought into line, except in someone crippled by a pathological condition that subverts the natural sovereignty of reason? The success of psychotropic medication in the treatment of psychosis raises questions for some about whether reasoning is the paramount ruler of the passions. Such medication seems to assuage the passions directly, bypassing the reasoning process. See Anastaplo, *American Moralist,* 492–93. See also note 274 above, note 282 below.

277. I deal at greater length with these two addresses in Chaps. 15 and 16 of this Collection. See, on Lincoln as Homer, note 267 above.

278. See, on Pickett at Gettysburg, note 476 below. Also something of a coincidence, but in a minor mode, is that our Quincy lawyer, who sometimes had his name spelled without a "t," happened to have the same name as the Vice President who succeeded Lincoln when he finally succumbed to death in 1865. See note 269 above.

279. Here is one of many versions of the Gettysburg Address in verse form that editors have offered up during the past century (Oldroyd, *The Poets' Lincoln,* xiii, see note 262 above):

Speech at Gettysburg

Four score and seven years ago
Our fathers brought forth on this continent
A new nation,
Conceived in liberty,
And dedicated to the proposition
That all men are created equal.

Now we are engaged in a great civil war,
Testing whether that nation,
Or any nation so conceived and so dedicated,
Can long endure.
We are met on a great battle-field of that war.
We have come to dedicate a portion of that field
As a final resting-place

For those who here gave their lives
That that nation might live.
It is altogether fitting and proper
That we should do this.
But, in a larger sense,
We cannot dedicate—
We cannot consecrate—
We cannot hallow—
This ground.
The brave men, living and dead,
Who struggled here,
Have consecrated it far above our poor power
To add or detract.
The world will little note nor long remember
What we say here,
But it can never forget
What they did here.
It is for us, the living, rather,
To be dedicated here to the unfinished work
Which they who fought here have so nobly advanced.
It is rather for us to be here dedicated
To the great task remaining before us—
That from these honored dead
We take increased devotion to that cause
For which they gave the last full measure of devotion;
That we here highly resolve
That these dead shall not have died in vain;
That this nation, under God,
Shall have a new birth of freedom;
And that government of the people,
By the people, and for the people
Shall not perish from the earth.

280. Does Matthew Gentry live on in (if not even more because of) Lincoln's poem? See George Anastaplo, *The Artist as Thinker: From Shakespeare to Joyce* (Athens: Ohio University Press, 1983), 310 f.

281. Lincoln, *Complete Works*, 1: 384.

282. This may be a Classical case of dementia praecox. See notes 274 and 276 above.

283. Is Matthew Gentry an example of the type of which the afflicted Friedrich Nietzsche is our most dramatic example? Were the Classical Greeks, on the other hand, more sensitive to the potentialities of the walking dead?

284. I do not refer here to Alzheimer's disease, distressing though that can be, but rather to the fragility of reason in its particular manifestations in one human being after another.

285. See George Anastaplo, "On Freedom: Explorations," 17 *Oklahoma City*

University Law Review 604 f. (1992). Compare Laurence Berns, "The Classicism of George Anastaplo," 26 *Political Science Reviewer* 90, 96 f. (1997). See also George Anastaplo, "First Impressions," 26 *Political Science Reviewer* 248, 250 f. (1997); "Samplings," 389. See as well note 504 below. Compare note 532 below.

286. Three stanzas of the Matthew Gentry poem—the eighth, tenth, and last—have been singled out by one critic as "of the first order." The Poet Hunter, *Lincoln's Poems* (New Orleans: Harvey Press, 1941), 14. I believe this is debatable, not least because of the sentimental tendency of the first two of these three stanzas. See Charnwood, *Abraham Lincoln,* 105. See also the text at note 299 below. See as well note 464 below.

An Illinoisan, transplanted from Texas (who still cherishes a connection to the antisecessionist Sam Houston), has put in poetic form her death-haunted eulogy of Abraham Lincoln:

> Lincoln's Birthday is another year.
> Americans, renounce your daily mail,
> And, child, desert your scratchy desk
> To play. No school keeps nor postman walks
> This sabbath day.
>
> A hundred years have dried each tear
> Death brought forth and stilled the wail
> Of orphaned men. Though they all rest,
> We live, and his truth ever talks,
> While children play.

Sara Prince Anastaplo, "February 12," in *Law and Philosophy,* 2: 1033, ed. John A. Murley, Robert L. Stone, and William T. Braithwaite (Athens: Ohio University Press, 1992). See notes 38 and 218 above, and the text at note 507 below. See as well the text at note 141 above.

The fate of Lincoln's lineage is recorded in the following response to a recent inquiry in the press as to whether there are any living Lincoln descendants (*Parade Magazine,* June 21, 1998, 2):

> No. Robert Lincoln (1843–1926)—oldest of our 16th President's four sons and the only one to reach adulthood—had three children: Mary, Abraham and Jessie. Mary had a son, Lincoln Isham (1892–1973); and Jessie had two children, Mary Lincoln Beckwith (1893–1975) and Robert Todd Lincoln Beckwith (1904–85). All three died without leaving any offspring.

All this bears upon what it is that one may reasonably expect "shall not perish from the earth." See note 52 above. See also notes 474 and 493 below.

Chapter 10. The "House Divided" Speech

287. This Jaffa talk, "The Speech That Changed the World," which I delivered for him and then drew on for my remarks at the 1993 Ottawa symposium, has been published in 24 *Interpretation* 363 (1997). The opening paragraphs of Lincoln's "House Divided" Speech may be found in the text at note 327 below. See also the text at note 432 below. See as well notes 74 and 75 above, note 333 below, the text at note 350 below, and the latter part of Sec. VI of Chap. 4 of this Collection.

288. See, e.g., Thomas Carlyle, *On Heroes, Hero-Worship, and the Heroic in History* (Berkeley and Los Angeles: University of California Press, 1993), 12–13:

> I am well aware that in these days Hero-worship, the thing I call Hero-worship, professes to have gone out, and finally ceased. . . . Shew our critics a great man, a Luther for example, they begin to what they call "account" for him; not to worship him, but take the dimensions of him,—and bring him out to be a little kind of man! He was the "creature of the Time," they say; the Time called him forth, the Time did everything, he nothing—but what we the little critic could have done too? This seems to me but melancholy work. The Time *call* forth? Alas, we have known Times *call* loudly enough for their great man; but not find him when they called! He was not there; Providence had not sent him; the Time, *calling* its loudest, had to go down to confusion and wreck because he would not come when called. For if we will think of it, no Time need have gone to ruin, could it have *found* a man great enough, a man wise and good enough: wisdom to discern truly what the Time wanted, valour to lead it on the right road thither; these are the salvation of any Time.

Consider also Aristotle, *Nicomachean Ethics* 1096a11–16; note 338 below. Consider as well the text at note 220 above, the text at note 295 below.

289. See note 492 below.

290. See, on the *Somerset* case, George Anastaplo, *The Amendments to the Constitution: A Commentary* (Baltimore: Johns Hopkins University Press, 1995), 341–44, 464. See also the Prologue to this Collection.

291. See, e.g., Oliver Warner, *William Wilberforce and His Times* (London: B. T. Batsford, 1962), 166; John Pollock, *Wilberforce* (London: Constable, 1977), 308–9.

292. In the United States, however, the African slave trade had to be tolerated by the Constitution until 1808. See Chap. 4 of this Collection.

293. See, for Mr. Jaffa's pioneering work on Lincoln, notes 26, 210, and 237 above, note 492 below. See also the concluding section of Chap. 7 of this Collection. See, on Mr. Jaffa, George Anastaplo, *The Artist as Thinker: From Shakespeare to Joyce* (Athens: Ohio University Press, 1983), 476–80; notes 177 and 289 above.

294. See, on the limits of George Orwell's depiction of totalitarian regimes, George Anastaplo, *The American Moralist: On Law, Ethics, and Government* (Athens: Ohio University Press, 1992), 161–80.

295. See, on Calhoun, Chap. 7 of this Collection. The career of James Louis Petigru, another South Carolinian, is instructive here. See note 214 above.

296. Consider, for example, the account of the development provided by Tocqueville. See Chap. 6 of this Collection. See also note 39 above.

297. See, on Marcus Brutus, Anastaplo, *Artist as Thinker,* 22–23. See, on Junius Brutus, George Anastaplo, *The Thinker as Artist: From Homer to Plato & Aristotle* (Athens: Ohio University Press, 1997), 361–66. Consider also Justice Black's caution about taking "too much of the responsibility of preserving [one's country's] freedom" upon oneself. *The Bar Admission Cases,* 366 U.S. 82, 114 (1961). Consider as well Roger K. Newman, *Hugo Black: A Biography* (New York: Panthern Books, 1994), 503–7; note 35 above, note 430 below. It can be instructive, in comparing the United States and England, to compare the rules of baseball and the rules (or, rather, the "understandings") of cricket.

298. See Lincoln, *Complete Works,* 3: 1 (August 21, 1858). See also note 306 below.

299. Jaffa, "The Speech That Changed the World," 363. This may be another instance of transforming an unhappy necessity into "a positive good," at least in speech. See the text at note 492 below.

Chapter 11. The Lincoln–Douglas Debates

300. See, e.g., notes 26, 210, and 293 above, note 492 below. See, also Chap. 10 of this Collection.

301. Harry V. Jaffa, *Crisis of the House Divided: An Interpretation of the Issues in the Lincoln–Douglas Debates* (Garden City, N.Y.: Doubleday, 1959), 296.

302. Ibid., 299. See note 74 above. One can be reminded here of how addictions may be understood.

303. An eminently useful study of the *Dred Scott* litigation is Don E. Fehrenbacher, *The Dred Scott Case: Its Significance in American Law and Politics* (New York: Oxford University Press, 1978). See also *Encyclopedia of the American Constitution,* 2: 584; Harry V. Jaffa, *Original Intent and the Framers of the Constitution* (Washington, D.C.: Regnery Gateway, 1994), 172–73; *The Center Magazine,* December 1986, 15; notes 2 and 86 above. Lincoln's 1860 Cooper Institute Address attempts to establish the opinions and actions of the Founding Fathers with respect to the status of slavery in this Country. See note 2 above, and the text at note 312 below. See also note 393 below.

304. See, e.g., Lincoln, *Collected Works,* 3: 9, 216, 296–97. See also for how this point was dealt with in the Federal Convention of 1787, Chap. 4 of this Collection.

305. People of African descent in this Country, whether free or enslaved, were (according to Chief Justice Taney in *Dred Scott,* 407) "so far inferior, that they had no rights that the white man was bound to respect." See Robert W. Johannsen, ed., *The Lincoln–Douglas Debates of 1858* (New York: Oxford University Press, 1965), 33, 34. See also Lincoln, *Collected Works,* 3: 9. The rights of Indians were somewhat more ambiguous than those of Africans and Asians. For example, the Constitution

anticipated civilized dealings by the United States with "Indian Tribes." See also note 25 above, note 526 below. See as well the text at note 90 above.

306. Lincoln, *Collected Works,* 3: 10. See also ibid., 3: 216–17, 296–97. Douglas's speeches, in the course of the Lincoln–Douglas Debates, are included by Roy P. Basler in Vol. 3 of his edition of Lincoln's *Collected Works.*

307. See, e.g., ibid., 3: 10–12.

308. Ibid., 3: 254.

309. Ibid., 3: 254–55. Did not *Dred Scott* tacitly call into question Congress's power to abolish slavery even in the District of Columbia? See note 241 above.

310. Lincoln, *Collected Works*, 3: 255.

311. Ibid., 3: 226 (October 7, 1858).

312. See, e.g., ibid., 3: 306–8. See also ibid., 3: 18, 180–81. See as well notes 215 and 303 above. Lincoln's most "scholarly" discussion of the status of slavery from the beginning of the Country may be found in his 1860 Cooper Institute Address in New York City. Ibid., 3: 522 (February 27, 1860).

313. Ibid., 2: 501 (a speech in Chicago, July 10, 1858). See also ibid., 3: 300.

314. Ibid., 2: 405–6 (a speech at Springfield, June 26, 1857) (the emphases are Lincoln's). See also ibid., 3: 301. The decision in *Dred Scott* had been announced in March 1857. See note 2 above.

315. See note 44 above.

316. Ibid, 3: 15 (quoting from a speech at Peoria, 16 October 1854, ibid., 2: 256). Lincoln's recognition here is at the heart of the prudential policies he developed both as candidate and as President. See, for example, Chaps. 13 and 16 of this Collection. See also note 28 above.

317. Ibid., 3: 27 (August 21, 1858).

318. Ibid., 3: 66 (August 27, 1858). See also ibid., 3: 66–67, 106–7, 215–16. Compare ibid., 3: 71, 179–80.

319. Ibid., 3: 261 (October 13, 1858). See the text at note 450 below. See also Plato, *Republic* 414D ff.; notes 190 and 275 above, notes 450 and 473 below. See also the text at note 1 above.

320. See, e.g., Lincoln, *Collected Works,* 3: 5, 32, 36, 40–42, 260–62, 288–89, 323–24.

321. Ibid., 3: 10 (August 21, 1858).

322. Ibid., 3: 16 (the emphasis is Lincoln's). See note 26 above, note 493 below. See also ibid., 3: 204–5; note 523 below.

323. Quoted by T. G. Hayden, *Phillips Exeter Bulletin,* Winter 1983, 75. See the epigraph for Chap. 8 of this Collection.

324. Lincoln, *Collected Works,* 3: 14 (quoting, on August 21, 1858, from Lincoln's Peoria speech of October 16, 1854, ibid., 2: 225). See, on the significance of self-interest, Chap. 6 of this Collection. See further, on Douglas's "don't care" policy, ibid, 3: 325–26.

325. Ibid., 3: 22–23. See also ibid., 3: 251–52.

326. Ibid., 3: 315 (October 15, 1858). Douglas's "poor tongue" was silenced three years later (in 1861); Lincoln's, seven years later (in 1865).

327. Ibid., 2: 461–62 (the emphases are Lincoln's). See, on the "House Divided" Speech, Chap. 10 of this Collection. See also the text at note 432 below.

328. See ibid., 3: 318 f.

329. See Chap. 9 of this Collection. See also Chaps. 15 and 16 of this Collection.

330. See notes 39 and 58 above.

331. See, e.g., Lincoln, *Collected Works,* 2: 255–56 (where Lincoln speaks of "the monstrous injustice of slavery itself"). See also ibid., 3: 212–16; Charnwood, *Abraham Lincoln,* 14 (on the perhaps apocryphal story about the young Lincoln's almost instinctive response to a New Orleans slave auction: "By God, boys, let's get away from this. If I ever get a chance to hit that thing, I'll hit it hard."). See as well George Anastaplo, "Justice Brennan, Natural Right, and Constitutional Interpretation," 10 *Cardozo Law Review* 201 (1988); George Anastaplo, *Human Being and Citizen: Essays on Virtue, Freedom, and the Common Good* (Chicago: Swallow Press, 1975), 46 f., 74 f.; note 344 below.

332. Lincoln, *Collected Works,* 3: 325. Compare ibid., 2: 400–403. See, for an indication that the *legal* should be the *just,* Max Farrand, ed., *The Records of the Federal Convention* (New Haven: Yale University Press, 1937), 2: 268, 628. See, on positivists today, note 26 above.

333. Lincoln, *Collected Works,* 3: 274 (October 13, 1858). See note 324 above. See, for some support for Douglas's assessment, the text at note 287 above.

334. See, on the Northwest Ordinance, Chap. 3 of this Collection.

335. See note 60 above. See also note 220 above, note 470 below.

336. Lincoln, *Collected Works,* 3: 220 (October 7, 1858). This was greeted by "great applause and cries of 'Hit him again,' 'good,' 'good.'" See also Anastaplo, "Slavery and the Constitution," 686–87.

337. Lincoln, *Collected Works,* 8: 333. See the text at note 505 below.

338. See, on the proper relation between the high and the low, Leo Strauss, *Spinoza's Critique of Religion* (New York: Schocken Books, 1965), 2 (quoted by Harry Jaffa in note 492 below). See also George Anastaplo, *The Constitution of 1787: A Commentary* (Baltimore: Johns Hopkins University Press, 1989), x. See as well notes 76 and 288 above. See, on the prosaic enlisted in a noble cause, the Prologue to this Collection.

Chapter 12. The First Inaugural Address

339. See Lincoln, *Collected Works,* 4: 262 f. See also Sec. III of Chap. 17 of this Collection. Compare the prospect today of Quebec "secession" (or separation) from Canada, which seems far less of a threat to the cause of liberty and the rule of law than was Southern Secession in 1860 and 1861. See George Anastaplo, *Human Being and Citizen: Essays on Virtue, Freedom, and the Common Good* (Chicago: Swallow Press, 1975), 139 f.; note 60 above. See also Anthony DePalma, "Canadian Court Rules Quebec Cannot Secede on Its Own," *New York Times,* August 21, 1998, A3. Fundamental to the August 1998 Opinion of the Supreme Court of Canada is the recognition that connections among the Canadian provinces and peoples are now so complicated that, even with the best will in the world, separation by Quebec from the rest of Canada would be, although not impossible, quite

difficult. See *Reference re Secession of Canada,* File No. 25506, August 20, 1998. See as well note 393 below.

340. See note 303 above.

341. Jefferson Davis had already been inaugurated as president of the Confederate States of America. On March 11, 1861, a new constitution, patterned for the most part upon the Constitution of 1787, would be "[a]dopted unanimously by the Congress of the Confederate States of South Carolina, Georgia, Florida, Alabama, Mississippi, Louisiana and Texas, sitting in Convention at the capitol, in the city of Montgomery Alabama." See George Anastaplo, *The Amendments to the Constitution: A Commentary* (Baltimore: Johns Hopkins University Press, 1995), 361. See also ibid, 125 f. See, on the Texan secession crisis, notes 218 and 286 above.

342. See Chap. 13 of this Collection. See, on Stephen A. Douglas as a minority Senator, note 350 below.

343. See, e.g., the text at notes 308 and 309 above.

344. Lincoln, *Collected Works,* 4: 264. It was one of the peculiar, if not unnatural, anomalies of slavery in the United States that whatever might be done to seize Africans living unenslaved in Africa there were legal limits to what could be done to seize men and women of African descent who, for one reason or another, had come to be regarded as "free" in this Country. This anomaly, if properly studied, should be instructive about the relation of the natural to the conventional or legal. See the text at note 528 below.

345. See ibid., 4: 264, 267–68.

346. See ibid., 4: 267–68.

347. Ibid., 4: 268–69. See, on the Thirty-seventh Congress, note 365 below.

348. Ibid., 5: 267.

349. See ibid., 3: 38 f. See also the text at note 287 above.

350. This is the same man who, sitting close to the new President on the platform as a fellow Illinoisan (and a still influential member of the Senate), held Lincoln's hat while he made his Inaugural Address. Douglas had run second in popular votes in the 1860 Presidential election and a distant fourth in Electoral College votes. He vigorously opposed Secession and, before his death in 1861, urged Lincoln to call out enough troops to defend the Union. See *Encyclopedia of the American Constitution,* 2: 578–79. It is said that Douglas wore himself out trying to prevent Secession. See, on the merits of our Electoral College system, Anastaplo, *Constitution of 1787,* 333. Did not an arrangement comparable to the Electoral College system prevail when United States Senators were elected by State legislatures? In 1858, the total popular vote for State legislative candidates pledged to Lincoln was larger than the total popular vote for State legislative candidates pledged to Douglas, but Douglas had ended up with more votes in the State legislature and hence could be reelected to the United States Senate.

351. See, on Secession and the rule of law, Anastaplo, "Slavery and the Constitution," 754 f.

352. See Carl Sandburg, *Abraham Lincoln: The War Years* (New York: Harcourt, Brace, 1939), 1: 9.

353. Is it merely a coincidence that Lincoln's First Inaugural Address has thirty-four paragraphs before the final one was added as a flourish looking to the

future? His own State, Illinois, had been admitted in 1818 as the twenty-first State. See note 66 above. The Country, it can be said, came of age with the admission of Illinois.

354. Lincoln, *Collected Works,* 4: 268. See, on Lord Mansfield's deference to Parliament, the text at note 10 above. See also note 357 below.

355. Compare, e.g., the detailed provision for the exercise of the veto power by the President. See, on judicial review, Anastaplo, *Constitution of 1787,* 335; Anastaplo, *Amendments to the Constitution,* 460.

356. All this is aside from what the powers of the United States Supreme Court, as well as of the Congress and of the President, may be in assessing and correcting the doings of the States. (These powers, but *not* judicial review of acts of Congress, are confirmed, in effect, by the Supremacy Clause in Art. VI of the Constitution of 1787.) It should also be noticed that courts are most in their element (and least "political") when they develop and apply the common law, perhaps more than when they interpret and apply legislation or even the Constitution. See note 155 above. See also Chap. 5 of this Collection. See, on the exclusive power of the legislature to interpret "these Rites and liberties" the conclusion of the 1641 Massachusetts Body of Liberties; Anastaplo, *Liberty, Equality, and Modern Constitutionalism,* 1: 195.

357. See Anastaplo, "The Supreme Court Is Indeed a Court," in *Is the Supreme Court the Guardian of the Constitution?* ed. Robert A. Licht (Washington, D.C.: American Enterprise Institute Press, 1993), 22. See also the text at notes 10 and 354 above.

358. See, e.g., note 58 above. See also note 39 above.

359. See Lincoln, *Collected Works,* 4: 265.

360. See ibid., 4: 262.

361. See ibid., 4: 266–67.

362. See Anastaplo, *Amendments to the Constitution,* 344. See also ibid., 125 f. See as well Sec. II of Chap. 13 of this Collection.

363. Lincoln, *Collected Works,* 4: 271. It is said that parts of this passage were suggested to Lincoln by others.

364. See, on Lincoln's use of his religious heritage, Chaps. 15 and 16 of this Collection.

Chapter 13. The Fourth of July Message to Congress

365. The Thirty-sixth Congress adjourned sine die on the morning of March 4, 1861 (before the inauguration, later that day, of the new President). The first regular session of the Thirty-seventh Congress (elected in November 1860) was scheduled to begin in December 1861. The Senate of the Thirty-seventh Congress was available to meet in executive session (to consider Presidential nominations of officers, etc.) from March 1861 on. See the text at note 347 above.

366. Those seven States of the Lower South included South Carolina, Geor-

gia, Florida, Alabama, Mississippi, Louisiana, and Texas. See the text at note 341 above.

367. Fort Sumter was manned at that time by a contingent of the Army of the United States under the command of a major who happened to be a slaveowner from Kentucky who remained loyal to the United States. On the other hand, I was intrigued, during a visit to Fort Sumter a few years ago, to hear an official guide of African-American descent explain how "we" (that is, we South Carolinians) had been obliged in the 1860s to resist Federal encroachments upon States' Rights. See note 218 above.

368. The four "seceding" States of the Upper South included Virginia, North Carolina, Tennessee, and Arkansas. Lincoln argued, in his Fourth of July Message, that the majority sentiment in Virginia was *not* secessionist. See Lincoln, *Collected Works,* 4: 598–99. See, on Texas, note 218 above.

369. See Abraham Lincoln, *Collected Works,* ed. Roy P. Basler (New Brunswick, N.J.: Rutgers University Press, 1953), 4: 421 f. See also Chap. 12 of this Collection.

370. See ibid., 4: 431 f. Detailed studies are available about both what Lincoln did on his own and what he asked Congress to do.

371. See Lincoln, *Collected Works,* 4: 429.

372. Ibid., 4: 438.

373. Ibid., 4: 438.

374. See, for the text of the provisional Confederate Constitution, Alexander H. Stephens, *A Constitutional View of the Late War between the States* (Philadelphia: National Publishing, 1870), 2: 714 f. See, for the text of the permanent Confederate Constitution, ibid, 2: 722 f.; George Anastaplo, *The Amendments to the Constitution: A Commentary* (Baltimore: Johns Hopkins University Press, 1995), 243, 344 f. See also note 483 below. See as well note 389 below.

375. Ratification of the 1787 Constitution depended upon the acquiescence of conventions in at least nine States. It could not be known, at the time that the Constitution was drafted, which States should be listed in the Preamble (in the way they had been in the Articles of Confederation, which had required for ratification the unanimous consent of all thirteen States). Eleven States *had* ratified the Constitution by the time the new government began in 1789. Was it not assumed that the other two States (North Carolina and Rhode Island) remained parts of the United States, however anomalous their status for the time being? See Anastaplo, *The Constitution of 1787,* 220–21. See also note 482 below.

376. The Ninth and Tenth Amendments were placed in Art. IV of the Confederate Constitution. See George Anastaplo, *The Constitution of 1787: A Commentary* (Baltimore: Johns Hopkins University Press, 1989), 361. See also ibid., 132.

377. Lincoln, *Collected Works,* 4: 438.

378. See, ibid., 4: 423, 425, 439.

379. See, e.g., ibid., 4: 514.

380. See Anastaplo, *Amendments to the Constitution,* 344–45, 363; George Anastaplo, "The Preamble," in *The Constitution and Its Amendments,* ed. Roger K. Newman (New York: Macmillan, 1999), 14–15. See also William W. Crosskey, *Politics and the Constitution in the History of the United States* (Chicago: University of

Chicago Press, 1953), 370 f.; Anastaplo, *Constitution of 1787,* 13 f.; Anastaplo, *Amendments to the Constitution,* 97 f., 125 f. See as well notes 383 and 384 below.

381. Related qualifications may be seen throughout the 1861 Confederate Constitution.

382. See, e.g., *Encyclopedia of the American Constitution,* 2: 906. See, on the case *for* States' Rights, George Anastaplo *The Constitutionalist: Notes on the First Amendment* (Dallas: Southern Methodist University Press, 1971), 171 f.

383. The Commerce Clause (in Art. 1, Sec. 8) was expanded by the Confederates to read:

> The Congress shall have power . . . To regulate commerce with foreign nations, and among the several States, and with the Indian tribes [*the expansion begins here:*] but neither this, nor any other clause contained in the constitution, shall ever be construed to delegate the power to Congress to appropriate money for any internal improvement intended to facilitate commerce; except for the purpose of furnishing lights, beacons, and buoys, and other aids to navigation upon the coasts, and the improvement of harbors and the removing of obstructions in river navigation, in all which cases, such duties shall be laid on the navigation facilitated thereby, as may be necessary to pay the costs and expenses thereof. (Anastaplo, *Amendments to the Constitution,* 349)

See, on internal improvements, note 384 below. See also Sec. IV of Chap. 7 of this Collection.

384. The opening clause of Art. 1, Sec. 8 was changed by the Confederates to read:

> The Congress shall have power—1. To lay and collect taxes, duties, imposts, and excises, *for revenue necessary* to pay the debts, [and] provide for the common defence [and general welfare of the United States], *and carry on the government of the* [United] *Confederate States; but no bounties shall be granted from the treasury; nor shall any duties or taxes on importations from foreign nations be laid to promote or foster any branch of industry;* [but] *and* all duties, imposts, and excises shall be uniform throughout the [United] *Confederate* States. (Anastaplo, *Amendments to the Constitution,* 349)

The bracketed words in this passage were stricken from the United States Constitution by the Confederates. Changes in capitalization are not noted here. The italicized words were added by the Confederates to their 1861 constitution. See also the text at note 380 above.

385. See, e.g., Sec. IV (i) of Chap. 14 of this Collection. Lincoln was anticipated in his "theory" by John Quincy Adams.

386. We can see in the epigraph for Chap. 13 of this Collection that Alexander H. Stephens, who had been the Vice President of the Confederate States of America, also believed that sophistry should be avoided. Stephens, like Lincoln, had

been a Whig member of the House of Representatives. Lincoln wrote home (to William H. Herndon, on February 2, 1848):

> I just take up my pen to say, that Mr. Stephens of Georgia, a little slim, pale-faced, consumptive man, with a voice like [Stephen T.] Logan's has just concluded the very best speech, of an hour's length, I ever heard.
>
> My old, withered, dry eyes, are full of tears yet. (Lincoln, *Collected Works*, 1: 448)

This Stephens speech vigorously denounced the Mexican War as an aggression to "force and compel" the people of Mexico to sell their country. See *Congressional Globe,* Thirtieth Congress, 1st sess., vol. 17, 159–63. See also note 389 below. See, on sophistry and positivism, note 26 above.

387.   Lincoln, *Collected Works,* 4: 434. See also note 482 below.

388.   See, e.g., Lincoln, *Collected Works,* 4: 426, 428 ("the border States, so called—in fact, the middle states").

389.   See note 427 below. Alexander Stephens, on the other hand, could even entitle his history of the Civil War *A Constitutional View of the Late War between the States.* Northerners tended to speak of the Insurrection, of the War of the Rebellion, and, of course, of the Civil War. The "constitutional view" from which Stephens presents his account is one that attempts to justify a violent effort to relieve Southern States of their constitutional obligations. It is instructive to consider how much more George Washington made of the *nation* and its principles. See, e.g., that great Virginian's First Inaugural Address and Farewell Address. See, also note 26 above, note 397 below.

390.   See, e.g., Lincoln, *Collected Works,* 4: 438. Compare, as Lincoln prepared for peace-time reconciliation, his Second Inaugural Address. See Chap. 16 of this Collection. See also note 533 below.

391.   See, e.g., Stephens, *Constitutional View of the Late War,* 425 f., 748 f. (the opinion of Chief Justice Taney in the *Merryman* case, note 407 below). Herman Belz ends a chapter, "Lincoln and the Constitution: The Dictatorship Question Reconsidered," with this sensible assessment: "We may conclude, therefore, that Lincoln was neither a revolutionary nor a dictator, but a constitutionalist who used the executive power to preserve and extend the liberty of the American Founding." Belz, *Abraham Lincoln, Constitutionalism, and Equal Rights in the Civil War Era* (New York: Fordham University Press, 1998), 43. See note 60 above. Also eminently sensible (including his recognition of the "idiosyncratic") is Belz, Book Review, *American Journal of Legal History,* July 1996, 395–96. See notes 485 and 521 below.

392.   Is there something innate about the moral sense? What is the relation of nature to morality? See, on Lincoln and a national common law, Lord Charnwood, *Abraham Lincoln* (Garden City: Garden City Publishing, 1917), 377–80. See also Anastaplo, "Teaching, Nature, and the Moral Virtues," 23 f.; Anastaplo, *Constitution of 1787,* 127 f. See as well Chap. 5 of this Collection; notes 58 and 155 above.

393.   See, on the debt owed by all of the United States, Lincoln, *Collected Works,* 4: 435 f. The lawyer somewhat mechanically at work may also be seen in

the Cooper Institute Address. Was not that New York City address designed to reassure the Eastern "establishment"? See notes 2 and 303 above, note 430 below. Would not Quebec's share of the Canadian national debt have to be negotiated in the event of Separation? See note 339 above. See also Sec. VII of Chap. 3 of this Collection.

394.   See note 64 above, notes 447, 468, 473, 490, and 533 below. See also note 81 above, and the text at note 496 below.

395.   See, e.g., George Anastaplo. "Lessons for the Student of Law: The Oklahoma Lectures," 20 *Oklahoma City University Law Review* 198 f, 206 f. (1995). .

396.   Although it is said that only a small proportion of Southerners held slaves, the pro-slavery faction (which tended to be wealthier) evidently dominated Southern politics. See note 501 below. It was *that* institution (not, for example, tariffless imports, which affected many more people directly) that the South was willing to go to war to protect. See note 213 above. See, on the self, George Anastaplo, *Human Being and Citizen: Essays on Virtue, Freedom, and the Common Good* (Chicago: Swallow Press, 1975), 87 f.

397.   Alexander Stephens, a lifelong defender of slavery, identified his residence, in Crawfordsville, Georgia, as "Liberty Hall." John Wilkes Booth proclaimed, upon shooting Abraham Lincoln, "*Sic semper tyrannis.*" See the Matthew Arnold epigraph at the beginning of this Collection. See also note 60 above. See as well the epigraph for Chap. 13 of this Collection. Both "liberty" and "constitutional" seem to be taken by Stephens from the same somewhat unreliable political lexicon. See note 389 above, note 470 below. See also Chap. 7 of this Collection. See as well note 26 above, note 533 below.

398.   See, for the emphasis placed by Lincoln upon the oath he took as President, *Collected Works,* 4: 271.

399.   See, e.g., ibid., 605, 607.

400.   See, e.g., the epigraph for Chap. 13 of this Collection. See also note 275 above.

401.   See Lincoln, *Collected Works*, 5: 35 f. (1861), 5: 513 f. (1862), 7: 36 f. (1863), 8: 136 f. (1864). See, on Lincoln and Homer, note 267 above.

402.   We can see a similar approach in the way that Winston Churchill dealt with Parliament during the Second World War.

403.   See, for President James Buchanan's last annual message to Congress (on December 3, 1860), *Congressional Globe,* 36th Cong., 2d sess., vol. 30, part 2, app., 1 f. See also the text at note 342 above.

404.   See, e.g., Lincoln's remarks to several Ohio regiments in August 1864. Lincoln, *Collected Works,* 7: 504–5, 512, 528–29.

405.   This immigration and its military and economic consequences are referred to by Lincoln in one of his annual messages to Congress. See ibid., 8: 141, 145, 150–51, 153 (1864). See also note 75 above.

406.   See ibid, 4: 429 f.

407.   See *In re Merryman,* 17 F. Cas. 144 (1861). See also note 391 above.

408.   Are the abuses of our considerable liberty to own guns somewhat like the abuses of our free press—and, as such, are they not regarded by some as part of the price to be paid for our considerable overall freedom? See, on gun control and

the Second Amendment, Anastaplo, *Amendments to the Constitution,* 59 f. See, on the gunning down of America, Anastaplo, "'McCarthyism,'" 128 f. See also notes 41 and 147 above. See, on Lincoln and newspapers, note 435 below.

409. See Anastaplo, *Constitution of 1787,* 299. Lincoln referred to this proposal in his First Inaugural Address. *Collected Works,* 4: 270. I have never understood why he had never been shown the proposal, *unless he did not want to see it* before his Inauguration, leaving him free to speak of it as he did on that occasion:

> I understand a proposed amendment to the Constitution—which amendment, however, I have not seen, has passed Congress, to the effect that the federal government shall never interfere with the domestic institutions of the States, including that of persons held to service. To avoid misconstruction of what I have said, I depart from my purpose not to speak of particular amendments, so far as to say that, holding such a provision to now be implied constitutional law, I have no objection to its being made express, and irrevocable.

410. See, e.g., Confederate Constitution, Art. IV: Sec. 2: "The citizens of each State shall be entitled to all the privileges and immunities of citizens in the several States; and shall have the right of transit and sojourn in any State of this Confederacy, with their slaves and other property; and the right of property in said slaves shall not be thereby impaired." Anastaplo, *Amendments to the Constitution,* 358–59. This provision ratifies in effect the position of Chief Justice Taney in *Dred Scott.* Does it not add to the Constitution an assurance for slaveowners that had not really been there before, whatever the *Dred Scott* Court may have believed? See also Anastaplo, *Amendments to the Constitution,* 173 f.

411. See, e.g., Chap. 11 of this Collection.

412. See Chaps. 3 and 4 of this Collection. See also Anastaplo, "Slavery and the Constitution," 717 f.

413. See the epigraph for Chap. 1 of this Collection.

414. See note 448 below.

415. Lincoln, *Collected Works,* 4: 440, 435.

416. See George Anastaplo, *The Artist as Thinker: From Shakespeare to Joyce* (Athens: Ohio University Press, 1983), 275 f.; George Anastaplo, *The Thinker as Artist: From Homer to Plato & Aristotle* (Athens: Ohio University Press, 1997). 46 f., 74 f. See also note 392 above, note 492 below. See as well the end of the Prologue and the end of Chap. 7 of this Collection.

Chapter 14. The Emancipation Proclamation

417. See, on the Confederate Constitution, Anastaplo, *Amendments to the Constitution,* 125 f., 344 f. See, on the Southern preference for "Confederated" over "United," note 482 below.

418. The texts of the Preliminary Proclamation (of September 22, 1862) and

of the Final Proclamation (of January 1, 1863), which together constitute the Emancipation Proclamation and which are completely set forth (in italics) in Chap. 14 of this Collection, are taken from Lincoln, *Collected Works,* ed. Roy P. Basler (New Brunswick, N.J.: Rutgers University Press, 1953), 5: 433–36; 6: 28–30.

419. Jaffa, *The Conditions of Freedom* (Baltimore: Johns Hopkins University Press, 1975), 8. See George Anastaplo, *The Artist as Thinker: From Shakespeare to Joyce* (Athens: Ohio University Press, 1983), 476 n. 285; note 448 below. See also George Anastaplo, *The Amendments to the Constitution: A Commentary* (Baltimore: Johns Hopkins University Press, 1995), 388 n. 11, 432 n. 168, 450–52. See as well note 26 above, note 492 below (including observations quoted by Mr. Jaffa from Leo Strauss about the proper relation of the high to the low).

420. Vernon Jarrett, "Why We Must Re-evaluate Heroes of the Past," *Chicago Tribune,* February 20, 1974, sec. 1, p. 14. See also note 423 below.

It should be remembered that Lincoln always had to contend with the anti-Negro prejudices of Unionists in the Northern and Middle States. See, e.g., John G. Randall, *Lincoln the President* (New York: Dodd, Mead, 1945), 2: 133 ("The Africanization of our Society"), 172; John T. Morse Jr., *Abraham Lincoln* (Boston: Houghton, Mifflin, 1893), 2: 126–27. See, for Lincoln's periodic, deliberate recourse to talk about "colonization of blacks" as his way of lulling the racial fears of white Unionists, Stephen B. Oates, *With Malice toward None: The Life of Abraham Lincoln* (New York: Harper & Row, 1977), 268, 297–99, 307, 312–13, 322, 325–26, 330–31, 339–42; Randall, *Lincoln the President,* 1: 138 f. Compare Robert Dale Owen, *The Wrong of Slavery, The Right of Emancipation* (Philadelphia: J. B. Lippincott, 1864). How these matters could be seen, whether or not correctly, is indicated by the account of Karl Marx (in November 1862): "Of Lincoln's emancipation [proclamation, of September 1862,] one still sees no effect up to the present, save that from fear of a Negro inundation the Northwest [what we today know as the Midwest] has voted Democratic [that is, against Lincoln's party]." John Hope Franklin, *The Emancipation Proclamation* (Garden City, N.Y.: Anchor Books, 1963), 85. See the text at note 423 below. See also note 455 below. See as well the text at note 1 above.

421. Editorial, *Chicago Tribune,* February 15, 1974, sec. 1, p. 12. This editorial was a response to Mr. Jarrett's column of February 13, 1974.

422. Sandburg, *Abraham Lincoln: The War Years* (New York: Harcourt, Brace, 1939), 2: 21–22. Seward had just said, "I mean that the Emancipation Proclamation was uttered in the first gun fired at Fort Sumter, and we have been the last to hear it." Ibid., 2: 21. See also John G. Randall, *Constitutional Problems under Lincoln* (New York: D. Appleton, 1926), 378–80. See as well note 451 below.

423. Herbert J. Storing, ed., *What Country Have I? Political Writings of Black Americans* (New York: St. Martin's, 1970), 52–53 (emphasis added). See note 420 above. Frederick Douglass's mature appraisal of the President may usefully be compared to what Martin Luther King Jr. said about him the night before King was murdered in Memphis in April 1968: "[In 1863] a vacillating president by the name of Abraham Lincoln finally [came] to the conclusion that he had to sign the Emancipation Proclamation." James M. Washington, ed., *A Testament of Hope: The Essential Writings of Martin Luther King Jr.* (San Francisco: Harper & Row, 1986), 279. We

see here, in the use of "vacillating," still another lamentable misreading of Lincoln's career. See George Anastaplo, "Lawyers, First Principles, and Contemporary Challenges: Explorations," 19 *Northern Illinois University Law Review* (1999), part 16 ("Martin Luther King and his Letter from Birmingham Jail").

424. Lincoln, *Collected Works,* 7: 281 (letter to Albert G. Hodges). See Anastaplo, *Amendments to the Constitution,* 450–52 n. 259.

425. Storing, *What Country Have I?* 51–52 (emphasis added). See also Randall, *Lincoln the President,* 2: 201–3. See as well Anastaplo, *Amendments to the Constitution,* 396 n. 45, 425 n. 142, 450–52 n. 259; note 450 below. See, on the significance of the telegraph during the Civil War, note 1 above.

426. Lincoln, *Collected Works,* 5: 388–89.

427. Ibid., 5: 389. See, for Lincoln's comments on his letter to Greeley, ibid., 7: 499–501. This letter was in response to Greeley's published criticism of "the policy [Lincoln seemed] to be pursuing with regard to the slaves of Rebels." This criticism had included the complaint, "We think you are unduly influenced by the counsels . . . of certain fossil politicians hailing from the Border Slave States." Ibid., 5: 389. (It is well to be reminded here of what is implied in Lincoln's salutary preference for "Middle States" over "Border States." An exception may be found at ibid., 7: 282. See the text at note 389 above, note 443 below.) See notes 430 and 455 below.

428. Ibid., 8: 152 (Annual Message to Congress, December 6, 1864). By this time "a proposed amendment of the Constitution abolishing slavery throughout the United States" had passed the Senate. Ibid., 8: 149. Lincoln had expressed similar sentiments in his Annual Message to Congress of December 1863. Ibid., 7: 51. See also ibid., 6: 411, 7: 81.

429. Harry V. Jaffa, *Equality and Liberty: Theory and Practice in American Politics* (New York: Oxford University Press, 1965), 157. See also George Anastaplo, *Human Being and Citizen: Essays on Virtue, Freedom, and the Common Good* (Chicago: Swallow Press, 1975), 203 f. See as well ibid., 61 f.

430. Jaffa, *Equality and Liberty,* 158. See note 427 below.

Lincoln's "historical" view of slavery, and of what was to be done about it in the American constitutional system, had been set forth in this manner on October 13, 1858 (in the course of the Lincoln–Douglas Debates):

> When Judge Douglas undertakes to say that as a matter of choice the fathers of the government made this nation part slave and part free, *he assumes what is historically a falsehood.* [Long continued applause.] More than that; when the fathers of the government cut off the source of slavery by the abolition of the slave trade, and adopted a system of restricting it from the new Territories where it had not existed, I maintain that they placed it where they understood, and all sensible men understood, it was in the course of ultimate extinction ["that's so"]; and when Judge Douglas asks me why it cannot continue as our fathers made it, I ask him why he and his friends could net let it remain as our fathers made it? [Tremendous cheering.]
>
> It is precisely all I ask of him in relation to the institution of slav-

ery, that it shall be placed upon the basis that our fathers placed it upon. Mr. Brooks, of South Carolina, once said, and truly said, that when this government was established, no one expected the institution of slavery to last until this day; and that the men who formed this government were wiser and better men than the men of these days; but the men of these days had experience which the fathers had not, and that experience had taught them the invention of the cotton gin, and this had made the perpetuation of the institution of slavery a necessity in this country. Judge Douglas could not let it stand upon the basis upon which our fathers placed it, but removed it and *put it upon the cotton gin basis.* [Roars of laughter and enthusiastic applause.] It is a question, therefore, for him and his friends to answer—why they could not let it remain where the fathers of the Government originally placed it. [Cheers, and cries of "Hurrah for Lincoln!" "Good!" "Good!"]

I hope nobody has understood me as trying to sustain the doctrine that we have a right to quarrel with Kentucky, or Virginia, or any of the slave States, about the institution of slavery—thus giving the Judge an opportunity to make himself eloquent and valiant against us in fighting for their rights. I expressly declared in my opening speech, that I had neither the inclination to exercise, nor the belief in the existence of the right to interfere with the States of Kentucky or Virginia in doing as they pleased with slavery or any other existing institution. [Loud applause.] Then what becomes of all his eloquence in behalf of the rights of States, which are assailed by no living man? [Applause. "He knows it's all humbuggery."] (Lincoln, *Collected Works,* 3: 276–77) (emphasis in the original)

Lincoln, in his 1860 Cooper Institute Address provided a more technical discussion of some of the points touched upon here. See notes 2 and 393 above. See notes 215 and 393 above, notes 443, 451, and 455 below.

See, for a brilliant use of the "created equal" language of the Declaration of Independence, Harry V. Jaffa, "Equality, Justice, and the American Revolution," *Modern Age,* Spring 1977, 114. See also George Anastaplo, "Mr. Justice Black, His Generous Common Sense and the Bar Admission Cases," 9 *Southwestern University Law Review* 1042 (1977). "The other part of our freedom consists in the civil rights and advancements of every person according to his merit: the enjoyment of those never more certain, and the access to these never more open, than in a free commonwealth." John Milton, "The Ready and Easy Way to Establish a Free Commonwealth," in *Complete Poems and Major Prose of John Milton,* ed. Merritt Y. Hughes, (Indianapolis: Odyssey Press, Bobbs Merrill, 1957), 896.

431. Jaffa, *Equality and Liberty,* 163. Consider this Unionist account of the proposed recourse by the Confederates themselves to their slaves as fighting men:

In the autumn and winter of 1864, the cause of the South was already lost and the collapse of the Confederate Government plainly foreshadowed to all except the leaders, whose infatuation and wounded vanity made them unwilling to acknowledge and accept defeat. Yet this effort to avoid confession of error in one direction compelled them to admit it in another. They had seceded for slavery, had made it the corner-stone of their Government, had anathematized President Lincoln for his decrees of emancipation, had pronounced the ban of outlawry, and had prescribed the sentence of death against every white officer who might dare to command negro troops; but now, in their extremity, some of them proposed to throw consistency to the winds and themselves commit the acts upon which they had invoked the reprobation of mankind, and for which they had ordained extreme punishment.

It would be difficult to estimate the benefit they had derived from the direct military labor of the slave, especially in building fortifications. They now proposed not only to put arms in his hands and make him a soldier to fight in the ranks, but also, as a final step, to emancipate him for the service. Even the flexible political conscience of Jefferson Davis, however, winced a little at the bold abandonment of principle which the policy involved, and in his message of November 7, 1864, to the Confederate Congress he argued the question with the reluctance of a man preparing to walk over live coals. . . .

Mr. Davis's hesitating and tentative recommendation was seed sown on barren ground. If the dose was unpalatable to him it appears to have been yet more bitter to the Members of the Confederate Congress, who doubtless felt, as has been pithily expressed by a Confederate writer, that it was an admission of the inherent injustice of slavery; that *"if the negro was fit to be a soldier he was not fit to be a slave"*; that *the proposition "cut under the traditions and theories of three generations of the South"*; and that "by a few strokes of the pen the Confederate Government had subscribed to the main tenet of the abolition party in the North and all its consequences, standing exposed and stultified before the world." As the fall of the Confederacy drew nigh the stress of disaster compelled his acceptance of the distasteful alternative, though even then he could not refrain from expressing the hope that the grim necessity would somehow be averted. . . .

They debated the unwelcome subject with qualms and grimaces through November, December, January, and most of February. On the 11th of January [1865], and again on the 18th of February, the proposal received a notable support in letters from General Lee, in which he declared the measure of employing negro soldiers "not only expedient but necessary," and recommended that the Confederate President be empowered "to call upon individuals or States for such as they are willing to contribute, with the condition of emancipation to all enrolled." (John G. Nicolay and John Hay, *Abraham Lincoln: A History* [New York: Century, 1914], 6: 484–87) (emphasis added)

(The lines I have italicized remind us of the anthropology upon which Southern pro-slavery political principles depended.) See also Grant, *Personal Memoirs,* 636;

Sec. IV (xiv) of Chap. 14 of this Collection; note 529 below. See as well Ellen G. Wilson, *The Loyal Blacks* (New York: Capricorn Books, 1976) (on the promises of emancipation of soldier-slaves by the British during the American Revolution).

Transformation of the burdens of slavery can take different forms. See, e.g., Thucydides, *The Peloponnesian War,* 4: 80; William Faulkner, *The Sound and the Fury* (1929) (Jason Compson's "emancipation").

432.   Lincoln, *Collected Works,* 2: 461–62. See, for the lines that preceded this prophecy, the text at note 327 above. See also Chap. 10 of this Collection.

433.   Similarly, it can be said that Christian thought (as we have come to know it) may be better seen in someone such as St. Augustine than in Jesus, if only because Jesus (insofar as he was human) was raised as a Jew with relatively little exposure to that part of the philosophical tradition of the Greeks that has been incorporated in Christianity. See, on St. Augustine, George Anastaplo, "Teaching, Nature, and the Moral Virtues," 1997 *The Great Ideas Today* 9 f. (1997). See, on St. Paul (who was born a Roman citizen), Anastaplo, "Rome, Piety, and Law: Explorations," 39 *Loyola of New Orleans Law Review* 32, 39 (1993). See also Anastaplo, *Amendments to the Constitution,* 422 n. 133, 452–53 n. 260. See as well note 485 (end) below.

434.   Sandburg, *The War Years,* 2: 20. Among the things that Lincoln's "paper" did, when he let it "go forth," was to provoke these responses:

> Southern reaction to the proclamation was predictably negative, damning it as an invitation to slaves to murder their masters. The reaction in the north was mixed, with the legislature of Lincoln's own state, Illinois, declaring the proclamation "a gigantic usurpation . . . converting the war . . . into a crusade for the sudden . . . violent liberation of 3,000,000 Negro slaves." (*Family Encyclopedia of American History* [Pleasantville, N. Y.: Reader's Digest, 1975], 383)

See note 447 below. See, on Illinois and the Thirteenth Amendment, note 455 below. See also note 353 above. Three million, we recall, was roughly the number of free men and women in the United States in 1776. It is far less than the number of Americans currently in prison, on parole, and on probation.

435.   Nicolay and Hay, *Abraham Lincoln,* 6: 161–62. See, for Lincoln's public discussion of emancipation prior to his issuance of the Proclamation, *Collected Works,* 5: 419–25. See, for his comments upon and review of the effects of the Proclamation, ibid., 6: 192, 407–9, 7: 49–52, 281–82, 499–501, 506–7.

See, on emancipation generally and its legal consequences (as well as on the Emancipation Proclamation itself), Randall, *Constitutional Problems under Lincoln,* Chaps. 15 and 16. "Back in Washington, meanwhile, Hay brought Lincoln a sampling of editorial opinion [on the Emancipation Proclamation] from the leading papers, but Lincoln wasn't too interested in their comments. He'd studied the emancipation problem so long, he said, that he knew more about it than the papers did." Oates, *With Malice toward None,* 321. See also notes 443 and 455 below.

See, on John Milton Hay, Judith H. Dobrzynski, "A Young Mr. Lincoln? Auction May Shed Light," *New York Times,* August 20, 1998, B3: "Hay and Lincoln were close. During the Civil War, Hay moved into the White House, and Hay, some historians say, was the only person there who referred to Lincoln by his first name." Hay, who was Lincoln's private secretary, served as Secretary of State under Presidents William McKinley and Theodore Roosevelt.

436. See, for the sources for Lincoln of these documents, note 392 above. Their deepest sources were, for Lincoln, the Declaration of Independence and his training and experience in Anglo-American law. See the Prologue to this Collection. See, for the texts of the two stages of the Emancipation Proclamation, note 418 above.

437. There are collected in the appendix to the *United States Statutes* thirteen of Lincoln's proclamations prior to this one. Both Emancipation Proclamation documents bear the signatures, "By the President: Abraham Lincoln/William H. Seward, Secretary of State."

Earlier drafts of these two documents may be found in Lincoln, *Collected Works,* 5: 336–37 (July 22, 1862), 6: 23–26 (December 30, 1862). Lincoln usually referred to these documents, as I do in this commentary, as "the preliminary Emancipation Proclamation" and as "the final Emancipation Proclamation." See, e.g., ibid., 6: 186, 7: 49. But, on one occasion at least, he referred to the Preliminary Proclamation as "the Summer Proclamation" Ibid., 6: 186. See note 451 below.

438. See Randall, *Lincoln, the President,* 4: 162. Too much is made these days of the President as "*our* Commander in Chief." He is, according to the Constitution, merely "Commander in Chief of the Army and Navy of the United States, and of the Militia of the several States, when called into the actual Service of the United States." Consider here an excerpt from the concurring opinion by Justice Jackson in *Youngstown Sheet & Tube Company v. Sawyer,* 343 U. S. 579, 643–44 (1952):

> There are indications that the Constitution did not contemplate that the title Commander-in-Chief *of the Army and Navy* will constitute him also Commander-in-Chief of the country, its industries and its inhabitants. He has no monopoly of "war powers," whatever they are. While Congress cannot deprive the President of the command of the army and navy, only Congress can provide him an army or navy to command. It is also empowered to make rules for the "Government and Regulation of land and naval forces," by which it may to some unknown extent impinge upon even command functions. That military powers were not to supersede representative government of internal affairs seems obvious from the Constitution and from elementary American history. (emphasis in original)

See note 441 below.

It is salutary to keep in mind here what can be said to be massive antitheses, grinding one another in gigantic contention, that go back to the earliest decades of this Republic:

The Antifederalists complained [in 1787–1789] of the absence of a bill of rights, but, more than that, of the presence (or the likely presence) of a standing army. That army would be used to enforce the laws because, they said, in a territory so extensive, comprising people with interests, habits and customs so diverse, [the laws] could not be enforced in any other way.

But the Federalists saw the necessity of a strong executive, making him commander in chief of the Army (which, on a few occasions—Little Rock, Ark., in 1957 and Oxford, Miss., in 1962—has indeed been used to enforce the laws). The Constitution "has an awful squinting," Patrick Henry said; "it squints toward monarchy," and for the Antifederalists monarchy meant the possibility of tyranny. . . .

The Antifederalists lost the debate on the Constitution, and probably ought to have lost it, but their arguments were not without merit and deserve careful consideration even (and perhaps especially) today. (Walter Berns, Book Review, *Washington Times,* July 4, 1993, B7–B8.)

See, on standing armies, Anastaplo, *Amendments to the Constitution,* 95. Should there not be added to the "few occasions [when the army] has indeed been used to enforce the laws," the massive response by President Lincoln and his colleagues to Southern secessionist efforts? See also ibid., 41–42, 440 n. 216.

Cannot it be said that Lincoln skillfully marshaled all his forces, political as well as military, to put an effective yet just end to slavery (a "golden" objective) within the conventional ("silver") setting provided by the Constitution (and its underpinning, the Declaration of Independence)? See the epigraph for Chap. 14 of this Collection and the text at note 455 below.

Consider the tribute paid the martyred President by two of his younger associates, "Fame is due Mr. Lincoln, not alone because he decreed emancipation, but because events so shaped themselves under his guidance as to render the conception practical and the decree successful. Among the agencies he employed none proved more admirable or more powerful than this two-edged sword of the final proclamation, blending sentiment with force, leaguing liberty with Union, filling the voting armies at home and the fighting armies in the field. In the light of history we can see that by this edict Mr. Lincoln gave slavery its vital thrust, its mortal wound. It was the word of decision, the judgment without appeal, the sentence of doom." Nicolay and Hay, *Abraham Lincoln,* 6: 437. See note 448 below. See also note 435 above. (The martyrdom of Lincoln resulted, in part, from casual security measures. On the other hand, the massive security measures to which we have become accustomed on behalf of Presidents today verge on the absurd. Here, as elsewhere, moderation would be instructive for the Republic.)

439. Lincoln, *Collected Works,* 6: 408 (letter to James C. Conkling in Illinois). There are echoes here of one of the grievances in the Declaration of Independence: "He has . . . endeavoured to bring on the Inhabitants of our Frontiers, the merciless Indian Savages, whose known Rule of Warfare, is an undistinguished Destruction, of all Ages, Sexes and Conditions." See William Blackstone, *Commentaries on the Laws of England* (Oxford: Clarendon Press, 1765–1769), 4: 312. See also

Harry V. Jaffa, *Crisis of the House Divided: An Interpretation of the Issues in the Lincoln–Douglas Debates* (Garden City, N.Y.: Doubleday, 1959), 233. See as well note 25 above. See, on the barbarity and cruelty of the international slave trade, Sec. IV of Chap. 4 of this Collection.

440. One need read only the youthful Lincoln's Temperance Speech in Springfield, Illinois on February 22, 1842, to sense his lifelong concern about moral passion. See Lincoln, *Collected Works,* 1: 271. See also Jaffa, *Crisis of the House Divided,* 233 f.; Anastaplo, *Amendments to the Constitution,* 200–201, 450–52. See, on how Americans regard their "interest," Chap. 6 of this Collection.

441. We should remember that Lincoln had even repudiated unauthorized decrees or acts of emancipation by generals in the field. See, e.g., Lord Charnwood, *Abraham Lincoln* (Garden City: Garden City Publishing, 1917), 268–70, 313–37; Lincoln, *Collected Works,* 4: 530–31. Ultimate political control of the military was evidently taken for granted throughout the Civil War, in both the North and the South, however much civilians were abused by armies on both sides. See note 438 above.

442. Morse, *Abraham Lincoln,* 2: 109.

443. The two "consent" qualifications are said to have been inserted in the Preliminary Proclamation at the suggestion of Secretary of State Seward. Lincoln, *Collected Works,* 5: 434n. "As the pro-slavery extremists utterly disregarded the humanity of the Negro, so did the abolitionists disregard utterly the element of consent required for the just acts of government. . . . What both disregarded was at bottom the same thing—the principle of equality." Jaffa, *Equality and Liberty,* 167. See note 7 above.

Consider also the element of consent, or "voluntarism," in Lincoln's efforts to persuade nonrebellious slaveholders in the Middle States to sell their slaves to the United States before they were deprived of them. See Morse, *Abraham Lincoln,* 32; Jaffa, *Equality and Liberty,* 166. (On the Middle States, see the text at notes 389 and 447 below. See also note 427 above.) "In a sense, it is true that Lincoln never intended to emancipate the Negro: what he intended was to emancipate the American republic from the curse of slavery, a curse which lay upon both races and which, in different ways, enslaved them both." Jaffa, *Equality and Liberty,* 166. See note 214 above. (I do *not* mean to suggest, by my use here in the text and elsewhere of our fashionable term "appreciate," that judgments about good and bad and about right and wrong are merely matters of taste. But "appreciate" can recognize the attractiveness of that which is being considered. See, on the status of beauty, the text at notes 478 and 479 below. See also note 172 above.)

444. The Emancipation Proclamation refers to all slaves in a rebellious State or part of a State, whereas Congress, in Sec. 9 of its July 1862 act, had referred primarily to "all slaves of persons who shall hereafter be engaged in rebellion against the government of the United States, or who shall in any way give aid or comfort thereto." See note 447 below.

445. See Randall, *Lincoln, the President,* 156–57; Franklin, *Emancipation Proclamation,* x, 43–44, 46–47; Oates, *With Malice toward None,* 311, 317–20.

It should be noticed, however, that Lincoln had issued, on July 25, 1862, a proclamation based on the Act of Congress (approved July 17, 1862), "An act to suppress insurrection, and to punish treason and rebellion, to seize and confiscate property of rebels, and for other purposes." Lincoln, *Collected Works,* 5: 341. (Parts of that act were later incorporated in the Preliminary Proclamation. See Sec. IV (v) of Chap. 14 of this Collection.) Lincoln's proclamation of July 25, 1862, drew upon the first paragraph of his first draft (July 22, 1862) of the Preliminary Emancipation Proclamation. See Lincoln, *Collected Works,* 5: 336–37. The section of the act of Congress relied upon by Lincoln in his Proclamation of July 25, 1862, "provided that property of persons in States in rebellion, who did not cease to give aid to the rebellion within sixty days after proclamation by the president, would be liable to seizure." Ibid., 5: 337 n. 2. The Emancipation Proclamation of September 22, 1862 went much further than did either the draft proclamation of July 22, 1862, or the proclamation of July 25, 1862. (Thus, under the Emancipation Proclamation, all slaves in the areas designated were immediately affected, not just the "property of persons . . . who did not cease to give aid to the rebellion" and not just the property actually seized.) The issuance of the more sweeping Emancipation Proclamation may well have waited upon a Union victory to prepare the way for it.

But the sixtieth day from July 25 does happen to be September 22 (counting both days). Did Lincoln settle upon the September 22 date, once the remarkably bloody "victory" of Antietam of September 17 had become available, in order to tie his Preliminary Proclamation (if that should later become necessary) to the sixty-day interval provided by Congress in its act of July 17 and keyed to his proclamation of July 25? See Owen, *The Wrong of Slavery,* 157. See also the quotation from Senator Douglas in the text at note 450 below. See as well Randall, *Lincoln the President,* 186–87.

See, on the Confiscation Acts, Nicolay and Hay, *Abraham Lincoln,* 6: 97–104, 151; Morse, *Abraham Lincoln,* 2: 14–15; Randall, *Constitutional Problems under Lincoln,* 457–65; Randall, *Lincoln the President,* 2: 131; Jaffa, *Equality and Liberty,* 142, 164–65; Oates, *With Malice toward None,* 309–10.

446. The clerk had written in everything at the end of what is otherwise Lincoln's handwritten original of the Preliminary Proclamation (beginning at "In witness whereof"). See Lincoln, *Collected Works,* 5: 433, 436; Franklin, *Emancipation Proclamation,* 52, 56 ("and sixty two, and sixty two").

447. Lincoln, *Collected Works,* 6: 428–29. See Morse, *Abraham Lincoln,* 2: 3, 99–100; Nicolay and Hay, *Abraham Lincoln,* 6: 405, 416 f. Lincoln's letter to Chase (whom he appointed Chief Justice of the United States in 1864) continues: "Would not many of our friends shrink away appalled? Would it not lose us the elections, and with them, the very cause we seek to advance?" Lincoln, *Collected Works,* 6: 429. See Anastaplo, *Amendments to the Constitution,* 396 n. 45; the text at note 430 above; note 434 above. See also Franklin, *Emancipation Proclamation,* 85–86; Oates, *With Malice toward None,* 323. See as well note 456 below.

We have noticed that a respect for the Constitution may be seen in Lincoln's provision that the decisive indication that a State is not in rebellion is that it is properly represented in Congress. The republican form of government is thereby deferred to. See Anastaplo, *Amendments to the Constitution,* 450–52. See also Lincoln, *Collected Works,* 6: 440, 7: 50–52, 66, 476–77. Is not such deference to be seen as well in the uses of *people* throughout the Emancipation Proclamation? But does not that apparent deference to the people seen in the current recourse to initiatives and referenda in various states threaten traditional republican government? See Nicholas Laman, review of *Paradise Lost,* by Peter Schrag, *New York Times Book Review,* May 3, 1998, 7. Compare John H. Fund, "Will Politicians Take the Initiative?" *Wall Street Journal,* June 1, 1998, A18. Related to this development may be the dubious recourse these days to term limits. See Anastaplo, *Amendments to the Constitution,* 465. See also the text at note 46 above.

    448. William Lloyd Garrison, *The Liberator,* no. 1, January 1, 1831, in *The Liberator: William Lloyd Garrison: A Biography,* by John L. Thomas (Boston: Little, Brown, 1963), 128. See, for Garrison's "extremist" position, Truman Nelson, ed., *Documents of Upheaval: Selections from William Lloyd Garrison's "The Liberator,"* *1831–1865* (New York: Hill & Wang, 1966), xiii. See, on John Brown, note 533 below. Another "extremist," but far less obviously so, is the Lord Mansfield of the *Somerset* case (1772). See Anastaplo, *Amendments to the Constitution,* 341 f.; Blackstone, *Commentaries,* 1: 412–13, 4: 29. See also the Prologue to this Collection.

    Consider as well Ralph Waldo Emerson's November 1862 address, "The Emancipation," which includes these sentiments: "The extreme moderation with which the President advanced to his design—his long-avowed expectant policy, as if he chose to be strictly the executive of the best public sentiment of the country, waiting only till it should be unmistakably pronounced—so fair a mind that none ever listened so patiently to such extreme varieties of opinion—so reticent that his decision has taken all parties by surprise, whilst yet it is just the sequel of his prior acts—the firm tone in which he announces it, without inflation or surplusage— all these have bespoken such favor to the act that, great as the popularity of the President has been, we are beginning to think that we have underestimated the capacity and virtue which the Divine Providence has made an instrument of benefit so vast. *He has been permitted* to do more for America than any other American man." *The Selected Writings of Ralph Waldo Emerson,* ed. Brooks Atkinson (New York: Modern Library, 1950), 886 (emphasis added). See the text at note 416 above. See also Anastaplo, *Human Being and Citizen,* 260 n. 3; notes 466 and 474 below. See, on Emerson and the Declaration of Independence, the text at note 17 above.

    449. Matthew 10:16.

    450. Lincoln, *Collected Works,* 3: 261. See also the text at note 319 above. Compare ibid., 3: 249–50, 277, 279–81. See, on salutary concealments, Plato, *Republic* 414E; Thucydides, *The Peloponnesian War,* 2: 65; Blackstone, *Commentaries,* 1: 238, 2: 117, 4: 33; Edward Gibbon, *The Decline and Fall of the Roman Empire,* Chap. 15 (opening and closing paragraphs); Morse, *Abraham Lincoln,* 2: 209 ("Temporarily the great Republic was under a 'strong government,' and Mr. Lincoln was the strength. Though somewhat cloaked by forms, there was for a while in the United States a condition of 'one-man power,' and the people instinctively recognized it, though they would on no account admit it in plain words."). See also Jules Gleicher, "Deception and Ennoblement in *Henry V,*" in *Law and Philosophy,* ed. John A. Murley, Robert L. Stone, and William T. Braithwaite (Athens: Ohio University Press, 1992), 2: 959; Stanley D. McKenzie, "The Prudence and Kinship of Prince Hal and John of Lancaster in *2 Henry IV,*" ibid., 2: 937; Anastaplo, *Amendments to the Constitution,* 405 n. 68, 425 n. 142, 445–46 n. 251; the text at note 319

above. See as well note 1 above. Compare, on the perhaps misguided campaign to change "an arcane House [of Representatives] procedural rule that allows members to block legislation in secret while supporting it in public," Clifford Krauss, "Conservatives Push to End Secrecy in House Rules," *New York Times,* September 14, 1993, A15; "Outflanked by Talk Shows, House Drops Secrecy Rule," *Chicago Tribune,* September 29, 1993, sec. 1, p. 6. See also Adam Clymer, "Broad Change Proposed in How Congress Works," *New York Times,* November 23, 1993, A14.

451.   Lincoln, *Collected Works,* 5: 358. See also the text at note 1 above. Lincoln explained the good relied upon for, and sought through, the Emancipation Proclamation: "I never did ask more, nor ever was willing to accept less, than for all the States, and the people thereof, to take and hold their places, and their rights, in the Union, under the Constitution of the United States. For this alone have I felt authorized to struggle; and I seek neither more nor less now. . . . After the commencement of hostilities I struggled nearly a year and a half to get along without touching the 'institution' [of slavery]; and when finally I conditionally determined to touch it, I gave a hundred days fair notice of my purpose, to all the States and people, within which time they could have turned it wholly aside, by simply again becoming good citizens of the United States. They chose to disregard it [the Preliminary Proclamation], and I made the peremptory proclamation [the Final Proclamation] on what appeared to me to be a military necessity. And being made, it must stand." Ibid., 6: 48–49 (January 8, 1863). See ibid, 4: 530–31; note 430 above, note 455 below. See, for Lincoln's annual assessments of the workings of the Emancipation Proclamation, *Collected Works,* 5: 527–37 (1862), 7: 49–51 (1863), 8: 152 (1864). See, on national reconciliation, note 533 below.

452.   James C. Austin, *Artemus Ward* (New York: Twayne Publishers, 1964), 107–8. See Oates, *With Malice toward None,* 318–19; Franklin, *Emancipation Proclamation,* ix, 47; Sandburg, *The War Years,* 1: 583; Charnwood, *Abraham Lincoln,* 324.

453.   I take the full text of "High-Handed Outrage at Utica" from Charles Farrar Browne, *The Complete Works of Artemus Ward* (New York: G. W. Dillingham, 1898), 36–37:

> In the Faul of 1856, I showed my show in Utiky, a trooly grate sitty in the State of New York.
>
> The people gave me a cordyal recepshun. The press was loud in her prases.
>
> 1 day as I was givin a descripshun of my Beests and Snaiks in my usual flowry stile what was my skorn disgust to see a big burly feller walk up to the cage containin my wax figgers of the Lord's Last Supper, and cease Judas Iscarrot by the feet and drag him out on the ground. He then commenced fur to pound him as hard as he cood.
>
> "What under the son are you abowt?" cried I.
>
> Sez he, "What did you bring this pussylanermus cuss here fur?" and he hit the wax figger another tremenjis blow on the hed.
>
> Sez I, "You egrejus ass, that air's a wax figger—a representashun of the false 'Postle."
>
> Sez he, "That's all very well for you to say, but I tell you, old man,

that Judas Iscarrot can't show hisself in Utiky with impunerty by a darn site!" with which observashun he kaved in Judassis hed. The young man belonged to 1 of the first famerlies in Utiky. I sood him, and the Joory brawt in a verdick of Arson in the 3d degree.

See, for an anticipation of the "big burly feller," Edward Gibbon, *Decline and Fall* (New York: Modern Library, n.d.), 2: 390–91 (the "indiscreet fury" of Clovis). See also Anastaplo, *Amendments to the Constitution*, 403–5 n. 66. The Artemus Ward volume includes a number of instructive pieces on slavery, Lincoln, and the Civil War. See, for the crippling consequences of not taking Lincoln seriously enough, ibid., 450–52 n. 259. See also note 479 below.

454. See, for Lincoln's political sense from early in his career, Chap. 8 of this Collection. See also note 497 below, Chap. 8, and Sec. IX of Chap. 4 of this Collection.

455. See Proverbs 25: 11 (the epigraph for Chap. 14 of this Collection). Lincoln, aware that the Emancipation Proclamation was necessarily limited in scope and not without problems as to its authority, encouraged in due time the Constitutional amendment (the Thirteenth) prohibiting slavery for which his Emancipation Proclamation and the Gettysburg Address can be said to have prepared the way. He announced on June 9, 1864 that he approved his party's "declaration of so amending the Constitution as to prohibit slavery throughout the nation":

> When the people in revolt, with a hundred days of explicit notice, that they could, within those days, resume their allegiance, without the overthrow of their institution [of slavery], and that they could not so resume it afterwards, elected to stand out, such an amendment of the Constitution as is now proposed, became a fitting, and necessary conclusion to the final success of the Union cause. Such [an amendment] alone can meet and cover all cavils. *Now, the unconditional Union men, North and South, perceive its importance, and embrace it.* In the joint names of Liberty and Union, let us labor to give it legal form, and practical effect. (Lincoln, *Collected Works,* 7: 380) (emphasis added)

See, for the party platform on which Lincoln was commenting, ibid., 7: 381–82, 411. See also Anastaplo, *Amendments to the Constitution*, 450–52 n. 259. See, for the salutary Aesopian lessons taught to Lincoln's generation about the limits of the equality principle, ibid., 422–24 n. 134.

A newspaper account of February 1, 1865, reports Lincoln's response to a serenade—a response that develops further his opinion about the relation between his great Proclamation and what is now the Thirteenth Amendment:

> The President said he supposed the passage through Congress of the Constitutional amendment for the abolishment of Slavery throughout the United States, was the occasion to which he was indebted for the honor of this call. [Applause.] The occasion was one of congratulation to the country and to the whole world. But there is a task yet before us—to go forward and consummate by the votes of the States that

which Congress so nobly began yesterday. [Applause and cries—"They will do it," &c.] He had the honor to inform those present that Illinois had already to-day done the work. [Applause.] Maryland was about half through; but he felt proud that Illinois was a little ahead. He thought this measure was a very fitting if not an indispensable adjunct to the winding up of the great difficulty. He wished the reunion of all the States perfected and so effected as to remove all causes of disturbance in the future; and to attain this end *it was necessary that the original disturbing cause should, if possible, be rooted out.* He thought all would bear him witness that he never had shrunk from doing all that he could to eradicate Slavery by issuing an emancipation proclamation. [Applause.] But that proclamation falls far short of what the amendment will be when fully consummated. A question might be raised whether the proclamation was legally valid. It might be added that it only aided those who came into our lines and that it was inoperative as to those who did not give themselves up, or that it would have no effect upon the children of the slaves born hereafter. In fact it would be urged that it did not meet the evil. But this amendment is a King's cure for all the evils. [Applause.] It winds the whole thing up. He would repeat that it was the fitting if not indispensable adjunct to the consummation of the great game we are playing. He could not but congratulate all present, *himself,* the country and the whole world upon this great moral victory. (Ibid., 8: 254–55) (emphases added)

See note 434 above. Notice in Lincoln's response his continued use of "abolishment" (see Sec. IV[ii] of Chap. 14 of this Collection) and the echoes from his Gettysburg Address. See note 438 above. See also the text at note 450 above. Compare the original response in Illinois to the Emancipation Proclamation recorded in note 434 above. See note 353 above.

The powers, or at least the use of the powers, of the Presidency had to be substantially expanded during the Civil War, with the Emancipation Proclamation a dramatic illustration of how far the constitutionalist might have to go in order to "preserve, protect and defend" both the Constitution of the United States and the Country which that Constitution serves. Compare, for the libertarian Bork, Graglia & Company position, note 26 above. But see note 391 above. The Iran-arms and Contra-aid controversy during the Reagan administration reminded us, as had the Watergate controversy during the Nixon administration, of the supremacy of Congress among the branches of government in our constitutional system. See George Anastaplo, *The Constitution of 1787: A Commentary* (Baltimore: Johns Hopkins University Press, 1989), 32–33, 312, 317–19; Anastaplo, *Amendments to the Constitution,* 79, 215, 445. The sexual and other improprieties exposed during the Clinton administration again reminded us of the supremacy of Congress and, even more, of the importance of moral character (both apparent and actual) in a republican political order. This is not to deny that there were serious abuses of the Independent Counsel Act and of the powers of grand juries in the effort to pin down a remarkably elusive President. See George Anastaplo, "What Do We Really Want to Learn about the President?" *Public Interest Law Reporter* (Loyola University of Chicago School of Law), April 1998, 2 f.; George Anastaplo, "Crisis and Continuity in the Clinton Presidency," *Public Interest Law Reporter,* July 1998, 1 f. (incorporating a talk given at the University of Dallas, February 27, 1998); George Anastaplo, "Presidential Prerogatives and Civil Suits, Indictments, and Impeachments," *Chicago Daily Law Bulletin,* February 24, 1998, 2; George Anastaplo, letter to the editor, *Chicago Sun-Times,* February 25, 1998, p. 40, *New York Times,* September 11, 1998, A26. The more "vulnerable" the Presidency is made in our circumstances, the better it is likely to be for all of us, and especially for any President who wants to do the right things in the right way. A President should always take care lest his friends be obliged to "shrink away appalled." See note 447 above, notes 456 and 464 below.

Chapter 15. The Gettysburg Address

456. See "The Perpetuation of Our Political Institutions—An Address Before the Young Men's Lyceum of Springfield, Illinois," January 27, 1837, in Lincoln, *Complete Works,* 1: 108 f. See, for an extended analysis of this address (something of a tour de force?), Harry V. Jaffa, *Crisis of the House Divided: An Interpretation of the Issues in the Lincoln–Douglas Debates* (Garden City, N.Y.: Doubleday, 1959), 181–232; note 26 above. Mr. Jaffa's may well be the most challenging book written in the twentieth century by an American-born political scientist. See Willmoore Kendall, "Source of American Caesarism" (a review of Mr. Jaffa's book), *National Review,* November 7, 1959, p 461; Laurence Berns, "Lincoln's Perpetuation Speech," in *Abraham Lincoln, The Gettysburg Address, and American Constitutionalism,* ed. Leo Paul S. de Alvarez (Irving, Texas: University of Dallas Press, 1976), 7 f.

See, on the theme of Lincoln's "Perpetuation Speech," Plato, *Gorgias* 483E–484A, *Republic,* Bk. 1 (the argument of Thrasymachus and its tentative refutation). See also Mark Twain, *The Adventures of Tom Sawyer,* Chap. 8 ("They said they would rather be outlaws a year in Sherwood Forest than President of the United States forever.") Compare "Tom Sawyer: Hero of Middle America," in Jaffa, *The Conditions of Freedom,* 207 f.; John C. Calhoun, "South Carolina Exposition and Protest," in *The Political Thought of American Statesmen,* ed. Morton J. Frisch and Richard G. Stevens (Itasca, Ill.: F. E. Peacock, 1973), 121, 140 ("preservation is perpetual creation"). The wartime Lincoln can remind one in various ways of Julius Caesar (the Caesar of the *Gallic Wars* more than of the *Civil Wars*). See, on contemporary Caesarism, Oswald Mosley, *My Life* (London: Nelson, 1968). President Clinton, with his talents, recklessness, romanticized heroism, deviousness, and charm, can remind one of Mark Twain's Tom Sawyer, who *can* become hard to live with (as Huck and Jim found out). We can sometimes see here the perpetual adolescent.

See, on the true statesman, Plato, *Statesman,* 293B, 305E. See also Plato, *Statesman* 259A–B, *Gorgias* 521D, *Epinomis* 992C–D, *Greater Hippias* 284–85. Compare Plato, *Gorgias* 473E–474A, 480E–481B.

457. See Abraham Lincoln, *Collected Works,* ed. Roy P. Basler (New Brunswick, N.J.: Rutgers University Press, 1953), 1: 109 f.

458. Ibid., 1: 114. See, on John Calhoun, Chap. 7 of this Collection. See, on John Brown, note 533 below.

459. Ibid.

460. Ibid.

461. Ibid., 1: 112.

462. Ibid., 1: 115.

463. Ibid., 7: 17 f. See, for the text of the Gettysburg Address, note 279 above. See, for one of Lincoln's anticipations of the Address, the text at note 49 above. See, for a preliminary discussion of the Address, Chap. 9 of this Collection.

464. See Plato, *Statesman,* 259A–B. "Reason, cold, calculating, unimpassioned reason" can alienate one from "one's own" if they should sense how "personally uninvolved" one may really be as a reasoner. See the opening pages of Judah Halevi's *The Kuzari* (the exchange with the philosopher); George Anastaplo *The Constitutionalist: Notes on the First Amendment* (Dallas: Southern Methodist University Press, 1971), 788 n. 16, 739 n. 141, 766 n. 181; George Anastaplo, "American Constitutionalism and the Virtue of Prudence," in *Abraham Lincoln, The Gettysburg Address, and American Constitutionalism,* ed. Leo Paul S. de Alvarez (Irving, Texas: University of Dallas Press, 1976), 135 n. 11, 147 n. 33; note 469 below. See, for Lincoln's interest in Shakespeare's *Macbeth, Collected Works,* 6: 392. See also note 1 above, the text at note 212 above.

The remarkable features of the Gettysburg Address may be best seen against the background of the Constitution and its sobriety. (One must, in such circumstances as Lincoln found himself, guard against both callousness and sentimentality. See note 286 above.)

Has not Lincoln been, among American politicians, *the* Constitutionalist? See Anastaplo, *The Constitutionalist,* 421 n. 2, 625 n. 62. The remarkably competent lawyer in Lincoln (noticed in the Prologue to this Collection) may be seen in his Message to Congress of July 4, 1861, and in the Emancipation Proclamation. See ibid., 477 n. 54, 602 n. 15; Lincoln, *Collected Works,* e.g., 6: 547, 7: 380. See also Chaps. 13 and 14 of this Collection.

The similarity of Lincoln's constitutional thought to that of the mature Daniel Webster can be striking. See Anastaplo, "American Constitutionalism and Prudence," 106 f.

Would Webster have thought Lincoln's promises with respect to perpetuity illusory? Would he have believed that Lincoln himself "believed" them? Was not Lincoln markedly affected by the suffering and sacrifices of the war? Would he have been "inhuman" not to have been thus affected? Did his ability to move his fellow-citizens depend upon something in addition to the "cold, calculating, unimpassioned reason" which he did employ? See note 455 above, notes 468, 474, 476, 485, 489, and 492 below.

465. See, for the Lord's Prayer, Matthew 6:9–13, Luke 11:2–4. See also Anastaplo, "Law and Literature and the Bible: Explorations," 23 *Oklahoma City University Law Review* 700 (1998). See, e.g., ibid, the text at n. 601.

466. See, e.g., Luke 2:36. Compare the First Inaugural Address: "It is seventy-

two years since the first inauguration of a President under our national Constitution." Lincoln, *Collected Works,* 4: 264. See Chap. 12 of this Collection.

Lincoln also observed in the First Inaugural Address that the Union was "much older" than the Constitution. (See ibid., 4: 265; Anastaplo, "American Constitutionalism and Prudence," 143 n. 25.) "Much older" meant, in this case, a mere seventeen years at most. Did not Lincoln, again and again, buttress with signs both of antiquity and of the divine the useful constitutional arrangement that chance had permitted reasonable men (who were somewhat aware of the nature of things) to establish? See notes 394 and 448 above.

"[The Gettysburg Address] tacitly obscures the rational foundations of the proposition to which it says the nation was dedicated. It associates the new birth of freedom with the idea of the release of the spirit from the bondage of sin, the idea with which the people were familiar from their ancient revealed religion. By this very association Lincoln gave the idea of political freedom, which was so new to the Western world, a sense of the dignity which is naturally associated only with things that are old." Jaffa, *Crisis of the House Divided,* 230. See also ibid., 229: "Lincoln, however, achieved, on the level of the moral imagination, a synthesis of the elements which in Jefferson remained antagonistic. He incorporated the truths of the Declaration of Independence into a sacred and ritual canon, making them objects of faith as well as of cognition. Through his interpretation of the Civil War as both a Hebraic and Christian ritual atonement, this canon was made sacred to the American people as the Declaration of Independence, of itself, could not be made. This interpretation did not depend for its conviction upon the intellectual acknowledgment of the truth alone—an acknowledgment which, of itself, Lincoln in 1838 showed was a feeble barrier to the passions—but upon a passionate and passion-conquering conviction born of the sense of the awful price exacted by that truth of its votaries." See as well ibid., 145; note 489 below.

"Again, what is long established seems akin to what exists by nature." Aristotle, *Rhetoric* 1387a16. See Anastaplo, "American Constitutionalism and Prudence," 140 n. 20; notes 485 and 492 below. Compare Shakespeare, *Henry VI,* III, iii, 3: "But for the rest, you tell a pedigree / Of threescore-and-two years; a silly time / To make prescription for a kingdom's worth." (It was said in reply, thereby again exposing for us the tension between the contractual and the natural [which the venerable or prescriptive suggests?], "Why, Warwick, canst thou speak against thy liege, / Whom thou obeyed'st thirty-and-six years, / And not bewray thy treason with a blush?")

467. See, on Genesis, Anastaplo, "Beginnings," 1998 *The Great Ideas Today* 149 (1998); George Anastaplo, "On Trial: Explorations," 22 *Loyola University of Chicago Law Journal* 767 f., 854 f. (1991).; Anastaplo, "Law and Literature and the Bible," 23 *Oklahoma City University Law Review* 548–91 (1998); note 165 above. See, on Moses, ibid., 591–640.

468. See, on arguments based on similitude, Quintilian, *Institutio Oratoria,* 5: xi, 2 ff.; 8: 3: 72 ff. See also the essays on Lincoln in H. L. Mencken, *Prejudices, Third Series* (New York: A. Knopf, 1922); in Richard M. Weaver, *The Ethics of Rhetoric* (Chicago: Henry Regnery, 1953); and in Edmund Wilson, *Patriotic Gore* (New York: Oxford University Press, 1962). See as well Harold Zyskind, "A

Rhetorical Analysis of the Gettysburg Address,"4 *Journal of General Education* 202 (1950); and Eva T. H. Brann, "A Reading of the Gettysburg Address," in *Abraham Lincoln, American Constitutionalism and the Gettysburg Address,* ed. Leo Paul S. de Alvarez (Irving, Texas: University of Dallas Press, 1976), 15 f. (also, in its way, something of a tour de force? see note 456 above). See, on rhetoric, note 473 below.

Does not the last sentence of the Gettysburg Address anticipate, and contribute to, the pervasive authority of the People and hence to such developments as the exaltation of the Presidency among us. See Anastaplo, *The Constitutionalist,* 655. See, on the significance of public opinion in the United States, Lincoln, *Collected Works,* 2: 256, 282, 385, 3: 27, 4: 17. See also ibid., 8: 52 (October 19, 1864): "[The people's] will, constitutionally expressed, is the ultimate law for all. If they should deliberately resolve to have immediate peace even at the loss of their country, and their liberty, I know not the power or the right to resist them. It is their own business, and they must do as they please with their own." This is not good either to believe or to say? Compare ibid., 8: 152 (December 6, 1864): "I repeat the declaration made a year ago, that 'while I remain in my present position I shall not attempt to retract or modify the emancipation proclamation, nor shall I return to slavery any person who is free by the terms of that proclamation, or by any of the Acts of Congress.' If the people should, by whatever mode or means, make it an Executive duty to reenslave such persons, another, and not I, must be their instrument to perform it." Compare, also, ibid., 7: 488: "Nothing justifies the suspending of the civil by the military authority, but military necessity, and of the existence of that necessity the military commander, and not a popular vote, is to decide." Compare, as well, Confucius, *Analects,* 11: xxiii; note 447 above, note 485 below.

Do we not see dimly reflected in the concluding lines of the Gettysburg Address a faith in progress that is rooted in the Enlightenment, and perhaps in the technology that the Enlightenment depended upon and promoted? See Anastaplo, *The Constitutionalist,* 666 n. 122. See also Anastaplo, "American Constitutionalism and Prudence," 140 n. 20; notes 479 and 492 below; Chap. 6 of this Collection. "The work of the Plymouth emigrants was the glory of their age. While we reverence their memory, let us not forget how vastly greater is our opportunity." Lincoln, *Collected Works,* 8: 170 (December 19, 1864). See as well ibid., 4: 190.

It is "a new world," one in which men have by now gotten used to hearing such remarkable things as this: "What are galaxies? No one knew before 1900. Very few people knew in 1920. All astronomers knew after 1924." L. N. Mavrides, ed., *Structure and Evolution of the Galaxy* (Dordrecht, Holland: D. Reidel, 1971), 10. See also ibid., 208: "[W]e are entering a new era in which, thanks to radio, microwave and infrared astronomy, the direct observational information on the medium from which we believe that stars are born and on the initial phases of their lives will become increasingly abundant and precise." (P. Ledoux) But see ibid., 215, 284, 288, 293 ("From what has been discussed here it can be concluded that we are a long way from understanding the evolution of the Galaxy. We cannot understand its early history until we are able to deduce what kind of a universe we live in."). See George Anastaplo, "Thursday Afternoons," in *S. Chandrasekhar: The Man behind the Legend,* ed. Kameshwar C. Wali (London: Imperial College Press, 1997), 122 f.;

George Anastaplo, review of the Chandrasekhar study of Isaac Newton's *Principia*, 1997 *The Great Ideas Today* 448 f. (1997); George Anastaplo, review of Aristotle's *Physics*, trans. Joe Sacks, 26 *Interpretation* 275 (1999). See also note 474 below.

Perhaps even more remarkable, and indicative of the "kind of universe [we believe ourselves to] live in," is "our" beaming into "deep space" of a radio message that should take at least 48,000 years for our descendants here to receive an answer to. See *New York Times*, November 20, 1974, 77; *Time*, December 2, 1974, 12. Is there not about this ambitious effort something wonderfully Odyssean as well as deeply generous—that is to say, essentially human? See, e.g., Dante, *Inferno*, Canto 26. Some, of course, would prefer to see such moneys spent on the poor. Compare John 12: 8. What does all this say about the supposed American emphasis upon "interest" discussed in Chap. 6 of this Collection? See note 190 above.

469.   Compare Luke 2:4, where Mary is said to have brought forth her first-born. Lincoln ignored at Gettysburg the role of females, stressing instead the role of fathers. But see his speech at a sanitary fair in 1864. *Collected Works*, 7: 254–54. It was Edward Everett who voiced at Gettysburg the "tribute to our noble women." Ibid., 7: 24, 7: 236. See, for an emphasis on "fathers," ibid., 3: 307–8. See, for the presumption in favor of *the* Fathers, ibid, 1: 488, 3: 532–35. See also note 430 above. The Gettysburg Address moves from "our fathers" to "the people"—from the ancestral (if not natural) and "instinctive" to the national (if not universal) and "rational." Is there not about such a movement *something* unpatriotic? See Anastaplo, "American Constitutionalism and Prudence," 150 n. 38; note 464 above, notes 474, 479, and 482 below. Compare note 466 above, notes 477, 489, 490, and 492 below.

We are reminded both of the virtual absence of references to the daughters' mother in Shakespeare's *King Lear* and of the relation between Zeus and Athena. See Laurence Berns, "Gratitude, Nature and Piety in *King Lear*," 3 *Interpretation* 27 (1972); Anastaplo, *The Constitutionalist*, 790 n. 20.

470.   See Lincoln, *Collected Works*, 2: 250, 3: 254. Hobbes observed that men "naturally love Liberty and Dominion over others." *Leviathan*, 2: xvii. See, in note 473 below, the remarks on Plato's *Gorgias*. See also Lincoln, *Collected Works*, 7: 301 (on the need for "a good definition of the word liberty"); the text at note 335 above; notes 60 and 220 above.

Consider as well the following passages from Lincoln's inaugural addresses: "One section of our country believes slavery is *right*, and ought to be extended, while the other believes it is *wrong*, and ought not to be extended. This is the only substantial dispute. The Fugitive Slave Clause of the Constitution, and the law for the suppression of the foreign slave trade, are each as well enforced, perhaps, as any law can ever be in a community where the moral sense of the people imperfectly supports the law itself. The great body of the people abide by the dry legal obligation in both cases, and a few break over in each. This, I think, cannot be perfectly cured; and it would be worse in both cases *after* the separation of the sections, than before. The foreign slave-trade, now imperfectly suppressed, would be ultimately revived without restriction, in one section; while fugitive slaves, now only partially surrendered, would not be surrendered at all, by the other." Lincoln, *Collected Works*, 4: 268–69 (1861). See Chap. 12 of this Collection. "One eighth of the whole population were colored slaves, not distributed generally over the Union, but localized in the Southern part of it. These slaves constituted a peculiar and powerful interest. All knew that this interest was, somehow, the cause of the war. To strengthen, perpetuate, and extend this interest was the object for which the insurgents would rend the Union, even by war; while the government claimed no right to do more than to restrict the territorial enlargement of it." Ibid., 8: 332 (1865). See Chap. 16 of this Collection. (President-elect Lincoln observed, in a private letter of December 11, 1860, "You know I think the fugitive slave clause of the constitution ought to be enforced—to put it on the mildest form, ought not to be resisted." Ibid., 4: 150. See Webster, *Works*, 6: 562.) See also note 482 below. See as well Anastaplo, "American Constitutionalism and Prudence," 154 n. 45 (concluding paragraph); note 26 above.

471. See, for a far less inspired version of the Gettysburg Address, Lincoln, *Collected Works*, 6: 319–20; and for private remarks on the death of a Union Army officer, ibid., 5: 385. See also ibid., 2: 121–22, 8: 116–17; Daniel Webster, *Works* (Boston: Little, Brown, 1869), 6: 601; note 473 below. (We are reminded of Robert Louis Stevenson's comment on Henry Thoreau's poems, "As to his poetry, Emerson's word shall suffice for us, . . . 'The thyme and marjoram are not yet honey.'" Robert Louis Stevenson, *Works* [New York: P. F. Collins & Sons, 1912], 7: 100.)

Also less inspired is the (unconscious?) 1955 version of the Gettysburg Address by William Faulkner, "To the Youth of Japan," in *American Literary Essays*, ed. Lewis G. Leary (New York: Crowell, 1960), 313. Does not this Faulkner version make too much of divergences in "economy and culture" and not enough of serious political principles?

The historicist, and hence potentially nihilistic, implications of a shift (for the acknowledged foundations of a community) from truths that are self-evident to propositions that are to be tested (by battle and political developments?) need to be cautiously considered. See, on the Declaration of Independence and its "self-evident lie," note 492 (beginning) below.

472. Notice also the self-restraint—the limitations upon liberty—that may be implied by the insertion at this point (in the closing sentence of the Gettysburg Address) of "under God," as if the exercise of liberty and the insistence upon equality are to be moderated by recourse to divine guidance. See, on "liberty" and "freedom," Anastaplo, *The Constitutionalist*, 11 f, 128; Lincoln, *Collected Works*, 2: 250, 7: 243, 301–2. Compare Gouverneur Morris, *A Diary of the French Revolution*, ed. B. C. Davenport (Boston: Houghton Mifflin, 1939), 2: 581, for his uses of "freedom" and "liberty." See also note 60 above.

See, on useful discipline for authors and readers, Anastaplo, *The Constitutionalist*, 787 n. 12 (which includes the observation by Marcel Proust about great poets, that "the tyranny of rhyme [may] force them into the discovery of their finest lines"). One of Lewis Carroll's best poems—the one with which he concludes *Through the Looking-Glass*—had the added discipline of being an acrostic. See, on the making of stained-glass windows for Rockefeller Chapel at the University of Chicago, George Anastaplo, *The Artist as Thinker: From Shakespeare to Joyce* (Athens:: Ohio University Press, 1983), 301 f. See, on Lewis Carroll, ibid., 166 f.

473. In its application to everyday life, equality is to mean that a man may eat

the bread that he has earned. See Lincoln, *Collected Works,* 2: 265–66, 270–71, 520, 3: 479–80, 4: 9–10. See also the text at note 322 above. Thus, Lincoln argued on July 4, 1861, "This is essentially a People's contest. On the side of the Union, it is a struggle for maintaining in the world, that form, and substance of government, whose leading object is, to elevate the condition of men—to lift artificial weights from all shoulders—to clear the paths of laudable pursuit for all—to afford all, an unfettered start, and a fair chance, in the race of life. Yielding to partial, and temporary departures, from necessity, this is the leading object of the government for whose existence we contend." Ibid., 4: 438. See also ibid., 5: 52–53, 8: 512; note 506 below.

A noble rhetoric helps men put up with the "partial and temporary departures" from the "leading object of the government"—departures that "necessity" sometimes imposes upon a community. In fact, does not rhetoric implicitly deny the existence of equality among men? That is, does it not assume (even in the best of circumstances) that there are two kinds of human beings in the world, those who know (or can be led to know) and those who do not know (or who cannot be led to know) but who have to be otherwise guided to do what is good or sensible? See, e.g., Aristotle, *Rhetoric* 1382bl–8, 1415a37–1415b20 ("It is plain that such introductions are addressed not to ideal hearers, but to hearers as we find them."), 1419b7 ("Irony better befits a gentleman than buffoonery; the ironical man jokes to amuse himself, the buffoon to amuse other people."). See the text at note 319 above. See also the Epilogue to this Collection. Rhetoric means, in practice, *no footnotes:* that is, qualifications, sustained substantiation, and documented evidence are neither necessary nor useful; a "first reading" (and that often on the run) suffices for most people. See Anastaplo, "American Constitutionalism and Prudence," 128 n. 1, 135 n. 11, 143 n. 25. See also Anastaplo, *The Constitutionalist,* 735 n. 135, 776 n. 181. See as well note 1 above.)

The conclusion of the *Rhetoric,* which shows Aristotle himself doing what he describes as appropriate for the conclusion of a rhetorical address (that is, "For the conclusion, the disconnected style of language is appropriate, and will mark the difference between the oration and the peroration. 'I have done. You have heard me. The facts are before you. I ask for your judgment'") suggests that the *Rhetoric* as a whole is in a sense, rhetorical (on behalf of a genuinely good-intentioned rhetoric?) and that it itself is organized according to rhetorical principles and must be examined accordingly. (This approach anticipates and curbs Machiavelli's *Prince.*) See, on Aristotle's *Rhetoric,* Larry Arnhart, *Aristotle on Political Reasoning* (DeKalb: Northern Illinois University Press, 1981); George Anastaplo, "On Freedom: Explorations," 17 *Oklahoma City University Law Review* 685 f. (1992).

The power, as well as the limitation, of rhetoric may be seen in what Edward Everett had to say in a biographical memoir of Daniel Webster: "A speaker could not, if he attempted it, anticipate in his study the earnestness and fervor of spirit induced by actual contact with the audience; he could not by any possibility forestall the sympathetic influence upon his imagination and intellect of the listening and applauding throng. However severe the method required by the nature of the occasion, or dictated by his own taste, a speaker like Mr. Webster will not often confine himself 'to pouring out fervors a week old.' . . . He must entirely possess himself beforehand of the main things which he wishes to say, and then throw himself upon the excitement of the moment and the sympathy of the audience. . . .The unforeseen incident or locality furnishes an apt and speaking image; and the discourse instinctively transposes itself into a higher key." Webster, *Works,* 1: lxx–lxxi. See Plato, *Ion* 535D–E. Compare Anastaplo, *The Constitutionalist,* 362–65; note 489 below. But does the Everett "method" helps us with the Gettysburg Address?

It is illuminating that the *Gorgias,* which may be Plato's principal dialogue on rhetoric, should open with a worldly politician (an admirer of rhetoricians) invoking (if only in jest) a proverb that takes personal selfishness for granted (and even legitimates it). Rhetoric, since it does not have intrinsic to it an end (unlike, say, the art of medicine), is at the service of its user's particular desires (desires that may even be "unpatriotic": for example, the desire to arrive at a battle at its conclusion, when it is safest to be there, instead of when one can help one's city).

Rhetoric can be touted as permitting one to free oneself and to enslave others. See Plato, *Gorgias* 452D. See also Plato, *Meno* 71E, 76B; the quotation from Hobbes in note 470 above. Thus, users of rhetoric try to get the better of one another as practitioners of their "art." (The just man, on the other hand, does not try to get the better of other just men, any more than one doctor tries to get the better of other doctors. See Plato, *Republic* 349A ff.) In this respect, then, the "art" of rhetoric is like the art of war, with each practitioner (unless properly instructed) looking out primarily for what he believes to be his interests. Socrates does recognize, however, that Gorgias can do things that Socrates himself is "temperamentally" unable to do, things that could, if wisely directed, serve Socrates' philosophical concerns. See Anastaplo, "American Constitutionalism and Prudence," 140 n. 20. See also Plato, *Republic* 459C–460A.

Consider the salutary blending, for self-confident republican government, of "freedom" and "equal" in Gouverneur Morris's description of America as "a Nation, every Individual of which in the Pride of Freedom thinks himself equal to a King." Morris, *Diary,* 1: 2. See Lincoln, *Collected Works,* 7: 528–29. Compare Plato, *Crito* 44C, 49D, *Republic* 473C ff., *Statesman* 293B, *Epistles,* 2: 314A.

Consider as well Morris's endorsement of the relative equality among Americans: "Oh! my Country, how infinitely preferable that equal Partition of Fortune's Gifts which you enjoy! Where none are Vassals, none are Lords, but all are Men." *Diary,* 1: 73. (See, for the context of these remarks, Anastaplo, "American Constitutionalism and Prudence," 97.)

See, for another form of the Trinity in politics, Sec.VI of Chap. 1 of this Collection. See also the text at note 490 below.

474. This may have been the first of the modern wars to end all war.

The timelessness of the Gettysburg Address is suggested by the absence of proper names and dates. The "four score and seven years ago" could be any time. Not even the identity of the speaker is indicated. Is not the eternal characterized by its lack of dependence upon particulars? Compare notes 477, 478 below.

The yearning of the political man, for *his* kind of immortality, may be seen in the closing sentence of the Gettysburg Address. See Anastaplo, *The Constitutionalist,* 796 n. 30. See also note 286 above. There are, in the closing passage of the Address a half-dozen uses of *"here."* It seems to be suggested thereby that the proper attention to the here and now can lead to something that endures forever. Is not this, in modernity, the essentially political claim (or expectation or delusion)? God *is* brought in to ratify and reinforce the political effort, but is it all essentially man's doing? Thus, God does help those who help themselves, and especially those who know how to help themselves to God? Thus, also, Nikos Kazantzakis can have one of his characters say, in his 1910 play, *Protomasteras*, "Why prattle about God, when man is omnipotent, or can be?" See note 468 above. See also note 493 below.

But, on the other hand, the central sentences of the Address ("It is altogether fitting and proper that we should do this. But, in a larger sense, we can not dedicate—we can not consecrate—we can not hallow—this ground.") may reflect the essential ambivalence aroused by political things: one aspires and yet one recognizes that one cannot really do *it*, that the enterprise cannot have the perfection or even the permanence for which one yearns. There is a sense, however, in which the political man must believe his own rhetoric insofar as he takes at all seriously what he is doing in devoting his life to public service.

Thus, does not Lincoln do with the Civil War what the South had been obliged to do, a generation earlier, with slavery? See Lincoln, *Collected Works,* 1: 267–68, 2: 131–32, 5: 403–4, 7: 281–82. That is, is it not an expression of confidence in the underlying order of the universe (if not a move of desperation) to regard a great affliction as a positive good? To what extent is this a response shaped by Christian (or Biblical) sentiment? See, e.g., Webster, *Works,* 3: 78; Lincoln, *Collected Works,* 8: 333 ("The Almighty has His own purposes."). See Anastaplo, "American Constitutionalism and Prudence," 143 n. 26; notes 448 and 464 above, note 485 below. Compare, for the sanctified and sanctifying sufferer, the *Philoctetes* and the *Oedipus at Colonus* of Sophocles. Consider, on the other hand, the devastating (even though often wry) desperation of Franz Kafka. See, on the Idea of the Good, George Anastaplo, *The Thinker as Artist: From Homer to Plato & Aristotle* (Athens: Ohio University Press, 1997), 303 f.

475. This passage is also discussed in note 474 above. Compare Lincoln, *Collected Works,* 4: 242 (where Lincoln does "proceed to the very agreeable duty assigned [to him of raising a flag]"). Compare, also, Genesis 50:25–26, Exodus 13:19, Joshua 24:32. But see Matthew 8:22. See also Matthew 26:12–13.

Consider, in William Faulkner's *As I Lay Dying,* the family that comes alive in its comically desperate (if not heroic) effort to bury its dead. (Should one be reminded somewhat of Antigone?) See George Anastaplo, *Human Being and Citizen: Essays on Virtue, Freedom, and the Common Good* (Chicago: Swallow Press, 1975), 317 n. 3. See also note 271 above, note 479 below.

476. Pericles' famous funeral address is part of a total account that shows the "victory" (that is, the grandeur) of Athens. That address, unlike Lincoln's, shuns the subject of death. See Strauss, *The City and Man* (Chicago: Rand McNally, 1964), 194–95. Lincoln, we have suggested, can be said to have both extolled and abandoned the dead.

See, on the relation of public to private interest in Athens (and in Pericles' thought), ibid., 192–209. Lincoln's address, unlike Pericles', shuns the subject of private interest; that is, he seems to proceed on the assumption that private interest can be completely "dedicated to the great task remaining before us." Does, however, the affirmation of equality tend to induce each man to make more of his private interests, even at the expense of the very public which sanctifies that affirmation? We Americans need to consider, among other things, what we mean by "need." To what extent can a community such as ours continue to rely upon what Lincoln called "the patriotic instinct of the plain people"? *Collected Works,* 4: 439. See, on the sources of the virtues, Plato, *Meno* 70A. See also Anastaplo, "American Constitutionalism and Prudence," 93–94, 133 n. 6, 149 n. 36; note 473 above. See, on the importance of, and what can be said *for,* private interest in the United States, Chap. 6 of this Collection.

See, on the funeral address in Plato's *Menexenus,* Anastaplo, *The Constitutionalist,* 801 n. 36; on Sophocles' *Antigone,* ibid., 798 n. 32; on Plato's *Meno,* ibid., 534 n. 94, 782 nn. 22, 32. See also Anastaplo, *Human Being and Citizen,* 74 f.; Anastaplo, *Thinker as Artist,* 192 f.; Anastaplo, "Teaching, Nature, and Moral Virtues," 4 f.

It should be noticed, with respect to the distinction between words and deeds, that once Lincoln settled into the Presidency he seldom made the long, discussion-like speeches grounded in the Declaration of Independence that he had frequently made earlier. That is, his speeches (including his long annual messages to Congress) became, as reports or pronouncements, more like deeds. See Lincoln, *Collected Works,* 7: 302 ("It is not very becoming for one in my position [as President] to make speeches at great length"). See also note 1 above, note 479 below. Consider as well Confucius, *Analects,* 15:40: "The Master said, In official speeches all that matters is to get one's meaning through." (But may not an appearance of good character lend support to, if it is not even part of, one's meaning? See note 464 above.)

See, on unheard melodies, John Keats, "Ode on a Grecian Urn." "The hidden harmony is better than the obvious." Heraclitus, Fr. 54. See, on the relation of poetry to history, Anastaplo, *Human Being and Citizen,* 248 n. 13. See, on the poetry of Abraham Lincoln, Chap. 9 of this Collection. Are the deeds of Civil War Southerners more memorable than their words? See William Faulkner, *Intruder in the Dust* (New York: Vintage Books, 1972), 194–95 ("For every Southern boy fourteen years old," the Battle of Gettysburg remains to be fought.). See also William Faulkner, *Absalom, Absalom!* (New York: Modern Library College Editions, n.d.), 361 (an exchange between a level-headed Canadian and a suicidal Southerner: "So that forevermore as long as your children's children produce children you wont be anything but a descendant of a long line of colonels killed in Pickett's charge at Manassas?" "Gettysburg. You cant understand it. You would have to be born there."). See also ibid., 217, 277, 345–356, 377, 378. See as well Anastaplo, *The Constitutionalist,* 651 n. 91; the text at note 278 above. See, for the state of mind of "every healthy-minded Northern boy," the epigraph for Chap. 15 of this Collection. Are boys more apt to be moved by the *noble* than by the *just* or the *wise*?

477. We recall that the worldwide scope of Lincoln's vision emerges from attention to a particular "portion of that field." Parallel to this development is the movement from eternal rest (after the earlier motion of "our fathers") to perpetual motion. The universal, in Lincoln's thought, seems to be reflected in, perhaps is dependent upon, the particular. Is this an inspiration that the practical man shares

with the poet? Compare note 474 above. See Anastaplo, *Human Being and Citizen,* 135 f. Do not both Lincoln and the Marxists draw upon the same post-Classical doctrines in their yearning for a comprehensive vision that can be realized in practical affairs? See Anastaplo, "American Constitutionalism and Prudence," 150 n. 39; note 468 above, notes 479, 485, and 492 below. See also note 493 below.

See, as an anticipation of Lincoln's closing words in the Gettysburg Address, remarks by Webster in 1824 in support of the revolution in Greece against Turkish despotism: "The civilized world has done with 'the enormous faith, of many made for one.' Society asserts its own rights, and alleges them to be original, sacred, and unalienable. It is not satisfied with having kind masters; it demands a participation in its own government; and in states much advanced in civilization, it urges this demand with a constancy and an energy that cannot well nor long be resisted. There are, happily, enough of regulated governments in the world, and those among the most distinguished, to operate as constant examples, and to keep alive an unceasing panting in the bosoms of men for the enjoyment of similar free institutions." Webster, *Works,* 3: 70. Compare Anastaplo, *The Constitutionalist,* 732 n. 127.

Is there not something salutary in this use by Webster of the term "regulated governments"? It suggests, that is, the prudence that should moderate the claims of both liberty and equality, thereby making republican government durable. But Webster did not consider the United States the only model of good government then available. See Lord Charnwood, *Abraham Lincoln* (Garden City: Garden City Publishing, 1917), 41: "Daniel Webster must have been nearly a great man"; Anastaplo, "American Constitutionalism and Prudence," 106 f. See, on critical testing of this form of government, *Federalist No. 1* (opening paragraph) and George Washington's First Inaugural Address (epigraph for Chap. 2 of this Collection).

478. Plutarch, in *The Comparison of Pelopidas with Marcellus* (Loeb Classical Library), expresses "frank indignation" that good men would "waste all their other virtues upon that of bravery [by] throwing away their lives." See the epigraph for Chap. 16 of this Collection. See, for a most sensible analysis of the ambiguous virtue of courage, the extended discussion in Aristotle's *Nicomachean Ethics.* That discussion was usefully summed up for us in the 1960s in a tale by a second-grader of uncommon common sense: "Once upon a time there was a brave little mouse who lived in a living room. One day he was walking and he saw a cat. The little brave mouse ran away." Compare Anastaplo, *The Constitutionalist,* 239 f. (on the noble folly of John Quincy Adams with respect to the antislavery petitions submitted to and suppressed by Congress). But see ibid., 730 n. 122; note 490 below. See also Plato, *Republic* 486A–B. See as well, on Adams and the antislavery petitions, Scot J. Zentner, review of *Arguing About Slavery: The Great Battle in the United States Congress,* by William Lee Miller, 25 *Interpretation* 282 (1998). Consider note 213 above, note 490 below.

Consider, with respect to the test of "endurance," Lincoln, *Collected Works,* 3: 416: "There are two ways of establishing a proposition. One is by trying to demonstrate it upon reason; and the other is, to show that great men in former times have thought so and so, and thus to pass it by the weight of pure authority." Can events (or "the competition of the market") be relied upon? Only if "the Almighty Ruler of Nations, with his eternal truth and justice," referred to by Lincoln in his First Inaugural Address (ibid., 4: 270), does manage the affairs of men? Are events likely to depend ultimately upon chance, no matter how prudent one has been? See, e.g., Niccolò Machiavelli, *The Prince*, Chap. 7 (on the fate of Cesare Borgia); also, ibid., Chap. 26 (on Fortuna). Lincoln's name does survive in part as a result of what he chose to do with the Gettysburg Address. But so does that of an otherwise undistinguished Mr. Getty. Consider also the dubious origins of the name "America." Does philosophy alone seem to be able to free itself from the here and now and hence from chance? Compare Aristotle, *Rhetoric* 1379a34–35. See Anastaplo, *The Constitutionalist,* 763 n. 177, 805 n. 39. See also Anastaplo, "American Constitutionalism and the Virtue of Prudence," 129 n. 2, notes 464, 474, and 477 above, note 492 below. See, on Machiavelli, Leo Paul S. de Alvarez, *The Machiavellian Enterprise: A Commentary on "The Prince"* (DeKalb: Northern Illinois University Preess, 1999).

See, on the status of beauty, note 443 above.

479. One exception to the utilitarian note may seem to be Lincoln's remarkable talent for humorous stories. His wit could somehow assert itself, although transposed, even in grim circumstances. See, e.g., *Collected Works,* 5: 474, 6: 78–79, 7: 11, 111, 239–40, 338, 8: 361. See also ibid., 2: 250, 269–70, 408, 3: 146, 279; sec. III of Chap. 8 of this Collection. See as well the entry for "Phrases, quaint conceits" in the index for John G. Nicolay and John Hay, eds., *Abraham Lincoln, Complete Works* (New York: Century, 1902), 2: 737–38; sec. VII of Chap. 14 of this Collection. Also remarkable (but unphilosophical?) was Lincoln's periodic melancholy. See Chap. 9 of this Collection. (See, for instructive, if sometimes perverse, comments on wit and melancholy, Hobbes, *Leviathan,* 1: 8. See also Allan Bloom, trans., *The Republic of Plato* (New York: Basic Books, 1968), 469: "[M]elancholy, although dangerous, is apparently an attribute of most exceptional men. [See] Aristotle [*Problems,*30:1], who says that all men remarkable in philosophy, politics, poetry, or the arts are melancholic." But can this be said, for example, of Socrates? See, on paranoia, Anastaplo, "American Constitutionalism and Prudence," 147 n. 33.)

See, on the relation of the useful to the noble, Aristotle, *Rhetoric* 1389a33–35, 1389b35–1390a5, 1393al3–16; Anastaplo, *The Constitutionalist,* 651 n. 91, 670 n. 2; *Thinker as Artist,* 182; note 7 above. See also the discussion of Tocqueville's paras. 4, 6, and 7 in Chap. 6 of this Collection. See as well note 521 below. Is not the ruthless, single-minded and uprooted Thomas Sutpen of William Faulkner's *Absalom, Absalom!* an incipient aristocrat? See, on how even the most unbecoming Founders are regarded when they succeed in establishing and endowing their line, Machiavelli's *Prince.* On the other hand, the Father of his Country is transformed, in *Absalom, Absalom!,* into local white trash, Wash Jones. See, on Thomas Jefferson and aristocratic imperatives in a democratic age, George Anastaplo, *The American Moralist: On Law, Ethics, and Government* (Athens: Ohio University Press, 1992), 103 f. Compare George Anastaplo, *The Amendments to the Constitution: A Commentary* (Baltimore: Johns Hopkins University Press, 1995), 107–24. See, on the relation of politics to philosophy, Anastaplo, *Human Being and Citizen,* 8 f. See, on utility, Chap. 6 of this Collection.

Lincoln, with his lifelong interest in technology and progress, which seems to fit in temperamentally with a dedication to effective equality, would have "appreciated" such "pushing back of the frontiers of knowledge" as is reported and promised by modern astronomy. (See note 468 above.) But would not his appreciation have been directed primarily to the practical, not to the speculative? Would not deeds be paramount, not words, except as words serve deeds? That is, words for their own sake look to an emphasis upon understanding for its own sake as something superior to nobility and even to morality. See Jacob Klein and Leo Strauss, "A Giving of Accounts," *The College* (St. John's College), April 1970, 1. See also Anastaplo, *The Constitutionalist,* 803 n. 38, 805 n. 39; note 492 below; the text at note 1 above. Compare Anastaplo, "American Constitutionalism and Prudence," 108.

480. See Anastaplo, *The Constitutionalist,* 499 n. 116, 500 n. 117. See also Anastaplo, "American Constitutionalism and Prudence," 142 n. 23; note 473 above.

A religion, political or otherwise, to be effective must be, to some degree, single-minded and even ruthless: the prerogative generously exercised by Jesus in healing on the Sabbath may have threatened Israel no less than did those in the desert who selfishly worshiped the Golden Calf. See Anastaplo, *The Constitutionalist,* 436 n. 38, 667 n. 124, 677 n. 14, 784 n. 10. See also Anastaplo, "On Trial," 882 f.; Anastaplo, "Law & Literature and the Bible," 604–13.

481. See, for the anomalies that still have to be dealt with and learned from, George Anastaplo, "'Racism,' Political Correctness, and Constitutional Law: A Law School Case Study," 42 *South Dakota Law Review* 108, 113 (1997); note 25 above. Consider, as passionate (but not truly thoughtful) challenges to the argument made in the text, the instructive work of James Baldwin.

482. Shades of an unreconstructed Governor George Wallace! Consider, however, General Grant's reflections at Appomattox Court House: "What General Lee's feelings were I do not know. As he was a man of much dignity, with an impassible face, it was impossible to say whether he felt inwardly glad that the end had finally come, or felt sad over the result, and was too manly to show it. Whatever his feelings, they were entirely concealed from my observation; but my own feelings, which had been quite jubilant on the receipt of his letter, were sad and depressed. I felt like anything rather than rejoicing at the downfall of a foe who had fought so long and valiantly, and had suffered so much for a cause, though that cause was, I believe, one of the worst for which a people ever fought, and one for which there was the least excuse. I do not question, however, the sincerity of the great mass of those who were opposed to us." U. S. Grant, *Personal Memoirs* (New York: Charles L. Webster, 1894), 629–30. See note 43 above. See also note 60 above.

Lincoln had, in his July 4, 1861 Message, questioned "this magical omnipotence of 'State rights,'" having already asserted, "This sophism derives much—perhaps the whole—of its currency from the assumption, that there is some omnipotent, and sacred supremacy, pertaining to a *State*—to each State of our Federal Union. Our States have neither more, nor less power, than that reserved to them in the Union, by the Constitution—no one of them ever having been a State *out* of the Union." *Collected Works,* 4: 433–34. (See also the text at note 387 above.) Does not this underestimate somewhat (however usefully for the occasion) the role of the States in the 1776–1789 period? Does it not conveniently ignore, for example, the implications of the "power" of the States at that time both to frame and to reject the Constitution of 1787? Still, would not the States that failed to ratify it still have been somehow in the Union? See note 375 above. Compare Harry V. Jaffa, "Equality as a Conservative Principle," 8 *Loyola of Los Angeles Law Review* 471, 502–5 (1975). Compare, also, the exchange between Thomas Jefferson and James Madison about the founding of the University of Virginia, in which the Declaration of Independence was referred to as "the fundamental act of Union of these States." See note 395 above. The very name "United States" seems to have troubled the would-be Secessionists, for they preferred to look back before the Constitution to the Articles of Confederation, if not even further back. See the text at note 417 above.

Lincoln's attitude against States' Rights comes down to our day. Its transmittal to us may be seen in such forms as that evident in a letter of November 23, 1912, from Theodore Roosevelt to Charles E. Merriam (University of Chicago Archives): "I was very anxious to get the Republican Party back to what it was in the days of Abraham Lincoln and make it the real progressive party of the country; because I do not believe that the Democratic Party can ever become such a progressive party because it is tied to absolutely outworn principles, especially to the ruinous principle of States' rights." Are not States' Rights, which are now much more the cause of the Republican Party, threatened ultimately by the "rationalizing" tendencies of the Enlightenment? See Anastaplo, *The Constitutionalist,* e.g., 664 n. 119; See also Anastaplo, "American Constitutionalism and Prudence," 150 n. 38. (See, on enduring differences between the Republican and Democratic Parties, George Anastaplo, review of *Roosevelt, the Soldier of Freedom,* by James M. Burns, *Critic,* January–February 1971, 71; George Anastaplo, "What Can Be Said for the Nixon Administration," *Chicago Tribune,* Sept. 22, 1973, sec. 1, p. 16; Anastaplo, "American Constitutionalism and Prudence," 147 n. 33.

Compare Anastaplo, *The Constitutionalist,* esp. Chap. 7, "A More Perfect Union"; ibid., 216 (on "an overriding concern for industrial prosperity induc[ing] our people toward a consolidated government"). Compare, also, Anastaplo, "American Constitutionalism and Prudence," 13; note 471 above.

The "in the course of ultimate extinction" language may be found at, among other places, Lincoln, *Collected Works,* 3: 276 (note 430 above). See Anastaplo, "American Constitutionalism and Prudence," 133 n. 6. Compare Lincoln, *Collected Works,* 2: 492.

483. See Anastaplo, *Human Being and Citizen,* 61 f. See also note 456 above, note 492 below. To what extent did the belittling of liberty addressed in the text (more than thirty years ago) contribute, as a reaction, to the abuses of liberty if not even licentiousness to which we have had to become accustomed? What form will the reaction in turn to this take? Are we moving back to the conditions addressed in Lincoln's Lyceum Speech?

"Our adversaries have adopted some Declarations of Independence, in which, unlike the good old one, penned by Jefferson, they omit the words 'all men are created equal.' Why? They have adopted a temporary national constitution, in the preamble of which, unlike our good old one, signed by Washington, they omit

'We, the People,' and substitute, 'We, the deputies of the sovereign and independent States.' Why? Why this deliberate pressing out of view, the rights of men, and the authority of the people?" Lincoln, *Collected Works,* 4: 438 (July 4, 1861). (See, for the Preamble settled upon for the Confederate Constitution of 1861, Sec. II of Chap. 13 of this Collection.) Does not the doctrine of equality, once accepted, tend to be harmonizing, even though it runs the risk of legitimating mediocrity? Does not the doctrine of liberty tend to promote distinction, even though it runs the risk of provoking disruption? See Anastaplo, "American Constitutionalism and Prudence," 133 n. 6; note 473 above.

484. See, on the right of revolution, Chaps 1, 2, 12, and 13 of this Collection. See also notes 64 and 219 above, the text at note 513 below. Harry Jaffa has argued: "It is significant that the seceding States of the South, in 1861, did not appeal to the right of revolution. They appealed—however speciously—to the right to secession as a constitutional right. They went to great lengths to avoid appealing to a right whose exercise would obviously apply far more to their slaves than to themselves." Harry V. Jaffa, *Original Intent and the Framers of the Constitution,* (Washington, D.C.: Regnery Gateway, 1994), 386. Even, so, Lincoln did address in his First Inaugural Address and thereafter the question of the proper exercise of the right of revolution. See as well Anastaplo, *Amendments to the Constitution,* x, 386.

485. Do not the ancient lights kindled in Greece and Rome somehow shine through the Declaration of Independence more than through the Gettysburg Address? See notes 464, 466, 468, 476, and 479 above, note 489 below. See also the text at note 521 below. (Is not pity, or compassion, made more of by the moderns than by the ancients? And is this related to the recourse by the moderns to technology to relieve human want? See, e.g., George P. Grant, *Technology and Empire* [Toronto: House of Anansi, 1969] 97 f., 103 ["It is not by accident that as representative and perceptive a modern political philosopher as [Ludwig] Feuerbach should have written that 'compassion is before thought.'"])

Is it not one ancient teaching, with which Americans (insofar as they are moderns) are somewhat uncomfortable, that "men have no right to what is not reasonable, and to what is not for their benefit"? See Edmund Burke, *Works* (London: World Classics, Oxford University Press, n.d.), 4: 68. Something of the ancient teaching *is* indicated in Lincoln's observation that "nothing should ever be implied as law, which leads to unjust, or absurd consequences." *Collected Works,* 4: 435. But if the law should happen to be explicit in ordaining "unjust or absurd consequences," what then? And what if the "sovereign people" should insist upon injustice or absurdities? That is, would not both Daniel Webster and Abraham Lincoln agree with Gouverneur Morris that "the Basis of our own Constitution is the indefeasible Right of the People to establish it"? *Diary,* 2: 533. See Webster, *Works,* 5: 433; Lincoln, *Collected Works,* 8: 52 (note 468 above). Compare ibid., 3: 315 ("But if it is wrong, he cannot say people have a right to do wrong."), 7: 486 ("If the people should, by whatever mode or means, make it an Executive duty to reenslave such persons, another, and not I, must be their instrument to perform it."), 7: 51, 8: 152; note 468 above. Compare also Plato, *Apology* 32B–D; Morris, *Diary,* 1: xliv; Anastaplo, *The Constitutionalist,* 418 n. 35.

Is it not another ancient teaching, with which pious Americans are somewhat uncomfortable, that only human reason can (but that *it* can) truly guide human conduct, even with respect to the proper place among us of divine worship? (See, e.g., the passage from Lincoln, *Collected Works,* 7: 282, quoted in note 492 below.) The post-Classical view takes two curiously related forms, that of modern relativism and that of precise (if not continuing) revelation. Consider, for example, the pronouncement (made from a Christian perspective) by George Santayana: "Shakespeare's world . . . is only the world of human society. The cosmos eludes him; he does not seem to feel the need of framing that idea. He depicts human life in all its richness and variety, but leaves that life without a setting, and consequently without a meaning." *Selected Critical Writings of George Santayana,* ed. Norman Henfrey (Cambridge: Cambridge University Press, 1968), 1: 65. Consider as well the admonition of Pope Paul VI in his Christmas 1973 message: "Today, many people substitute anthropology for theology. They see in Christianity a human value that is acceptable to all. They do not see the divine truth that gives this human value its reason for being and its infinite worth." Or, to put the ancients–moderns distinction in another way, the ancients, even when they sensed the impermanence of all things, including human existence, were not so self-centered as to indulge themselves in an apocalyptic view of the world. See Anastaplo, "American Constitutionalism and Prudence," 147 n. 33. Or, to put the ancients–moderns distinction in still another way, "It is baffling to reflect that what men call honour does not correspond always to Christian ethics" (Winston Churchill, as quoted by Harry V. Jaffa, *Thomism and Aristotelianism* [Chicago: University of Chicago Press, 1952], ii). See Anastaplo, "American Constitutionalism and Prudence," 140 n. 20; note 489 below.

It is my opinion, it might be noted in passing, that Churchill is himself "post-Classical" in certain decisive respects, just as is (I argue in note 492 below) Lincoln himself. And it might be noted as well, with a view to the discussion below, that Shakespeare may also be, although perhaps to a lesser degree, "post-Classical": this may be seen in the emphasis in Shakespeare's work upon the "conscience" (that conscience which is so much a part of modern "individuality"). Compare the discussion in Aristotle's *Nicomachean Ethics* of "shame," something that is decisively more social than is "conscience." Thus, the difference between "conscience" and "shame" is essential to any serious assessment of, say, the fate of Sir Thomas More. See Anastaplo, *Human Being and Citizen,* 275 n. 39; "On Trial," 950 f. See, on shame, Anastaplo, *Artist as Thinker,* 475 n. 282. See also Confucius, *Analects* 2:3. See, for the distinction between "guilt" and "folly," Anastaplo, "American Constitutionalism and Prudence," 146 n. 30. See, on Shakespeare as "the great vehicle within the Anglo-American world for the transmission of an essentially Socratic understanding of the civilization of the West," note 492 below.

See, on Churchill as observed over many decades by a Labour Party adversary, Emanuel Shinwell, *I've Lived through It All* (London: Gollancz, 1973), 14–15, 44–45, 85–86, 104–5, 119–20, 134–35, 145–47, 157–65, 169–70, 178–80, 184–85, 204, 208, 210, 216–17, 218–19, 240–42, 266–67. See also ibid., 30–32, 34, 39–40, 50–51, 107–8, 147–49, 249–57. See as well F. W. Winterbotham, *The Ultra Secret*

(New York: Harper & Row, 1974), e.g., 39 ("The well-known voice was always courteous."), 64–65, 81–82.

Curiously enough, one reviewer has seen my argument in *The Constitutionalist* as assuming that "principles must be given priority over consequences." 68 *American Political Science Review* 775 (1974). Such a self-centered assumption, however noble it can sometimes appear, would have as one consequence the virtual elimination of prudence and hence of responsible politics. (See Anastaplo, "American Constitutionalism and Prudence," 138 n. 17. See also note 7 above.) Even more bizarre is the polemicist who concluded his review of *The Constitutionalist:* "In short, Professor Anastaplo, despite his surface admiration of Plato and Aristotle, does not have a Classical perspective of politics. In this regard he is truly representative of the Straussian school of political theory." 17 *Modern Age* 94 (1973). Compare Willmoore Kendall's endorsement of the same Classical studies, 61 *American Political Science Review* 783 (1967). Compare, also, 16 *Revue de Science Politique* 115 (1966); 4 *Political Science Reviewer* 169 n. 8, 189–90 (1974). Compare as well George Anastaplo, "The Occasions of Freedom of Speech," 5 *Political Science Reviewer* 383 (1975); the text at note 521 below.

Is not the Gettysburg Address more distinctively "American" than either the Declaration of Independence or the Constitution in that it was crafted by someone who had been an American all his life, unlike the authors of 1776 and 1787? See note 433 above.

486. Lincoln, *Collected Works,* 1: 382. See, for the complete text of this handbill, note 497 below. See also George Anastaplo, "Church and State: Explorations," 19 *Loyola University of Chicago Law Journal* 86 f., 148 (1987); Anastaplo, *Human Being and Citizen,* 117 f.; Anastaplo, *The Constitutionalist,* 610 n. 34. See as well note 492 below, the text at note 91 above, the text at note 497 below.

487. Lincoln, *Collected Works,* 6: 34 (January 2, 1863).

488. Ibid., 7: 86 (December 22, 1863). See also ibid., 7: 178–79, 223.

489. In this respect, the authors of 1776 may have been more like the Classics, mindful of the observation in Matthew 6:24, that no man can serve two masters. I have noticed, however, that the attitude of Gouverneur Morris differed in this respect from that of Thomas Jefferson. See Anastaplo, "American Constitutionalism and Prudence," 101 f. See also the chapter, "Religion and the Social Order," as well as the appendix, in Paul F. Boller Jr., *George Washington and Religion* (Dallas: Southern Methodist University Press, 1963). Washington's sentiments are indicated in the passage cited in note 490 below. See, for Webster's public reliance upon Christianity, *Works,* e.g. 3: 75, 4: 234, 371 f., 5: 330, 331. Consider, for Lincoln's views, such *public* statements as that found in the First Inaugural Address (*Collected Works,* 4: 271): "Intelligence, patriotism, Christianity, and a firm reliance on Him, who has never yet forsaken this favored land, are still competent to adjust, in the best way, all our present difficulty." See also ibid., 5: 497–98, 7: 48, 169.

What *were* Lincoln's private opinions on this subject? Does the truly political man eventually cease to have serious private reservations with respect to the most important questions? Can he preserve, that is, a deep-rooted reliance upon "cold, calculating, unimpassioned reason"? Ibid., 1: 115 (January 27, 1838). Should we want him to do so? So perceptive an observer as Alexander H. Stephens, the Vice

President of the Confederacy, said of Lincoln that "the Union with him in sentiment, rose to the sublimity of a religious mysticism." (See the epigraph for Chap.
13 of this Collection. See also Anastaplo, "American Constitutionalism and Prudence," 142 n. 21.) This is not to say that mysticism rules out considerable political skill. Is not Moses a case in point? See Machiavelli, *The Prince,* Chap. 6. Charles
Péguy is said to have characterized religion as "beginning in mysticism and ending
in politics" (quoted in the *Chicago Sun-Times,* December 29, 1973, 36). Cannot a
case be made as well for the opposite movement? See Plato, *Republic* 415C–D. See,
on reading carefully, de Alvarez, *The Machiavellian Enterprise,* x, 75–79.

In any event, neither Lincoln nor Webster was so doctrinaire in this respect,
or so reckless, as to permit himself to be labeled by his contemporaries as was the
author of the Declaration of Independence, "Mr. Jefferson, the atheist Virginian."
See *Encyclopedia Americana,* 29: 147 (1956 ed.). Does modern republicanism depend
upon that political impotence of religion that tends to result from a multiplicity of
sects even while it relies upon the moral character and, on occasion, even the
intense fervor promoted by religious sentiment? Consider the pious hope
expressed by Webster in 1833 (*Works,* 1: 306): "Heaven grant that it may be the
glory of the United States to have established two great truths, of the highest
importance to the whole human race; first, that an enlightened community *is* capable of self-government; and, second, that the toleration of all sects does *not* necessarily produce indifference to religion." (Webster had said, shortly before, "So far as
we can trace the designs of Providence, the formation of the mind and character,
by instruction in knowledge, and instruction in righteousness, is a main end of
human being." Ibid., 1: 305.)

I have been discussing in this note the relation of the life of reason to the life
of faith. It has been observed:

> The most impressive alternative to philosophy in the life of Leo Strauss
> is summoned up by the name of a city, Jerusalem, the holy city. What if
> the one thing most needful is not philosophic wisdom, but righteous-
> ness? This notion of the one thing most needful, Mr. Strauss argued, is
> not defensible if the world is not the creation of the just and loving
> God, the holy God. Neither philosophy nor revealed religion, he
> argued, can refute one another; for, among other reasons, they disagree
> about the very principles or criteria of proof. Leo Strauss was a Jew, a
> Jewish scholar, and, if I know anything about the meaning of the word,
> he was a philosopher; but he insisted that strictly speaking there is no
> such thing as Jewish philosophy. This mutual irrefutability and tension
> between philosophy and Biblical revelation appeared to him to be the
> secret of the vitality of Western Civilization. (Laurence Berns, "On Leo
> Strauss," *The College* [St. John's College, Annapolis, Maryland], April
> 1974, 5)

See George Anastaplo, review of *Jewish Philosophy and the Crisis of Modernity,* by Leo
Strauss,1998 *The Great Ideas Today* (1998). (The complete version of this book
review is appended to Anastaplo, "Law & Literature and the Bible," 778–86 [note

465 above].) See also George Anastaplo, "Leo Strauss at the University of Chicago," in *Leo Strauss, the Straussians, and the American Regime*, ed. Kenneth L. Deutsch and John A. Murley (Lanham, Md.: Rowman & Littlefield, 1999), 3–30.

Compare David Hume, *An Enquiry Concerning Human Understanding*, sec. 10: Chap. 2 ("Of Miracles"): "Eloquence, when at its highest pitch, leaves little room for reason or reflection; but addressing itself entirely to the fancy or the affections, captivates the willing hearers, and subdues their understanding. Happily, this pitch it seldom attains. But what a Tully [Cicero] or a Demosthenes could scarcely effect over a Roman or Athenian audience, every *Capuchin*, every itinerant or stationary teacher can perform over the generality of mankind, and in a higher degree, by touching such gross and vulgar passions." Compare, also, Anastaplo, *Human Being and Citizen*, 135 f.; note 493 below. See the text after note 191 above.

Is it not revealing that Socrates, in the course of a discussion in Plato's *Theages* with an aspiring politician about the wisdom or knowledge appropriate for governing a democratic people, should make so much of his daemonic thing? Only the inarticulate daemonic thing, rather than any *techne*, can be counted upon to save the truly principled man who finds himself engaged in the political life of a democratic city. Compare Plato's *Republic* in this respect. See, on Socrates' daemonic thing, Anastaplo, *Human Being and Citizen*, 325; Anastaplo, *Thinker as Artist*, 394.

See notes 466 and 473 above.

490. See Sec. VI of Chap. 1 of this Collection; Anastaplo, *Constitution of 1787*, 21–22, 308 n. 16; the text at note 473 above. See also Jaffa, *Crisis of the House Divided*, 229 (quoted in note 467 above). Had not the Declaration presented divinity in the image of the political? Did not Lincoln, on the other hand, present the political in the image of divinity? Did the passions and memories of the Revolution temporarily (for some three-score years?) take the place of religion? And then did "conventional" religious passions reassert themselves, often in bizarre forms? That is, did the different circumstances in 1776 and 1863 require different "rhetorical" responses on the part of public-spirited statesmen? Grandeur and daring, as well as mere expediency, may be seen on both occasions. (Euripides's *Bacchae* reminds prudent men to be aware of, and careful about, other people's passions. See, on the Declaration of Independence and divinity, Sec. VI of Chap. 1 of this Collection.)

This shift in the character of public sentiment is indicated by Webster's observation of May 15, 1850 (*Works*, 6: 551): "Circumstances have occurred, within the last twenty years, to create a new degree of feeling, at the North, on the subject of slavery; and from being considered, as it was at the adoption of the Constitution, mainly as a political question, it has come to be regarded, with unusual warmth, as a question of religion and humanity." Did not this mean that men and women, both North and South, would be less apt than their grandparents to act sensibly? Consider, for example, the (sometimes intemperate?) post-Presidential career in the House of Representatives of John Quincy Adams. See note 478 above. Compare note 213 above. See, for counsels of moderation addressed especially to intellectuals, George Anastaplo, review of *Political Prisoners in America*, by Charles Goodell, *Chicago Sun-Times, Book Week*, July 8, 1973, 1; George Anastaplo, "An Amnesty on Discussions of Amnesty?" *Chicago Tribune*, Feb. 25, 1973, sec. 2, p. 2 (reprinted at 119 *Cong. Rec.* H3280–H3281 [May 2, 1973]);

George Anastaplo, review of *John Strachey,* by Hugh Thomas, *Chicago Sun-Times, Book Week,* January 6, 1974, 14; Anastaplo, *The Constitutionalist,* 735 n. 135; Anastaplo, Preface to *Human Being and Citizen,*; Anastaplo, "American Constitutionalism and Prudence," 147 n. 33.

491. We find two of Lincoln's sons with non-Biblical names, in marked contrast to the names of his forebears. See Anastaplo, "American Constitutionalism and Prudence," 129 n. 2. It should be noticed that Lincoln's sons were born before the Civil War—before, that is, whatever influence toward the revival of a greater recourse to Biblical language that the passions of the war might have had on Lincoln. See note 256 above.

492. "Our republican robe is soiled and trailed in the dust. Let us repurify it. Let us turn and wash it white, in the spirit, if not the blood of the Revolution." Lincoln, *Collected Works,* 2: 276 (October 16, 1854). (A prominent Indiana senator, John Pettit, we recall, had even called the "created equal" language in the Declaration of Independence "a self-evident lie." Ibid., 2: 275 [1854], 3: 205, 301–2 [1858]. Lincoln said about Pettit's heresy, "What would have happened if he had said it in old Independence Hall? The door-keeper would have taken him by the throat and stopped his rascally breath awhile, and then have hurled him into the street." Ibid., 2: 283–284 [1854]. See Sec. III of Chap. 1 of this Collection.) Consider Jaffa, *Crisis of the House Divided,* 228 f.; note 456 above. (One sees even the free-thinking Jefferson [note 489 above] resorting to the theological and the supernatural when most moved by the slavery question. See ibid., 242–43.) Consider as well the inscription above the statue in the Lincoln Memorial (the true national cathedral in Washington, D.C.): "In this temple as in the hearts of the people for whom he saved the Union the memory of Abraham Lincoln is enshrined forever." (Notice that the emphasis is put here where Lincoln, as President, had been obliged to put it: on saving the Union, not on abolishing slavery.)

I have assigned to Lincoln a very high place in the pantheon of American constitutional heroes. See, e.g., note 464 above. But having done so, I find myself obliged and, I trust, equipped and entitled, to question those who would assign him an even higher place. May not this make too much of chance opportunities and developments? (See, on Lincoln's ambition, Anastaplo, "American Constitutionalism and Prudence," 128 n. 1. See also Chaps. 8 and 9 of this Collection.)

It is difficult to canonize Lincoln without playing down the Declaration of Independence and its Constitution. But a Lincoln we do not have with us always, or if we do, it is a Lincoln who must, in large part, be understood in terms of the immediate problems confronting him, whereas constitutional principles should provide more enduring guidance. A good constitution is, in a sense, prudence institutionalized. It should be more the product of deliberation, and less of chance, than any particular statesman, his character, or his career. See Anastaplo, *The Constitutionalist,* 581 n. 43. See also Anastaplo, "American Constitutionalism and Prudence," 138 n. 17. See as well Sec. IX of Chap. 4 of this Collection.

We as citizens must be, as were both Webster and Lincoln, *somewhat cautious* in directing most of our fellow citizens to a "higher authority which sits enthroned above the Constitution and above the law." Webster, *Works,* 6: 558. Thus Lincoln could instruct his political lieutenants, May 17, 1860, "I agree with Seward in his

'Irrepressible Conflict,' but I do not endorse his 'Higher Law' doctrine." *Collected Works,* 4: 50. See Randall, *Lincoln the President,* 1: 146–153, 231–237. See, on John Brown's "enterprise," Lincoln, *Collected Works* 2: 538–40, 4: 12. See also note 39 above, note 533 below. See, on the rule of law, Plato, *Statesman* 294A–295D, 279D ff. One can learn from Plato's dialogues that the best regime is not one in which the rule of law ultimately governs. This means, for example, that there need be no fixed terms of office for rulers and hence no provision for formal impeachment. See Anastaplo, "American Constitutionalism and Prudence," 83–94, 143 n. 26. But must we not make do with the rule of law until the reign is instituted among us of philosopher–kings, not of one chance philosopher–king *but of a reliable series of them*? See Anastaplo, *The Constitutionalist,* 581 n. 43. See, on the problem here of Marcus Aurelius, George Anastaplo, "Samplings," 27 *Political Science Reviewer* 394 (1998).

Consider, as an instructive challenge, the elevation of Abraham Lincoln evident in Harry Jaffa's 1973 talk on Leo Strauss (*Conditions of Freedom,* 7–8):

I have been asked to say a word about my own studies of Lincoln, and the American regime, in their relationship to Strauss. The most obvious connection is between Strauss's many expositions of Locke, and Locke's massive influence on America. Locke certainly represented modernity in its soberest form, although Strauss was careful to emphasize Locke's ultimate, if concealed, insobriety. But Strauss also thought that American politics, at its best, showed a practical wisdom that owed much to a tradition older than Locke. Indeed, Locke's esoteric teaching, which emphasized that older tradition, was taken with the greatest seriousness in America. But the American regime was not formed only by Locke. Many a frontier log cabin, which had in it no philosophical works whatever, had the King James Bible—and Shakespeare. And Shakespeare was the great vehicle within the Anglo-American world for the transmission of an essentially Socratic understanding of the civilization of the West. [See, on Shakespeare as "post-Classical," note 485 above.]

Most American studies begin, and properly so, with the Constitution. The Constitution does not define the regime, but it is the most public and visible expression of it. It is part of the defect of modern politics that it looks to the character of the law, more than to the character of the men who make and enforce the law, however intimate the connection between them necessarily is. However admirable the character of the American Constitution, it was not, I thought, the most admirable expression of the regime. The Constitution is the highest American thing, only if one tries to understand the high in the light of the low. It is high, because men are not angels, and because we do not have angels to govern us. Its strength lies in its ability to connect the interest of the man with the duty of the place. But the Constitution, in deference to man's nonangelic nature, made certain compromises with slavery. And partly because of those compromises, it dissolved in the presence of a great crisis. The man—or the character of the man—who bore the nation through that crisis, seemed to me—and Strauss gave me every encouragement to believe it—the highest thing in the American regime. The character of Lincoln became intelligible, not on the basis of *The Federalist*—profound as that work is—but on that of the *Nicomachean Ethics*. In the final analysis, not only American politics, but all modern politics, must be clarified on the basis of Classical political philosophy. That is because [quoting Leo Strauss; see note 338 above], "It is safer to try to understand the low in the light of the high than the high in the light of the low. In doing the latter one necessarily distorts the high, whereas in doing the former one does not deprive the low of the freedom to reveal itself fully as what it is."

Does not Mr. Jaffa, in his noble partisanship, sometimes go too far? However that may be, it is not what Mr. Jaffa says which is questioned below *so much as what he might be taken by the careless to have said*. (We are confident [I first said in the 1970s] that if there should happen to be anything both novel and of merit in the comments prompted here by Mr. Jaffa's talk, he will be able to take due account of it as he continues that study of Lincoln which he has thus far so nobly advanced.)

In the first place, it should be noticed that the Constitution simply did *not* "dissolve in the presence of a great crisis." (Nor had Lincoln, in his "House Divided" Speech expected it to dissolve? Compare the judgment of Thaddeus Stevens, in the text at note 442 above.) Rather, a terrible storm was weathered by the regime, partly because of what had been accomplished theretofore pursuant to the Constitution. American constitutionalism had provided a Lincoln the opportunities and guidance he needed to develop his great natural talents; it had permitted and encouraged the development of the resources, both spiritual and material, with which the Country could *(with or without Lincoln)* conduct and endure a great civil war; it had developed a people willing and able to be led, through much uncertainty and many sacrifices, to do what was necessary to preserve institutions that had shown themselves worthy of and beneficial to free men. Thus, Lincoln could say on April 4, 1864, "I claim not to have controlled events, but confess plainly that events have controlled me." *Collected Works,* 7: 282. Certainly, it would be a mistake to underestimate the resiliency and fundamental good sense of the American people, both the people who gave us Lincoln and the people given us by Lincoln and his fellow soldiers in the Civil War. See Anastaplo, "American Constitutionalism and Prudence," 103. See, on Lincoln and determinism, note 497 below.

In the second place, it should be noticed that the "compromises with slavery" made by the Constitution were ratified and even repeated by Lincoln. See, e.g., note 470 above. Is there any reason to believe that a Lincoln, in like circumstances, would not have made the 1787 compromises or that the more thoughtful framers of the Constitution would not have acted as Lincoln did in *his* circumstances? That is, is there not an essential sameness to truly prudent men? Thus, Webster insisted in 1850, "firmness, steadiness of principle, a just moderation, and unconquerable preservance, are the virtues the practice of which is most likely to correct whatever is wrong in the constitution of the social system." *Works,* 6: 561. See the end of note 477 above.

In the third place, it should be noticed that Lincoln himself (especially by his virtual sanctification of equality) was obliged, in turn, to make compromises of his own and to leave expectations and hence problems which may lead to greater crises among us than those we have already endured, crises affecting not only the American people but even the fate of mankind. It does not deny a political hero's memorable contribution to his regime if one should have to question both his uniqueness and his infallibility. Consider, for example, the political intemperance of Churchill during the First World War, that most foolish war which led both to many of the horrors of the twentieth century and to Churchill's own inspiring efforts during the Second World War. See Anastaplo, *The Constitutionalist,* 784 n. 11; also, note 209 above. See, on the modernity of Churchill and, to a lesser extent, of Shakespeare, note 485 above. Lloyd George could say of Churchill, "Winston likes wars, I don't." Mosley, *My Life,* 106. See note 209 above, note 504 below.

Indeed, among the problems left by Lincoln, my fellow Illinoisan, is that he may well have, as one result of his egalitarian teachings and example, helped turn serious American thought *away from* that Classical political philosophy recommended by Mr. Jaffa. Does not the "divine" take the place, in Lincoln's thought (not only, as among the more cautious ancients, in public discourse), of "nature," that nature upon which Classical political philosophy rests? See Plato, *Sophist* 265E. Does not the sacred, notwithstanding its association with and dependence upon the traditional, look (or seem to look) to the essence of things? But the pious votary cannot understand this fully. He has lost sight of nature, the causes of things, and chance. (Compare Xenophon's *Memorabilia,* 4: 3; also, Plutarch on Plato in his *Nicias.*) In addition, does not the liberty that the ancients seem to have preferred to equality look more than does equality to virtue (to human excellence) and hence to nature? See the book review cited in note 483 above. See also note 485 above.

Consider, in assessing Lincoln's religion-based sentiments, the "republican robe" quotation with which this note opens. Consider also the element of mysticism (induced in part, no doubt, by the great passions of the war) already referred to. See notes 466 and 489 above. Consider as well the Christian imagery and tone that permeate much of Lincoln's later public statements, perhaps even his most private thoughts. See, e g., *Collected Works,* 5: 403–4. See, on the "positive good" of the wartime affliction, note 474 above. Douglas had observed, by 1858, that Lincoln had "a proneness for quoting scripture." Ibid., 2: 510. Whatever the political usefulness or the ultimate sincerity of such sentiments, they do seem somehow more impassioned, somewhat less urbane, than those which one associates with Classical political philosophy or (for that matter) with the Declaration of Independence. See, e.g., note 479 above. See also Sec. VI of Chap. 1 of this Collection. Do not these sentiments differ in critical respects from that godlike virtue of which a Cicero spoke? Certainly, there is to Lincoln's sentiments a familiar Midwestern accent. See Chaps. 8 and 9 of this Collection.

Thus, philosophy—the "essentially Socratic understanding"—seems, by the end of Lincoln's life, not to have (if it ever did have) the status one finds assigned to it in Classical political thought or even among the Founding Fathers of the eighteenth century. See, e.g., Lincoln, *Collected Works,* 7: 542 (September 7, 1864): "All the good the Saviour gave to the world was communicated through this book [the Bible]. *But for it we could not know right from wrong.* All things most desirable for man's welfare, here and hereafter, are to be found portrayed in it." (These remarks are taken from Lincoln's "Reply to Loyal Colored People of Baltimore upon Presentation of a Bible [to the President].") The sentence I have italicized is hardly Classical in its inclination. Compare Plato, *Republic* 414B ff., 427B ff. However, the circumstances in which Lincoln made these remarks bear upon how they are to be understood, as is true of the handbill found in note 497 below and discussed in the text of this Collection at note 486 above, in Sec. IX of Chap. 4, and in Sec. III of Chap. 16 of this Collection. See also Lincoln, *Collected Works,* 1: 315 (March 4, 1843): "He whose wisdom surpasses that of all philosophers, has declared that 'a house divided against itself cannot stand.'" (Aesop was identified on that occasion as a "great fabulist and philosopher.") See as well ibid., 2: 510, 3: 445, 462.

Lincoln seems to have been, in decisive respects, a child of the Enlightenment, dedicated to the hope, if not the expectation, of continuous and unlimited progress. (See note 468 above.) In this way, too—independent of the effects upon him of a soul-searing war—he seems to have been open to modern influences that are distantly grounded in Christian doctrines. Modernity, if not also existentialism, may be detected as well in the sentiment, "But the game is caught; and I believe it is true, that with the catching, end the pleasures of the chase." Ibid., 1: 113 (January 27, 1838). See, for Lincoln's Lockean inclinations, Anastaplo, "American Constitutionalism and Prudence," 134 n. 8. See, on existentialism, Anastaplo, *American Moralist,* 139. See also Sec. VII of Chap. 7 of this Collection.

It may well be true, of course, that "the character of Lincoln [becomes] intelligible not on the basis of *The Federalist*—profound as that work is—but on that of the *Nicomachean Ethics.*" But that should be true of all complex characters, good and bad, noble and base, just and unjust, to say nothing of ancient and modern—since Aristotle's *Ethics* does provide us a serious study of character. It would be quite another thing to say, however, that something like the *Ethics,* which may indeed be needed to understand a Lincoln, was itself in effect understood, especially in its teachings about the intellectual virtues, by Lincoln. But without a solid awareness of the intellectual virtues, and of the preeminent status of the contemplative life (so critical to Aristotle's overall argument), can there be a sufficient opening toward a respect for Classical political philosophy? One is reminded, by the cast of Lincoln's mind, of the highly moral and quite practical sense of Confucian thought: if philosophy provides an underpinning for that thought, it is well concealed and hence is not as instructive as philosophy can be. See Anastaplo, "An Introduction to Confucian Thought," 1984 *The Great Ideas Today* 124 (1984). (Much the same can be said about Hindu thought, which is much more vivid than Confucian thought, however "metaphysical" it sometimes seems. See Anastaplo, "An Introduction to Hindu Thought," 1985 *The Great Ideas Today* 258 [1985]. A collection of my introductions to non-Western thought is to be published by Rowman & Littlefield.)

There may have been in the United States more of an opening toward Classical political philosophy before 1800 than after 1860. (See Anastaplo, *Amendments to the Constitution,* 107 f.) Consider such developments, after 1860, as pragmatism and behaviorism. (Americans have had the benefit, since the 1930s, of European refugees trained in serious Classical studies.) However that may have been, should not we say that the founders of good regimes are not *above* the constitutions they bring forth, in that they are but midwives? That is, they do not create or innovate, but rather they discover and help realize what is called for in the circumstances they confront. And, whatever they may find it prudent to say, they surely do not believe, if they are truly prudent men, that only one form of government is legitimate or that any particular form of government can possibly last forever. See Anastaplo, "American Constitutionalism and Prudence," 150 n. 39.

Are we not obliged, because of Mr. Jaffa's usefully provocative suggestions, to consider further our "unwritten constitution," the regime that shaped both Lincoln and the Constitution? Are not the Constitution and Lincoln, properly understood, both means to an end that transcends political men and political institutions? For a proper understanding of that end, must not the *American* student of Classical political philosophy come to terms with the Declaration of Independence?

Or would Mr. Jaffa quietly compel us to concede that they who really understand Lincoln—those happy few—are, with Lincoln, "the highest thing in the American regime"? But what about those among us, perhaps even fewer, who perceive what was perhaps wrong, as well as what was wonderfully right, with Lincoln? Dare we conclude that *they* are higher than *all* regimes, including the American regime? This would surely be, if not a "concealed insobriety," an unobtrusive enthronement by implication. "Ambition should be made of sterner stuff." Compare, on the case of Julius Caesar, the epigraph for Chap. 13 of this Collection. Some responses by Mr. Jaffa to my comments on his work may be found in the exchanges between us included in his book *Original Intent and the Framers of the Constitution,* 167 f., 303 f., 359 f., 369 f. See also Harry V. Jaffa, *American Conservatism and the American Founding* (Durham: Carolina Academia Press, 1984), 48 f., 140–41. See as well note 299 above. See, for Mr. Jaffa's most recent work, the concluding section of Chap. 7 of this Collection. See also note 210 above.

493. See, for an informed critique of the most notorious of the students of politics to have developed this warning, Leo Strauss, *Thoughts on Machiavelli* (Glencoe, Ill.: Free Press, 1958). There is something down-to-earth and hence refreshing about the way the Strauss critique begins. See the epigraph for Chap. 7 of this Collection. See, on the yearning for personal immortality, Anastaplo, "Law & Literature and the Bible," 783–51. See also notes 286 and 489 above.

494. One must wonder what it is that the contemporary statesman has to draw upon comparable to the materials Lincoln had at hand in the Declaration of Independence, Shakespeare, and the Bible. Do we have (of these) primarily the Declaration, and a somewhat neglected Declaration at that, to serve as a popular underpinning of our venerable Constitution? Lincoln, on the other hand, could still depend upon a substantial uniformity in the literary tastes and in the orthodox religious sentiments of his community—tastes and sentiments (imbedded in his language, as they still are in some degree in ours) which the respectable literature and the influential intellectuals of his day did not openly challenge. See, in David Hume's *Enquiry Concerning Human Understanding,* the closing pages of sec. 10 and the opening pages of sec. 11.

We may detect these basic problems in our current church-and-state concerns. Are we most explicitly concerned *today* about "the separation of church and

state" because it is an epoch when the blending of these two by the creative statesman is much more difficult than it has ever been among us? The particular legislative measures and judicial decisions that have aroused controversy among us in
recent decades may relate merely to essentially desperate skirmishes in a battle
already over. One faction [I could say in the 1970s] has a victory that it may not
yet know it has won; the other has suffered a defeat that it may be futilely trying
to reverse. The victor overestimates the strength of political institutions; the vanquished underestimates the relentless skepticism of modern relativism. See, e.g.,
Grant, *Technology and Empire*, 43 f., 108 f.

The problem of "church and state" may have become so acute because we
are at last in an era when the relation between the "state" and the "church" is
coming to reflect more than formal or legal separation. What had once been
taken for granted—a seemingly inexhaustible quarry of religious sentiment independent of government control or concern—has had to be abandoned. The
attempt to encourage by law what had once been produced by the community
at large raises far-reaching issues of public policy and constitutional law. Also far-
reaching, and difficult to determine, are the effects of the opinions that a people
has. Thus, the beliefs among the ancient Germans and Gauls (just as among modern Muslims?) in personal immortality may have promoted military valor. But
may not such beliefs, even when not coupled with softening injunctions to charity, incapacitate a people for war by deflecting it from extensive temporal concerns and hence from the development of the technology often necessary to support its valor against the mechanized onslaughts of a more worldly people? On
the other hand, technology can promote self-indulgence that may also be softening us. See Julius Caesar, *Gallic Wars*, 6; Montesquieu, *The Spirit of the Laws*, 20:
1. See, on Islam, George Anastaplo, "An Introduction to Islamic Thought," 1989
The Great Ideas Today 234 (1989). (The salutary aspects in this Country of such
measures as Sunday Closing Laws are apt to be neglected these days. See, e.g., note
50 above. See also notes 63 and 81 above.)

No doubt, the Gettysburg Address will continue to move men so long as the
English language is read. But one must wonder whether the Address can continue
to have its intended effect now that its theological foundations have been worn
away. Even so, is not the Gettysburg Address likely to remain more captivating to
moderns than Lincoln's Second Inaugural Address, in that it is less explicitly theological and more obviously political than that political sermon? (Compare Lincoln,
Collected Works, 8: 356.) Moreover, the Second Inaugural Address seems designed
primarily for immediate concerns and thus stands, with respect to the Gettysburg
Address, much as the Constitution does with respect to the Declaration of Independence.

Chapter 16. The Second Inaugural Address

495. Comparable codes, earlier in this century, would have been rules of eti-
quette. See, on hate-speech codes, George Anastaplo, *Campus Hate-Speech Codes,*

Natural Right, and Twentieth-Century Atrocities (Lewiston, N.Y.: Edwin Mellen Press, forthcoming), part 1. See, on parliamentary rules, Anastaplo, "On *Robert's Rules of Order*," 1996 *The Great Ideas Today* 232 (1996). Consider also the rules used by the Federal Convention of 1787 (ibid., 248) and the rules evident in the Lincoln–Douglas Debates of 1858. (One manifestation of the nationalizing aspects of the Civil War is the development of a set of parliamentary rules that could be relied upon everywhere in the Country. It may someday become apparent that the Civil War was for the United States its uniformity-promoting "Norman Conquest." See George Anastaplo, "The Natural Right Component of American Law: *Swift v. Tyson* Revisited," *Legal Studies Forum*, note 7 [forthcoming]. See also note 155 above.)

496. See, e.g., note 25 above. See also the text at note 394 above.

497. The complete text of this handbill, which touches upon matters developed two decades later in the Gettysburg Address and the Second Inaugural Address, is set forth here (Abraham Lincoln, *Collected Works*, ed. Roy P. Basler [New Brunswick, N.J.: Rutgers University Press, 1953], 1: 382):

> To the Voters of the Seventh Congressional District
> FELLOW CITIZENS:
>
> A charge having got into circulation in some of the neighborhoods of this District, in substance that I am an open scoffer at Christianity, I have by the advice of some of my friends concluded to notice the subject in this form. That I am not a member of any Christian Church, is true; but I have never denied the truth of the Scriptures; and I have never spoken with intentional disrespect of religion in general, or of any denomination of Christians in particular. It is true that in early life I was inclined to believe in what I understand is called the "Doctrine of Necessity"—that is, that the human mind is impelled to action, or held in rest by some power, over which the mind itself has no control; and I have sometimes (with one, two or three, but never publicly) tried to maintain this opinion in argument. The habit of arguing thus however, I have, entirely left off for more than five years. And I add here, I have always understood this same opinion to be held by several of the Christian denominations. The foregoing, is the whole truth, briefly stated, in relation to myself, upon this subject.
>
> I do not think I could myself, be brought to support a man for office, whom I knew to be an open enemy of, and scoffer at, religion. Leaving the higher matter of eternal consequences, between him and his Maker, I still do not think any man has the right thus to insult the feelings, and injure the morals, of the community in which he may live. If, then, I was guilty of such conduct, I should blame no man who should condemn me for it; but I do blame those, whoever they may be, who falsely put such a charge in circulation against me.
>
> July 31, 1846. A. Lincoln

See ibid, 1: 383–84. See also note 492 above, the text at notes 91 and 486 above.

See as well George Anastaplo, "Church and State: Explorations," 19 *Loyola University of Chicago Law Journal* 148 (1987); notes 256 and 259 above.

498. Lincoln did manage to get elected to the House of Representatives in 1846, serving one term there (by a prior intraparty arrangement). See, on how a leader should talk, Odysseus's rebuke of Agamemnon, Homer, *Iliad,* 14: 82 ff. See, on religion and morality, the text at note 48 above, and the epigraph for Chap. 2 of this Collection.

499. See George Anastaplo. "Lessons for the Student of Law: The Oklahoma Lectures," 20 *Oklahoma City University Law Review* 187 f., 198 f., 206 f. (1995). See also George Anastaplo, "Heaven's Gate Suicides Probably Include Murder Victims, Murderers," letter to the editor, *USA Today,* 8 May 1997, 14A (reprinted in its entirety in George Anastaplo, "The O. J. Simpson Case Revisited," 487 n. 59).

500. This could be seen in Stephen A. Douglas's "don't care" policy with respect to the status of slavery in the Territories of the United States. See Chap. 11 of this Collection. See also note 492 (beginning) above.

501. Consider, e.g., the *Chicago Tribune* editorial of January 3, 1861, two months before Abraham Lincoln was inaugurated (as reprinted in the *Chicago Tribune,* June 10, 1997, sec. 1, p. 19) (this editorial begins with a comment on the Southern wing of the Democratic Party):

The Real Issue

What a sight! The leading politicians of a great and once liberty-loving and patriotic party, the chief executive officers of the government, a full half of the people of one section of the Republic, all plotting and conspiring against the perpetuity of the fairest political fabric ever built by human hands, and provoking civil war between brothers— for what? That the representatives of a little Oligarchy of 347,000 slave-holders may have the privilege, not authorized by the Constitution, of buying, selling, working without pay and whipping at will, men, women and children in the Territories which God made free; that the Constitution which was purposely framed so that the word "slave" might not occur therein, may be so amended, after seventy years successful working, as to recognize property in man; that the States which have rid themselves of the crime and curse of in-voluntary bondage shall be compelled to accept it again; and that the moral sense of the people of the North, now rebelling against man-selling, shall correct itself, and begin to affirm that the Atheism which makes one man own another is the new evangel for the civilization of mankind.

What a sight! What a theme for the historian who writes the Rise and Fall of the Republic of the United States! What a commentary on the civilization of the age! What a burning reproach to the cause of Democracy throughout the world! Yet we state fairly the causes of the quarrel. No difference of race and lineage, of religious faith, nor save in one thing, of political policy, has brought on the struggle. We are one people, with one hope and men have believed, with one destiny. That

People is to be divided, that hope given up, and that glorious destiny overruled, that the business of man stealing and woman-whipping may grow with our nation's growth.

It is well enough in times like these, to keep the real issues steadily before the people. We state them above in language that all may understand.

See note 396 above.

502. Lincoln, *Collected Works*, 8: 332.

503. See, for Lincoln's Reconstruction policies, Richard H. Sewell, *A House Divided* (Baltimore: Johns Hopkins University Press, 1983), 186 f. See also note 533 below.

504. Could there have been, after the First World War, anything like Lincoln's speeches explaining and justifying the sacrifices of that war, a war perhaps harder to justify? See notes 209 and 492, above. Much the same can be asked about the Vietnam War. See, e.g., George Anastaplo, "First Impressions," 26 *Political Science Reviewer* 250 f. (1997); The Second World War has proved much easier to justify, with Nazism taking the place of slavery as a dreadful institution in need of being checked. See note 145 above. Then, of course, there was the incredible folly of the Japanese surprise attack on Pearl Harbor. See Anastaplo, "The Vices of Treachery and of Revenge," in "On Freedom," 645 f. Revenge, unfortunately, seems to be the primary motive in our August 20, 1998, cruise-missile surprise attack on Afghanistan and Sudan. See Anastaplo, "Overwhelming Power and a Sense of Proportion," in "On Freedom," 604 f. See also the Orwell discussion cited in note 294 above. See as well note 285 above; the text at note 415 above; Sec. V of Chap. 14 of this Collection. Compare note 532 below.

505. Lincoln, *Collected Works*, 8: 333. See also the text at note 337 above.

506. Much the same can be said about whites in this Country when compared to their relatives in Europe. See, on the opportunities available in the United States, the text at note 508 below. See also note 473 above.

507. See, e.g., notes 44, 73, and 137 above. Compare notes 212, 214, and 215 above. See also note 286 above. See as well note 286 above.

Chapter 17. Abraham Lincoln's Legacies

508. Lincoln, *Collected Works*, 4: 438. See note 506 above. See, on Lincoln's liberalism, the Randall quotation in note 533 below.

509. Ibid., 6: 438.

510. See George Anastaplo, "Nature and Convention in Blackstone's Commentaries," 22 *Legal Studies Forum* 161 (1998). See also Chap. 5 of this Collection.

511. Plutarch, *Lives* (New York: Modern Library, n.d.), 70. See also Richard M. Weaver, *Ideas Have Consequences* (Chicago: University of Chicago Press, 1948). The "need" to fill up dozens of channels brought to us by cable television and satellites means that all kinds of "strange people" with "strange words" are bound

to be given free rein. See, on Plutarch, George Anastaplo, "Lessons for the Student of Law: The Oklahoma Lectures," 20 *Oklahoma City University Law Review* 44 f. (1995).

512.   See Lincoln, *Collected Works*, 1: 108 f. See also note 237 above.

513.   See, on the right of revolution, Sec. IV of Chap. 1 of this Collection. See also notes 64, 219, and 484 above.

514.   Nature also strives to constrain that self-expression which liberals tend to make so much of. See, e.g., note 63 above. See also note 492 (beginning) above. See, on the First Inaugural Address, Chap. 12 of this Collection. See, on natural law/natural right, note 39 above. See, on nature, the Epilogue to this Collection.

515.   See, on the July 4, 1861, Message to Congress, Chap. 13 of this Collection.

516.   See Lincoln, *Collected Works*, 4: 426, 427, 428.

517.   See ibid., 4: 433.

518.   Ibid., 4: 438. See, for the first draft of the Preamble of the Confederate Constitution, Sec. II of Chap. 13 of this Collection.

519.   See, on the proposed abolition of broadcast television in the United States, note 63 above. See also note 221 above. See as well note 511 above.

520.   See, on Lincoln's First Inaugural Address and his Fourth of July Message to Congress, Chaps. 12 and 13 of this Collection. See, on Lincoln's upbringing, Chaps. 8 and 9 of this Collection.

Epilogue

521.   See, e.g., notes 26, 29, 485 (end), 492 and 493 above. See also Laurence Berns, "The Classicism of George Anastaplo," 26 *Political Science Reviewer* 92–93 (1997). George Anastaplo, "First Impressions," 26 *Political Science Reviewer* 249 f. (1997). See as well George Anastaplo, "The Founders of Our Founders: Jerusalem, Athens, and the American Constitution," in *Original Intent and the Framers of the Constitution,* ed. Harry V. Jaffa (Washington, D.C.: Regnery Gateway, 1994), 181° George Anastaplo, *The Amendments to the Constitution: A Commentary* (Baltimore: Johns Hopkins University Press, 1995), 124; note 207 above. These diverse approaches may be reflected in Tocqueville's distinguishing the new democratic way from the old aristocratic way. This may be related to the question of whether the moral virtues are grounded in nature and hence worthy of choice for their own sake. See Chap. 6 of this Collection. See also notes 65 and 479 above. See, on the usefulness of bringing Classical doctrines to bear upon American constitutional discourse, the Belz book review cited in note 391 above. See, on Lincoln as Homer, note 267 above.

522.   See, e.g., note 39, and the text at note 515 above. See also George Anastaplo, *The American Moralist: On Law, Ethics, and Government* (Athens: Ohio University Press, 1992), 412–15, 616.

523.   Aristotle's systematic discussion of slavery begins in Chap. 3 of Book. 1 of his *Politics*. The Laurence Berns translation of that discussion may be found in George Anastaplo, *Liberty, Equality, and Modern Constitutionalism,* 1: 215–21. See, for

a useful introduction to that discussion, Harry Jaffa's article on Aristotle in the first and second editions of the *History of Political Philosophy* collection edited by Leo Strauss and Joseph Cropsey. (This article has been reprinted in Jaffa, *The Conditions of Freedom.*) See, for another useful introduction to Aristotle, Mortimer J. Adler, *Aristotle for Everybody* (New York: Macmillan, 1978). See also Anastaplo, *The American Moralist,* 20–26; Anastaplo, *The Thinker as Artist,* 318–34. See, on the nature and limitations of "equality," Plato, *Laws* 757A–758A.

See, for a reminder of how slavery could be regarded in antiquity, the extraordinary (yet typical?) episode recorded in Plutarch, *Titus Flamininus,* 13: 4. See also George Anastaplo, "Law, Education, and Legal Education: Explorations," 37 *Brandeis Law Journal* (1999), app. A, sec. V. We can be reminded here of how much slavery depends upon, even as it degrades, law-abidingness. See note 7 above.

524. See, on modern individualism, Chap. 6 of this Collection. See also note 485 above.

525. This is the kind of observation that Lincoln made in various ways in challenging the self-centeredness, if not even the hypocrisy, of the typical arguments for slavery. See also note 60 above. Lincoln observed, evidently in 1858, "As a *good* thing, slavery is strikingly peculiar, in this, that it is the only good thing which no man ever seeks the good of, for *himself.*" *Collected Works,* 3: 205. See the text at note 322 above.

526. Compare, on that spiritedness of the North American Indians which left them ill-fitted for slavery, note 25 above. This was not, for them, an unmixed blessing. See note 305 above.

527. Aristotle would have been horrified, as were most late-eighteenth-century Americans (in the South as well as in the North), by the inhumanity of the trans-Atlantic African slave trade. Its gross injustice would also have been obvious to him. See Sec. IV of Chap. 4 of this Collection. See also note 44 above.

528. See note 344 above.

529. If the differences between master and slave can be reinforced by marked differences in color, so much the "better," as we know from the history of the United States. But we also know that the presence in pre–Civil War America of more and more emancipated slaves who were quite able to take care of themselves called into question the legitimacy of any race-based slavery in the United States. See note 431 above.

Aristotle knew as well that there were far more slaves around than were evident. That is, he would have endorsed this sentiment recorded in Henry Thoreau's journal on the eve of the Civil War:

> Talk about slavery! It is not the peculiar institution of the South. It exists wherever men are brought and sold, wherever a man allows himself to be made a mere thing or a tool, and surrenders his inalienable rights of reason and conscience. Indeed, this slavery is more complete than that which enslaves the body alone. It exists in the Northern States, and I am reminded by what I find in the newspapers that it exists in Canada. I never yet met with, or heard of, a judge who was not a slave of this kind, and so the finest and most unfailing weapon of injustice. He fetches a

slightly higher price than the black man only because he is a more valuable slave. (Carl Bode, ed., *The Best of Thoreau's Journals* [Carbondale: Southern Illinois University, 1967], 318–19 [entry of December 4, 1860])

See also the beginning of Chap. 4 of this Collection. Also expressed in the Thoreau journals is his opinion that John Brown was rare in being truly free (that is, in being able to act on high principle). Compare note 533 below. Consider, for the dictates of prudence, note 28 above. Consider as well the choice of Odysseus recorded in book 10 of Plato's *Republic*. See, on the Good, the True, and the Beautiful, note 172 above. See, on Thoreau, notes 80 and 471 above.

530. See, for the perniciousness that can be encountered here, Chap. 7 of this Collection.

531. See, e.g., Leo Strauss, *Thoughts on Machiavelli* (Glencoe, Ill.: Free Press, 1958), 14: "Machiavelli would argue that America owes her greatness not only to her habitual adherence to the principles of freedom and justice, but also to her occasional deviation from them." See, on beginnings, note 165 above. See also notes 76 and 108 above.

532. We notice, for example, that the Thirteenth Amendment *does* permit "slavery" in the United States "as a punishment for crime whereof the party shall have been duly convicted." See George Anastaplo, *The Amendments to the Constitution: A Commentary* (Baltimore: Johns Hopkins University Press, 1995), 437 n. 195. See, for blatant abuses of this exception in the Thirteenth Amendment (which exception may be found also in the Northwest Ordinance), Ralph Korngold, *Thaddeus Stevens: A Being Darkly Wise and Rudely Great* (New York: Harcourt, Brace, 1955), 377. Much more extensive and effective in one form or another, until the middle of the twentieth century, were the white supremacists' efforts described in Michael Perman, *Struggle for Mastery: Disfranchisement in the South, 1888–1908* (Chapel Hill: University of North Carolina Press, forthcoming).

We are reminded of the need to keep in view, when interpreting and applying constitutional provisions, the spirit and purpose implicit from the outset in such provisions. These provisions can be as diverse as the Commerce Clause (which empowers Congress to regulate the economy of the Country), the First Amendment (which protects the frank and full discussion by the Country of its affairs), and the Fourteenth Amendment (which ratifies, in effect, the military and political results of the Civil War on behalf of one Country). Then there is the much-neglected Republican Form of Government Guarantee. See George Anastaplo, *The Constitution of 1787: A Commentary* (Baltimore: Johns Hopkins University Press, 1989), 172–75, 337; Anastaplo, *Amendments to the Constitution,* 463. See also the epigraphs for the Prologue to this Collection and for Chap. 13 of this Collection. See as well the text at note 8 above. Compare, for Calhoun's constitutional teaching, note 220 above. (It can be argued, with some plausibility, that it is a variant of our Republican Form of Government Guarantee that the NATO countries invoked in their 1999 Kosovo campaign to discipline Serbia as a de facto member of the European community. Compare notes 285 and 504 above. One can also be reminded here of Lord Charnwood's characterization of the victory of the North in the Civil War as "the costly and imperfect triumph of the right." See the text at note 226 above. See as well the discussion of Serbian atrocities in Bosnia in George Anastaplo, *Campus Hate-Speech Codes, Natural Right, and Twentieth-Century Atrocities* (Lewiston, N.Y.: Edward Mellen Press, 1997). Be all this as it may, the more that Europeans control the NATO Kosovo campaign, the better for the incipient United States of Europe.

533. Lincoln, in his attempt to secure this redemption, had before him to draw upon, as extreme antislavery approaches, the armed crusade of a John Brown (note 492 above; also, the epigraph for Chap. 15 of this Collection) and the healing ministry of a John Woolman. See, on Brown and Woolman, James G. Randall, *Dictionary of American Biography* (New York: Charles Scribner's Sons, 1929 [vol. 3], 1936 [vol. 20]), 3: 131, 20: 516. See also the text at notes 240, 448, and 458 above. See as well the text following note 337 above; note 529 above. Lincoln relied upon prudence in drawing on these and other resources upon undertaking the great task he accepted as a son of the Northwest Territory who was dedicated (with thousands of his fellow-citizens) to the defense and implementation, in a constitutional manner, of the great promises of the Declaration of Independence. Had Lincoln survived the war, he might have been able to insist upon the policy of national reconciliation implicit in this 1933 appraisal of him by a distinguished historian (James G. Randall, *Dictionary of American Biography* [New York: Charles Scribner's Sons, 1933] 11: 258):

> The early crystallization of the enduring Lincoln tradition was illustrated by [Edwin M.] Stanton's comment [at his death], "Now he belongs to the ages." That he was among the "consummate masters of statecraft" may be disputed, but such was the impression he left that this distinction has been accorded him. In the shortest list of American liberal leaders he takes eminent place: liberalism with him was no garment; it was of the fiber of his mind. His hold upon the affections of his own people had not been due merely to the fact that he, a backwoods lad, rose to the highest office in the land. It is doubtful whether any other leader of the North could have matched him in dramatizing the war in the popular mind, in shaping language to his purpose, in smoothing personal difficulties by a magnanimous touch or a tactful gesture, in avoiding domestic and international complications, in courageously persisting in the face of almost unendurable discouragements, in maintaining war morale while refusing to harbor personal malice against the South. Not inappropriately, he has become a symbol both of American democracy and the Union.

See, for limits on Lincoln's "liberalism" in the face of political heresy, note 492 (beginning) above, on how Senator Pettit should have been dealt with. See, on the youthful Lincoln as a peacemaker, Sec. VI of Chap. 8 of this Collection.

Lincoln's last public address (of April 11, 1865) discussed prospects for Reconstruction. It included these observations (*Collected Works*, 8: 403):

We all agree that the seceded States, so called, are out of their proper practical relation with the Union; and that the sole object of the government, civil and military, in regard to those States is to again get them into that proper practical relation. I believe it is not only possible, but in fact, easier, to do this, without deciding, or even considering, whether these states have even been out of the Union, than with it. Finding themselves safely at home, it would be utterly immaterial whether they had ever been abroad. Let us all join in doing the acts necessary to restoring the proper practical relations between these states and the Union; and each forever after [can] innocently indulge his own opinion whether, in doing the acts, he brought the States from without, into the Union, or only gave them proper assistance, they never having been out of it.

(That speech may also be found, along with most of Lincoln's principal statements as President, in George Anastaplo, *Liberty, Equality, and Modern Constitutionalism*, vol. 2, sec.V.) Lincoln had said that the question, "whether the seceded States, so called, are in the Union or out of it . . . is bad, as the basis of a controversy, and good for nothing at all—a merely pernicious abstraction." (Lincoln, *Collected Works*, 8: 402–3) Perhaps Abraham Lincoln enjoyed formulating the advice he gave on this occasion—that "each forever after [can] innocently indulge his own opinion" on the question—a suggestion that may have provided him some of the innocent pleasure he had had, at the other end of his public career in the Illinois General Assembly, when he suggested that a prematurely appointed County Surveyor he kept in reserve "so that if the old surveyor should hereafter conclude to die, there would be a new one ready made without troubling the legislature." Ibid., 1: 31. See the text at note 229 above. See also note 451 above. See, on Lincoln's constantly reworking his materials, note 267 above. See also the text at note 1 above.

Be all this as it may, we should not leave the Civil War–centered dialogue on statesmanship and the pursuit of a proper happiness offered by this Collection without reminding ourselves once again of that gallant love of liberty and that deep abhorrence of slavery natural to the Old South. These noble responses are evident in a passage from Patrick Henry's most celebrated speech, a passage which anticipates the solid Union that would be required for the people of this Country to be able truly to govern themselves. The passage is taken from this 1775 speech before a meeting of the Second Revolutionary Convention of Virginia:

There is a just God who presides over the destinies of nations, and who will raise up friends to fight our battles for us. The battle, sir, is not to the strong alone, it is to the vigilant, the active, the brave. Besides, sir, we have no election. If we were base enough to desire it, it is now too late to retire from the contest. There is no retreat but in submission and slavery! Our chains are forged. Their clanking may be heard on the plains of Boston! . . . The war is actually begun! The next gale that sweeps from the north will bring to our ears the clash of resounding arms! Our brethren are already in the field! Why stand we here idle? What is it that gentlemen wish? What would they have? Is life so dear, or peace so sweet, as to be purchased at the price of chains and slavery? Forbid it, Almighty God!—I know not what course others may take; but as for me, give me liberty, or give me death!

See William Wort, *Sketches of the Life and Character of Patrick Henry,* 3d ed. (Philadelphia: James Webster, 1818), 115–25. Compare Chap. 7 of this Collection. But see notes 60 and 297 above, and especially Chap. 1 of this Collection.

Index

abolition act, British (1833), 6–8,
151–52, 268
abolitionism/abolitionists, 5, 52–53,
113, 115, 117, 128–30, 132, 151,
164, 171, 175, 195, 199–202, 208,
213, 214, 225, 319–26
abortion controversy, 7, 52–53, 62–64,
79, 293
absolutes, 19, 66–67, 255. *See also* natural law/natural right
accident. *See* chance
acquisitiveness. *See* avarice
Adams, Henry, 282
Adams, John, 12, 26, 28, 111, 268
Adams, John Quincy, 290, 335, 343
Adler, Mortimer J., 257, 355
advertising, 192, 255. *See also* avarice;
rhetoric; sophistry
Aesop, 323, 348
affirmative action controversy, 6, 35,
52, 75, 154, 274, 319
Agamemnon, 352
Alcibiades, 113, 115
Alexander the Great, 231
aliens (UFOs), 246
Alschuler, Albert W., 1
anarchy, 22, 253
Anastaplo, Sara Maria, 335
Anastaplo, Sara Prince, 300
Angle, Paul M., 297
Antigone, 334
apocalyptic view of the world, 340
"appreciate," definition of, 319
aristocracy. *See* nobility
Aristophanes, 290
Aristotle, 12, 32–33, 257–63, 266, 274,
285, 286, 295, 301, 328–29, 331,

336–37, 340, 345, 348, 355
Arnhart, Larry, 331
Arnold, Matthew, 110, 288
Articles of Confederation, 40, 46, 54,
59, 61, 75, 189, 267, 275, 307, 338
Athena, 329
Augustine, Saint, 316
Aurelius, Marcus, 345
avarice, 57, 62, 67, 98, 103, 122, 133,
282–83. *See also* free market econo-
my; self-interest.
Axtell case (1660), 70, 283

Baker, John E., 10
Baldwin, James, 337
Bane, Charles A., 30, 101, 167, 170
Barrett, Jay A., 277–79
baseball, 302
Basler, Roy P., 11, 39, 243, 269, 303
beauty, 84, 86, 88–90, 91, 96, 100,
104–5, 156, 237, 285, 319, 336
Becker, Carl L., 268, 273
behaviorism, 348
Bels, Herman, 309, 354
"Berlin Wall," 56
Berns, Laurence, 257, 286, 296, 300,
325, 329, 342, 354
Berns, Walter, 317
Beveridge, Albert W., 281
Bible, 25, 53, 111, 122, 133–34, 172,
197, 226–27, 232, 235, 240, 247,
252, 255, 285, 296, 323–24, 326–29,
333, 341–42, 344–45, 347–49, 351.
See also divinity
biological war, 66, 291
Black, Hugo L., 289, 302

Black & White Taxicab Co. v. Brown & Yellow Taxicab Co. (1928), 77, 283
Blackstone, William, 1, 252, 283, 318, 321, 353
Blassingame, John W., 284
Blücher, Gebhard L. von, 264
Bloom, Allan, 336
Boller, Paul F., Jr., 341
Booth, John Wilkes, 9, 310
Borgia, Cesare, 336
Bork, Robert H., 269–70, 324
Bouvier, John, 269
Braithwaite, William T., 283, 300, 321
Brann, Eva T. H., 328
Brown v. Board of Education (1954), 19, 52, 238, 266, 271
Brown, John, 174, 229–30, 321, 326, 345, 356–57
Browne, Charles Farrar, 322
Brutus, Junius, 302
Brutus, Marcus, 154, 302
Buchanan, James, 178, 193, 265, 310
Burke, Edmund, 295, 339
Burns, James M., 338
Burns, Robert, 135
Bush, George H. W., 146–47
Butler, Pierce, 55
Butler, William, 131–32
Butterfield, Fox, 274
Byron, Lord 135

Caesar, Julius, 154, 185, 231, 325, 347–50
Calhoun, John C., 6, 67, 113–22, 153, 230, 264, 266, 282, 286, 288–94, 302, 326, 356
cannibalism, 293
Cappon, Lester J., 273
Carlyle, Thomas, 149, 301
Carroll, Lewis, 330
Carson, James Louis, 290
Cato, 286
censorship, 244, 252, 285
Cephalus, 285
Cervantes, Miguel de, 297
chance, 9, 32, 74, 123, 134, 152, 219, 223, 225, 227, 261, 293–94, 326, 344, 346–47
Chandrasekhar, Subrahmanyan, 328–29, 332–33
Charles I, King, 70
Charnwood, Lord, 119, 123, 229, 288, 293, 296, 300, 304, 309, 318, 356–57
Chase, Salmon P., 218, 320
Christianity, 84, 137, 151, 160, 232, 237–38, 240, 241, 245, 248, 252, 272, 285, 316, 327, 339–43, 347–50, 351. *See also* divinity
Churchill, Winston S., 144, 265, 287, 310, 341, 347
Cicero, 12, 69, 274, 343, 347
Clay, Henry, 117, 292
Clinton, Stanford, 10
Clinton, William J., 324–25
Clovis, 323
Collins, Ronald K. L., 197
Columbus, Christopher, 265
commerce, commerce power, 34, 47, 51, 53, 55–58, 63–64, 69, 272, 296
common law, 69–77, 275, 280, 283–84, 295, 306
Confederate Constitution (1861), 182–83, 187–89, 194, 197, 305, 307–8, 339, 354
Confiscation Acts, 320
Confucius, 328, 334, 340, 348
conscience, 104–5, 198, 199, 204, 222, 227, 340
consent of the governed, 24, 49, 52, 57–58, 209, 319
Constitution (U.S.): Preamble, 189–90, 254; Article I, 13, 54, 59–60, 189–90, 254, 278, 280, 282, 296, 307–8, 339, 356; Article IV (Fugitive Slave Clause), 6, 55–56, 68, 78, 159–61, 174–75, 209, 212–13, 276, 278, 329; Article IV (Republican Form of Government Guaranty), 320, 346; Article V, 57–58, 293; Article VI, 306; Bill of Rights, 47, 56, 74, 204, 278; Amendment I, 118, 271, 356; Amendment II, 271, 310;

Amendment IV, 16, 76; Amendment IX, 76, 188, 307; Amendment X, 188, 307; Amendment XIII, 7, 18, 194, 224, 270, 281, 313, 316, 323–24, 356; Amendment XIV, 4, 18, 60, 217, 270, 281, 356; Amendment XV, 18, 270, 281; Amendment XVIII, 281; Proposed Amendment (1861), 194, 310–11

Corbett, Richmond M., 50

cotton gin, influence of, 62, 164, 282–83, 313–14

Cox, Richard H., 265, 267, 273, 275, 279

"created equal" phrase (Declaration of Independence), 8, 17–18, 26, 48, 56, 82, 115, 121–22, 142, 143, 151, 156, 159, 165, 181, 183, 187, 234, 235, 239, 254, 258–59, 262, 338, 343–44

cricket, 302

Cropsey, Joseph, 284, 355

Crosskey, William W., 278, 280, 283, 288, 307

culture, 67, 108, 257–62, 264, 284, 330

Cutler, Manasseh, 271

daemonic thing, 343. *See also* Socrates

Dana, William F., 268, 270

Dante Alighieri, 329

de Alvarez, Leo Paul S., 229, 292, 325–28, 336, 342

Declaration and Resolves of the First Continental Congress (1774), 14

Declaration of Independence (1776), 2, 8–38, 52, 56, 58, 60–61, 64, 66, 72, 76, 95, 108, 110, 118, 121–22, 142, 151, 154–55, 158–60, 165, 168, 172–73, 175, 177, 180–87, 191, 195, 204, 215, 227, 232, 234–35, 239–40, 257, 265, 267–75, 287–88, 290, 310, 315–18, 321, 327, 330, 334, 337–39, 341, 343, 347–50, 356–57

Declaration of the Causes and Necessity of Taking Up Arms (1775), 14

Declaration (or Bill) of Rights (1689), 14, 269

Declaration of the Rights of Man and Citizen (1789) (France), 87, 288

Declaratory Act (1766), 14

De Gaulle, Charles, 99

DeHart, Joan, 287

Demosthenes, 343

Dennis v. United States (1951), 19, 271

Descartes, René, 83, 87, 92, 97, 102, 105, 284–85, 287

despotism. *See* tyranny

Deutsch, Kenneth L., 343

Dickens, Charles, 287

divinity, 12, 14–15, 17–18, 20, 25–26, 31–32, 34–35, 47–48, 52, 54, 83–84, 105–6, 111, 122, 133–34, 147–51, 156, 167, 171, 173–74, 183, 190, 222, 231, 235, 239–41, 227, 243–51, 270, 275, 284, 288, 296, 306, 313–14, 321, 326–27, 330, 333, 335–37, 339, 342–44, 346–47, 349, 350–51, 358–59

Douglas, Stephen A., 18, 40, 125–26, 129–130, 149–50, 154–55, 157–75, 177, 180–81, 223, 226, 269, 300–304, 313–14, 320, 352, 358

Douglass, Frederick, 115, 168, 173, 199, 223, 266, 284, 312, 351

Dred Scott v. Sandford (1857), 2–3, 120, 158–59, 160, 169, 171, 177, 179–82, 193, 265, 270, 279, 302, 311

duty/duties, 31–38, 63, 109, 173–75, 293

education, 40, 75, 108–9, 111, 125–28, 170–72, 220, 256

efficiency, 43, 161, 172. *See also* free market economy

Electoral College, 305

emancipation, compensated, 6, 54, 153, 162, 198, 208, 214, 217, 220–21, 319

Emerson, Ralph Waldo, 12, 229, 268, 321, 330

enlightenment, 87, 103, 108–9, 111, 151, 328, 338, 348

envy, 100, 255

Epictetus, 157
Erie Railroad Co. v. Tompkins (1938),
    283–84
Euclid, 143, 172, 234, 252
Euripides, 343
Everett, Edward, 329, 331–32
Ewing, William L. D., 296
existentialism, 347–48
expediency, 36, 44, 245

Farrand, Max, 51, 280
Faulkner, William, 294, 316, 330,
    333–34
Federalist, The (Publius), 275–76, 279,
    286, 335, 346–47, 353–54. *See also*
    rhetoric
Fehrenbacher, Don E., 150, 302
Feuerbach, Ludwig, 339
Fichte, Johann G., 264
First World War, 289, 347, 353. *See also*
    governmental insanity; paranoia
Forquer story, 295
Fort Sumter, 192, 307
Fort, Tomlinson, 290, 292
fortune. *See* chance; divinity; provi-
    dence
Fox, Charles, 152
Franklin, Benjamin, 28, 266
Franklin, John Hope, 312, 319–20, 322
free market economy, 8, 98, 160, 172,
    290. *See also* avarice; property
freedom of expression, 275, 353
freedom of speech, of the press, 35, 38,
    118, 274, 278, 285, 353
freedom of the will, 265
friendship, 17, 27
Frisch, Morton J., 325
Fulkerson, Elbert, 294
Fulkerson, June, 294

Galbreath, C. B., 276–78
gambling, 287
Garrison, William Lloyd, 225, 321. *See
    also* abolitionism, abolitionists
Gentry, Matthew, 131, 139, 143–45,
    298–300

George III, King, 4, 13–15, 21, 23, 27,
    121, 272
Gibbon, Edward, 321–23
Gleicher, Jules, 321
Goethe, Johann Wolfgang von, 264
Good, True, and Beautiful, 285, 356
Goodell, Charles, 343
Gorgias, 332
governmental insanity, 113, 119–20,
    289
Graglia, Lino A., 332
Grant, George P., 339, 350
Grant, Ulysses S., 22, 119, 124, 247,
    272, 293, 315, 337
Grayson, William, 42
Greeks and Turks, 335
Greeley, Horace, 201, 313
Grotius, Hugo, 266, 297
guns, use and abuse of, 193, 271–72,
    274, 283, 310–11
Gup, Ted, 292

habeas corpus, writ of, 2–7, 56, 193,
    194, 266
Halevi, Judah, 326
Hall, Brian, 292
Hallam, Henry, 269
Hamilton, Alexander, 53
Harrison, William Henry, 277
Hatch, Orrin B., 251
hate speech and codes, 243–49, 350
Hay, John Milton, 314–15, 316–18,
    320, 336
Hayden, T. C., 303
Hayne, Robert Young, 40
Heaven's Gate cult, 352
Hegel, Georg W. F., 264
Heidegger, Martin, 114, 263–65, 289,
    291
Henfrey, Norman, 339
Henry, Patrick, 9, 65, 318, 358–59
Herndon, William H., 142, 298, 309
Heston, Charlton, 271. *See also* guns,
    use and abuse of
Higginson, Thomas W., 157
Hill, Robert S., 69

historicism, 264, 330
history. *See* providence
Hitler, Adolf, 97, 99–100, 108, 109, 153, 239, 353
Hoar, George F., 276
Hobbes, Thomas, 98, 137, 269, 329, 332, 336
Hodges, Albert G., 313
Holmes, Oliver Wendell, Jr., 77, 283
Homer, 297–98, 352, 354
honor, 26, 28–29, 87–90, 92, 98, 103, 114, 116, 161, 165, 169, 274, 295. *See also* immortality, yearning for; shame
Hooker, Richard, 271
Houston, Sam, 292, 300
Huidekoper's Lessee v. Douglass (1805), 283
Humboldt, Wilhelm von, 264
Hume, David, 285, 343, 349
Huckleberry Finn, 325
hypo. *See* melancholy
hypocrisy, 17–18, 84, 159–60, 161, 168, 354–55

Idea of the Good, 274, 288, 333
Ideas, 111, 273
ideology, 23, 95, 121–22
Illinois, Southern, 123–34, 294–96
immortality, yearning for, 137, 141, 152, 238, 332, 349–52. *See also* Abraham Lincoln: Poetry; Abraham Lincoln: Lyceum Speech
Independent Counsel Act, 324
Indians, North American, 47, 74–75, 246, 269, 279, 302, 318, 355
individualism, 33, 42, 52, 81–111, 258–59, 271, 340, 355
initiatives and referenda, 320
Iran aid–Contra arms controversy, 324
irony, 9, 92, 166, 226, 237, 331
Islam, 350

Jackson, Andrew, 114–16, 118, 153, 266
Jackson, Robert H., 317

Jaffa, Harry V., 114, 120–22, 149–52, 155–56, 158, 198, 202, 269–70, 285, 288–89, 295, 301–2, 304, 312–14, 319, 320, 325–27, 338–39, 340, 343–49, 354–55
James II, King, 14
Jarrett, Vernon, 198, 312
Jefferson, Thomas, 12, 22, 25–26, 28, 40, 111, 121, 155, 161, 172–73, 185, 187–88, 237, 268, 273–74, 276, 327, 336–38, 340–42, 344. *See also* Declaration of Independence
Jensen, Merrill, 275, 278
Jesus, 145, 232, 316, 336. *See also* Bible
Jewish disabilities, 266–67, 293
Joan of Arc, 285
Johannsen, Robert W., 302
John, King, 1, 4, 44
Johnson, Andrew, 298
Johnson, Lyndon B., 290
Johnston, Andrew, 136–43, 297–98
Jones, Wash, 336
Jowitt, William, 269
Judas Iscariot, 226–27, 322
judicial review, 4, 7, 159, 181–82, 265, 306
judiciary, 47, 52, 179–82, 265
justice, 16, 24, 27–28, 33, 35–37, 43, 47, 56, 65, 70, 74–76, 79, 94–95, 105, 106, 107–8, 117–18, 121, 143–45, 152–53, 159, 161–63, 168, 175, 196, 206, 214, 222, 224–25, 237–38, 243, 254, 260, 261, 266, 275, 277, 285, 304, 315, 318, 332, 334, 337, 345, 355–56

Kafka, Franz, 333
Kant, Immanuel, 264, 284
Kazantzakis, Nikos, 333
Kearns, Doris, 290
Keats, John, 334
Keitt, Laurence, 291
Kendall, Willmoore, 325, 341
Kennedy, John F., 154
Kennington, Richard, 284

King, Martin Luther, Jr., 154, 266,
   312–13
Klein, Jacob, 289, 337
Kleist, Heinrich von, 264
Knox, William, 136–39, 145
Kolarik, Gera-Lind, 287
Korngold, Ralph, 356
Kosovo campaign, 289, 356–57

law-abidingness, 128, 191, 209,
   230–31, 253, 355
Lee, Richard Henry, 268
Lee, Robert E., 119, 315, 337
legislative supremacy, 7, 25, 320, 324
Lerner, Ralph, 289, 292
Levi, Edward H., 10, 101, 167, 170. *See
   also* rhetoric
Levy, Leonard A., 271
Licht, Robert A., 306
Lincoln, Abraham (texts): Election
   Manifesto (1832), 124–25, 134;
   Stone–Lincoln Protest (1837),
   128–30; Lyceum Speech (The Perpetuation of Our Political Institutions) (1838), 26, 128, 142, 230–31,
   252–53, 290, 297, 325, 338; Temperance Address (1842), 318; poetry
   (1846?), 28, 135–47, 219, 236, 241,
   296–300; Infidelity Handbill (1846),
   66, 239, 245, 248, 301, 350–51;
   "House Divided" Speech (1858),
   149–56, 169–70, 180, 203, 265,
   300–302; Lincoln–Douglas Debates
   (1858), 40, 125–26, 129–30, 149,
   154–55, 157–75, 177, 180–81, 255,
   269, 302–4, 313–14, 351; Cincinnati
   Speech (1859), 39, 49; Cooper
   Institute Address (1860), 265, 277,
   302–3, 309–10, 315, 325; Independence Hall Remarks (1861), 11,
   195; First Inaugural Address (1861),
   31, 177–83, 185–86, 192, 194–95,
   238–39, 243, 246, 253, 254–56, 295,
   304–6, 310–11, 314, 329, 335, 339,
   341, 353–54; Fourth of July Message to Congress (1861), 178,
185–86, 243, 246, 247, 251, 254–56,
   306–11, 326, 330, 337, 354; Emancipation Proclamation (1862, 1863),
   2, 4, 6–7, 18, 187, 190, 195,
   197–227, 243, 268, 270, 311–25,
   346; Gettysburg Address (1863), 2,
   18, 26, 35, 53, 135, 142–43, 146,
   147, 156, 170, 182, 192, 195–96,
   207, 215, 238–39, 240, 243, 247,
   248, 255, 265, 270, 298–99, 323,
   325–51; Annual Messages to Congress (1861, 1862, 1863, 1864), 192,
   310, 313, 322, 334; Second Inaugural Address (1865), 26, 53, 132,
   142, 145, 147, 156, 170, 173–74,
   190, 195, 240, 243–49, 309, 329,
   350–53; Reconstruction Remarks
   (1865), 357–58
Lincoln, Mary Todd, 130, 131, 294
Lincoln, Robert T., 309
Lloyd George, David, 347
Lochner v. New York (1905), 287
Locke, John, 4, 12, 72, 122, 268, 345,
   348
Logan, Stephen T., 308
Logue, Calvin M., 287
Lomax, J. Harvey, 287
Lord's Prayer, 232, 326
Lott, John R., Jr., 271
Luther, Martin, 301
Lycurgus, 40, 252
Lynd, Stanton, 280

Macaulay, Thomas B., 266–67
Macbeth, 114, 326
Machiavelli, Niccolò, 97–98, 111, 113,
   262, 286, 331, 336, 342, 349, 356
Madison, James, 53–57, 64–66,
   281–82, 291, 338
madness. *See* melancholy
Magna Carta (1215), 1–2, 4, 9, 40, 266,
   271, 278
Mansfield, Lord, 2–9, 69, 151, 259,
   263–67, 293, 306, 321
Marshall, John, 58, 281
Marshall, Thurgood, 266

Martin, Luther, 53–54
Marx, Karl; Marxists, 121–22, 312, 335
Mason, George, 57
Massachusetts Body of Liberties
    (1641), 306
Masugi, Ken, 81
Mavrides, L. N., 328
Maxcy, Virgil, 291
Mayer, J.–P., 284, 292
McCarthy period, 269, 290
McClay, Wilfred M., 295
McClellan, John L., 290
McHatton, Samuel, 126, 258
McKenzie, Stanley D., 321
McKinley, William, 316
McLaughlin, Andrew C. 275–79
Meiklejohn, Donald, 284
melancholy, 100, 130, 132, 138–44,
    145–46, 194, 197–98, 246, 336
Mencken, H. L., 329
Merriam, Charles E., 338
Merryman, In re (1861), 309–16
Mexican War, 62, 309
Miers, Earl S., 297
Mill, John Stuart, 266
Milton, John, 266, 314
Mink, Patsy T., 289
Missouri Compromise (1820), 63, 159
Mitchell, Stephen A., 10, 101, 167, 170
moderation and the rule of law, 5–6,
    118, 132, 225, 318, 335, 343, 346.
    See also justice; prudence, wisdom
Monroe, James, 42, 122, 289
Montaigne, Michel Eyquem de, 90–92,
    104–5, 286, 287
Montesquieu, Baron de La Brède et de
    (Charles-Louis de Secondat), 92,
    286, 337–38, 350
Moorhead, Hugh S., 286
Moran, Richard, 271
More, Thomas, 285
Morris, Gouverneur, 53–54, 57, 330,
    332, 339–40
Morrish, Richard, 279
Morse, John T., 312
Moses, 152, 154, 210, 232, 327, 336, 342

Moses, Walter H., 68
Mosley, Oswald, 325, 347
Murley, John A., 283, 300, 321, 343

Napoleon Bonaparte, 231, 264
national debt, 48, 191, 309
National Rifle Assocation, 271–72. *See
    also* guns, use and abuse of
natural law/natural right, 4, 6–7, 20,
    70, 74, 77, 95, 100, 106, 107, 116,
    153–54, 171, 196, 199, 222, 244,
    252–55, 257–68, 287
natural rights, 22, 27, 87, 154, 224,
    234, 269, 272, 293
nature/natural, 2, 16–17, 19, 21, 25, 28,
    34–35, 42–43, 46, 52, 57, 65, 71–76,
    79, 95, 100, 103, 106–7, 108, 109,
    110, 111, 116, 121–22, 136, 143,
    145, 147, 150, 158, 171–72, 182–83,
    217, 219, 221, 224, 231, 235, 239,
    254–55, 260, 262, 264, 267, 271–72,
    274, 277, 270, 286–87, 290, 298,
    304–5, 309, 324, 329, 346–47, 350,
    353–54
necessity, 251–52, 265, 286, 296, 302,
    330–31, 351
Nevins, Allan, 279
Newman, Roger K., 302, 307
Newton, Isaac, 329
Nicolay, John G., 314–16, 318, 320,
    336
Nietzsche, Friedrich, 287, 299
nihilism, 270, 330
Nixon, Richard M., 324, 338
nobility/noble, 33, 38, 58, 83–89,
    98–101, 105, 106, 109–11, 124, 146,
    175, 237, 262, 266, 275, 281, 288,
    334, 336, 340, 348, 354, 358. *See
    also* justice
noble lie, 166, 226, 321
non-Western thought, introductions
    to, 348
Northwest Ordinance (1787), 6,
    39–49, 54–55, 69–79, 124, 163, 172,
    215, 267, 273–79, 283, 313, 357

nuclear war, 66, 174, 291, 293–94
Nuremberg Trial, 70, 283

Oates, Stephen B., 312, 316, 319, 322
obscenity, 287. *See also* censorship
O'Connor, John M., 80
Odysseus, 297, 329, 352, 356
Oedipus, 333
Ogilvie, Richard, 278
Oklahoma City bombing, 246
Oldroyd, Osborn H., 297
Organic Laws of the United States, 267
Orwell, George, 301
Otrompke, John, 283
Owen, Robert Dale, 312
Owens, Mary, 131, 296

paranoia, 336. *See also* melancholy
Paton, Alan, 119
Paul, Saint, 316
Paul VI, Pope, 340
Pensoneau, Taylor, 278
Pericles, 15, 27, 333
Perman, Michael, 356
Perpetual Union, 267
Petigru, James Louis, 290, 302
Petitt, John, 344, 357
Phideas, 110
Philoctetes, 333
philosophy, 1, 9, 23, 37, 94–96,
    100–102, 105, 109, 110, 111, 114,
    125, 133, 157, 237, 253, 262, 265,
    316, 336–37, 339, 341–42, 345,
    346–49
Pickett, George E., 142, 298, 334
Pickering, Timothy, 277
Pieper, Josef, 122
Pinckney, Charles Cotesworth, 51, 280
Pitt, William, 152
Plato, 36, 122, 155, 257, 270, 274, 286,
    292, 297, 303, 321, 325–26, 329,
    332, 334–355, 339–42, 345, 348,
    355–56
plebiscite, 273
Plutarch, 253, 274, 335, 354–55

political religion, 26, 231. *See also*
    divinity
Pol Pot, 99–100, 153
Poole, William F., 277
"positive good" of slavery, 8, 54, 114,
    117, 260, 289, 302, 312, 333, 347.
    See also melancholy; paranoia
positivism, positivists, 161–66, 171–72,
    174, 255, 269–70, 282, 309
pragmatism, 348
Pritchett, C. Herman, 281
privacy, 92, 106, 287. *See also* philoso-
    phy; self-interest
property, 5, 7–8, 18, 27, 42–45, 47,
    59–60, 65, 71–73, 78–79, 83, 122,
    158–62, 166, 173–74, 198–99,
    202–3, 206–7, 210, 214, 230, 260,
    279, 282–83, 312, 338. *See also*
    avarice; culture; leisure
prosperity, 8, 18, 34, 37, 108, 114, 258,
    282. *See also* culture; tyranny
Proust, Marcel, 330
providence, 83–84, 106, 216, 265, 284,
    288
prudence, 9, 17, 21–24, 28, 35, 37, 43,
    52–53, 62, 66–67, 87, 92, 104,
    109–11, 119–20, 122, 136, 147,
    164–67, 171, 174–75, 181–82,
    199–200, 203, 225, 237, 249, 262,
    270, 279, 288, 289–90, 303, 321,
    340, 343, 345–46, 348–49, 355–57,
    358. *See also* nature; philosophy
public sentiment, importance of, 125,
    166, 191, 224, 263. *See also* rhetoric
Publius. *See Federalist, The;* rhetoric

Quebec separatism, 304
Quintilian, 327
Quixote, Don, 297

Randall, John G., 296, 312, 316,
    319–20, 344, 353, 357
Randolph, Edmund, 282
rationality. *See* reason
Reagan, Ronald W., 324

realism/realists so-called, 35, 41–42, 44, 77, 88, 94, 99, 107, 109, 122, 171, 236, 255, 280, 282

reason, rationality, 9, 21, 25, 28, 36, 65, 77, 88, 91, 93, 106, 111, 141, 143–45, 190, 204, 219, 231, 257, 259–60, 277, 298–99, 326, 329, 338–39, 341–42

rebellion sugarcoated, 246, 254. *See also* sophistry

Reconstruction policies, 309, 352, 357–58

Rehnquist, William H., 269–70

relativism, 19, 77, 239, 271, 339, 349

religion, 265, 273, 287. *See also* divinity

religious liberty, 43, 47–48, 239–40, 271, 349

resoluteness, 289, 291

revenue power, 58–60, 64–67, 278, 289–90

revisionism, 31, 270

revolution, right of, 13, 15–16, 19–23, 33, 35–38, 49, 113, 172, 174, 191, 239, 253, 255, 271–75, 292, 339, 354, 358

rhetoric, 7–8, 15, 34, 94, 97, 330–33, 342–43. *See also* sophistry

Riesman, David, 295

rights. *See* natural rights

Robert's Rules of Order, 43, 244, 351

Roe v. Wade (1973), 293. *See also* abortion controversy

Romulus, 154

Roosevelt, Theodore, 317, 338

Rosenberg espionage case, 113, 289

Rousseau, Jean-Jacques, 103, 105, 266, 286

Rush, Benjamin, 281

Rutledge, Ann, 296

Sachs, Joe, 263, 329

Sandburg, Carl, 177, 295–96, 305, 312, 316

Santayana, George, 340

Santo Domingo slave uprising, 62

Scalia, Antonin E., 269–70, 281

Schelling, Friedrich W., 263–64

Schiller, Johann C. F. von, 264

Schleiermacher, Friedrich E. D., 264

Schoeman, Karel, 293

Second World War, 347, 353

Seiter, Francis J., 112

self-expression, 274, 353

self-interest, 38–39, 75, 81–111, 168, 172, 173, 175, 254, 261–62, 275, 278, 283–88, 303, 310, 318, 328–29, 331–34, 345, 354–55

separation of powers, 25–26, 46, 73, 224, 240, 324

Serbians, 211, 289, 357

Seward, William H., 344, 352

Shakespeare, William, 7, 100, 111, 135, 172, 252, 266, 321, 326–27, 329, 339–40, 345–46, 349

shame, 86, 105, 108, 192, 194, 340. *See also* conscience; honor

Sharp, Malcolm P., 113, 288

Sherman, Roger, 55, 61

Shinwell, Emanuel, 340

Sidney, Algernon, 12

Simon, John, 296

Simon, Paul, 127–28, 295

Simpson, O. J., 274

skepticism, 134, 349

Skinner, B. F., 283

slave trade, international, 54–56, 63, 151, 163, 272–73, 280–82, 295, 301, 305, 313, 318, 329, 355

Smith, Len Young, 148

Socrates, 131, 155, 169, 257, 285, 297, 332, 336, 343, 345, 347

Solomon, 197

Solon, 40

Solzhenitsyn, Alexander, 286

Somerset v. Stewart (1771–1772), 2–9, 152, 190–92, 259, 263–67, 284, 301, 321

sophistry, 185, 190–92, 246, 253, 270, 282, 308–9, 337

Sophocles, 100, 334

Spirit, the, 64, 264–65

Sprecher, Robert A., 196

Stalin, Joseph, 99, 100, 153, 239
Stambaugh, Joan, 263
Stanton, Edwin M., 357
Stephan, Edmund A., 101, 167, 170, 184
Stephens, Alexander H., 121, 185, 266, 304, 308–10, 341
Stevens, Richard G., 283, 325
Stevens, Thaddeus, 207, 345, 356
Stevenson, Robert Louis, 330
Stone, Daniel, 128–30
Stone, Robert L., 284, 300, 321
Storing, Herbert J., 312
Story, Joseph, 69, 284
Strauss, Leo, 9, 113, 227, 269, 284–85, 288, 304, 312, 333, 337, 340, 343, 344–45, 349, 355–56
Sunday Closing Laws, 350
Sutpen, Thomas, 336
Swift v. Tyson (1842), 69, 284, 300, 351

Taney, Roger B., 18, 179, 193–94, 267–70, 302
television, abolition of, 255, 274, 277, 278, 293, 353–54
term limits, 320
Thales, 252
Thomas Aquinas, 122, 271
Thomas, D. Robert, 228
Thomas, Hugh, 344
Thoreau, Henry, 278, 330, 356
Thrasymachus, 282, 325
Thucydides, 269, 273, 316, 321
Titus Flamininus, 266, 355
Tocqueville, Alexis de, 2, 30, 81–111, 262, 284–88, 292, 302, 354
Todd, Mary. *See* Lincoln, Mary Todd
Tribe, Laurence, 281
truths, self-evident, 4, 13, 15–16, 17–21, 108, 109, 115, 172, 234, 252, 267, 330. *See also* Euclid
Twain, Mark, 71, 281, 286, 325
tyranny, 13, 16, 18, 20, 23, 27, 33, 38, 56, 71, 85, 115, 120, 152–53, 172–74, 253, 282, 293, 301, 310, 318, 330, 335. *See also* Aristotle; philosophy

utility, 34, 85–86, 89–91, 93, 96, 104, 106, 237, 336. *See also* prudence

Van Buren, Martin, 114
Vietnam War, 290, 352
Vinson, Fred M., 19
Virgil, 81, 135
Virginia and Kentucky Resolutions, 292
Virginia Bill of Rights, 268

Wali, Kameshwar C., 328
Wallace, George C., 290, 337
Walling, James C., 279
Ward, Artemus, 226–27, 322
Warren, Lous, 297
Washington, George, 25, 28, 31, 61, 188, 223, 309, 335–36, 341
Washington, James M., 312
Watergate controversy, 324
We the People, 267
Weaver, Richard M., 293, 327, 353
Webster, Daniel, 12, 40, 268, 276, 292, 326, 330–32, 333–35, 339–42, 344, 346
Weingartner, Steven, 289
Weiss, Jerome S., 101, 167, 170, 242
Wesley, John, 152, 246, 266
Weston, Russell, 272
Wiecek, William M., 266
Wilberforce, William, 151–52, 154, 301
Williamson, Hugh, 61
Wills, Garry, 272
Wilmot Proviso, 120
Wilson, Clyde N., 111, 290
Wilson, Edmund, 128, 327
Wilson, Ellen G., 316
Wilson, James, 55
Wilson, Woodrow, 17
Wirt, William, 358–59

wisdom, 17, 24, 95, 332, 334. *See also* prudence
women, rights of, 130, 155, 258, 276, 329
Woolman, John, 357
World Soul, 264

Xenophon, 273, 341

Young, Horace A., 250
Youngstown Sheet & Tube Company v. Sawyer (1952), 317

Zentner, Scot J., 335
Zetterbaum, Marvin, 284
Zeus, 329
Zyskind, Harold, 327

About the Author

George Anastaplo was born in St. Louis, Missouri, in 1925 and grew up in Southern Illinois. After serving three years as an aviation cadet and flying officer during the Second World War, he earned the A.B., J.D., and Ph.D. degrees from the University of Chicago. He is currently lecturer in the liberal arts at the University of Chicago, professor of law at Loyola University of Chicago, and professor emeritus of political science and of philosophy at Dominican University.

His publications include ten books and a dozen book-length law review collections. His scholarship was reviewed in seven articles in the 1997 volume of the *Political Science Reviewer*. A two-volume Festschrift, *Law and Philosophy*, was issued in his honor by the Ohio University Press. Between 1980 and 1992 he was nominated annually for the Nobel Peace Prize by a Chicago based committee that had as its initial spokesman Malcolm P. Sharp (1897–1980), professor emeritus of the University of Chicago Law School.

Professor Anastaplo's career is assessed in a chapter in *Leo Strauss, the Straussians, and the American Regime* (Rowman & Littlefield, 1999). He has observed that he learned early in his life, and has been reminded on several occasions since, that instructive accusations of heresy or infidelity come in a variety of forms. He has also learned that even the least informed and most impassioned actor in these controversies does aim at some good.